# SPENSER'S POETRY

## AND THE

## REFORMATION TRADITION

# SPENSER'S POETRY
# AND THE
# REFORMATION TRADITION

*John N. King*

PRINCETON UNIVERSITY PRESS

PRINCETON, NEW JERSEY

COPYRIGHT © 1990 BY PRINCETON UNIVERSITY PRESS

PUBLISHED BY PRINCETON UNIVERSITY PRESS, 41 WILLIAM STREET,

PRINCETON, NEW JERSEY 08540

IN THE UNITED KINGDOM: PRINCETON UNIVERSITY PRESS, OXFORD

*LIBRARY OF CONGRESS CATALOGING-IN-PUBLICATION DATA*

KING, JOHN N.

SPENSER'S POETRY AND THE REFORMATION TRADITION / JOHN N. KING.

P.   CM.

INCLUDES BIBLIOGRAPHICAL REFERENCES (P.    ).

ISBN 0-691-06800-3 (ALK. PAPER)

1. SPENSER, EDMUND, 1552?–1559—CRITICISM AND INTERPRETATION.

2. SPENSER, EDMUND, 1552?–1599—RELIGION. 3. CHRISTIAN POETRY,

ENGLISH—HISTORY AND CRITICISM. 4. PROTESTANTISM IN LITERATURE.

5. REFORMATION IN LITERATURE. I. TITLE.

PR2367.R4K56  1990   821'.3—DC20  89–29137  CIP

THIS BOOK HAS BEEN COMPOSED IN PALATINO

PRINCETON UNIVERSITY PRESS BOOKS ARE PRINTED
ON ACID-FREE PAPER, AND MEET THE GUIDELINES FOR
PERMANENCE AND DURABILITY OF THE COMMITTEE ON
PRODUCTION GUIDELINES FOR BOOK LONGEVITY
OF THE COUNCIL ON LIBRARY RESOURCES

PRINTED IN THE UNITED STATES OF AMERICA BY
PRINCETON UNIVERSITY PRESS, PRINCETON, NEW JERSEY

1  3  5  7  9  10  8  6  4  2

IN MEMORY OF

*William A. Ringler, Jr.*

# CONTENTS

# LIST OF FIGURES

# ACKNOWLEDGMENTS

THIS BOOK REPRESENTS the second part of a consideration of
the emergence and development of the English Protestant literary tradition during the sixteenth and seventeenth centuries.
As such, it is the sequel to my study of literature and culture during
the reign of Edward VI: *English Reformation Literature: The Tudor Origins of the Protestant Tradition* (Princeton, 1982).

I am particularly indebted to the late William A. Ringler, Jr., in
whose Spenser seminar at the University of Chicago this book found
its inception many years ago, and to Barbara Kiefer Lewalski, whose
1982–83 postdoctoral seminar on Renaissance Genres and Genre Theory at Brown University provided a splendid opportunity for preliminary research and for airing ideas. A fellowship from the National
Endowment for the Humanities made that work possible, and I have
continued the project with the support of an ACLS Grant-in-Aid
(1983), a Huntington Library-NEH Fellowship (1984), and a Folger
Shakespeare Library-NEH Senior Resident Fellowship (1986–87).
Bates College has supported this work by extending a sabbatical
leave and other released time, and by awarding me two Roger C.
Schmutz grants and a grant for photographic expenses from the Pres-
ident's Discretionary Fund (Fund for Scholarly Research).

Many scholars have offered helpful advice, criticism, assistance,
and encouragement. Among them I count James Bednarz, David
Bevington, Patrick Collinson, Robert C. Evans, A. C. Hamilton,
Thomas Hayward, Anne Imbrie, Peter and Sheila Lindenbaum, Leah
S. Marcus, Barry Menikoff, Maryclaire Monroney, David Paisey,
Thomas P. Roche, Jr., John T. Shawcross, Hallett Smith, Susan Sny-
der, and George Walton Williams. Barbara K. Lewalski and Anne
Lake Prescott have provided a bountiful reservoir of good counsel. I
am especially grateful for the thorough and detailed readings of the
entire text by Darryl Gless, Gordon Kipling, Anne Lake Prescott,
George Rowe, and an anonymous reader for Princeton University
Press. David Norbrook has had a particularly strong influence
through private conversation and through his *Poetry and Politics in the
English Renaissance* (London, 1984), which appeared as I was completing Chapter One in its preliminary form. Robert E. Brown and
Sherry Wert have once again devoted meticulous care to guiding my
work through the process of editing and publication. Sterling Bland
assisted at the Press. The unflagging support of Linda Spugnardi
made it possible for me to make a mid-book shift out of CPM and

Wordstar and into MS-DOS and Wordperfect. Julianna Leveridge collaborated diligently in the preparation of the indices. Toward the end, we received sharp-eyed assistance from Quentin Martin and Robin Smith. I am deeply grateful for their help.

The completion of this project owes much to the support, encouragement, and conversation of the directors, fellows, and readers at the Huntington and Folger Libraries. Librarians and other staff members at both institutions were most helpful, as were their colleagues at the Bodleian Library, British Library, English Faculty Library at Oxford University, Houghton and Widener Libraries at Harvard University, Rockefeller Library at Brown University, and Ladd Library at Bates College.

A number of editors have granted permission for the inclusion of previously published work in suitably abridged, revised, or expanded form. The bulk of Chapter One and the Appendix is drawn from "Spenser's *Shepheardes Calender* and Protestant Pastoral Satire," in *Renaissance Genres: Essays on Theory, History, and Interpretation*, ed. Barbara K. Lewalski, Harvard English Studies 14 (Cambridge, Mass., 1986), pp. 369–98; and "Was Spenser a Puritan?" *SSt* 6 (1985): 1–31. Short excerpts from the following essays appear in different parts of this book: "Queen Elizabeth I: Representations of the Virgin Queen," *Renaissance Quarterly* 43 (1990): 30–74; "Milton's Bower of Bliss: A Rewriting of Spenser's Art of Married Love," *Renaissance and Reformation*, n. s. 10 (1986): 289–99; and "Reformation" and "sacraments," in *The Spenser Encyclopedia*, ed. A. C. Hamilton, et al. (Toronto, 1990), pp. 1174–78, 1233–34. Portions of this book have been presented in papers delivered at the Folger Shakespeare Library, Harvard University Seminar on Renaissance Studies, Huntington Library, and the 1986 and 1987 meetings of the Modern Language Association of America.

Book-length studies by Sean Kane, David Lee Miller, and John N. Wall, Jr., were published too late to have had an impact on the present argument.

The modern use of i/j, u/v, and w is followed. Contractions in early printed books are silently expanded. I am of course responsible for all remaining errors and deficiencies.

Above all, I would like to thank my wife, Pauline, for her constant support. Without her forbearance, this book would still be in progress.

# ABBREVIATIONS

U NLESS OTHERWISE STATED, London is the place of publication and reference is to first editions. The abbreviation *sig.* is omitted from signature references. Except for biblical passages quoted in early printed books, scriptural texts are from *The Geneva Bible*, facsimile of the 1560 edition with introduction by Lloyd E. Berry (Madison: University of Wisconsin Press, 1969). Spenserian quotations are either from *The Poetical Works of Edmund Spenser*, ed. J. C. Smith and Ernest de Sélincourt, 3 vols. (Oxford: Clarendon Press, 1909–10); or from *Var.* Miltonic texts are from *The Poems of John Milton*, ed. John Carey and Alastair Fowler (London: Longman, 1968).

| | |
|---|---|
| *A&M* (1563) | John Foxe, *Actes and Monuments of these Latter and Perillous Dayes* (1563) |
| *A&M* (1570) | John Foxe, *Actes and Monumentes of Thynges Passed in Every Kynges Tyme in this Realme*, 2nd ed., rev. and enlarged, 2 vols. (1570) |
| *A&M* (1877) | John Foxe, *Actes and Monumentes* ed. S. R. Cattley, rev. and corrected by J. Pratt, 8 vols. (1877) |
| *Am.* | Edmund Spenser, *Amoretti* (1595) |
| *Article(s)* | *The Thirty-nine Articles of Religion* (1563 [Lat.], 1571 [Eng.]), from Charles Hardwick, *A History of the Articles of Religion* (London: George Bell and Sons, 1888), pp. 289–353 |
| *BCP* | *The Book of Common Prayer, 1559: The Elizabethan Prayer Book*, ed. John E. Booty (Charlottesville: University Press of Virginia, for the Folger Shakespeare Library, 1976) |
| *Book of Homilies* | *Certaine Sermons or Homilies Appoynted to be Read in Churches*, 2 vols. (1633); personal copy. Contains the text of *Certayne Sermons, or Homilies* (1547) and *The Seconde Tome of Homelyes* (1563) |
| "Book of Martyrs" | The popular title of Foxe's *Acts and Monuments* |
| *Calender* | Edmund Spenser, *The Shepheardes Calender* (1579) |

| | |
|---|---|
| Dixon, *Commentary* | John Dixon, *The First Commentary on "The Faerie Queene,"* ed. Graham Hough (Stansted: privately published, 1964) |
| *ELH* | *A Journal of English Literary History* |
| *ELR* | *English Literary Renaissance* |
| *Epith.* | Edmund Spenser, *Epithalamion* (1595) |
| *ERL* | John N. King, *English Reformation Literature: The Tudor Origins of the Protestant Tradition* (Princeton: Princeton University Press, 1982) |
| *Essential Articles* | A.C. Hamilton, ed., *Essential Articles for the Study of Edmund Spenser* (Hamden, Conn.: Archon Books, 1972) |
| *FQ* | Edmund Spenser, *The Faerie Queene*, 2 vols. (1590, 1596) |
| *FQ*, ed. Hamilton | Edmund Spenser, *The Faerie Queene*, ed. A. C. Hamilton (London: Longman, 1977) |
| *FQ*, ed. Roche | Edmund Spenser, *The Faerie Queene*, ed. Thomas P. Roche, Jr. (Harmondsworth: Penguin Books, 1978) |
| *HLQ* | *Huntington Library Quarterly* |
| *JEGP* | *Journal of English and Germanic Philology* |
| *JWCI* | *Journal of the Warburg and Courtauld Institutes* |
| Kellogg and Steele | Edmund Spenser, *Books I and II of "The Faerie Queene," the Mutability Cantos, and Selections from the Minor Poetry*, ed. Robert Kellogg and Oliver Steele (New York: Odyssey Press, 1965) |
| *MLN* | *Modern Language Notes* |
| *N&Q* | *Notes and Queries* |
| *OED* | *A New English Dictionary on Historical Principles*, ed. J.A.H. Murray et al., 11 vols. (Oxford: Oxford University Press, 1884–1933) |
| *Orl. fur.* | Ariosto, *Orlando furioso*, trans. Sir John Harington (1591), ed. Robert McNulty (Oxford: Clarendon Press, 1972) |
| *PL* | John Milton, *Paradise Lost* (1667, 1674) |
| *PMLA* | *Publications of the Modern Language Association of America* |
| *RQ* | *Renaissance Quarterly* |
| *SSt* | *Spenser Studies* |
| *SP* | *Studies in Philology* |

STC

*A Short-Title Catalogue of Books Printed in England, Scotland, and Ireland, and of English Books Printed Abroad, 1475–1640*, first compiled by A. W. Pollard and G. R. Redgrave; 2nd ed., rev. and enlarged, begun by W. A. Jackson and F. S. Ferguson, completed by Katharine F. Pantzer, 2 vols. (London: The Bibliographical Society, 1976–86)

Var.

*The Works of Edmund Spenser: A Variorum Edition*, ed. Edwin A. Greenlaw, C. G. Osgood, F. M. Padelford et al., 10 vols. in 11 pts. (Baltimore: Johns Hopkins University Press, 1932–57)

YES

*Yearbook of English Studies*

# SPENSER'S POETRY
## AND THE
## REFORMATION TRADITION

# INTRODUCTION

THIS BOOK PRESENTS the first extended treatment of Edmund Spenser's place in the Reformation literary tradition and his employment and redefinition of artistic practices, iconographical formulas, and royalist praise associated with Protestant poets and apologists. It supplements the familiar view of the epic poet of Elizabethan England as a rival of Continental literary predecessors by situating his work within the context of English culture of the middle and latter parts of the sixteenth century. While this study does not attempt to dislodge the writings of Virgil, Ovid, Ariosto, and Tasso as the poet's major literary models, it does aim to show how Spenser infuses the sophisticated standards of the European Renaissance, which were based upon classical precedents, with unpretentious devices of native satire and allegory that were adopted by English Protestant authors.[1]

Because most studies of Renaissance literature and iconography "still face toward Italy,"[2] it is essential to define the domestic cultural context that supplies Spenser with late medieval formulas for complaint and satire, and allegorical structures akin to the *psychomachia* combat of early Tudor interludes. Under the impact of the Reformation, many sixteenth-century English authors grafted Protestant ideology onto literary and artistic conventions and techniques that predated and/or coexisted with the newly imported classical and Italianate standards of the Continental Renaissance. The present study therefore scrutinizes Spenser's habit of drawing upon and transforming a variety of conventions, topoi, and iconographical devices from English Protestant literature and art, which coexist with humanistic and Italianate elements in his works. Certain of these practices inhere in late medieval English verse that was in vogue during the early phase of the English Reformation and in mid-Tudor satire and allegory. Spenser's thinking is in tune with the criticism of religious corruption associated with Chaucer and the *Piers Plowman* poet; indeed, he joins other Protestants in appropriating the views of late medieval dissidents like the Lollards and of those Catholics who identified the pope with Antichrist and the Church of Rome with the Whore of Babylon. Although these viewpoints are neither new nor

---

[1] See Anne Lake Prescott, "Spenser's Chivalric Restoration: From Bateman's *Travayled Pylgrime* to the Redcrosse Knight," *SP* 86 (1989): 194.

[2] Ernest Gilman, *Iconoclasm and Poetry in the English Reformation: "Down Went Dagon"* (Chicago: University of Chicago Press, 1986), p. 2.

distinctively Protestant, Spenser and his contemporaries feature them in their arsenal of anti-Catholic propaganda. The Reformation was still relatively young when Spenser began his poetic career, however, and "native" and "Protestant" had tension as well as overlap.

Spenser's emulation of the archaic diction, style, and characterization of *The Canterbury Tales* and *The Plowman's Tale*, a radical satire that had been drawn spuriously into the Chaucer canon, indicates his place within English Protestant tradition. He shares the widespread Tudor reverence for Chaucer both as a poetic paragon and as a reputed disciple of Wyclif. The Middle English master's portraits of worldly clerics accord with some elements of the Reformation attack against the Church of Rome. Chaucer's works were aligned with *Piers Plowman* and reformist texts associated with it, which spawned a host of anticlerical dialogues, estates satires, and millennial prophecies during their vogue under the permissive Protestant regime of Edward VI (1547–53).[3] At that time Protestant authors also exhibited intense interest in the vernacular Bible as a model for poetic imagery, genres, allusions, parables, and rhetorical structures. Although it is true that scripturalism permeated fifteenth- and sixteenth-century Catholic poetry,[4] authors as various as the Wakefield Master and Robert Southwell demonstrated how the Catholic tradition is shaped by apocryphal additions, Mariology, sacramentalism, and elements of the old church calendar that were shunned by Protestants.

The literary milieu for Spenser's active poetic career (1569–99) is more varied than the generally uncomplicated nativism, scripturalism, and didacticism of the preceding decades. Although readers continued to seek out Edwardian gospelling poetry and drama at London bookstalls,[5] Queen Elizabeth forbade the public dramatization of religious and political topics at the outset of her reign.[6] Even though *Piers Plowman* was out of print for 250 years following a single early Elizabethan edition, black-letter folio printings of Chaucer's works continued to appear. Old-fashioned modes of complaint, satire, and invective retained their dynamism in the Marprelate pamphlets.[7] Although critics like Sir Philip Sidney and George Puttenham

[3] See *ERL*, chs. 5–7.

[4] On the continuity of scripturalism before and after the Reformation, see Janel M. Mueller, *The Native Tongue and the Word: Developments in English Prose Style, 1380–1580* (Chicago: University of Chicago Press, 1984).

[5] *ERL*, pp. 428–32. See also Norbrook, *Poetry and Politics*, p. 59.

[6] Murray Roston, *Biblical Drama in England: From the Middle Ages to the Present Day* (Evanston, Ill.: Northwestern University Press, 1968), p. 114.

[7] See Ritchie D. Kendall, *The Drama of Dissent: The Radical Poetics of Nonconformity, 1380–1590* (Chapel Hill: University of North Carolina Press, 1986), pp. 187–94.

began to attack the validity of nativist style and matter as models for imitation, Spenser followed the pattern of those contemporaries who amalgamated native and imported literary modes. This strategy of poetic inclusion provoked Sidney's censure of the "old rustick language" of *The Shepheardes Calender* on the ground that its humble vernacular idiom lacked precedent "sith neyther *Theocritus* in Greeke, *Virgill* in Latine, nor *Sanazar* in Italian did affect it."[8] Nevertheless, a collection like Barnabe Googe's *Eglogs, Epytaphes, and Sonettes* (1563) afforded a sturdy native precedent for Spenser's amalgamation of Continental pastoral, Protestant religious allegory, and humble vernacular idiom in the ecclesiastical eclogues of the *Calender*. Elizabethan syncretism also gave rise to works like Googe's *The Shippe of Safegarde* (1569) and Stephen Bateman's *The Travayled Pylgrime* (1569), which share with *The Faerie Queene* an encyclopedic combination of romance, quest narrative, didactic allegory, and Protestant polemics.[9]

Spenser relies upon the modification of genres in his attempt to harmonize competing elements drawn from classical, biblical, medieval, Renaissance, pre- and post-Reformation, imported, and native literary and iconographical traditions. This inclusionist strategy treats the repertoire of historical genres (e.g., epic, tragedy, pastoral eclogue, sonnet) not as a fixed set of prescriptive precedents and rules, but rather as a framework for generic hybridization and mutation that entails a "fruitful questioning" of received literary models. Claudio Guillén accordingly defines literary genre (or kind) as "a problem-solving model, a standing invitation to the matching of matter and form." In place of the older dependence of literary history upon content, themes, sources, and analogues, he argues that "the central thrust of generic definition is the association of matter with form," whereby new genres come into being that incorporate or allude to old genres, conventions, and techniques as their subject matter.[10] The combination of genres enabled Renaissance authors who tended not to believe in prescriptive rules to create "encyclopedic works of 'mixed genre' which incorporate and juxtapose virtually the entire range of generic conventions." As a "set of interpretations, of 'frames' or 'fixes' on the world," the genre system furnishes a means

[8] G. Gregory Smith, ed., *Elizabethan Critical Essays*, 2 vols. (Oxford: Oxford University Press, 1904), 1: 196. Angus Fletcher addresses the need to avoid condemnation of "the tonal rusticity in the Spenserian renewal of Chaucer's 'antique' diction" in *The Prophetic Moment: An Essay on Spenser* (Chicago: University of Chicago Press, 1971), p. 99.

[9] See Prescott, "Spenser's Chivalric Restoration," pp. 166–97.

[10] Guillén, *Literature as System: Essays toward the Theory of Literary History* (Princeton: Princeton University Press, 1971), pp. 109–13, 122, 386.

of commenting upon human experience.[11] Furthermore, one may approach the historical genres in terms of a "family of generic indicators" whose presence in a sufficient density indicates the membership of a work in a particular category. These overlapping indicators may include external and metrical structure, magnitude, subject, values, mood, occasion, character, style, and like features.[12]

Generic mixture offers Spenser a versatile tool for his syncretic attempt to reconcile the competing claims of the various components of his literary heritage. Despite this effort to synthesize discordant parts, no doubt remains concerning the insufficiency of many of the literary models that he assimilates into a wider Christian pattern. Some of his modifications indicate a sectarian position, for example the grafting of native plowman satire onto imported pastoral conventions in the ecclesiastical eclogues of the *Calender*. These poems are rooted not only in classical and neo-Latin precedent, but also in the native tradition of complaint and satire spawned by *Piers Plowman*.[13] The alignment of Spenser's religious satires with the homiletic style of Hugh Latimer's "Sermon on the Plowers" (1548) places the *Calender* within the mainstream of Tudor Protestant thought (see p. 22).

As counterparts to the modification and variation of many genres under the impact of Reformation ideology, certain "countergenres"[14] came into existence that criticized literary practices associated with Catholicism. In line with this movement, Spenser fashioned a distinctively Protestant version of the saint's life in Book 1 of *The Faerie Queene*; he rejects many elements in medieval lives of saints, notably those in *The Golden Legend*, which Protestants regarded as superstitious. Intimately related to countergenre are parody and inversion, which are closely associated with satire. Parody involves the transference of conventions from one genre to another. While such imitation was often employed to burlesque an original and make it appear ridiculous, it had not yet acquired exclusively derogatory associa-

---

[11] Rosalie Colie, *The Resources of Kind: Genre-Theory in the Renaissance*, ed. Barbara K. Lewalski (Berkeley and Los Angeles: University of California Press, 1973), pp. viii, 8, 76–77. See also Lewalski's overview of Milton's use of an encyclopedic array of literary genres and modes as a rhetorical vehicle for education and discovery in *"Paradise Lost" and the Rhetoric of Literary Forms* (Princeton: Princeton University Press, 1985).

[12] Alastair Fowler, *Kinds of Literature: An Introduction to the Theory of Genres and Modes* (Cambridge, Mass.: Harvard University Press, 1982), pp. 37–74.

[13] See Hallett Smith, *Elizabethan Poetry: A Study in Conventions, Meaning, and Expression* (Cambridge, Mass.: Harvard University Press, 1952), pp. 208–16; and Norbrook, *Poetry and Politics in the English Renaissance* (London: Routledge and Kegan Paul, 1984), p. 69.

[14] See Guillén, *Literature as System*, pp. 133, 146–47. Fowler employs the term "antigenre" in *Kinds of Literature*, pp. 174–75, 216.

tions.[15] Examination of Spenser's use of these devices is helpful for understanding how the iconoclastic movement to extirpate "idolatry" leaves its mark on the ecclesiastical eclogues of the *Calender* and many episodes in *The Faerie Queene*.

By way of contrast to the longstanding view that Protestant iconoclasm is inherently opposed to fiction and visual art, Spenser assumes the existence of a complex dialectic in which a destructive attack against "false" images gives rise to a corresponding movement to construct acceptable forms of "true" literature and art (see *ERL*, pp. 144–60). Stephen Greenblatt's identification of Guyon's dismantling of the Bower of Bliss with "the principle of regenerative violence," whereby the "act of tearing down is the act of fashioning," permits us therefore to pinpoint the internalization within *The Faerie Queene* of the Reformation attack against idolatry as a force that is aesthetically *constructive* as well as *destructive*. The related insight that the Protestant Tudor monarchs rely upon a pattern of "displacement and absorption"[16] in improvising their strategy of assimilating the external forms of prohibited Catholic ritual and literature enables us to see how Spenser fills the generic space left empty by a pattern of iconoclastic destruction with iconic images that praise Queen Elizabeth as a religious leader—as well as with the array of "demonic" parodies of her authority that includes Lucifera and Duessa. The ground-breaking findings of Frances Yates and Roy Strong concerning the incorporation of Mariological imagery into Elizabeth's portraiture and heraldry may be extended to Spenser's practice in *The Faerie Queene*,[17] where the uneasy symmetry between positive and negative queenly images reflects the poet's fascination with apocalyptic images of religious "truth" and "error." Symbolic woodcuts in Stephen Bateman's *Christall Glasse of Christian Reformation* (1569) and other contemporary illustrated books provide a rich source of Protestant visual satire that illuminates iconic allegories in *The Faerie Queene*.

A number of important critical studies have begun to explore Protestant poetic theory and practice during the English Renaissance.

[15] See Rosemond Tuve, "Sacred 'Parody' of Love Poetry, and Herbert," *Studies in the Renaissance* 8 (1961): 249–90; Fletcher, *The Prophetic Moment*, p. 99; and *ERL*, p. 214.

[16] Greenblatt, *Renaissance Self-Fashioning: From More to Shakespeare* (Chicago: University of Chicago Press, 1980), pp. 188, 230.

[17] Yates, "Queen Elizabeth as Astraea," *JWCI* 10 (1947): 27–82, reprinted in idem, *Astraea: The Imperial Theme in the Sixteenth Century* (London: Routledge and Kegan Paul, 1975), pp. 29–87; and Strong, *The Cult of Elizabeth: Elizabethan Portraiture and Pageantry* (London: Thames and Hudson, 1977), pp. 46–52. For an application of the theories of Yates and Strong, see Robin H. Wells, *Spenser's "Faerie Queene" and the Cult of Elizabeth* (London: Croom Helm, 1983).

The present investigation builds upon the work of Barbara K. Lewalski concerning later poetic tradition,[18] and it extends David Norbrook's examination of the relation of Spenser's literary practice to Protestant political and ideological concerns.[19] Other critics have also indicated ways in which Spenser's verse incorporates devotional and satirical attitudes of the sixteenth-century Protestant movement.[20] The historical assumptions of recent studies have given rise to questions concerning cultural poetics, literary genres, conventions, and topoi that were ignored by A.S.P. Woodhouse and Virgil Whitaker when they accomplished the necessary task of defining the theological doctrines at work in Spenser's verse.[21] Although Anthea Hume has rightly directed our attention to contemporary sermons and commentaries as a context for understanding Spenser's poems, she tends to reduce the satirical eclogues to tractarian arguments by insisting that the poet shares the goals of Puritan divines. Her concern with doctrinaire thematic categories helps to explain why her book fights anew the long-since victorious battle to disprove the dichotomy that Woodhouse draws between the Christian concerns of Book 1 and the secular frame of the remainder of *The Faerie Queene*.[22] Agreeing that Spenser is a "puritan humanist," Alan Sinfield makes an ahistorical effort to demonstrate the poet's movement toward "a general disillusion with protestant values." By simply reversing the Woodhouse hypothesis that Spenser sharply differentiates between nature and grace, for example, Sinfield misunderstands his commitment to Christian syncretism as "a happy confusion" of Christian and pagan categories.[23] Sinfield's thesis leads Gary Waller to claim that lyric

[18] Lewalski, *Protestant Poetics and the Seventeenth-Century Religious Lyric* (Princeton: Princeton University Press, 1979).

[19] Norbrook, *Poetry and Politics*, chs. 3–5; and his "Panegyric of the Monarch and Its Social Context under Elizabeth I and James I," dissertation, Oxford University, 1978.

[20] See Andrew Weiner, *Sir Philip Sidney and the Poetics of Protestantism: A Study of Contexts* (Minneapolis: University of Minnesota Press, 1978); Greenblatt, *Renaissance Self-Fashioning*, pp. 188–91; Lynn Staley Johnson, "Elizabeth, Bride and Queen: A Study of Spenser's April Eclogue and the Metaphors of English Protestantism," *SSt* 2 (1981): 75–91; and Louis A. Montrose, " 'Eliza, Queene of shepheardes,' and the Pastoral of Power," *ELH* 10 (1980): 153–82.

[21] Woodhouse, "Nature and Grace in *The Faerie Queene*," *ELH* 16 (1949): 194–228; reprinted in *Essential Articles for the Study of Edmund Spenser*, ed. A. C. Hamilton (Hamden, Conn.: Archon Books, 1972), pp. 58–83; and Whitaker, *The Religious Basis of Spenser's Thought*, Stanford University Publications, University Series, Language and Literature, vol. 7, no. 3 (Stanford: Stanford University Press, 1950).

[22] Hume, *Edmund Spenser: Protestant Poet* (Cambridge: Cambridge University Press, 1984), pp. 59–71, esp. pp. 59–60 for a summary of this critical controversy.

[23] Sinfield, *Literature in Protestant England, 1560–1660* (London: Croom Helm, 1983),

verse is "a site of intense cultural struggle" between Protestant attitudes and Petrarchan topoi and conventions.[24]

Scholars continue to debate Spenser's exact religious position even though the headnotes for the ecclesiastical eclogues in the *Calender* identify him explicitly with the progressive Protestant movement to continue the process of church reform. The glosses that E.K. supplies for those satires consistently contrast "Catholic," "popish," or "papist" practices with "protestant" reforms in public worship and individual devotion (*Var.* 7, i: 46, 57–58, 75, 84). Efforts to align the poet with "Puritan,"[25] "Catholic,"[26] or "Anglican"[27] camps have failed because of the existence of a broad consensus concerning official theology. It is inappropriate, furthermore, to define the Elizabethan church settlement in terms of "Anglicanism" because that system derives largely from the nineteenth-century Oxford Movement and John Henry Newman's promotion of an "Anglican" *via media* between Protestantism and Roman Catholicism prior to his conversion. The recent findings of ecclesiastical historians have discredited anachronistic efforts to discover a conflict between "Anglicanism" and "Puritanism" during the sixteenth century.[28] During Spenser's

---

pp. 29–30; see also pp. 1–19, 27–50. Sinfield ignores positions concerning church discipline and polity that ecclesiastical historians generally identify with the Elizabethan Puritan movement.

[24] Waller, *English Poetry of the Sixteenth Century* (London: Longman, 1986), pp. 93–104, 136.

[25] See *Var.* 7, i: 600–609; Hume, *Protestant Poet*, pp. 3–9, 14–15, 17–27; and Appendix, below.

[26] Paul McLane, "Spenser's Political and Religious Position in the *Shepheardes Calender*," *JEGP* 49 (1950): 332; *Spenser's "Shepheardes Calender": A Study in Elizabethan Allegory* (Notre Dame, Ind.: University of Notre Dame Press, 1961), pp. 117–18, et seq.; and "Spenser and the Primitive Church," *English Language Notes* 1 (1963): 6–11. For a critique of McLane's position, see Norbrook, *Poetry and Politics*, p. 297 nn. 10–11.

[27] Daniel W. Doerksen criticizes the "Anglican" interpretation in "Recharting the *Via Media* of Spenser and Herbert," *Renaissance and Reformation*, n.s. 8, no. 3 (August 1984): 215–25. The nomenclature of Whitaker's *Religious Basis* is problematic because he applies the term "Anglican" to what E.K. terms "protestant." Whitaker rightly concludes that although Spenser objects to Roman Catholic ritual and ceremonial, he sympathizes with the "Catholic" tradition that encompasses "pre-Reformation elements" that Catholics and English Protestants shared in common (p. 8 n. 31, and pp. 3–8, passim).

[28] See Patrick Collinson, "A Comment Concerning the Name Puritan," *Journal of Ecclesiastical History* 31 (1980): 483–88. Concluding that "moderate puritan" best describes the "predominant style current in the Elizabethan church," Peter Lake rejects as a false dichotomy the choice of "*either* a rigidly defined, party-based conflict or opposition, *or* a conflict-free consensus" in *Moderate Puritans and the Elizabethan Church* (Cambridge: Cambridge University Press, 1982), pp. 279–80, and 281–92, passim. Although "Puritan" came into play during the sixteenth century as a term of abuse, no usage of "An-

lifetime a sharp cleavage had not yet emerged in the Church of England between conformists and separatists. Thomas Cranmer's *via media* survived in the Elizabethan church, but it mediated chiefly between Roman Catholicism and Protestant dissenting groups, like the Anabaptists whose beliefs were rejected by the "magisterial" reformers.[29] Until Archbishop Laud encouraged a shift toward Arminianism and Roman Catholic religious practices under Charles I, the broadly inclusive doctrine of the Church of England continued to accommodate early Puritans.[30]

During Spenser's lifetime, Protestant groups united in opposition to key teachings of medieval or Tridentine Catholicism concerning papal supremacy, clerical intercession, purgatory, pardons, adoration of images and relics, invocation of saints, transubstantiation, and the concept of the mass as a continuing sacrifice. These views were incorporated into the official formularies of the Church of England, including the codification of doctrine in the *Thirty-nine Articles*, which provided Spenser and his contemporaries with a readily accessible compendium of Protestant theology. The poet grew up knowing the official doctrine and ritual of the Elizabethan church as it was transmitted through reading and hearing the *Book of Common Prayer*, which set forth the order of worship and the attendant reading of sermons from the *Book of Homilies* and scriptural texts drawn from the Great Bible or its successor, the Bishops' Bible.[31] Like other learned Protestants (including Matthew Parker, Queen Elizabeth's first Archbishop of Canterbury), he presumably read the Geneva Bible, which incurred official disapproval because of its polemical annotations. Based upon Cranmer's original documents, Elizabethan formularies accord with the predestinarian theology of grace of Continental reformers like Ulrich Zwingli, Martin Bucer, Pietro Martire Vermigli (Peter Martyr), and Heinrich Bullinger.[32] Because Richard Hooker's

---

glican" in Newman's sense of the term existed prior to the mid-nineteenth century (*OED*, *s.v.* "Anglicanism").

[29] Patrick Collinson, *The Elizabethan Puritan Movement* (Berkeley and Los Angeles: University of California Press, 1967), pp. 34–35. See also *ERL*, pp. 86, 90, 92, 152.

[30] Norbrook, *Poetry and Politics*, p. 65. See also Weiner, *Sidney and the Poetics of Protestantism*, pp. 5–7, 190–91 n. 8.

[31] John N. Wall, Jr., argues that the official formularies of the Church of England had a considerable impact upon Book 1 of *The Faerie Queene* in "The English Reformation and the Recovery of Christian Community in Spenser's *The Faerie Queene*," *SP* 80 (1983): 150–51, 155. See also his "Godly and Fruitful Lessons: The English Bible, Erasmus' Paraphrases, and the Book of Homilies," in John E. Booty, ed., *The Godly Kingdom of Tudor England: Great Books of the English Reformation* (Wilton, Conn.: Morehouse-Barlow Co., 1981), pp. 47–135; and *ERL*, pp. 122–38, 429.

[32] See Dewey D. Wallace, Jr., *Puritans and Predestination: Grace in English Protestant*

*Of the Laws of Ecclesiastical Polity* (1593, 1597) was published too late
to have had an appreciable impact upon Spenser's verse, the present
study employs the doctrinal sermons in the first *Book of Homilies*, John
Jewel's *An Apology of the Church of England*, Martyr's *Common Places*,
and Calvin's *Institution of the Christian Religion* as normative sources
for Elizabethan theology.

Spenser's verse demonstrates a distinctively Elizabethan glorification of the monarch as an instrument of divine providence against
vestiges of "papistry," the formulations of the Council of Trent, and
the attempt to reconvert England by means of the Jesuit Mission. His
works provide every indication that he favors an episcopacy owing
obedience to the queen as Supreme Governor of the Church of England. He celebrates the monarchal authorization of the Bible as the
self-sufficient means of divine revelation in this world, one indepen-
dent of the traditional authority of the Roman Catholic Church. Such
attitudes underlie Spenser's praise of Elizabeth in her early guise of
Eliza ("April") and in her many guises in *The Faerie Queene*.

The vicissitudes of Elizabethan politics and religion during the
1580s and 1590s help to account for some of the sharp differences
between the relative optimism of the first two books of *The Faerie
Queene* and the deep-seated pessimism revealed by the harsh realities
of Books 5 and 6.[33] Spenser's celebration of the Protestant values held
by many members of the privy council, whose inner circle was dominated by Leicester and Walsingham until the late 1580s, gives rise to
unresolved tensions in the epic between conservative ideology and
progressive goals. This gap becomes pronounced in the Belge episode in Book 5 of *The Faerie Queene*, which idealizes the militant policy
of intervention in behalf of beleaguered Protestants in the Low Countries despite the queen's evident disapproval. David Norbrook notes
that the "Legend of Justice" contains not only a "sustained defence
of the Leicester-Essex foreign policy," but also the representation in
the Mercilla episode of the execution of Mary, Queen of Scots, in
accordance with Parliamentary opinion but in direct violation of Elizabeth's publicly expressed wishes. Even though it was published
many years after the disgrace of Spenser's patron, Arthur Lord Grey
de Wilton, Lord Deputy of Ireland, for the 1580 massacre of Spanish

---

*Theology, 1525–1695* (Chapel Hill: University of North Carolina Press, 1982), pp. viii, x–
xi, et seq.; and Patrick Collinson, "England and International Calvinism, 1558–1640,"
in *International Calvinism, 1541–1715*, ed. Menna Prestwich (Oxford: Clarendon Press,
1985), pp. 214–15.

[33] Richard Helgerson, *Self-Crowned Laureates: Spenser, Jonson, Milton, and the Literary
System* (Berkeley and Los Angeles: University of California Press, 1983), pp. 83–84, 90–
91.

and Irish troops at Smerwick, the "Legend of Justice" defends the harshly punitive colonial policy of the Protestant militants.[34]

The present study investigates Spenser's poetic *oeuvre* neither exhaustively nor chronologically. Because it deals only with major works or episodes where Protestant ideology, conventions, iconography, and transformations of literary genres and modes are a guiding force, this book leaves to others the task of accounting for the importance of patristic, Neoplatonic, Christianized Aristotelian, and pre-Reformation elements in Spenser's verse. This study begins with a consideration of the poet's debut as an emulator of "Chaucerian" precedent for ecclesiastical satire in the *Calender* (Chapter 1). The ensuing argument concentrates on *The Faerie Queene*, Books 1 and 5 in particular, in an extended consideration of the interplay of iconoclasm, iconography, the debate over celibacy and marriage, and generic modification. The *constructive* side of Reformation iconoclasm underlies the pervasive inversion and mutation of iconic tableaux throughout most of *The Faerie Queene*. Among important sites associated with the iconoclastic destruction of "false" art and construction of "true" alternatives are Orgoglio's Castle, the Bower of Bliss, the House of Busirane, the Temple of Venus, Isis Church, and the shrine that Geryoneo dedicates to his late father, Geryon (Chapter 2). A complementary analysis of many queenly "icons," notably Gloriana, Una, Belphoebe, Britomart, and Mercilla, joins the debate over the iconography of Elizabeth I as a political and religious leader (Chapter 3). The study next considers Spenser's complicated presentation of ideals of married chastity. When the poet redefines romantic love in *Amoretti and Epithalamion* and *The Faerie Queene*, he incorporates important elements of Protestant ideology (Chapter 4). A detailed reading of Book 1 (and some parts of Book 5) of *The Faerie Queene* concludes this study by addressing Spenser's reformation of deficient and worldly forms of romance, pastoral, and tragedy into a set of purged and elevated Christian counterparts, within the all-inclusive frame of allegorical romantic epic (Chapter 5).

This book argues that Tudor Protestant literature constituted not a set of material *sources* and *influences* upon Spenser's literary career, but a *tradition* that set firmly in place a constellation of assumptions concerning genres, countergenres, iconography, and iconoclasm. By "tradition" I mean not a teleological continuum of structural influ-

---

[34] Norbrook, *Poetry and Politics*, pp. 112, 132, 139–42, etc. See also Simon Adams, "Eliza Enthroned? The Court and Its Politics," in *The Reign of Elizabeth*, ed. Christopher Haigh (London: Macmillan, 1984), pp. 55–56, 67–68, 75.

ences that assumes simple continuity and repetition of "the same,"[35] but rather a system like that described by Claudio Guillén, one which contains a dynamic field of forces and counterforces. Guillén directs our attention to "conventions and traditions" as " 'fields' or 'systems' where the main unifying factor is accepted usage."[36] I subscribe to the view that "conventions of technique are the essentials of literary tradition and the proper subject of literary history."[37] The presence of a cluster of prominent generic and/or sectarian indicators, along with textual or structural allusions to specific works, provides a literary shortcut that signals the presence of embedded genres or invokes well-known subtexts or topoi. The disguising of Archimago in monastic attire and the provision of his sobriquet, Hypocrisy, are therefore sufficient to associate this false magus with conventional anticlerical characters in Protestant moral interludes of the kind written by John Bale and his contemporaries (see pp. 51–52). An awareness of Reformation iconography should further enable us to recognize in Errour an inversion of the topos of "Truth, the Daughter of Time" when the monster emerges as a perverse *Veritas* from her cave of disfame (see p. 146). This study presupposes a concept of literary tradition based upon topoi, conventions, genres, countergenres, inversions, and parodies rather than the interplay of sources, analogues, and influences. It situates Spenser's achievement within the broad context of Elizabethan Protestant culture.

[35] See Michel Foucault, *The Archaeology of Knowledge*, trans. A. M. Sheridan Smith (New York: Harper and Row, 1976), pp. 4–6, 21–27.

[36] Guillén, *Literature as System*, p. 60.

[37] Arthur Heiserman, *Skelton and Satire* (Chicago: University of Chicago Press, 1961), p. 3.

# ONE

## THE SHEPHEARDES CALENDER

## AND PROTESTANT PASTORAL SATIRE

**P**RAISE OF SPENSER as "our new Poete," in the words of E.K. (*Var.* 7, i: 7), stresses the clear innovation of *The Shepheardes Calender* (1579) as a collection that represents a sharp break with English literary tradition.[1] Accordingly, one can deny neither the self-conscious modishness of its emulation of imported standards of the Continental Renaissance nor its dazzling array of metrical, stanzaic, and generic features that lack precedent in native English literature. The *Calender*'s Continental antecedents include avant-garde French poetry.[2] Nevertheless, it is essential to recognize that Spenser adopts not only Virgil's pastoral pose of poetic apprenticeship but also the recognizable voice of the English religious reformer for his poetic debut under the anonymous guise of Immerito. Although the *Calender* pays homage to Virgil's *Eclogues* as the preeminent model for stylized poetry dealing with the lives and loves of shepherds, the ecclesiastical eclogues are aligned with an alternative Renaissance tradition of pastoral satire. E.K. views them as poems "which for the most part be mixed with some Satyrical bitternesse" (*Var.* 7, i: 12).

Spenser's eclogues on church affairs are rooted in pre-Reformation satire against clerical abuses. A major impulse came from the Continent, where Petrarch directed speeches by pastors, in the double sense of herdsmen and clerics, against the corruption of the Avignon popes. These attacks led Elizabethans to view the Italian poet as a proto-Protestant reformer.[3] When Baptista Spagnuoli (Mantuan)

---

[1] This chapter contains findings originally presented in "Was Spenser a Puritan?" *SSt* 6 (1985): 1–31; and "Spenser's *Shepheardes Calender* and Protestant Pastoral Satire," *Harvard English Studies* 14 (1986): 369–98. Although they were written prior to the publication of Norbrook, *Poetry and Politics,* I have revised the text in light of his argument. Our views are complementary, and we share many of the same problems and conclusions.

[2] On Spenser's imitation of Clément Marot's eclogues on Louise de Savoie and François I^re as Pan in "November" and "December" respectively, see Anne Lake Prescott, *French Poets and the English Renaissance: Studies in Fame and Transformation* (New Haven: Yale University Press, 1978), pp. 10–12.

[3] Petrarch, *Bucolicum carmen*: "Pastorum pathos" ("The Shepherds' Suffering") and

wrote *Adolescentia seu Bucolica* (Mantua, 1498), he elaborated upon Virgilian precedent and Petrarch's satirical application of biblical texts in ten neo-Latin eclogues that were read in English grammar schools. Mantuan's honorable standing as a Carmelite friar lent credence to pastoral satire that conventionally dealt with the problems of clerical greed and ignorance. The association of Mantuanesque pastoral[4] with satire, archaism, and dialectical usage may be noted in England as early as Alexander Barclay's *Egloges* (c. 1515). John Bale anglicized Mantuan as a model for Protestant satire before Spenser's birth, when the Protestant activist viewed him as an anti-Scholastic who "smelled out more abuses in the Romysh churche, then in those daies he durst wele utter." Bale praises Mantuan's first and ninth eclogues in particular for their attack on clerical corruption.[5]

The invocation of Chaucer's verse, the pseudo-Chaucerian *Plowman's Tale*, and *Piers Plowman* in E.K.'s commentary and the envoi of the *Calender* indicates that Spenser's departure from English literary tradition is not so great as it may at first appear. Tudor authors and readers interpreted—and emulated—those native vernacular works as powerful appeals for the correction of ecclesiastical abuses and the social ills stemming from them.[6] Furthermore, English poems of the 1560s and 1570s exemplify conventions that characterize the ecclesiastical eclogues of the *Calender*. Like that text, the eight eclogues in Barnabe Googe's *Eglogs, Epytaphes, and Sonettes* (1563) join together diverse material including imitations of Mantuan, translations from Montemayor's *Diana*, and didactic counsel concerning the entrapments of romantic love. Googe's third eclogue in particular provides a precedent for Spenser's combination of a plain vernacular style and Protestant religious allegory. Coridon laments the persecution of good shepherds by a neatherd with the same name, who has led the "selye Sheape" into error:

> O Cruell Clownish [i.e., rustic] Coridon,
>   O cursed Carlish Heade,
> Thy simple Shepe, constrayned he,
>   theyr Pasture swete to leave.

(B1)

---

"Grex infectus et suffectus" ("The Infected and Replenished Flock"). See Yates, "Queen Elizabeth as Astraea," in *Astraea*, pp. 41, 44, and 77 n. 3.

[4] See Patrick Cullen, *Spenser, Marvell, and Renaissance Pastoral* (Cambridge, Mass.: Harvard University Press, 1970), pp. 19–26.

[5] *A Lamentable complaynte of Baptista Mantuanus . . . wherin he famylyarly commoneth* [communes] *wyth his owne mynde, that Deathe is not to be feared* (c. 1551), sig. A2r-v; a translation of Mantuan's *De contemnenda morte carmen*.

[6] See H. Smith, *Elizabethan Poetry*, pp. 208–10. For convenience, I refer to the anonymous author of *Piers Plowman* by the traditional ascription, William Langland.

This account of the martyrdoms of "good shepherds" and deception of their "flock" alludes to Mary Tudor's effort to advance the Counter Reformation in England. Although George Turberville fails to add an overtly Protestant edge to his translation of Mantuan's *Eglogs* (1567), pastoral decorum does lead him to imitate rustic dialect in the manner of Spenser's ecclesiastical eclogues: "So have I shapt my stile and tempred it with suche common and ordinarie phrase of speach as Countreymen do use in their affaires" (A3ᵛ). A further precedent for the metrical and stanzaic variety of the *Calender* may be found in the panoply of traditional and experimental verse forms contained in Thomas Churchyard's *The First Parte of Churchyardes Chippes* (1575).

Underlying pastoral satire on religious topics is the Bible, which provides a standard of spiritual purity for criticizing a corrupt church establishment. Although all Christian groups share the scriptures as a model for literature and art, Spenser's adoption of plain vernacular diction and style accords with the Protestant principle that the broadest possible readership should have access to the Bible in the vernacular. The widespread dissemination of English translations of the Bible provided a counterweight to neoclassical standards and aureation. By contrast, Petrarch and Mantuan address an elite audience of clergy and scholars able to read the Vulgate Bible in Latin. Spenser furthermore follows the Protestant adaptation of late medieval satire by using specifically anti-Roman Catholic interpretations of scriptural texts in the *Calender*.

The envoi to the *Calender* incorporates the fundamental biblical metaphor for Christian pastoral by alluding to the Parable of the Good Shepherd (John 10:1–16) in defining the pastoral ideal:

> To teach the ruder shepheard how to feede his sheepe,
> And from the falsers fraud his folded flocke to keepe.
>
> (*Var.* 7, i: 120)

Good ministers and priests imitate Christ in fulfilling their clerical vocation, whereas their flawed colleagues endanger the spiritual health of their charges. Sheep and lambs provide enduring symbols both for Christ as a sheep led "to the slaughter" (Acts 8:32) and for individual Christians. Paradoxically, Christ as the Lamb of God is the shepherd of those who are saved (Rev. 7:17). The satirical eclogues repeatedly apply the Parable of the Good Shepherd in praise of an ideal Christian ministry (see Fig. 1). That parable, Psalm 23:1–3 ("The Lord is my shepherd, I shal not want"), and Christ's Parable of the Lost Sheep (Matt. 18:12–14) fuse with the *topoi* of biblical pastoral concerning dangers to the flock from wolves and thieves. Spenser

## The high way to Heauen.

Fiue talents didſt thou pay, wheron was framed,
  the ſeale of death, Impreſt with crimſon Blood:
Two in thy Hands, two in thy Feet remain'd,
  one in thy Side: thoſe bought that heauenly food,
  that feeds the Soule with his eternall good.
Laie mee downe then, ſweet Chriſt and let mee feed,
on that for which I ſigh, and thou didſt bleed.

**1.** *The Good Shepherd.* Richard Vennard, *The Right Way to Heaven* (1602)

accordingly looks beyond Mantuan's eighth eclogue ("Religio") to scriptural texts such as Matthew 7:15 ("Beware of false prophets, which come to you in shepes clothing, but inwardely they are ravening wolves") for the imagery of "September" and its equation of "Popish prelates" with wolves and foxes (ll. 141–55, et seq.).[7] Similarly the messianic prophecy of Isaiah 40:1–16 fuses with characters and themes from Mantuan's ninth eclogue ("Falco") as a model for "July," with its critical contrast between "proude and ambitious Pastours" and "good shepeheardes." Related scriptural parables and metaphors concerning the sowing of seed and divine husbandry were assimilated readily into the georgic modification of pastoral satire that is identified with the *Piers Plowman* tradition.

Even though all Protestant groups have anti-Catholicism in common, a belief stubbornly persists that Spenser served as a spokesman for Puritan zeal. Little more is offered in proof, however, than the circumstantial evidence that the Protestant pastors in the *Calender* speak in the "idiom . . . of Elizabethan Puritan propaganda" that was familiar from the 1560s dispute over clerical vestments and the 1570s Admonition controversy.[8] Piers's attack against the "tryfles," "bells," and "babes" of the Fox is therefore taken to contain well-worn catchwords and clichés from Puritan pamphlets. Nevertheless, E.K. interprets these standard subjects of Protestant propaganda—bells, idols, and paxes—as the "reliques and ragges of popish superstition" ("May," ll. 238–40 and gloss). Even though Puritans did use such language, it falls into the area of consensus among progressive Protestants who thought of themselves as "godly" and obedient Christians. Tudor readers doubtless identified contemporary religious issues in the satirical eclogues, yet their topical readings would have applied a frequently used set of types—the shepherds, sheep, wolves, and foxes of biblical pastoral—to broad Reformation problems of faith, spiritual regeneration, and salvation.[9] A plain style and highly charged biblical imagery were the common property of En-

---

[7] See Lewalski, *Protestant Poetics*, pp. 96–97, on pastoral metaphor as a trope for the Christian life. William Nelson comments on Petrarch's identification of priests with shepherds in *The Poetry of Edmund Spenser: A Study* (New York: Columbia University Press, 1963), p. 44.

[8] Hume, *Protestant Poet*, pp. 14, 21–23. By way of contrast, Norbrook concludes that Spenser was neither a presbyterian nor a separatist. Although the poet's views were broadly Protestant rather than narrowly Puritan, he was read with approval by Puritans. See Norbrook, *Poetry and Politics*, pp. 60–61, 64, 66–67, 76, and 89–90.

[9] According to William Webbe's *Discourse of English Poetrie* (1586), the respective "lessons" of the "July" and "September" eclogues concern "the commendation of good Pastors, and shame and disprayse of idle and ambitious Goteheardes" and "the loose and retchlesse lyving of Popish Prelates." See G. Smith, *Elizabethan Critical Essays*, 1: 264.

glish Protestant progressives, who agreed that sincere worship should be based upon the scriptures and that ministerial integrity should avoid pride, avarice, and ignorance. The effort to align Spenser with a Puritan camp imposes upon the *Calender* anachronistic assumptions about the state of Elizabethan religion and publishing practices (see Appendix, below). The "Puritan" slogans of the *Calender* differ in no material respect, however, from the official prohibition of "Papisticall superstitions and abuses" that was heard in churches throughout England when preachers read the "Sermon of Good Workes Annexed unto Faith" out of the *Book of Homilies*:

> as of Beads, of Lady Psalters, and Rosaries, of fifteene Oes, of Saint *Bernards* verses, of Saint *Agathes* letters, of Purgatory, of Masses satisfactory, of Stations, and Jubilees, of fayned Reliques, of hallowed Beades, Belles, Bread, Water, Psalmes [i.e., palms], Candles, Fire, and such other: of superstitious fastings, of fraternities or brotherheads, of pardons, with such lyke marchandise, which were so esteemed and abused to the great prejudice of Gods glory and Commandements.
>
> *(Book of Homilies* 1: 38)

Spenser deploys the Foxes and Wolves of the ecclesiastical eclogues as allegorical types for both Roman Catholic priests and crypto-Catholic clergy within the Church of England who prey upon an innocent "flock." Thomalin's application of the Parable of the Good Shepherd furnishes a contrasting exemplum concerning the ideal clerical vocation ("July," ll. 53–56). Such scriptures are expanded into extended fictions in "May," where the imagery of biblical pastoral is infused into the fable of the Fox and the Kid, and "September," where Diggon Davie's account of Roffy's watchfulness applies Christ's admonition in the Sermon on the Mount against "false prophetes, which come to you in shepes clothing, but inwardely they are rauening wolues" (Matt. 7:15). E.K.'s glosses supply appropriate Protestant moralizations.

The satirical eclogues integrate scriptural language with poems that function as literary fictions rather than theological arguments. Nevertheless, religious allegory is only one aspect of a collection concerned with enduring questions about life, love, hard work, leisure, poetry, and death. Because Spenser structures each eclogue as a genuine dialogue or debate rather than a one-sided tractarian formulation, reduction of his artistry to mere argumentation loses the dramatic interplay and dialectical tension within the various months of the *Calender*.[10] The satirical eclogues attack "papist" vestiges, but

[10] See Nelson, *Poetry of Edmund Spenser*, p. 46; and Cullen, *Spenser, Marvell, and Renaissance Pastoral*, pp. 29–32.

they also call into question forms of extreme piety and devotion that alienate some of the Protestant shepherd-pastors from more moderate and humane forms of conduct and belief. Although the ecclesiastical eclogues are of lively topical interest, they integrate broad issues of religious policy with detailed historical allegory concerning individual persons and contemporary events. Political events and motivations remain veiled and enigmatic, however, in even the most topical sections of the *Calender*, those stories alluding to the downfall of Archbishop Edmund Grindal ("July," ll. 215–28) and to Bishop John Young's exposure of a secret papist who was preying on the "flock" of devout Christian "sheep" ("September," ll. 180–225).

## The Protestant Plowman

Spenser was a great amalgamator who modeled himself on "auncient Poetes" like Chaucer and, presumably, Langland.[11] The homage that Spenser pays to the former under the name of Tityrus, as a model for poetic style, craftsmanship, and thought, alludes partly to the Reformation belief that the medieval master was a religious radical. Such praise extends to the identification in *The Faerie Queene* of "Dan *Chaucer*, well of English undefyled" (4.2.32) as a model for versification, uses of language, and moral earnestness. Immerito openly acknowledges his poetic mentor with affected modesty in the Chaucerian envoi to the *Calender*:

> Goe lyttle Calender, thou hast a free passeporte,
> Goe but a lowly gate emongste the meaner sorte.
> Dare not to match thy pype with Tityrus hys style,
> Nor with the Pilgrim that the Ploughman playde a whyle:
> But followe them farre off, and their high steppes adore,
> The better please, the worse despise, I aske nomore.

Spenser confers the classical name of Tityrus on both Chaucer and Virgil, as one means of affirming that England possesses a literary heritage equal to that produced by ancient and modern Continental

---

[11] *Var.* 7, i: 10. The few considerations of the *Calender*'s relationship to the native tradition of the late Middle Ages include Edwin A. Greenlaw's " 'The Shepheards Calender,' " *PMLA* 26 (1911): 437–45; and W. L. Renwick's commentary in his edition of *The Shepherd's Calender* (1930), pp. 200–206, passim. See also A. C. Hamilton, "The Visions of *Piers Plowman* and *The Faerie Queene*," in *Form and Convention in the Poetry of Edmund Spenser*, ed. William Nelson (New York: Columbia University Press, 1961), pp. 2–3, et seq.; Judith H. Anderson, *The Growth of a Personal Voice: "Piers Plowman" and "The Faerie Queene"* (New Haven: Yale University Press, 1976), pp. 1–2; and Norbrook, *Poetry and Politics*, pp. 59–60, et seq.

authors. The ambiguity of Tityrus, whose attributes as English Chaucer superimpose those of Roman Virgil, typifies the complicated nature of a collection whose many layers integrate simultaneous appeals to innovation and tradition. This overlaying of the English Tityrus upon "the Romish *Tityrus*" ("October," l. 55 and gloss) enables Spenser to lodge an exalted claim both to inherit and to surpass native and classical exemplars of poetic excellence. The Virgilian analogy implies that Spenser may ultimately become England's epic poet. As Colin Clout's master and the ancient model for vernacular poetry, the English Tityrus exemplifies the traits of the rustic truthteller. Thenot, for example, declares that in his youth he learned a "tale of truth" from him ("February," ll. 91–92). Colin acknowledges his discipleship to the English Tityrus as a singer of songs, a relationship cited repeatedly in E.K.'s glosses (see "June," ll. 81–82 and gloss).

Just as Tityrus represents a fusion of Virgil and Chaucer, Immerito refers to "the Pilgrim that the Ploughman playde a whyle," thus combining two works that many Tudor readers viewed as proto-Protestant satire: *Piers Plowman* and *The Plowman's Tale*.[12] The allusions and alliterative quotations from the pseudo-Chaucerian *Plowman's Tale* refer to a text that E.K. assigns to the canon (gloss on "February," l. 149). (By contrast, the *Calender* contains neither quotations from nor close textual allusions to *Piers Plowman*.) The Briar's "stirring up sterne strife" by appealing to the Husbandman for aid against the Oak ("February," l. 149) echoes, for example, the opening line of the *Tale* proper, "A Sterne stryf is stered newe" (l. 53). Thomalin's hostility to ostentatious Catholic vestments "ygyrt with belts of glitterand gold" ("July," l. 177) accords with the Pelican's attack on corrupt priests in the *Tale*:

> That hye on horse willeth ryde
> In glitterand golde of grete aray,
> I-paynted and portred all in pryde;
> No commun knight may go so gay.
> Chaunge of clothing every day,
> With golden girdles grete and small.

(ll. 133–38)

---

[12] Thomas Warton cites Spenser's general relationship to Chaucer and Langland in *Observations on the Fairie Queene of Spenser* (1754), pp. 89–90 and 99–142, passim. He treats their works as models for anticlerical satire in *The History of English Poetry*, 3 vols. and vol. 4 unfinished (1774–81), 1: 266, 278. See also Norbrook, *Poetry and Politics*, p. 59; and Alice Miskimin, *The Renaissance Chaucer* (New Haven: Yale University Press, 1975), pp. 93, 290.

E.K. notes that the participle "glitterand" is "used sometime in
Chaucer." In the "April" eclogue, Colin's aside, "Albee forswonck
and forswatt I am" ("April," l. 99), goes without an attribution to
Chaucer because E.K. simply explains that the phrase means "over-
laboured and sunneburnt." This allusion to the description of the
Plowman in the *Tale*'s prologue, "He was forswonke and all forswat"
(l. 14), covertly aligns Spenser's persona with the humble speaker
whom Tudor readers accepted as a member of the Canterbury pilgrimage.[13]

Spenser aligns himself with the sixteenth-century Protestant authors who continued the Lollard tradition of articulating appeals for
reform in the voice of a blunt, truth-telling character named Piers
Plowman. The extraordinary power of the plowman conceit during
this age of religious renewal and reform is manifest in the very popular sermons of Hugh Latimer, the evangelical reformer who advocated a preaching ministry and adopted the alliteration and archaic
vernacular diction associated with the *Piers Plowman* tradition. His
1548 "Sermon on the Plowers" applies a text from Christ's Parable of
the Sower, "He that soweth, the husbandman, the plowman, went
forth to sow his seed" (Luke 8:5), as an allegorical figure for the fulfillment of clerical vocation. In this analysis of the Protestant ministry, the simple gospel conceit for the divine Word of the Bible as
seed, the preacher as plowman, and the "faithful congregation" as
the sown fields of the Lord unites clergy, as common laborers, with
laity.[14] The continuing association of this parable with ecclesiastical
reform may be noted in "The Spiritual Husbandrie," a treatise by
Thomas Kirchmeyer that Barnabe Googe appended to his translation
of Kirchmeyer's satire *The Popish Kingdome* (1570).

By the early sixteenth century, visionary quest narratives and debates featuring the persona of the plain-speaking plowman or roam-
ing countryman had evolved into vehicles for religious and social
protest. The master authors of this tradition were Chaucer and Langland. Even though their works were theologically orthodox, many
Tudor readers viewed them as "Protestant" models because of the
association of their rustic figures with the relentless search for spiri-

---

[13] Quoted from Walter W. Skeat, ed., *Chaucerian and Other Pieces* (Oxford: Clarendon
Press, 1897). See Norbrook, *Poetry and Politics*, pp. 60–61. He suggests that E.K. remains silent about the allusion in "April" in order to avoid possible offense to the
queen, who favored a policy of religious conservatism (p. 87).

[14] Latimer, *Selected Sermons*, ed. A. G. Chester (Charlottesville: University Press of
Virginia, for the Folger Shakespeare Library, 1968), pp. 28–31. Robert Kelly argues that
Latimer uses Langland as a stylistic model in "Hugh Latimer as Piers Plowman," *Stud-
ies in English Literature* 17 (1977): 14–15.

tual truth. Although neither was a Wyclifite, both were praised during the Reformation for anticipating later attacks on the Roman church establishment.[15] The mute honesty of Chaucer's Plowman (*General Prologue*, ll. 529–41) was seen to represent an extension of the simple gospel ethic of his brother, the Parson, in potent contrast to the unsavory greed of the Monk, the Summoner, and the Pardoner, who are stock types from medieval anticlerical satire.

*Piers Plowman*, in particular, amalgamated simple colloquial speech and subjective inward piety in a manner that was thought compatible with the Protestant belief in justification by faith alone and the priesthood of all believers. This masterpiece was commonly accepted as the best-known model for connecting heavy alliteration and blunt vernacular dialect to satirical attack against the Roman Catholic Church. The work first appeared in print in 1550, soon after Latimer preached his "Sermon on the Plowers" at St. Paul's Cathedral in London; the appearance of three editions of the text during that single year attests to the poem's popularity during the radical Reformation of Edward VI's reign. The marginal glosses of the editor, Robert Crowley, ardently apply passages like the following as prophecies of the advent of the Reformation, when Henry VIII imposed royal control over the church and dissolved the monasteries:

> And there shal come a king, and confesse you religious
> And beat you as the bible telleth, for breking of your rule
> And amende moniales, monkes, and chanons
> And put hem to her penaunce.[16]

Crowley collaborated with another editor, John Bale, in reconstructing and publishing a library of complaint and satire that included many writings by Wyclif and his contemporaries. The reformers also drew Lollard additions to the *Piers Plowman* apocrypha, such as *Pierce the Ploughmans Crede* and *The Pilgrim's Tale*, into their expanding canon of radical poetry.[17] The composition of *The Plowman's Tale*—a revision of an early fifteenth-century original—exemplifies how Tudor Protestants embraced the apocryphal tradition.[18] The ad-

---

[15] *ERL*, pp. 50–52, 323, 325.

[16] Quoted from the third edition (*STC* 19907a), sig. N2ʳ; see *The Vision of William Concerning Piers the Plowman*, ed. W. W. Skeat, 2 vols. (Oxford, 1886), B.10.317–20. Crowley was still influential in London at the time that Spenser published the *Calender*, according to Norbrook, *Poetry and Politics*, p. 59.

[17] On the tradition of Lollard satire, see Kendall, *Drama of Dissent*, pp. 67–89.

[18] Andrew Wawn demonstrates in "The Genesis of *The Plowman's Tale*," *YES* 2 (1972): 21–40, that the work is a sixteenth-century reformist revision and expansion of an early fifteenth-century Lollard original.

dition of lexical notes and glossaries to the black letter editions of these texts suggests that contemporary readers would have recognized both the archaism of the *Calender* and E.K.'s explanatory notes on word meanings as constituent elements of Protestant satire.

In line with Chaucer's reputation both as England's chief model for vernacular poetry and as a proto-Protestant satirist, the canon of his poetry underwent radical expansion during the sixteenth century to include works by Lydgate, Hoccleve, anonymous Lollard reformers, and others. Chaucer was first linked to Langland as a Protestant prophet through the fraudulent publication of the apocryphal *Plowman's Tale* as a gathering out of an edition of *The Canterbury Tales* (c. 1535). *Jack Upland* was added to the canon c. 1540 as an antifraternal satire delivered by yet another bluntly outspoken lay speaker. Some Tudor scholars like John Leland even tried to credit *Piers Plowman* itself to Chaucer.[19] The frequent republication of Chaucer's complete works from the 1530s onward suggests that he was known universally as a native poetic model. Until the 1557 publication of Tottel's *Miscellany*, these expanded folio editions of Chaucer's works provided the major anthologies of English vernacular poetry. They presented *The Plowman's Tale* as a complement to Chaucer's *Parson's Tale*; by convention the two came to be located as a reformist coda at the end of *The Canterbury Tales*. In addition to accepting *The Plowman's Tale* as Chaucer's work, John Foxe assimilated *Jack Upland* into the "Book of Martyrs" as an "auncient treatise compiled by Geoffray Chawcer by the way of a Dialogue or questions moved in the person of a certaine uplandish and simple ploughman of the Countrey" (*A&M* [1570], pp. 341, 965–66). Another pseudo-Chaucerian satire against monasticism, *The Pilgrim's Tale*, achieved notoriety when it was circulated in the reformist *Court of Venus* along with the poetry of Sir Thomas Wyatt.[20]

On the model of works like *Piers Plowman* and *The Plowman's Tale*, Protestant satirists constructed their own appeals for ecclesiastical and social reform. A distinct subgenre of Reformation satire emerged in a prolific series of conventional debates between a bluntly honest

---

[19] Leland, *Commentarii de Scriptoribus Britannicis*, ed. Anthony Hall (Oxford, 1709), p. 423.

[20] *ERL*, pp. 50–52, 71, 226–27. For these remarks on Chaucer's sixteenth-century reputation, I am indebted to Caroline Spurgeon, ed., *Five Hundred Years of Chaucer Criticism and Allusion: 1357–1900*, rev. ed., 3 vols. (Cambridge: Cambridge University Press, 1925), 1: 80, 82–83, 105–6. The introduction and facsimile texts in Chaucer's *Works*, ed. D. S. Brewer, document the inclusion of apocryphal works within the Chaucer canon during the sixteenth century. Spenser could have read either the 1542 or the c. 1550 reprint of William Thynne's edition (1532), or John Stow's 1561 expansion of Thynne's collection. See also Miskimin, *The Renaissance Chaucer*, pp. 226–61.

Protestant peasant and a Catholic cleric whose attempts at sophisticated eloquence cannot mask his spiritual ignorance.[21] Typical of this
convention is the humble laborer's stubborn skepticism about transubstantiation in Luke Shepherd's *John Bon and Mast[er] Person* (1547),
because it can be neither tasted nor seen:

> Yea but mast parson thynk ye it were ryght
> That if I desired you to make my blake oxe whight
> And you saye it is done, and styl is blacke in syght
> Ye myght me deme a foole for to beleve so lyght.
>
> (A4r)

Spenser avoids using classical names for his shepherds, giving
them instead simple English names that establish native vernacular
works as a generic context. As the type of the Protestant pastor in
"May," Piers (or Pierce) invokes the alliterative tradition of *Piers
Plowman* and the apocryphal satires ascribed to both Chaucer and
Langland.[22] This character's name and occupation indicate that he is
a probing seeker engaged in a quest for spiritual understanding. Although Diggon Davie (i.e., Dickon Davy) is original to Spenser, the
name suggests an inheritance from "Dawe the dyker," a poor ditch-
digger whose prophesied death by starvation is cited in the attack on
avaricious clergy and landlords in *Piers Plowman*.[23] He is a literary
cousin of Chaucer's Plowman, of whom it is said, "He wolde
thresshe, and therto dyke and delve" (*General Prologue*, l. 536). *Piers
Plowman* spawned a truth-telling character named Davy Diker in
Thomas Churchyard's imitation of Langland, a millennial vision of a
perfect commonwealth titled *Davy Dycars Dreame* (c. 1552).[24] Piers as
a defender of poetry is linked to Colin Clout, whom he praises in
"October" as the embodiment of a Neoplatonic theory of poetic inspiration. Even this Spenserian pen name furnishes a vestigial link to
evangelical satire as a hybrid derived from Skelton's *Collyn Clout*
(composed 1521–22) and the pastorals of the poet Clément Marot.[25]

---

[21] See *ERL*, pp. 258–60, 286–87.

[22] See Norbrook, *Poetry and Politics*, p. 62. McLane's conjecture in *Study in Elizabethan
Allegory*, pp. 175–87, that the name Piers alludes to John Piers, Bishop of Salisbury, is
improbable given the conservatism of that prelate's views.

[23] 3rd. ed. (1550), G1v; see *Piers Plowman*, ed. W. W. Skeat, B.5.320.

[24] William Waterman's *Westerne Wyll* acknowledges Churchyard's debt to Langland:
"This Diker sems a thryving ladde, brought up in pieres scole / The plowman stoute,
of whom I thynke ye have often harde." See *The Contention bettwyxte Churchyeard and
Camell, upon David Dycers Dreame. Newlye Imprinted* (1560), A1r-v, C4v, G1.

[25] Even though Marot was reputed to be a Protestant, he tried to pass as an evangelical Catholic and was not a committed Calvinist. On his religious attitudes and relation to Spenser, see Prescott, *French Poets and the English Renaissance*, pp. 10–12, 15–

Despite Skelton's hostility to the Lutherans, reformers approved of his verse because they read his satire on Cardinal Wolsey and abuses in the church in the Lollard tradition of *The Plowman's Tale*.[26]

Spenser adapts the native tradition of "georgic" satire by conflating medieval English devices of language, characterization, and thought associated with the simple plowman who implicitly or explicitly represents Christian social ideals—poverty, hard work, piety, and humility—and the shepherd conventions of pastoral eclogue. Piers's attack against prideful clergy in "May" illustrates the flat plain style, archaic diction, and alliteration associated with the blunt English truth-teller:

> Some gan to gape for greedie governaunce,
> And match them selfe with mighty potentates,
> Lovers of Lordship and troublers of states.

> (ll. 121–23)

Spenser's use of native conventions enables him to achieve a synthesis that stresses not Theocritean idleness but the real hardships of recognizable peasant workers, who endure the seasons' labors and the conflicts of youth and age. This harsh, georgic strain has classical sources also, as far back as Hesiod's *Works and Days*.

Spenser associates Chaucer's rhetorical device of affected modesty with his employment of a plain style within individual eclogues. Thomalin's disclaimer—"How be I am but rude and borrell" ("July," l. 95)—reduplicates, without the irony of Chaucer's original, the Franklin's protest: "I am a burel man" (*Franklin's Prologue*, l. 8). Similarly, Diggon Davie's self-reflexive comment that his "english is flatt" confirms Hobbinol's opinion of the "plaine" speech of "September" (ll. 104–5, 136). Although the "medieval" conventions that Spenser adopts were in their origins complex and sophisticated, by the sixteenth century they seemed homely and provincial. The nine-syllable accentual verse of all but one of Spenser's religious satires reflects Chaucer's lines as the Tudors imperfectly read them, having lost the medieval pronunciation of the accented terminal "*e*." The use of fourteeners (a metrical cousin of ballad measure) in the remaining poem, "July," recalls the Reformation adaptation of traditional folk song to religious purposes in the Common Measure of Sternhold and Hopkins's Psalter. Robert Crowley, the first editor of *Piers Plowman*, was an early experimenter in the use of ballad measure for Psalm

---

16, 27–29. For an opposed view, see Annabel Patterson, "Re-opening the Green Cabinet: Clément Marot and Edmund Spenser," *ELR* 16 (1986): 44–70.

[26] John Bale, *Scriptorum illustrium maioris Brytanniae . . . catalogus*, 2 vols. (Basel, 1557–59), 1: 651.

paraphrase, as was Archbishop Matthew Parker in many of his English Psalms.

The religious satires contain debates between Protestant and Catholic type characters, which in turn enclose exemplary fables or tales. Reformist literature mediates between the embedded tales of "February" and "September" and the fabular paradigms of Aesop and the medieval Reynard tradition. The embedded tales of the Fox and the Kid, and Roffy and the Wolf, emulate not only medieval prototypes like the Reynard story in *The Nun's Priest's Tale*, but also the debate between the Pelican and the Griffin in *The Plowman's Tale*. Spenser's enclosure of tales exhibits the same format as the *Tale*, in which an outer dialogue articulates different religious viewpoints by way of introduction to a fable in which opposed allegorical types—a Pelican and a Griffin—personify the Reformation conflict. Sidney may well allude to Spenser's inclusion of beast fables within eclogues when he lists animal tales among the variations of pastoral: "Is the poore pype disdained, which . . . sometimes, under the prettie tales of Wolves and Sheepe, can include the whole considerations of wrong dooing and patience."[27]

That Spenser's contemporaries recognized a "Chaucerian" tradition of anticlerical satire is suggested by the marginalia of an edition of *The Plowman's Tale* published in 1606, within a decade of the poet's death.[28] The anonymous editor expands the work's title with an explanatory note: "Shewing by the doctrine and lives of the Romish Clergie, that the Pope is Antichrist and they his Ministers." The tale proper is presented as a "complaint against the pride and covetousnesse of the Cleargie: made no doubt by *Chawcer*, with the rest of the Tales." A marginal gloss on avaricious clergy who exploit their flock interprets the *Tale* explicitly as a subtext for Spenser's ecclesiastical eclogues by observing that "of such shepheards speakes maister *Spencer* in his Kalender" (A3v). A note on the "making of a Crede" (l. 1066) invokes other apocryphal texts: "Some thinke hee means the questions of *Jack-upland*, or perhaps *Pierce Ploughmans* Creede. For *Chaucer* speakes this in the person of the Pellican, not in his owne person" (G1r-v). The Plowman's retelling of the religious debate between the Pelican and Griffin was evidently interpreted in favor of the former, who is aided in victory by an apocalyptic Phoenix symbolic of both Christ and the advent of Christ's kingdom during the Reformation.

The presence in the *Calender* of the pose of the plain-spoken truth-

---

[27] G. Smith, *Elizabethan Critical Essays*, 1: 175.
[28] See Norbrook, *Poetry and Politics*, p. 60.

teller serves, almost in itself, to establish the religious eclogues as Protestant rather than Puritan satire. The "honest" peasant is just about to disappear totally from popular religious propaganda, to be replaced by a view of the unlettered countryman as an obstinate opponent of true religion whom the preacher must, if he can, convert. Although George Gascoigne honors "good *Peerce*, thou plowman by thy name"[29] during the era of the *Calender*, Thomas Nashe transforms the Protestant plowman into a malcontent rogue who rails against vices of which he is himself guilty in *Pierce Penilesse His Supplication to the Divell* (1592). Most authors would in the future see the religion of the common people as "ungodly" and anticlerical (i.e., anti-Puritan), in contrast to views of "godly" laity who side with the clergy. This generic shift came at a time when aspiring satirists like Marston, Donne, and Jonson abandoned the conventions of native satire to embrace neoclassical standards of formal verse satire modeled on the works of Juvenal, Horace, and Persius.[30]

The *locus classicus* for this harsh view of the obdurate laity is *The Countrie Divinitie* (1581)[31] by George Gifford, Sidney's chaplain and deathbed confessor. In this dialogue the Puritan preacher Zelotes aims to refute the attitudes of Atheos, who is not an atheist in the modern sense of the word, but rather an unlearned believer in witchcraft and other "ungodly" superstitions who nevertheless conforms to the Elizabethan Settlement. Gifford's *Sermon upon the Parable of the Sower* (1582) loses touch with the sympathy extended to the common people and their dialect in Latimer's exposition of the same parable in his "Sermon on the Plowers." Another "exposition of the parable of the Sowers" that is markedly antipopular in its tendency is *The Difference of Hearers* (1614) by William Harrison, one of the royal preachers in Lancashire. Arthur Dent's often-published *Plaine Mans Path-way to Heaven. Wherein every man may clearely see, whether he shall be saved or damned* (1601) echoes and quotes from Gifford's *Countrie Divinitie*. Although Dent sets his work "forth Dialogue-wise, for the

---

[29] *The Steele Glass* (1576), l. 1017; quoted from Richard S. Sylvester, ed., *The Anchor Anthology of Sixteenth-Century Verse* (New York: Anchor, 1974), p. 311.

[30] See John Peter, *Complaint and Satire in Early English Literature* (Oxford: Clarendon Press, 1956), pp. 132–56; and H. Smith, *Elizabethan Poetry*, pp. 216–56, passim.

[31] The complete title is *A Briefe Discourse of Certaine Points of the Religion, which is among the common sort of Christians, which may be termed the Countrie Divinitie*. See Dewey D. Wallace, Jr., "George Gifford, Puritan Propaganda and Popular Religion in Elizabethan England," *Sixteenth Century Journal* 9, no. 1 (1978): 28–38. Boyd Berry has informed me that the degeneration of the rustic truth-teller may also be noted in Sir John Ferne's *The Blazon of Gentrie* (1586), where an ignorant plowman, Columell, cannot enter into intelligent dialogue concerning gentility with a herald, a knight, a divine, a lawyer, and an antiquary.

better understanding of the simple," it also attacks popular lay religion. The unlearned layman Asunetus (Greek for "not intelligent") contradicts the values of Spenser's zealous shepherds, for he loathes sermons and remains ignorant of the scriptures. The arguments in all of these texts parallel beliefs that E.K. attributes, on the other hand, to speakers like Piers and Diggon Davie.

Acceptance of E.K.'s judgment that archaic English diction is "fittest for such rusticall rudenesse of shepheards" (*Var.* 7, i: 8) was by no means universal; indeed, Spenser presumably understood that his native English models would seem dated to avant-garde readers. E.K. clearly assumes that the *Calender* will disappoint believers in linguistic augmentation and Latinate aureation: "Other some not so wel seene in the English tonge as perhaps in other languages, if them happen to here an olde word albeit very naturall and significant, crye out streight way, that we speak no English, but gibbrish" (*Var.*, 7, i: 9). The neoclassical assumptions of Sir Philip Sidney and George Puttenham led to their exclusion of humble native speech as a model for stylistic imitation. Although Sidney's *Apologie for Poetrie* acknowledges Chaucer's "reverent antiquity," he finds that he had "great wants" and that his excellence is concealed to contemporary readers "in that mistie time." He similarly tempers his judgment that the *Calender* is the only collection by a contemporary poet that is "worthy the reading, if I be not deceived" by declaring that no precedent exists for poetic imitation of archaic language: "That same framing of his stile to an old rustick language I dare not alowe, sith neyther *Theocritus* in Greeke, *Virgill* in Latine, nor *Sanazar* in Italian did affect it." Puttenham joins his voice to Sidney's critique in *The Arte of English Poesie*: "Our maker therfore at these dayes shall not follow *Piers plowman* nor *Gower* nor *Lydgate* nor yet *Chaucer*, for their language is now out of use with us." He claims that the obsolescence of the diction ("termes hard and obscure") of *Piers Plowman* precludes poetic imitation because "in them is litle pleasure to be taken." The aristocratic and courtly assumptions of these critics may be noted in Puttenham's effort to restrict permissable poetic language to the dialect in use at the royal court and its immediate environs: "Ye shall therefore take the usuall speach of the Court, and that of London and the shires lying about London within lx. myles, and not much above."[32]

The circumstances of composition of the *Calender* may offer at least a partial explanation for why Spenser adopted an archaic "Chaucerian" style that met with disfavor from Sir Philip Sidney, to whom he dedicated the volume. This acknowledgment actually represented a

---

[32] G. Smith, *Elizabethan Critical Essays*, 1: 196; 2: 65, 150.

retrospective bid for approval that postdated the poet's move out of the household of John Young, whom he served as secretary at the time that he presumably composed his eclogues, into the service of the Earl of Leicester in London. In contrast to aristocratic patrons like Sidney and his uncle, Leicester, who were sympathetic to the presbyterians, Young persecuted those opposed to episcopal authority. Spenser had studied at Pembroke Hall, Cambridge, when Young was master. He entered into Young's service in 1578 soon after the scholar's appointment as Bishop of Rochester ("episcopus Roffensis"), which title Spenser commemorates in the name of the good shepherd Roffy (or Roffyn).[33] Hobbinol's praise of Roffy as "meeke, wise, and merciable" identifies him as Spenser's patron: "Colin clout I wene be his selfe boye" ("September," ll. 174–76). The proliferation of references to Kent throughout the *Calender* may reflect Spenser's familiarity with the area around the bishop's residence at Bromley in Kent.

The fashion for reading Chaucer and imitating his diction, which had found an honored place at the courts of Henry VIII and Edward VI, survived at Cambridge University during the reign of Queen Elizabeth, when Puttenham testifies that it was no longer fashionable for courtiers to imitate medieval style. When Spenser studied at Pembroke Hall during the early 1570s, at the time of Young's mastership, a living tradition of reading Chaucer, Langland, and Gower had been in place for at least a generation.[34] Young himself was schooled at Cambridge during Edward VI's reign, at about the time that university scholars like John Cheke and Roger Ascham found places at the court of the young king. Their colleague, Thomas Wilson, observed at that time that the "fine Courtier wil talke nothyng but Chaucer."[35]

[33] Israel Gollancz, "Spenseriana," *Proceedings of the British Academy* 3 (1907–8): 103. See Alexander C. Judson, *The Life of Edmund Spenser*, in *Var.* 8: 52.

[34] William Turner, a Protestant propagandist who was a fellow of Pembroke Hall during the mid-1530s, advocated the study of Middle English in order to understand Chaucer's original language. See pp. 37–39, below, on the relationship between his work and Spenser's *Calender*. Gabriel Harvey, who was a fellow of Pembroke Hall when Spenser studied there, commended Chaucer as an "excellent and unempeachable" source (c. 1585). Francis Beaumont the Elder mentions the university connection in his 1597 reminiscence that he and his friend, Thomas Speght, were taught to appreciate Chaucer by "those auncient learned men of our time in Cambridge, whose diligence in reading of his workes them selves, and commending them to others of the younger sorte, did first bring you and mee in love with him." Beaumont rebuts the charge that Middle English diction has "growne too hard and unpleasant" by citing Spenser's "much frequenting of *Chaucers* antient speeches." Speght, who had studied with Beaumont at Peterhouse c. 1560–70, published a new edition of Chaucer's works in 1598. See Spurgeon, *Chaucer Criticism and Allusion*, 1: 90–91, 127, 145–46.

[35] Wilson, *The Arte of Rhetorique* (1553), sig. Y2ᵛ. See Winthrop S. Hudson, *The Cam-*

Their archaic mannerism seems to have reflected what E.K. refers to as "the shewe of such naturall rudenesse" (*Var.* 7, i: 8). The style of the *Calender* reflects the academic taste that prevailed in a university setting that produced the tightly knit group of committed Protestant reformers, including bishops, privy councilors, and members of Parliament, who attempted to implement a religious settlement more radical than that desired by their cautious queen.[36] Sidney's disdain for such language may reflect the coming of age of a new generation of courtiers during Elizabeth's reign.

Sidney's censure of Spenser's imitation of "an old rustick language" in the *Calender* applies most notably to the "Chaucerian" style of the satirical eclogues. Contrary to Sidney and Puttenham, E.K. argues that the "most auncient Poetes . . . devised this kind of wryting, being both so base for the matter, and homely for the manner" (*Var.* 7, i: 10), as an appropriate medium for the fledgling poet. E.K.'s derivation of "aeglogue" from the Greek term for "Goteheards tales" (*Var.* 7, i: 12) justifies the *Calender*'s vernacular style by analogy to the stock association of satire (spelled "satyr" in the sixteenth century) with the rough shagginess of the satyrs and ancient Greek satyr plays.[37] Accordingly he glosses archaic "Chaucerian" diction as a lexical aid to the Tudor reader.

## The Satirical Eclogues

The repetition of a network of satirical conventions and techniques helps to shape the religious eclogues ("February," "May," "July," and "September") into a coherent subsection within the *Calender*. The religious poems are woven together further by the rudimentary narratives concerning the fate of Algrind and Palinode's pilgrimage to Rome. Formulaic features of these poems include the juxtaposition of blunt, truth-telling shepherds with pastors exhibiting a variety of clerical failings; the gospel ethos of the plain-speaking pastors; the use of typical English satirical names; and the use of the native plain

---

bridge *Connection and the Elizabethan Settlement of 1559* (Durham, N.C.: Duke University Press, 1980), p. 54.

[36] Patrick Collinson notes that Grindal, whom Spenser honors as Algrind in the *Calender*, seems to have secured Young's appointment to the mastership of Pembroke Hall after he had resigned that office himself, in *Archbishop Grindal, 1519–1583: The Struggle for a Reformed Church* (London: Jonathan Cape, 1979), p. 37.

[37] Alvin Kernan, *The Cankered Muse: Satire of the English Renaissance* (New Haven: Yale University Press, 1959), pp. 54–63.

style as well as the flat metrical and stanzaic structures of vernacular verse.

The recapitulation of the biblical pattern of the Fall also sets these eclogues within a wider Christian context. E.K.'s comment on the universality of the Fall makes it clear that individual tragedies reenact the primal sin of Adam, who, "by hys follye and disobedience, made all the rest of hys ofspring be debarred and shutte out from thence" (gloss to "July," ll. 63–70). This archetypal cycle is repeated in the experience of the Oak and the Briar, the Kid, and Algrind. A wary comment by Thomalin on the revolution of Fortune's wheel sets Algrind's experience within the context of *de casibus* tragedy:

> Ah God shield, man, that I should clime,
>    and learne to looke alofte,
> This reede is ryfe, that oftentime
>    great clymbers fall unsoft.

("July," ll. 9–12)

Despite Algrind's evident virtues, however, it is he rather than the "proude and ambitious" Morrell who falls. The prediction that "good *Algrin*" shall "be bett[er] in time" (ll. 229–30) holds out the prospect, however, that he may recover good fortune. This possibility for a positive outcome suggests that Spenser differentiates between two kinds of tragedy along the lines of Protestant contemporaries like John Bale and John Foxe, who counterbalance the eternal suffering of the "reprobate" with the limited, worldly tragedies of the faithful that will eventually be absorbed into the overarching, "comic" pattern of providential history (see below, pp. 222–26).

The argument of "February" claims that the debate between Cuddie and Thenot is "rather morall and generall, then bent to any secrete or particular purpose." Its ambiguity sets it apart from the other ecclesiastical eclogues and their specific controversial concerns. Aged Thenot, who accepts mutability and the attendant tragic nature of life, chides his youthful companion for a careless devotion to a life of ease, love, and pleasure. Thenot's homiletic counsel that he never "was to Fortune foeman, / But gently tooke, that ungently came" (ll. 21–22), despite his consciousness of mutability and flux, associates a Christian stoic response to misfortune with the clerical paradigm of the good pastor:

> Must not the world wend in his commun course
> From good to badd, and from badde to worse,
> From worse unto that is worst of all,
> And then returne to his former fall?

(ll. 11–14)

Thenot's acceptance of Fortune and awareness of the inevitability of sin and the Fall counterbalance Cuddie's thoughtless hedonism, as the elder herdsman conflates the counsel of the Old Testament Preacher to "remember now thy Creator in the daies of thy youth" (Eccles. 12:1) with St. Paul's admonition, "for the wages of sinne is death" (Rom. 6:23):

> *Cuddie*, I wote thou kenst little good,
> So vainely tadvaunce thy headlesse hood.
> For Youngth is a bubble blown up with breath,
> Whose witt is weakenesse, whose wage is death,
> Whose way is wildernesse, whose ynne Penaunce,
> And stoopegallaunt Age the hoste of Greevaunce.
>
> (ll. 85–90)

Thenot's allegorical tale recalls the outer dialogue in which "olde Shepheard" debates the meaning of life with the young and energetic "Heardmans boye." The attribution to Tityrus of the "Aesopic" fable of the Oak and Briar alludes to the apocryphal Chaucerian tradition. Unlike the Oak, Thenot provides a positive example of age and the possibilities of repentance and regeneration, in contrast to Cuddie, who resembles the Briar as an unrepentant youth. The inset fable functions as a moralized exemplum concerning the frailty of youth. The association between the "aged Tree" (l. 102) and the old religion introduces a controversial dimension into this universal conflict:

> For it had bene an auncient tree,
> Sacred with many a mysteree,
> And often crost with the priestes crewe,
> And often halowed with holy water dewe.
> But sike fancies weren foolerie,
> And broughten this Oake to this miserye.
>
> (ll. 207–12)

E.K.'s gloss directs the reader to associate the "finall decay of this auncient Oake" with a past when "the popishe priest used to sprinckle and hallowe the trees from mischaunce. Such blindnesse was in those times." Nevertheless, an interpretative crux results from the disparity between the presence of some degree of sympathy for the "goodly Oake" and the dissimulation of the manifestly flawed and "proude weede," who uses "painted words" to conceal his "colowred crime with craft" (ll. 103, 160–62). Spenser elsewhere links hypocrisy of this kind to Roman Catholic types like the false Wolves who devour sheep "under colour of shepeheards" ("May," l. 126).

Although the double tragedy of the Oak and Briar lacks an explicit topical application, it articulates a double-edged warning against the religious excesses of both radical Protestants and Catholic recusants. Although the Oak has earned its "miserye" through "foolerie" and false belief (ll. 211–12), its destruction leaves the Briar fatally exposed. Even though Protestantism claimed that it was the ancient "religion of the apostles and Catholicism a latter-day distortion,"[38] Reformation satirists used generational conflict as a conventional allegorical figure that could be directed against either "old" Catholic believers or headstrong Protestant youth. Their practice adapts the Pauline admonition to "cast of[f] . . . the olde man" and "put on the new man" (Eph. 4:22–24). In Wever's *Lusty Juventus*, for example, the youth (Juventus) is torn between the "young" faith of the Protestant and the "old" carnal corruption of the Catholic.[39] Donne similarly uses the transition from one generation to the next as a paradoxical metaphor for religious reform in "Satire III," whose speaker fears that Catholic forebears may be closer to salvation than those living in the present age of religious reform:

> . . . and shall thy fathers spirit
> Meet blind philosophers in heaven, whose merit
> Of strict life may be imputed faith, and hear
> Thee, whom he taught so easie ways and near
> To follow, damned?
>
> (ll. 11–15)

The "generational" nature of tradition and authority was a fundamental question during the Reformation, when Protestants claimed to return to the practices of the primitive church of the New Testament and apostolic age, while Roman Catholics claimed validity for the nonscriptural traditions or "unwritten verities" promulgated in later centuries by church councils or the papacy. Most assuredly Spenser issues no defense of recusancy, but he does align himself with reformist elements in medieval Christian thought. "February" takes a qualified stand on reform through its sentiment that it is best to retain whatever goodness inheres in religious tradition while throwing away abuses. Many Tudor readers assumed that the Protestant movement should preserve valid practices from the old religion.

The eclogues for May, July, and September associate ideals for religious reform with shepherd-pastors whose names contain ana-

---

[38] Nelson, *Poetry of Edmund Spenser*, p. 44.
[39] See *ERL*, pp. 280–81, 312–15.

grams that provide a thin veil for a circle of Elizabethan bishops who believed in an evangelical model for the church. This strategy of concealment accords with E.K.'s explanation that parts of the *Calender* contain "secret meaning in them" (*Var.* 7, i: 11). Chief among these pastors is Edmund Grindal, whose appointment as Archbishop of Canterbury in 1576 represented a throwback to the heyday of magisterial reform under Edward VI. His accession as primate of the Church of England seemed to hold out the possibility of resolving divisions that had emerged among presbyterians, other Puritan groups, and the religious establishment. Although Grindal sympathized with the Puritan commitment to continuing reform of the church, to increased emphasis on preaching, and to the ideal of a learned and humble clergy, he attacked nonconformity. He tried "to make presbyterianism unnecessary by reforming the church."[40] The Protestant speakers in the satirical eclogues similarly believe in sincere worship based upon the scriptures, and they attack clerical laxness based upon pride, avarice, and ignorance. They remain pointedly silent about Puritan disputes over ecclesiastical polity and discipline, the use of candles, kneeling during communion, and the playing of music during worship. In addition to Grindal, whose exclusion from royal favor is alluded to in the destruction of the idealized pastor, Algrind, we may identify the archbishop's protégé, John Young, under the guise of Roffy, the hero of "September." Probable cases can be made for identifying Thomalin and Diggon Davie with Thomas Cooper, Bishop of Lincoln, and Richard Davies, Bishop of St. David's, both of whom signed a letter to the queen in support of Grindal at the time of his fall.[41]

The argument of "May" invites the reader to interpret the eclogue in terms of the general conflict between "two formes of pastoures or Ministers, or the protestant and the Catholique." That is, it identifies the chief speaker, Piers, and his antagonist, Palinode ("countersong"), as personifications of Protestantism and Catholicism respectively. Piers's speeches are filled with scriptural metaphors concerning sheep and their vulnerability to wolves (see Jer. 5:6, Matt. 10:16, and Luke 10:3). For example, his attack against the worldliness of false pastors, whose greed destroys their flock, invokes the Sermon on the Mount (Matt. 7:15):

> Tho under colour of shepeheards, somewhile
> There crept in Wolves, ful of fraude and guile,

[40] Norbrook, *Poetry and Politics*, pp. 68–69.
[41] McLane, *Study in Elizabethan Allegory*, esp. pp. 140–74, 203–34; Viola Hulbert, "Diggon Davie," *JEGP* 41 (1942): 349–67.

> That often devoured their owne sheepe,
> And often the shepheards, that did hem keepe.

(ll. 126–29)

Piers's diatribe against hireling shepherds and those who abandon their flock by putting them out for hire (i.e., nonresident holders of benefices) is set against the background of Christ's Parable of the Lost Sheep and the history of the unworthy servant in Christ's Parable of the Talents (Matt. 18:12-14; 25:14–30):

> I muse, what account both these will make,
> The one for the hire, which he doth take,
> And thother for leaving his Lords taske,
> When great *Pan* account of shepeherdes shall aske.

(ll. 51–54)

E.K.'s gloss on Pan as "Christ, the very God of all shepheards, which calleth himselfe the greate and good shepherd" produces a syncretic fusion of biblical and classical pastoral.

Although Anthea Hume argues that the conflict between Piers and Palinode veils Spenser's Puritan hostility to semi-papists,[42] Peter Lake reminds us that hostility to "popery" was not a Puritan monopoly.[43] This position was axiomatic in the Elizabethan church. Puritans could have found covert confirmation for their zeal in the "May" eclogue's satire against Wolves and Foxes, but E.K.'s more literal interpretation applies those types with greater ease as embodiments of the errors of Roman clergy. E.K. explicitly guides the reader to interpret the text with reference to the Reformation conflict when he identifies the Fox with "the false and faithlesse Papistes" (gloss on l. 174). Contemporary readers of the *Calender* assumed this interpretation.

The immediate political context of the *Calender* supports E.K.'s view because the organization of the Jesuit Mission to England during the year of publication made Catholic priests and laity controversial subjects for Protestant satire. Spenser's other writings are devoid of Puritan propaganda. Indeed, the prominence of the Fox in *Mother Hubberds Tale* suggests that Spenser harbored little sympathy for religious nonconformity. The variety of disguises that the hypocritical beast assumes makes it difficult to reduce it to a stock Puritan type for a crypto-papist cleric. On the contrary, the Priest's recommendation that the Fox "fashion eke a godly zeale" in order to curry favor with a noble patron of "a zealous disposition" (*Var.* 7, ii: ll. 491–93) sounds very much like a slap against hypocritical sectarians.

---

[42] Hume, *Protestant Poet*, pp. 14–28, passim.
[43] Lake, *Moderate Puritans*, p. 280. See note 8 above.

Spenser's conversion of the biblical Wolf into the Fox of "May" alludes to the satirical tradition that the Wolves who could prey openly during a Roman Catholic regime conceal themselves as Foxes under Protestant monarchs. According to E.K., the Kid's tragic fall exemplifies the dangers of religious backsliding, warning "the protestaunt beware, howe he geveth credit to the unfaythfull Catholique" (gloss on l. 304). This conceit infiltrates the polemical hunting dialogues in which William Turner and John Bale applied the imagery of Romish Foxes and Wolves to the broad outlines of Reformation controversy during the reigns of Henry VIII, Edward VI, and Mary I.[44] The authors originally designed their series of polemical beast fables to attack Stephen Gardiner, Bishop of Winchester, as a Henrician Fox who thwarted religious reform through cunning concealment of his papal sympathies. Turner then claimed that the bishop revealed himself openly as a Roman Wolf under the aegis of Mary Tudor.[45] Although Anthony Gilby applied Turner's *Huntyng and Fyndyng Out of the Romishe Foxe* to the vestiarian controversy of the 1560s by adding a prefatory attack against "popish" vestments, it should be noted that its composition predates the emergence of the Puritan movement under Elizabeth I.[46]

A contemporary satirical engraving vilifies Gardiner visually as one who slaughters Christ as the Lamb of God (Fig. 2). The bishop leads the lay people at the left by rings in their noses. The miter-wearing Wolves at the right disguise their episcopal vestments beneath "sheep's clothing" as they drink the blood of the sacrificial Lamb in a lurid parody of the Roman Catholic mass and doctrine of transubstantiation. The attendant bishops, Bonner and Tunstall, are implicated along with Gardiner, as Queen Mary's Lord Chancellor, in the persecution of Protestant "lambs," whose piled carcasses bear the

[44] Although these works predate the first stirrings of the Puritan movement by ten to twenty years, Anthea Hume interprets them as "Puritan" tracts (*Protestant Poet*, pp. 21–23). For opposed views, see Harold Stein, "Spenser and William Turner," *MLN* 51 (1936): 350; Rainer Pineas, "William Turner's Polemical Use of Ecclesiastical History and His Controversy with Stephen Gardiner," *RQ* 33 (1980): 599–608; and Norbrook, *Poetry and Politics*, pp. 60–61, 72–74.

[45] When Bale's *Yet a Course at the Romyshe Foxe* (Zurich [i.e., Antwerp], 10 December 1543) appeared under the pseudonym of James Harrison, it imitated Turner's *Huntyng and Fyndyng Out of the Romishe Fox* (Basel [i.e., Bonn], 14 September 1543), which was issued as the work of William Wraghton. Turner later wrote sequels entitled *The Rescuynge of the Romishe Foxe Other Wyse Called the Examination of the Hunter Devised by Steven Gardiner* (Winchester [i.e., Bonn], 1545) and *The Huntyng of the Romyshe Wolfe* (Emden, c. 1555). *The Rescuynge of the Romishe Foxe* attacks a reply by Gardiner, which is now extant only insofar as it is quoted by Turner for purposes of refutation.

[46] Turner, *The Hunting of the Fox and the Wolfe* (c. 1565).

**2.** *The Roman Wolves.* c. 1555

names of the most famous of the Marian martyrs: Rogers, Bradford, Cranmer, Latimer, Ridley, and Hooper. Christ as the slaughtered Lamb protests: "Why do you crucifie me agen For with one oblation have I for ever made perfecte those that are sanctified." The "Winchester Wolfe" (i.e., Gardiner as Bishop of Winchester) replies:

> Whilome in youth a foxe that have byn
> In age am a Woolfe more valiant in synne
> A foxe when I was, the lambe and the henne
> Dyd them me content, but nowe I feede on men.[47]

John Bale interpolates a slur of this kind of scene into *Three Laws*, the Protestant moral interlude that he wrote in 1538 under the patronage of Thomas Cromwell. The Catholic Vice known as Infidelity provides a cue to Ambition, who is costumed "lyke a byshop," to demonstrate to the audience the resemblance between his miter and the "mouth of a wolfe":

> If thu stoupe downewarde,     loo, se how the wolfe doth gape.
> Redye to devoure     the lambes, least any escape.[48]

The negative position taken by Piers on Maying customs reflects the contemporary origins of English Sabbatarianism, yet even this movement to observe Sunday strictly as a day of worship, Bible reading, and rest is broadly Protestant rather than distinctively Puritan in nature. A contemporary petition of Justices of the Peace attacks "enormities of the Saboothe" such as "wakes, fayres, marketts, barebaits, Bulbaits, Ales, mayegames, resortinge to Alehouses in tyme of divyne service, pypinge and dauncinge, huntinge, and all manner of unlawfull gamminge" as vestiges of Roman Catholic practice rather than Protestant abuses.[49] Control of Sunday sports and entertainments would not become the focus of violent controversy until James I promulgated the *Book of Sports* authorizing Sunday recreations considered by many to be sacrilegious. The issue was not firmly identified with the crown during Spenser's time, however, because Queen Elizabeth held herself aloof from the argument. The privy council did exert control during Sunday services, but it tended to take a lenient

[47] The confession of the Winchester Wolf continues at the base: "Hole men that eate muche and drinke muche, have muche bludde and muche feede. But we are hole men eatinge muche and drinkinge muche, ergo we have muche bludde and muche feede. But suche as have muche bludde and muche feede if they lacke wyves of there owne, and are destitute of the gyfte of chastitie, do and must often grevouslie synne in advouterie [adultery] fornication, and pollutions in the nyght: But we are destitute of the gifte of chastite, and have no wyves of our owne, ergo we synne muche and often. And wheras without sheadinge of bludde is no remission of synne, therfore syth we synne so grevously, none ought to marvaile that we dayly shedde so heynously." See *Catalogue of Prints and Drawings in the British Museum*, 3 vols. in 4 pts. (1870–77), 1: 4–5. According to Harold Stein, "Spenser and William Turner," p. 344, the original engraving is in the Bodleian Library copy of the c. 1555 edition of Turner's *Huntyng of the Romishe Wolfe* (8° A. 122 Linc.).

[48] *The Complete Plays of John Bale*, ed. Peter Happé, 2 vols. (Cambridge: D. S. Brewer, 1985–86), 2: 99, ll. 1184–86; 2: 121.

[49] Duke of Sutherland, Ellesmere MS 6299 (c. 1582–89); punctuation added.

position on traditional festivities during the rest of the day so long as a modicum of public order and piety was maintained. Strict Puritans did prefer a twenty-four-hour observance, but until very late in Elizabeth's reign Sabbatarians accepted the government position.[50]

Although sharp factional divisions on Sabbath observances had not yet coalesced by 1579, rigorous Sabbatarians did believe that Sunday entertainment characterized Roman Catholic rather than English Protestant belief. Piers's opponent, Palinode, favors the proliferation of holidays and veneration of the saints in the sacred calendar of the Roman church ("May," ll. 15, 310). Elizabethan Sabbatarians emphasized the keeping of the Fourth Commandment rather than the prohibition of Maying, play-going, and other pastimes. Their foremost goal was to prevent profanation of Sunday. Rather than being a distinctively Puritan issue, this concern goes back to the origins of the English Reformation; it was shared by many devout Protestants who opposed the secular pastimes and festivities that dominated traditional saints' festivals. (Zealous reformers forgot that works like Robert Mannyng of Brunne's *Handlyng Synne* documented medieval efforts to impose restraints on Sunday celebrations.) Although Piers's views may resemble the Puritan attack against May games, he is a proponent of clerical reform rather than a Sabbatarian as such. He cites Algrind as his authority for imposing a higher moral standard on clergy than laity: "But shepheards (as Algrind used to say,) / Mought not live ylike, as men of the laye" ("May," ll. 75–76).[51]

In his railing attack on Maying customs, Piers articulates fundamental questions concerning clerical ignorance and avarice, and spiritual failures due to hireling shepherds who "playen, while their flockes be unfedde":

> Perdie so farre am I from envie,
> That their fondnesse inly I pitie.
> Those faytours little regarden their charge,
> While they letting their sheepe runne at large.
>
> (ll. 37–40, 44)

For half a century, similar attacks on nonpreaching clergy and the holding of multiple benefices had fueled reformist appeals in writings like Robert Crowley's apocalyptic satires and Hugh Latimer's "Sermon on the Plowers"; they also appear in *Mother Hubberds Tale*. Similarly, Roffy's portrayal in "September" as an ever-watchful shep-

---

[50] See Peter Milward, *Religious Controversies of the Jacobean Age: A Survey of Printed Sources* (London: Scolar Press, 1978), p. 44.

[51] See Norbrook, *Poetry and Politics*, p. 72.

herd who protects his flock from the depredations of the papist Wolf accords with the traditional yearning of reformist Protestants (and Catholics) for a learned and humble clergy devoted to pastoral care.

E.K.'s biases may judge the "May" argument in favor of Piers's strident attack; however, the poet himself takes no explicit stand. Palinode's call for tolerance is not altogether lacking in sympathy, and his position approaches that of Hobbinol, the idealized shepherd whose stoical counsel of acceptance and contentment is opposed in "September" to the unbending rigorism of Diggon Davie, a visionary cousin of Piers:

> Ah fon, now by thy losse art taught,
> That seeldome chaunge the better brought.
> Content who lives with tryed state,
> Neede feare no chaunge of frowning fate:
> But who will seeke for unknowne gayne,
> Oft lives by losse, and leaves with payne.
>
> (ll. 68–73)

Furthermore, Piers's attack against Maying customs is at this time associated with attacks on drama and fiction because they "lie" or exert a morally corrupting influence. Palinode's tolerance for dancing and entertainment, however, mirrors Spenser's evident approval of fictionality and artistry, as it is embodied in the complex interplay of narrative and dramatic structures in the *Calender*. This line of argument becomes explicit in "October," with its reasoned justification of poetry, paralleling in some ways Sir Philip Sidney's formal defense of fictional art in *An Apologie for Poetrie*. The open-endedness and ambiguity of "February" suggest that Spenser is willing to frame a complex dialectic in which both speakers and their arguments may contain a mixture of wisdom and folly. His pastoral dialogues are genuine discussions in which speakers disagree and valid arguments may be brought forward on both sides. We need to take seriously E.K.'s interpretation of the "May" eclogue in Piers's favor, but clearly the shepherd is neither flawless nor a simple mouthpiece for Spenser's religious opinions. The issues that Piers raises are, nevertheless, staple Protestant concerns.

During the period leading up to the publication of the *Calender*, Archbishop Grindal fostered hope for achieving reform from *within* the Church of England. His fall from favor under the guise of Algrind provides the historical kernel of "July," where Spenser bases Thomalin's attack against ecclesiastical corruption on the messianic prophecy that "Everie valleie shalbe exalted, and everie mountaine and hill shalbe made lowe" (Isa. 40:1–5). Tudor Protestants viewed this call for moral and spiritual renewal as a *locus classicus* for satirical attacks on avarice and clerical failure.[52] Grindal's appointment stirred up expectations of continued reform of the ministry and church discipline at a time when a powerful progressive faction within the privy council, at court, and among the bishops favored eradication of continuing vestiges of "papistry" and widespread Pelagianism, and when preachers and pamphleteers were displaying a new awareness of "sin" as it is manifested in theater, dance, Maying, dicing, and like activities. Zealous Protestants fervently supported gospel preaching, cooperation between gentry and clergy, and an evangelical episcopacy devoted to pastoral care rather than prelatic prerogative. By alluding to the archbishop's disgrace, Spenser reflects the concern of like-minded Protestants that a period of church reform had come to a close.

Although the Grindal allusion is daring, pastoral dialogue and disguise furnish the poet with a means of self-protection and of treating religious and ethical problems without taking a fixed side in factional argument. The faction associated with Grindal included all of the public figures alluded to in the *Calender* except John Aylmer, Bishop of London. The name of Thomalin's debating opponent in "July," Morrell, is very likely an anagram for this prelate, whose name was spelled variously as Elmer and Elmore.[53] E.K.'s "disprayse of proude and ambitious Pastours" ("July," argument) identifies hill-dwelling Morrell with "papist" vestiges in the church.

Christ's division between the elect sheep and reprobate goats (Matt. 25:32–33) underlies the conflict between Morrell's haughty pride and the simplicity of Thomalin, who tends his sheep in "the lowly playne" ("July," l. 7). The biblical imagery of the unfaithful goats links "May" and "July" by suggesting that the goatherd Morrell typifies the inadequate clerical leadership that made the Kid in the earlier eclogue vulnerable to the stratagems of the false Fox. As an immature goat, the Kid is presumably damned, despite its identification by E.K. as "the simple sorte of the faythfull and true Christians" (gloss on "May," l. 174). Thomalin's reference to Palinode's pilgrimage to Rome ("July," ll. 181–84) further interlaces the two dialogues by furnishing a narrative postscript to "May." Protestants favored the Erasmian attack against the superstitiousness involved with pilgrimages and shrines.

---

[52] Robert Crowley, for example, uses it as an epigraph for the series of reformist appeals to twelve hierarchical estates, including priests and clergy, in *The Voyce of the Laste Trumpet* (1549). According to the Stationers' Register, the *Voyce* was still on sale in London at the time that Spenser wrote the *Calender*.

[53] McLane, *Study in Elizabethan Allegory*, pp. 188–202.

The "July" eclogue dramatizes the conflict between the desire for a return to the simple, evangelical piety of the primitive church and the perceived abuses of Roman Catholic traditions and the church hierarchy. The humble shepherd, Thomalin, accordingly pays homage to "the great God *Pan*" (l. 49):

> O blessed sheepe, O shepheard great,
>     that bought his flocke so deare,
> And them did save with bloudy sweat
>     from Wolves, that would them teare.
>
> (ll. 53–56)

His words recall the application of the Parable of the Good Shepherd in "May," where E.K. identified Pan as "Christ, the very God of all shepheards, which calleth himselfe the greate and good shepherd" (gloss on l. 54). In an inversion of Christ's parable, sheep are "sold" to false shepherds by "theyr Pan," identified by E.K. as "the Pope, whom they count theyr God and greatest shepheard" ("July," l. 179 and gloss). Thomalin's tale of Algrind emphasizes the clerical ideal of humility exemplified by Christ, the Good Shepherd, and the Old Testament types for priesthood, Moses and Aaron.

Thomalin's fable about Algrind daringly alludes to Grindal's recent suspension from his duties as Archbishop of Canterbury and to his sequestration for refusing to execute Queen Elizabeth's order to suppress the "prophesyings," where zealous clergy gathered to expound biblical texts outside the context of the authorized homilies and licensed sermons permitted in Sunday services. These "prophesyings" constituted a kind of remedial training for clergy with deficient education. The tale articulates the yearning of Protestant progressives of the "Grindalian" era (1575–77) for a ministry and episcopacy characterized by poverty, humility, simplicity, and a devotion to pastoral care ("July," ll. 127–36). These reforms can hardly be termed Puritan, however, because they received backing from a sizeable body in the government. Although Grindal's commitment to Bible preaching and devoted pastoral care led him, on grounds of conscience, to refuse to transmit the queen's command to suppress the prophesyings, he had also protected those gatherings from being exploited by the Puritans.[54] Despite Algrind's obvious virtues as a cler-

---

[54] Patrick Collinson, "The Downfall of Archbishop Grindal and Its Place in Elizabethan Political and Ecclesiastical History," in his collected papers, *Godly People: Essays on English Protestantism and Puritanism* (London: Hambledon Press, 1983), pp. 375–76, et seq. See also his *Archbishop Grindal*, pp. 219–52. Grindal belongs to the Latimer tradition of the preacher-plowman, according to Davies, *From Cranmer to Hooker*, pp. 14–15.

gyman, it is he who suffers the tragic fall that would seem due instead to Morrell as a "Goteherd prowd." No hint is given that Algrind is tainted by the pride and ambition that *de casibus* tragedy usually features (see ll. 9–12, 101–4). Thomalin applies his tale, instead, as an exemplum that warns against high estate:

> He is a shepherd great in gree,
>    but hath bene long ypent.
> One daye he sat upon a hyll,
>    (as now thou wouldest me:
> But I am taught by *Algrins* ill,
>    to love the lowe degree.)
>
>           (ll. 215–20)

Although the hazardous analogy between the high-flying Eagle and Queen Elizabeth is clear enough, neither explanation nor blame is attached to the Eagle's decision to brain Algrind with a shellfish in the manner of the legendary account of Aeschylus's death. The self-protective praise of "the meane and lowly state" in the glosses and concluding emblem tactfully acknowledge both royal fiat and the conventional danger of rising high on Fortune's Wheel. Indeed, Protestant progressives like Leicester, Walsingham, and the circle of bishops identified in the *Calender*, who were in sympathy with Grindal's program, tempered their advocacy of church reform with a prudent awareness of the royal supremacy. The archbishop's disgrace became a "liability" for their cause.[55] At no point does Spenser criticize the queen for her handling of the incident, and the attribution of Algrind's destruction to "hap," "myshap," and "chaunce" (l. 229 and gloss on l. 213) accords with the fable's character as a *de casibus* tragedy. In its recognition of the queen's power and her potential ruthlessness, the episode functions as a moral tale rather than antigovernment satire.

"September" offers a variation of the biblical *topoi* of wolves in sheep's clothing and the lost sheep. The character of Diggon Davie combines the latter figure and that of the returned prodigal who sought to better his fortune in "a farre countrye," only to be disillusioned by the pride and greed of the false shepherds he found there. Although there is some evidence for identifying Wales as this distant land,[56] E.K.'s reference to the "abuses . . . and loose living of Popish prelates" ("September," argument) suggests Rome (the destination of Palinode's pilgrimage) as the likely locale. Diggon's tale of "Argus

---

[55] Collinson, "Downfall of Archbishop Grindal," in *Godly People*, p. 388.
[56] McLane, *Study in Elizabethan Allegory*, pp. 126, 216–34.

eyed" Roffy (l. 203) recalls Piers's emphasis in "May" on the need for watchfulness against the skillful dissimulation of the false Fox (a type for Antichrist, according to E.K.). Although the specific details of the incident remain enigmatic, Diggon's narrative styles Roffy as a type of the Good Shepherd, Christ. Roffy epitomizes the vigilance appropriate to the ideal cleric when he discerns the depradations against his flock of "a wicked Wolfe . . . / Ycladde in clothing of seely sheepe" and kills the predator ("September," ll. 184, 188; see Matt. 7:15).

"October," the last of the satirical eclogues, belongs in a category by itself because E.K. defines the object of its attack as "the comtempte [sic] of Poetrie, and the causes thereof" rather than religious abuses. This eclogue articulates the *Calender*'s most explicit statement concerning poetic imitation, because Cuddie epitomizes Spenser's manifest concern with surpassing his predecessors to become *the* English poet. The relation to Virgil, "the Romish *Tityrus*" (l. 55), is particularly complex, because Virgil's career furnishes the classical paradigm for Piers's exhortation to Cuddie to abandon the lowly style and matter of pastoral for the romantic epic. That it should be Piers, the plain-spoken shepherd-poet, who argues on behalf of "pierlesse Poesye" (l. 79) demonstrates Spenser's eclecticism in honoring native and foreign models of poetic achievement, at the same time that he attempts to surpass them. Cuddie's limited awareness of his own worth and that of poetry in general is set off against the moral earnestness and idealism of Colin Clout, which epitomizes for Piers the possibility of Neoplatonic ascent through love and poetry:

> . . . for love does teach him to climbe so hie,
> And lyftes him up out of the loathsome myre:
> Such immortall mirrhor, as he doth admire,
> Would rayse ones mynd above the starry skie.
> And cause a caytive corage to aspire,
> For lofty love doth loath a lowly eye.
>
> (ll. 91–96)

E.K. aligns the eclogue with Platonic terminology when he comments upon poetic inspiration and the conception of poetry as "a divine gift and heavenly instinct." (Of course, Catholics inspired by Neoplatonism, like Ronsard, said very much the same thing.)

The *Calender* exemplifies a self-conscious concern with genre, one that E.K. mirrors in his glosses. The collection is a virtuoso display of metrical and stylistic sophistication by a writer who follows precedent in adopting the pastoral pose of the apprentice poet to claim the title of England's "new Poete." It should be noted that Spenser carefully avoids introducing his own poetic voice, that of Colin Clout, into the satirical eclogues,[57] an absence that situates these poems as only one of several segments in the *Calender* as a whole. The lofty goals and heroic ideals articulated by Piers for Colin and his career look beyond that collection to final fulfillment in the great national epic, *The Faerie Queene*, which was already underway at the time that Spenser published the *Calender* (*Var.* 9: 17). Spenser's early proclivity for Protestant satire extends into the mature work of his romantic epic. Even though he follows the neo-Latin precedent of Petrarch and Mantuan in using the eclogue to discuss religious problems, and adapts eclogues by Marot in the plaintive laments of "November" and "December," the poet also pays homage to the native tradition of the plowman as an ardent seeker for spiritual renewal. The tribute paid to Tityrus, who encompasses both Roman Virgil and English Chaucer, marks Spenser's ability to combine old and new ways of writing into a distinctive kind of Protestant pastoral satire. Under the guise of Immerito, Spenser defines his place as both the heir and the peer of Chaucer. That he does so means that he styles himself as a Reformation satirist.

[57] Helgerson, *Self-Crowned Laureates*, p. 85 n. 37. See also Norbrook, *Poetry and Politics*, p. 86.

# TWO

## SPENSERIAN ICONOCLASM

### Monastic Parody

AT THE OUTSET of *The Faerie Queene*, following his relatively easy defeat of monstrous Errour, the Redcrosse Knight encounters a more covert enemy of holiness in the form of Archimago, whose friar's habit ("long blacke weedes") and seclusion in a "little lowly Hermitage" externally convey austere piety. Although this false cleric deceives both Redcrosse and Una—they accept an offer of lodging from "that old man of pleasing wordes"—his formalistic religious practices and necromantic studies of "Magick bookes and artes of sundry kindes" invite the reader to identify this variation of Ariosto's magician-hermit with reformist stereotypes concerning Roman Catholic hypocrisy and superstition (1.1.29, 34–36).[1]

Spenser incorporates a Protestant cultural code as a prominent layer in the identity of Archimago, who is modeled on the hermit met by Angelica in *Orlando furioso*. Sir John Harington makes this connection explicit in his 1591 translation of the Italian epic when he interprets Archimago's literary antecedent as "an unchast hermit or rather hypocrite in whose person he toucheth the holy Church men that spend so much devotion on such Saints" (*Orl. fur.* 2.13). By the reign of Queen Elizabeth recusant priests were commonly attacked as conjurers, wizards, and necromancers.[2] The alert reader may notice that Archimago's practice of wandering as a "member of the regular clergy" contradicts his feigned withdrawal from the world, even though this discrepancy escapes Redcrosse and Una.[3] Archimago's claim to live "in hidden cell / Bidding his beades all day for his trespas" (st. 30) brings to life popular devotional practices that Protestant

[1] See Richard Mallette, "The Protestant Art of Preaching in Book One of *The Faerie Queene*," *SSt* 7 (1986): 9–10.

[2] Keith Thomas, *Religion and the Decline of Magic: Studies in Popular Beliefs in Sixteenth- and Seventeenth-Century England* (Harmondsworth: Penguin Books, 1973), pp. 78, 326. See also D. Douglas Waters, *Duessa as Theological Satire* (Columbia, Mo.: University of Missouri Press, 1970), pp. 25–26; and Michael O'Connell, *Mirror and Veil: The Historical Dimension of Spenser's "Faerie Queene"* (Chapel Hill: University of North Carolina Press, 1977), p. 55.

[3] Darryl Gless, *"Measure for Measure," the Law, and the Convent* (Princeton: Princeton University Press, 1979), p. 72. Gless coins the term "parodic monastic" (p. 85).

reformers vilified as superstition. The book hanging from his belt should be the Bible worn by members of religious orders (see Figs. 3, 13), but his practice of telling tales of "Saintes and Popes" suggests instead that he reads from a collection of legendary lives of the kind that were banned under Edward VI and Elizabeth I (*FQ* 1.1.29–30, 35).[4] Archimago's mode of "preaching" corresponds to the image of "false" religion that was familiar during Spenser's adulthood in Protestant polemics like John Bale's *Image of Both Churches* (Antwerp, 1545) and the title page of Foxe's "Book of Martyrs," where the cleric at the lower right preaches on what appears to be a nonscriptural theme—no Bible is open before him—while ignorant members of the congregation tell their rosary beads (*ERL*, fig. 18).

Archimago personifies abuses that Protestants identified with the Church of Rome. Like other reformers, Spenser expands upon the late medieval critique of formalistic religion that identified the "holy" with material places and objects: shrines, relics, and images of saints and the Virgin Mary. Jean Gerson, the antischolastic philosopher, denounced superstitious abuses from the Sorbonne, for example, and the Devotio Moderna advocated inward piety rather than cult observances.[5] Erasmus sympathized with this view in writings like "A Pilgrimage for Religion's Sake" (1526), where he satirized the gullibility of pilgrims and the fantastic wealth of the shrine of Our Lady at Walsingham.[6] His views had limited effect, however, because they were geared to the intelligentsia and stopped short of the arguments used by reformers like Karlstadt and Zwingli to justify an iconoclastic attack against all aspects of the Catholic cult "as a human institution that was opposed to the worship revealed by God in scripture." The shattering of images and condemnation of the monastic orders was only the most visible aspect of this radical movement, which was particularly active at the outset of the reigns of Edward VI and Elizabeth I.[7]

The Protestants inherited a lively tradition of medieval satire against monastic abuses and pretensions, which thrived in the writings of Nigel Wireker, for example, and the goliardic poets. Unlike

---

[4] The *Book of Common Prayer* attacks "uncertain stories, legends, responds, verses, vain repetitions, commemorations, and synodals" on the ground that reading them prevented Catholic priests from educating the laity in the Bible (*BCP*, p. 14). See James Nohrnberg, *The Analogy of "The Faerie Queene"* (Princeton: Princeton University Press, 1976), p. 158.

[5] Carlos M. N. Eire, *War against the Idols: The Reformation of Worship fom Erasmus to Calvin* (Cambridge: Cambridge University Press, 1986), pp. 21–22.

[6] Erasmus, *Colloquies*, trans. Craig R. Thompson (Chicago: University of Chicago Press, 1965), pp. 292–308, passim.

[7] Eire, *War against the Idols*, pp. 1–3, 54–65, 73–86, passim.

## Of Enuie.

*Where Gods word preached is in place : vnto the people willingly :*
*Woe be to them that would deface : for if such cease, the Stones will crie.*

### ¶ The signification.

HE which preacheth in the pulpit, signifieth godly zeale, &
a furtherer of the gospel: and the two which are plucking
him out of his place, are the enemies of Gods word, threat-
ning by fire to cosume the professors of the same ; and that
company which sitteth still, are *Nullifidians*, such as are of no
religion, not regarding any doctrine, so they may bee quiet
to liue after their owne willes and mindes.

noho

3. *Of Envie.* Stephen Bateman, *A Christall Glasse of Christian Reformation* (1569)

Shakespeare, who alludes enigmatically to the destruction of the abbeys in the "bare ruin'd choirs" of Sonnet 73, Spenser invokes explicit memories of religious "error" by employing conventions familiar from medieval satire. In open discipleship of Chaucer, he models his false hermit on the medieval tradition that encompasses unsavory ecclesiastics in the *Canterbury Tales* like the Pardoner and Friar. Archimago's forebears populate Chaucerian and pseudo-Chaucerian satires like the *Summoner's Tale* and *Jack Upland*, as well as the translation of the *Romaunt of the Rose* by Guillaume de Lorris and Jean de Meun, which followed the militantly anti-Catholic *Plowman's Tale* in sixteenth-century editions of Chaucer's collected works. Even though Jean de Meun incorporates False Semblaunt into a work devoted to the renewal of the mendicant orders, Chaucer's Tudor reputation as a proto-Protestant conferred anti-Catholic coloring upon that character. False Semblaunt, as the embodiment of hypocrisy, disguises himself as a member of many different occupations and estates, but his chosen costume is that of a "holy heremyte" (l. 6481) and "the cope of a frer" (l. 7408).[8] From the time of Jean de Meun onward, it was conventional to cloak personifications of hypocrisy in religious habits. False Semblaunt's ironic confession that his attire disguises his worldly vices of avarice and pride belongs to a tradition of clerical self-confession shared by *The Pardoner's Tale* and *Doctor Double Ale*, a Reformation satire by Luke Shepherd.[9]

Although it may appear that the disestablishment of monasticism was a dead issue in Elizabethan England (after all, the Cromwellian campaign had taken place during the 1530s), members of religious orders walked abroad during Spenser's boyhood, when Queen Mary restored some of the monastic houses that her father had dissolved.[10]

[8] Chaucerian quotations follow *The Works of Geoffrey Chaucer*, ed. F. N. Robinson, 2nd ed. (Boston: Houghton Mifflin, 1957). William Thynne juxtaposed the *Romaunt* and the *Plowman's Tale* in the second edition of his *Workes of Geffray Chaucer* (1542), fols. 119–26. I am indebted to Darryl Gless's illuminating discussion of the *Roman de la Rose* and medieval antifraternal satire as a generic context for both Spenser and Shakespeare (*The Law, and the Convent*, pp. 67–72). Barnabe Googe designates Chaucer as a prototype for moral reform in *The Shippe of Safegarde* (1569), D7ᵛ–8, a militantly Protestant allegory concerning the quest for salvation. Googe quotes a passage from the *Romaunt* (ll. 413–48) with reference to the soul's passage by the island of Hypocrisy, which is personified by a statue of "Pope holye" (i.e., hypocritical) in the guise of a woman carrying a psalter and doing good works.

[9] See *ERL*, pp. 261–64.

[10] The first Parliament of Queen Elizabeth (1559) reconfirmed the disestablishment of the monasteries and chantries under Henry VIII and Edward VI. Anthony Gilby claimed that many Elizabethan clerics who had been ordained before Mary Tudor's death were "old monks and friars and old popish priests, notorious idolators, openly perjured persons, halting hypocrites, manifest apostates"; as quoted by Christopher

Archimago's presentation as a deceptive friar would have been unmistakable, furthermore, because it incorporates contemporary Protestant iconography. Satirists like Robert Crowley assigned Archimago's sobriquet of Hypocrisy (*FQ* 1.1 argument) to Catholic type characters whose skill at dissembling conveys an outward appearance of devotion.[11] (Crowley charges further that the friars are those "who receyved Antichriste fyrste" and that "Hypocrisi woundeth preachers" in his marginalia for *Piers Plowman* [3rd ed., 2E4, 2F4].) The stage convention of costuming personifications of Hypocrisy in monastic attire lodges the point that onlookers must learn to "see through" their spiritual disguises. Bale assigns clerical attire to the lurid personifications of Roman error in *The Three Laws*:

> Lete Idolatry be decked lyke an olde wytche, Sodomy lyke a monke of
> all sectes, Ambycyon lyke a byshop, Covetousnesse lyke a Pharyse or
> spyrituall [i.e., canon] law[y]er, False Doctryne lyke a popysh doctour,
> and Hypocresy lyke a graye fryre.

The Franciscan habit worn by Hypocrisy identifies him as a theatrical approximation of Archimago's initial representation. In Bale's *King Johan*, Dissimulation disguises himself first as the monk Raymundus and then as Simon, the murderous monk of Swynsett Abbey who reveals that he is falsely "taken of men for monastycall devocyon."[12] While the personification of "feigned or chosen holiness" in R. Wever's *Lusty Juventus* does not wear specifically clerical attire, this Catholic Vice associates himself with "Holy vesti[ments, holy copes,] / Holy hermits and friars, / Holy priests, holy bishops, / Holy monks, holy abbots."[13] The performance or publication of these earlier Tudor works in Elizabethan London helps to explain Spenserian allegory as

---

Haigh, "The Church of England, the Catholics and the People," in *Reign of Elizabeth*, ed. Haigh, p. 197.

[11] "*Philargyrie of Greate Britayne* by Robert Crowley," ed. John N. King, *ELR* 10 (1980): 59, ll. 359–64 et seq.

[12] *Complete Plays of John Bale*, ed. Happé, 1: 84, l. 2103; 2: 121. In *Life and Repentance of Mary Magdalene* (c. 1550; publ. 1566), Lewis Wager doubles the roles of four Catholic Vices with hypocritical Virtues: Pride (Nobility and Honor); Cupiditas (Utility); Carnal Concupiscence (Pleasure); and Infidelity (Legal Justice to priests and Pharisees; Prudence to publicans and people). Two other Protestant plays involve dramatizations of Hypocrisy: the anonymous *New Custom* (1573) and Nathaniel Woodes's *Conflict of Conscience* (1581). Glynne Wickham claims that Tudor spectators would look for concealed meanings in plays of this kind, where everything is "two-faced—a seeming exterior masking hidden truth," in *Early English Stages 1300 to 1660*, 4 vols. (London: Routledge and Kegan Paul, 1959– ), 2, i: 17.

[13] R. Wever, *Lusty Juventus*, in *Four Tudor Interludes*, ed. J.A.B. Somerset (London: Athlone Press, 1974), ll. 23, 409–12.

well as the costuming of Mephistophilis as a monk in Marlowe's *Doctor Faustus*.[14]

Hypocrisy and other vices are also attired as monks and friars in woodcuts found in many Protestant books, among the most important of which are two printed by the prominent Elizabethan publisher John Day, whose production of Reformation propaganda and apologetics went back to the reign of Edward VI. Many of the inflammatory illustrations in Foxe's "Book of Martyrs" implicate monks and friars in the martyrdoms of Protestant "saints." The woodcuts in Stephen Bateman's *Christall Glasse of Christian Reformation* similarly include friars among the lay people and clerics who personify the Seven Deadly Sins.[15] They are associated with the specific transgressions of lying, treason, deceit, sloth, envy, and murder (C3ᵛ, C4ᵛ, D4ᵛ, H1, H2). A gloss for one of these antifraternal woodcuts explains that "the Fryers weede and Beades signifieth hypocrisie and lothsomnes of the truth" (G2; Fig. 4). Other friars personify envy and wrath (Figs. 3 and 13). Furthermore, a cardinal personifies persecution, whereas a pope is proverbially prideful (H2, I2).

Archimago's presentation in the first canto of *The Faerie Queene* furnishes a paradigm for the satirical treatment of abuses of monasticism elsewhere in *The Faerie Queene*, notably the ideal of withdrawal from the world into contemplative "devotion." Idleness, who is the only clerical type among the counselors of Lucifera at the Palace of Pride, resembles Archimago in his wearing of dark clerical attire. Spenser gives a sharp polemical edge to his Chaucerian portrayal of the "nourse of sin" who heads the pageant of the Seven Deadly Sins "arayd in habit blacke, and amis thin, / Like to an holy Monck, the service to begin" (*FQ* 1.4.18). Spenser's personification allegory is aligned with the portrayal "Of Sloth" as a monk in the *Christall Glasse of Christian Reformation*, where Bateman's gloss explains that "He

---

[14] David Bevington comments that the "Legend of Holiness" parallels the formulaic structure of Tudor Protestant drama in its "progression from Catholic hypocrisy (Archimago, Duessa) and Avarice (Kirkrapine and others) to the proud tyranny of Orgoglio." See *From "Mankind" to Marlowe: Growth of Structure in the Popular Drama of Tudor England* (Cambridge, Mass.: Harvard University Press, 1962), p. 250. For examples of the entry of mid-Tudor editions in the Stationers' Register during the reign of Elizabeth, see *STC* 1288, 6089.5, 19908, 25149.

[15] On Day's role in the illustration of the *Christall Glasse* and "Book of Martyrs," see Samuel Chew, *The Pilgrimage of Life* (New Haven: Yale University Press, 1962), pp. 90–93, 124–27; and John N. King, *Tudor Royal Iconography: Literature and Art in an Age of Religious Crisis* (Princeton: Princeton University Press, 1989), pp. 118–21, 134n. Day presumably commissioned Bateman to write a text to accompany a set of woodblocks already in existence; unlike the brief "significations," Bateman's treatise bears no relation to the illustrations.

# *Of Sloth.*

*Great griefe it is the learned to see : in slothfull rest to spend their dayes:*
*Such may be likened to dronebees : that sucke the sweete and go their wayes.*

## ¶*The signification,*

HE which rydeth on the Asse signifieth sloth, as well amog
the chiefest as among the lowest : the Fryers weede and
Beades signifieth hypocrisie and lothsomnes of the truth.

G.ij.     Sloth

4. *Of Sloth.* Bateman, *A Christall Glasse of Christian Reformation* (1569)

which rydeth on the Asse signifieth sloth, as well among the chiefest as among the lowest" (Fig. 4). Idleness rides a "slouthfull Asse" (st. 18).

The bond between Idleness and Archimago is apparent not only in their clerical attire, but also the devotional manuals that they bear. Just as Archimago follows False Semblaunt's practice of flaunting a copy of the Bible, the portable breviary borne by Idleness symbolizes the liturgical deficiency of the old religion. Despite the well-worn condition of his "Portesse," Idleness "therein little red, / For of devotion he had little care" (1.4.19). The companionship of Idleness and Gluttony in Lucifera's pageant may provide a tenuous connection between the former and the fabled overindulgence of members of the mendicant orders. Chaucer's Monk typifies this failure with his fondness for fat roasted swans (*General Prologue* l. 206).

In contrast to Protestant satire and its medieval antecedents, clerical types tend to disappear in Counter-Reformation works. Although prayer books and rosaries may symbolize false devotion in Catholic visual satire, their bearers differ from Protestant portraits in their lack of clerical attire. Thus Cesare Ripa's *Iconologia* (Rome, 1603) portrays Hippocresia as a thin and weak woman ("donna magra, & pallida") who wears an ash-grey garment and reads from a breviary ("un offitiuolo" [i.e., ufficiolo]) as she ostentatiously gives alms to a beggar. The sole clerical figure portrayed in this emblematic text is the idealized priest ("huomo in habito di Sacerdote"), who personifies religious zeal (N2$^v$–3, 2K3$^v$).

Spenser alludes to the Dissolution of the Monasteries in episodes positioned near the beginning and end of *The Faerie Queene*: the interlude at the house of Corceca and the final onslaught of the Blatant Beast. The alleged failure of monasticism to devote alms and church wealth to the charitable care of the poor and needy may be noted in the first instance in Kirkrapine's inclination

> to robbe Churches of their ornaments,
> And poore mens boxes of their due reliefe,
> Which given was to them for good intents.

> (1.3.17)

The name and customs of Kirkrapine's lover, Abessa, associate her with both monastic devotion and a failure to observe the vow of celibacy taken by nuns. Her guiltiness of "whoredome" links her to Duessa as a type for "spiritual fornication," just as it echoes sensational allegations lodged by Protestant reformers that the religious orders nurtured sexual immorality.[16] Typical of these charges are the slurs about monastic licentiousness and perversion that John Bale gathers in *Actes of Englysh Votaryes* (1546–51; reprinted 1560). (The licentiousness of Chaucer's Friar portrays this failure in a more genial vein, as does the ironic reference of Spenser's Squire of Dames to the refusal of "an holy Nunne" to break her vow of chastity [*FQ* 3.7.58].)

---

[16] On the place of sexual innuendo in anti-Catholic satire, see *ERL*, pp. 381–87.

As a kind of "abbess," albeit one who heads a disorderly household, Abbessa personifies one effect of the spiritual blindness embodied by her mother Corceca, whose name presumably means "blind heart" (Lat. *cor* + *caecum*). Corceca's blindness and ceaseless dedication to formulaic acts of piety accord with John Dixon's interpretation of her as "blynd devotion" (Dixon, *Commentary* 1.1.29n), because

> that old woman day and night did pray
> Upon her beades devoutly penitent;
> Nine hundred *Pater nosters* every day,
> And thrise nine hundred *Aves* she was wont to say.

(1.3.13)

Spenser links Corceca to Archimago not only through their shared habit of telling rosary beads (see Fig. 4), but also through her supplication of him in the guise of the false Redcrosse Knight to take revenge against Una; Corceca lodges a deceitful charge of harlotry against she who "was the flowre of faith and chastity" (1.3.23–24).

The importance of the lion in Tudor heraldry suggests that Una's companion may allude partly to the exercise of monarchal power in the Dissolution of the Abbeys. Not only do lions symbolize English royalty, but the rampant posture of Una's protector (1.3.5) mimics the appearance of a supporter of the English royal arms.[17] It assumes this heraldic posture for a second time in guarding Una against Sansloy (st. 41).

The Lion's breaking down the door of Corceca's house and suppression of Kirkrapine ("church robbery") "under his Lordly foot" is richly suggestive of the Cromwellian campaign to suppress the monasteries during the 1530s. Even though Kirkrapine's liaison with Abessa involves him in the spiritual "whoredome" that the reformers associated with Catholic "superstition" (sts. 17, 19), his removal of church "ornaments," the "rich vestiments" of saints' images, and other "holy things" is problematic because it also gives him the appearance of a Protestant iconoclast. Kirkrapine may symbolize both

---

[17] John Upton states that "this defender of the Faith and of Una (the lion) suggests England, or the English king . . . ; or what if the allegory points more minutely to King Henry VIII, to whom this title was first given, and who opened the way for a thorough reformation of the church?" (*Var.* 1: 207). The glosses on *FQ* 1.3.5 and 7 in Dixon, *Commentary*, allude to Rev. 5:5 ("beholde, the lion which is of the tribe of Juda, the rote of David") in interpreting Una's relationship with her lion as a type for Queen Elizabeth's love of "Christe the sone of david." On the royalist symbolism of the lion, see Jane Apteker, *Icons of Justice: Iconography and Thematic Imagery in Book V of "The Faerie Queene"* (New York: Columbia University Press, 1969), p. 62; O'Connell, *Mirror and Veil*, pp. 50–51; and Thomas H. Cain, *Praise in "The Faerie Queene"* (Lincoln: University of Nebraska Press, 1978), p. 68. For an opposed view, see *FQ*, ed. Roche, 1.3.5n.

the misappropriation of ecclesiastical wealth by the monks of old and the excesses to which the Protestant movement was prone.[18]

Spenser adopts what may appear to be an ambiguous stance toward iconoclasm that seems to endorse the destruction of Catholic "idolatry" at the same time that it preserves and adapts "idolatrous" imagery to Protestant purposes. His position is dialectical rather than ambivalent, however, in a way that appropriates the energy of that which is "alien" at the same time that it is constructed "as a distorted image of . . . authority."[19] This polyvalence is even more pronounced in the iconoclastic onslaught of the Blatant Beast, who revealed depravity when he ransacked a "Monastere":

> the Monckes he chaced here and there,
> And them pursu'd into their dortours sad,
> And searched all their cels and secrets neare;
> In which what filth and ordure did appeare,
> Were yrkesome to report.

(6.12.24)

This double-edged satire is critical of both monastic abuses and the pillaging of the abbeys at the time of the Henrician dissolutions.[20] The negative potential of Protestant iconoclasm is apparent when the Blatant Beast's destructive course carried him "into the sacred Church" where he

> robd the Chancell, and the deskes downe threw,
> And Altars fouled, and blasphemy spoke,
> And th'Images for all their goodly hew,
> Did cast to ground, whilest none was them to rew;
> So all confounded and disordered there.

(st. 25)

The destruction of the old religion did not ensure its replacement by "pure" religious practices.[21]

Spenser's insight into the negative potential of the English Reformation need not imply any form of vestigial Roman Catholic sympa-

[18] Mother Mary Robert Falls finds no reference to monastic abuses in what she interprets as a one-dimensional attack against contemporary abuses in the Church of England in "Spenser's Kirkrapine and the Elizabethans," *SP* 50 (1953): 457–75. See also Jerome Oetgen, "Spenser's Treatment of Monasticism in Book I of *The Faerie Queene*," *American Benedictine Review* 22 (1971): 109–20.

[19] Greenblatt, *Renaissance Self-Fashioning*, p. 9.

[20] See Patrick Cullen, *Infernal Triad: The Flesh, the World, and the Devil in Spenser and Milton* (Princeton: Princeton University Press, 1974), p. 36.

[21] For the view that the Blatant Beast episode condemns abuses of monasticism rather than its institutional ideals, see Whitaker, *Religious Basis*, p. 18.

thy, because his stance is conventional in Protestant satire.[22] Not only does such satire predate Spenser's career, but it survives in the Miltonic warning in "On the New Forcers of Conscience under the Long Parliament" that "New *Presbyter* is but Old *Priest* writ Large." Protestant social reformers like Simon Fish and Henry Brinkelow blamed plundering courtiers and avaricious landlords for breaking the Henrician promise to redistribute monastic wealth to the poor in the form of charity and social reforms. Prominent Reformation preachers like Hugh Latimer and Thomas Lever attacked fellow clergymen for their failure to give up "monkish" idleness and clerical pluralism. Robert Crowley fictionalizes such views in *Phylargyrie of Greate Britayne* (1551), a satire whose epigraph cites the admonition against avarice in 1 Timothy 6:10 ("The rote of al mischife that ever dyd spring / Is carefull Covetise, and gredy Gathering") as sufficient sanction for the dismantling of monasteries and shrines. This text mocks the great wealth and fraudulent use of relics at the abbeys.[23]

The attack against avarice is an ancient one, as is its association with the Christian clergy. Crowley's choice of the favorite sermon text of Chaucer's Pardoner ("Radix malorum est Cupiditas") provides one indication of the continuity of anticlerical satire during the Middle Ages and Renaissance.[24] Crowley's title-page woodcut portrays the giant Philargyrie as a fur-clad Protestant aristocrat who adopts a hypocritical pose of piety as he avariciously rakes gold into a sack. His prominent use of a Bible to move his hoard makes it clear that external piety carries with it no assurance of inward faith. Although Philargyrie embodies the negative potential of monarchal acquisitiveness, which survived the Reformation unscathed, his portrayal implies no disapproval of kingship as such. Crowley's personification of Hypocrisy, Philargyrie's pre-Reformation minister, as a Roman Catholic anticipates Spenser's association of the same vice with Archimago. Nevertheless, his Protestant successor, Philaute, personifies the kind of "self-love" pursued by Henry VIII and the avaricious nobles who received the spoils of the monastic dissolutions. As a clear alternative to Crowley's charge that Protestants may be as bad as "papists," his ideal King personifies the positive capacities of Protestant kingship. At the close of the satire, the King's chief minister, Truth, advises him to embark upon a thoroughgoing iconoclastic program.[25] That Protestants lacked a monopoly on this

[22] See Norbrook, *Poetry and Politics*, pp. 123–24.

[23] Crowley, *Philargyrie*, ed. King, ll. 539–86.

[24] See Peter, *Complaint and Satire*, pp. 104–13.

[25] See *ERL*, pp. 346–55, and fig. 14; and Norbrook, *Poetry and Politics*, p. 50. *Phylargyrie* was sold in London during Spenser's youth (*STC* 6089.5).

kind of attack may be noted in *Respublica* (1553), a drama written by Nicholas Udall for production at the court of Queen Mary. This Christmas interlude includes a performance by Avarice as a Protestant vice.

In line with the complicated nature of Spenserian iconoclasm, the eremitical life retains some appeal in *The Faerie Queene*. This does not mean that Spenser adopts a "Catholic" position, because the Protestant reformers opposed the abuses of monasticism (among which they included the vow of celibacy), rather than what they regarded as its original altruistic ideals. Luther and his English followers agree that monasticism began as a reformist movement and a benevolent educational enterprise that was corrupted gradually by avarice and ritualism. Even John Bale concurs that "in all ages and in all congregacyons [i.e., monasteries], some godly men there were."[26] Calvin acknowledges that monks have abandoned a religious calling that was originally honorable to "set the chiefe parte of their holinesse in idlenesse" and admits that, their failures to the contrary, the monasteries "have yet some good men in their flocke."[27] John Jewel agrees that sloth is not intrinsically "Catholic" when he cites St. Augustine's denial that it is "lawful for a monk to spend his time slothfully and idly and under a pretensed and counterfeit holiness to live upon others."[28] Despite these concessions, the Protestant commitment to the active life of lay piety excludes the cloister as a positive ideal, and by shattering images and closing the monasteries the reformers denied "a central Catholic mode of generating inward reflection."[29]

## The House of Holiness

The House of Holiness provides an iconoclastic antidote to the "false" religious practices of Spenser's parodic monastics. Its theological allegory is grounded on the Protestant insistence that the Bible is the primary foundation for religious belief and that Christ is the sole mediator in human salvation, views that led directly to iconoclastic attacks against images of saints, shrines of the Blessed Virgin, and the entire monastic establishment of medieval Christendom.[30]

---

[26] Introduction to *A Lamentable complaynte of Baptista Mantuanus*, A3ᵛ.

[27] Calvin, *Institution*, trans. Norton (1561), 4.13.10, 15; fols. 86ᵛ, 88ᵛ. See Gless, *The Law, and the Convent*, p. 87; and Whitaker, *Religious Basis*, p. 25.

[28] Jewel, *Apology*, ed. Booty, p. 88.

[29] Greenblatt, *Renaissance Self-Fashioning*, p. 85.

[30] See Davies, *From Cranmer to Hooker*, pp. 17–25.

The reformers viewed such practices as "unwritten traditions" that lacked spiritual authority. Reformation iconoclasm represented a renewed outburst of an argument rooted in patristic and Byzantine controversies over the meaning of the Second Commandment and the status of religious icons. Pope Gregory I established the normative position of the Church of Rome that images may be substituted for the Bible as "books" (i.e., didactic vehicles) for the illiterate laity. When the Reformation reopened the attack against idolatry that had obsessed the eastern church during the eighth and ninth centuries, iconoclasts went back to the same scriptural and patristic texts that had figured in earlier disputes.[31]

Like their Byzantine predecessors, early English Protestants rejected the Gregorian sanction of icons, accepting only those religious pictures that were subordinate to the reading and understanding of the scriptures.[32] Both open and closed books therefore appear in Protestant literature and art as symbols of the supreme and self-validating authority of scriptural truth.[33] A polemical woodcut in Bateman's *Christall Glasse of Christian Reformation* accordingly personifies "godly zeale" as a Protestant clergyman who "preacheth in the pulpit" (Fig. 3). A friar joins the "enemies of Gods word" who pull down this "furtherer of the gospel" as he reads from an open Bible.[34] The New Testament that the Redcrosse Knight offers to his rescuer,

---

[31] Eire, *War against the Idols*, pp. 19–20, 59; Judith Herrin, *The Formation of Christendom* (Princeton: Princeton University Press, 1987), pp. 177–78, 307–43, 479. Gregory's argument may be found in *Patrologiae cursus completus. Series latina*, ed. J. P. Migne, 221 vols. (Paris, 1844–62), 77: col. 1128. Calvin rejects his defense of images in *Institution* 1.11.7

[32] *ERL*, pp. 144–60, passim.

[33] On the "book as symbol" from early Christian times until the Renaissance, see Ernst R. Curtius, *European Literature and the Latin Middle Ages*, trans. Willard Trask, 2nd ed. (New York: Harper and Row, 1963), pp. 310–40. On the relationship between iconoclasm and iconographical images of the divine Word in sixteenth- and seventeenth-century Protestant literature and art, see *ERL*, pp. 144–47, 152–55, 185–88; and John R. Knott, Jr., *The Sword of the Spirit: Puritan Responses to the Bible* (Chicago: University of Chicago Press, 1980), pp. 110–11. See also Chew, *Pilgrimage*, p. 123. The scriptures are employed as a dramatic prop in Wever's *Lusty Juventus*, a Protestant interlude in which the hero receives the text from Good Counsel; see ll. 276, 616–18. Similarly, the ideal king in Crowley's *Phylargyrie of Greate Britayne* wields a Bible in order to implement Protestant reforms (ll. 1379–84). See below, pp. 143, 145, concerning Queen Elizabeth's histrionic embrace of a Bible during her entry into London preceding her coronation.

[34] The fire that threatens "to consume the professors of the same [gospel]" may allude to the persecutions of the recent reign of Queen Mary. The dynamics of this woodcut are similar to those of the famous illustration in Foxe's "Book of Martyrs" that portrays friars and other Marian clerics pulling Archbishop Cranmer down from a platform "for the true confession of his fayth" (*A&M* [1570], p. 1781).

Prince Arthur, upon his release from Orgoglio's dungeon is a gospel image of this kind, one that is associated with the centrality of the vernacular Bible in Protestant devotion:

> Which to requite, the *Redcrosse* knight him gave
> A booke, wherein his Saveours testament
> Was writ with golden letters rich and brave:
> A worke of wondrous grace, and able soules to save.

(FQ 1.9.19)

Nevertheless, the "illiterate" knight who offers this gift is as yet unable to read the scriptures or to apply them to his own experience.[35] In his perception, the "golden letters" of this book convey little more than the talismanic magic associated with illuminated manuscripts and other books whose devotional illustrations conjured up Protestant fears of Catholic "superstition" and "idolatry." Such texts are included in Errour's "vomit full of bookes and papers," Archimago's library of saints' lives and "Magick bookes," and the breviary carried by Idleness as an outward sign of religious devotion (1.1.19, 36; 1.4.19). Because of his lack of understanding, Redcrosse cannot complete his spiritual education until he learns to read and understand the Bible.

The knight's sojourn at the House of Holiness allegorizes a "paradigm of salvation" that early Protestants extrapolated out of the epistles of St. Paul. It is divided into the stages of "election, calling, justification, adoption, sanctification, [and] glorification," which can sometimes be "concomitant rather than sequential." The distinctive feelings that accompany those stages include a conversion experience, which is an appropriate response to the divine calling; repentance; the experience of faith; and the fluctuating emotional states that accompany sanctification.[36] The overall movement of Redcrosse's experience traces the trajectory of Protestant spiritual life from the initial conviction of sin to confidence that one is the chosen recipient of divine grace. Although original sin leads Redcrosse, like any Christian, repeatedly into error, the unmerited gift of divine grace extends the promise of salvation. Thus when Despair sways Redcrosse to the point of suicide at the knowledge of his own sinfulness, Una pulls her knight back with a reminder of his election: "Why shouldst thou then despeire, that chosen art?" (1.9.53). Upon Redcrosse's arrival at the House of Holiness, Dame Caelia acknowl-

---

[35] Redcrosse "is spiritually illiterate and hard of hearing" according to Mallette, "The Protestant Art of Preaching," p. 9.

[36] Lewalski, *Protestant Poetics*, pp. 13–23. See also Kellogg and Steele, pp. 40–43.

edges his status as an elect "saint" (1.10.10). Under the tutelage of her daughter, Fidelia, Redcrosse comes to believe that divine grace has infused him with righteousness.

The House of Holiness functions externally as a metaphor for the church and internally as a figure for the mind or human spirit.[37] As an "auntient house," Dame Caelia's dwelling is aligned with the ideal of returning to the principles of the early Christian church. While the household resembles a monastery in its emphasis on humility, asceticism, and obedience, it exemplifies many religious principles that Catholics and Protestants share, notably the honor paid to the seven works of corporal mercy.[38] Although Dame Caelia may look like an alter ego of Corceca as she spends her nights "in bidding of her bedes," she corrects the spiritual blindness of the latter through her knowledge of "sacred lore, / And pure unspotted life." The House of Holiness provides the antithesis of the ignorance that thrives at the dwellings of Archimago and Corceca. The monastic vow of celibacy has no standing there because Caelia's virgin daughters, Fidelia and Speranza (faith and hope), are "spousd, yet wanting wedlocks solemnize" (sts. 3–4). The chaste fecundity of Charissa (charity) is traditional in Christian iconography.

Protestant theology helps to clarify a major crux in the House of Holiness. Why is Dame Caelia's youngest daughter, Charissa, the mother of a "multitude of babes" who was "late in child-bed brought," separated from her elder sisters (sts. 29, 31)? In contrast to the traditional portrayal of the theological virtues as a unified trio, Spenser detaches Charissa from her sisters. Spenser's variation of this Pauline allegory applies an influential text, "And now abideth faith, hope and love [i.e., charity], even these thre: but the chiefest of these is love" (1 Cor. 13:13), to the changed circumstances of the Reformation. The sisters' birth order reflects Luther's determination that faith has higher standing than charity in accordance with Romans 3:19–26 and that believers are saved by divine grace as it is apprehended through inward faith rather than by good works in the outward world.[39] The order in which Spenser introduces first Fidelia and then Speranza in an interlocking pair ("Ylinked arme in arme in

---

[37] John Hankins, *Source and Meaning in Spenser's Allegory: A Study of "The Faerie Queene"* (Oxford: Clarendon Press, 1971), pp. 55–56.

[38] See Whitaker, *Religious Basis*, p. 44. Gless argues that in the House of Holiness "monasticism becomes a metaphor for the proper ordering of individual souls" (*The Law, and the Convent*, pp. 87–88).

[39] *Luther's Works*, ed. Jaroslav Pelikan et al., 55 vols. (St. Louis: Concordia Publishing House, 1958–76), 25: 234–37. For a precedent in the writings of St. Thomas Aquinas, see Kellogg and Steele, pp. 41–42.

lovely wise"; st. 12), long before the reader encounters Charissa, furnishes an index for the relative valuation of each virtue. Fidelia's seniority as the eldest sister exemplifies the subordination of charity to faith in line with the dictum in the *Book of Homilies* that "true faith doth give life to the works" and "without fayth no worke is good before GOD" (*Book of Homilies* 1: 30). Calvin asserts further that hope necessarily accompanies faith: "Now whersoever this lively faith shalbe, it can not be possible but that it hathe with it the hope of eternal salvation, as an undividable companion" (*Institution* 3.2.4; fol. 125ᵛ). The importance of charitable deeds as posterior *signs* of faith may be noted further in the retention of an honorable place for the "holy Hospitall" (i.e., hospice) of the seven Bead-men (sts. 36–43). Their standing as men of prayer and true devotion complements Dame Caelia's ceaseless round of "doing good and godly deedes" (st. 3).

As the core doctrines of the Reformation, justification by faith alone (*sola fide*) and the complete dependence of the individual upon divine grace (*sola gratia*) represent a readjustment of universal Christian belief, shared by Catholics and Protestants, in both good works and faith.[40] According to Luther, the recovery of the primacy of faith and other church reforms represents not an innovation but a return to Christian ideals shared by St. Paul, the primitive church, and some medieval thinkers, notably those in the Augustinian tradition. By way of contrast, the doctrine of justification by good works, whereby humans could take an active part in the reception of divine grace, dominated the salvation theology of the later Middle Ages. The cautious sermons on salvation, faith, and works in the *Book of Homilies* advance the view promulgated by Luther that although works in themselves have no bearing upon salvation, they retain importance in the Christian way of life. These homilies distinguish between "a dead faith, which bringeth foorth no good workes, but is idle, barren, and unfruitfull," and a "true, lively and unfeigned Christian faith" that "worketh by charity." It is an apparent paradox that despite the absence of any human merit, true faith must result in good works: "Faith may not bee naked without good workes, for then it is no true Faith: and when it is adjoyned to workes, yet it is above the workes." Although "we must set no good works before fayth, nor thinke that before faith a man may doe any good works," good works necessarily follow faith as the "fruit" of the spirit.[41] Calvin's thinking

[40] Charles H. and Katherine George, *The Protestant Mind of the English Reformation: 1570–1640* (Princeton: Princeton University Press, 1961), p. 44.

[41] *Book of Homilies*, 1: 21–22, 30, 32. See Wall, "Godly and Fruitful Lessons," pp. 103–11; and *ERL*, pp. 133–34. Hugh MacLachlan concludes in "The Death of Guyon and

is aligned with this position: "For that which the Scholemen (i.e., Scholastic theologians) teache, that charitie is before faithe and hope, ys a mere madness. For it is faythe only that fyrste engendreth charitie in us." He concludes that "frutes of repentance" must include "charitie toward men, and therewithall a holinesse and purenesse in all our life."[42] Peter Martyr concurs: "For if faith without works be dead, much more are works dead without faith."[43]

The House of Holiness is the site of the Redcrosse's education concerning faith as it is personified by Fidelia in the "schoolehouse . . . of her heavenly learning." Like Una, her kindred catechetical figure, and Dame Caelia, Fidelia teaches "celestiall discipline" (i.e., religious knowledge). Una never carries a Bible, but she characteristically voices proverbs and admonitions drawn from the scriptures. By way of contrast, Fidelia holds aloft a copy of the "sacred Booke" associated with her pupil's spiritual indoctrination. "Signd and seald with blood" of Christ's atonement, this text symbolizes the Bible or the New Testament in general, or Revelation in particular.[44] Although the book contains mysterious truths—"darke things . . . hard to be understood"—Fidelia's opening of "his dull eyes, that light mote in them shine" (sts. 13, 18) accords with St. Paul's definition of evangelism (Acts 26:18). Through the illumination of heavenly grace, the previously inarticulate and illiterate knight eagerly learns to comprehend fundamental theological truths: "Of God, of grace, of justice, of free will" (st. 19). Fidelia's function as a wise tutor conforms to the Protestant doctrine of the priesthood of all believers, which defines clergy as learned individuals who provide spiritual education rather than as mediators between individuals and the divine. As a religious advisor rather than an absolving priest, Fidelia can counsel Red-

---

the *Elizabethan Book of Homilies,*" *SSt* 4 (1983): 98, 103, 109, that the authorized "Sermon on Good Workes" supplies an immediate context for the presentation of Guyon as one whose lack of "both a *true* and *lively* faith" places him "in the awkward position of being a Roman Catholic in a staunchly Protestant poem." He argues that it is not until after the Mammon episode that the hero abandons reliance upon the theology of good works.

[42] Calvin, *Institution* 3.2.19, 3.3.16; fols. 116ᵛ, 132. He argues further that "we do not justifie a man by workes before God; but we say that all they that are of God, are regenerate and made a newe creature, that they may passe out of the kingdome of sinne into the kingdome of righteousnesse, and that by this testimonie thei make their callyng certayne, and are judged as trees by the frutes" (3.16.8; fol. 196).

[43] Martyr, *Common Places*, trans. Anthony Marten (1583), pt. 3, 2N4 (fol. 151).

[44] Whereas the chalice carried by Faith is a standard device in medieval art, Tudor Protestant illustrations characteristically feature a book symbolic of part or all of the Bible (e.g., Fig. 16). Counter-Reformation art also features the book, as in the image of "Fede Cattolica," who holds the Ten Commandments (symbolic of the Old Law) and the New Testament in Ripa's *Iconologia*. See Norbrook, *Poetry and Politics*, p. 120.

crosse, but he must guide himself according to biblical interpretation and the inner dictates of his own conscience. His experience accords with the declaration of the official homily on Bible reading that "whatsoever is required to the salvation of man, is fully contained in the Scripture of GOD" (*Book of Homilies*, 1: 2).

The House of Holiness exemplifies the place of introspective self-examination and conversion in Protestant spirituality.[45] Overcome with the enormity of sin, the knight's immediate response to his growth in faith is a desire "to end his wretched dayes." Through Speranza's offer of "comfort sweet," however, he undergoes a therapeutic regimen devised by Patience, a skilled physician who attacks the source of spiritual sickness: original sin. Four attendants demarcate the stages of Redcrosse's conversion experience. Following the ministrations of Amendment, whose pincers pluck away "superfluous flesh," Redcrosse undergoes a formal progress from Penance to Remorse and, ultimately, Repentance, who completes the treatment "of his cured conscience" (sts. 21–29). Although penance retained a place in the Protestant devotional scheme, it lost the sacramental status that it had possessed in the Roman rite. The doctrine of justification by faith alone supplanted the Catholic penitential system based upon private confession and clerical absolution. True repentance is marked by sincere amendment of life rather than by external acts of penance.[46] According to Calvin, the conversion experience is identified with repentance as a "true turninge of pure lyfe unto God, whiche consisteth in the mortifyeng of the fleshe and of the olde man, and in the quyckening of the spirite" (*Institution* 3.3.5; fol. 128). He finds that repentance is the direct result of faith: "Repentance doth not only immediatly folow faith, but also spring out of it. . . .[The sinner] muste returne from the erroures of hys former life into the right way, and applie all his studie to the meditation of repentance" (*Institution* 3.3.1; fol. 126ᵛ).[47]

[45] See Kellogg and Steele, pp. 40–43.

[46] See Davies, *From Cranmer to Hooker*, pp. 18–19. On the Protestant insistence that true repentance is based upon faith and amendment of life instead of penitential works, see *Melanchthon on Christian Doctrine: "Loci Communes 1555,"* ed. and trans. Clyde L. Manschrek (New York: Oxford University Press, 1965), pp. 237–39.

[47] The theological stages of Redcrosse's progress correspond to a contemporary diagram showing "the Causes of Salvation and Damnation, according to God's Word" in William Perkins's *The Foundation of Christian Religion* (1588); facs. in H. C. Porter, *Puritanism in Tudor England* (Columbia, S.C.: University of South Carolina Press, 1971), pp. 295–300. This sketch indicates that the ultimate causes of salvation are God's foreknowledge and election of souls through the mediation of Christ. Divine calling, justification, and sanctification are the three causes of salvation during the life of the elect, prior to glorification following death. Human faith apprehends these operations in the

The life of true charity represented by Dame Caelia's establishment and the Hospital of the Seven Bead-men, although compatible in certain respects with the doctrine of good works, accords with the viewpoint of the *Book of Homilies* that good works are a necessary consequence of faith.[48] These establishments provide access to Mount Contemplation, a place of epiphany that marks Redcrosse's highest point of ascent and the culmination of his spiritual education. By reminding the reader of Roman Catholic devotional practices, Contemplation's blindness and retirement to "a litle Hermitage" demonstrate that meditation retains a positive place in Christian spirituality, be it Protestant or Catholic. Although his "earthly" eyes are blind to this world, "yet wondrous quick and persant [i.e., piercing] was his spright" (sts. 46–48). Nevertheless, we must remember that despite Redcrosse's yearning to withdraw from the world, hermit Contemplation sends him down from the mountaintop to fulfill his obligation of active service to Una and Gloriana (1.10.62–63).[49] This insistence upon a return to "deeds of armes" (st. 62) elevates the active over the contemplative life, "an emphasis shared by Protestantism and reforming elements of the medieval church."[50] By way of contrast, the deficiency of withdrawal from worldly action may be noted in Idleness, who "shunned manly exercise . . . for contemplation sake" (1.4.19–20). Despite its association with the necromancy of Archimago and the spiritual blindness of Corceca, contemplation retains a positive place in Protestant spirituality so long as the active life remains paramount.

## Iconoclastic Poetics

Spenser's poetry is inherently iconoclastic in its attack of the abuse or misapplication of art. Although he never equates art with idolatry, an iconoclastic pattern permeates *The Faerie Queene*, where "false"

---

following stages: "effectuall preaching and hearing, the mollifying of the heart, faith, remission of sinne, imputation of righteousnes, mortification, vivification, and repentance." Andrew D. Weiner applies this diagram to the stages of Redcrosse's quest in " 'Fierce Warres and Faithfull Loves': Pattern as Structure in Book I of *The Faerie Queene*," *HLQ* 37 (1973): 54–56.

[48] Whitaker, *Religious Basis*, p. 46.

[49] Contemplation is an "apocalyptic preacher" who provides Protestant homiletic counsel, according to Mallette, "The Protestant Art of Preaching," pp. 21–22.

[50] Kellogg and Steele, p. 43. Although the role played by another good hermit in the saving of Timias and Serena indicates that contemplation may be a valid alternative after a lifetime dedicated to active service (6.5.35–37), the active life is the chief concern of *FQ*.

projections of the artistic imagination are dismantled time after time, not simply Acrasia's Bower but also the Castle of Busirane and Geryon's shrine. In every case a destructive attack invokes the idiom of Reformation polemics against religious idolatry, which associate the Church of Rome with external devotion and the attendant ritualistic objects. Spenser's ramifying attacks against idolatry include not only Kirkrapine's destruction by Una's Lion but also Prince Arthur's savage suppression of "pagan" sacrifices at Orgoglio's Castle. The "blasphemous" associations of Geryoneo's "Church," with its "Altar" on which "daily sacrifize" is made, indicate that Arthur's assault on and destruction of the golden "Idole" objectify Protestant hostility against religious images, "relickes," and the Roman mass that they attack as "vaine fancies" of the imagination (5.11.18–21, 33).

Reformation scholars have commonly assumed that the iconoclastic movement to destroy works of art that were substituted for God as objects of worship had little if any impact on poetry and drama. They have seen the movement to redirect devotion from the created to the creator largely as an attack against roods and rood screens, statues of the Madonna and Child, images of saints, medieval Dooms and other wall paintings, and woodcuts in devotional texts.[51] A small explosion of recent studies has undertaken to correct this imbalanced view, however, by demonstrating the positive impact of iconoclasm on sixteenth- and seventeenth-century literature. Stephen Greenblatt attributes the constructive side of iconoclasm to "the principle of regenerative violence" whereby the "act of tearing down is the act of fashioning." According to this view, Spenser's emphasis on the imagistic status of poetic fiction defends him against any charge that his own art may be idolatrous:

> The answer lies in an art that constantly calls attention to its own processes, that includes within itself framing devices and signs of its own createdness. . . . If you fear that images may make a blasphemous claim to reality, that they may become idols that you will be compelled to worship, you may smash all images or you may create images that announce themselves at every moment as things made.[52]

---

[51] John Phillips perpetuates this narrow definition in *The Reformation of Images: Destruction of Art in England, 1535–1660* (Berkeley and Los Angeles: University of California Press, 1973), the most complete study of iconoclasm during the English Reformation.

[52] Greenblatt, *Renaissance Self-Fashioning*, pp. 188–90. See also James R. Siemon's *Shakespearean Iconoclasm* (Berkeley and Los Angeles: University of California Press, 1985), which convincingly relates "certain features of Shakespearean drama . . . [to the] struggles over imagery and likeness that vexed post-Reformation England" (p. 30); and Michael O'Connell's "The Idolatrous Eye: Iconoclasm, Anti-Theatricalism, and the Image of the Elizabethan Theater," *ELH* 52 (1985): 279–310.

Spenser shares the early Protestant assumption that iconoclasm involves a complex dialectic in which attacks on "false" images are connected to a countervailing effort to construct acceptable forms of "true" literary and visual art (see *ERL*, pp. 144–60). Patrick Collinson concludes that until at least 1580, English Protestants were united in their commitment to the constructive production of literature and art because:

> Iconoclasm implies a spirited attack, verbally violent or actually violent, on certain unacceptable images, but not the total repudiation of all images, which on my terms is Iconophobia. Indeed, Iconoclasm in this sense may imply the substitution of other, acceptable images, or the refashioning of some images for an altered purpose. It is hostile to false art but not anti-art, since its hostility implies a true and acceptable art, applied to a laudable purpose.[53]

Only recently has extensive study been devoted to the implications of Spenserian iconoclasm. Kenneth Gross argues, for example, that Spenser experiences a conflict between iconoclastic and idolatrous motives, which results in "the nearly obsessive repetition of scenes in which icons, statues, phantasms, illusions, and so on are first elaborately described and then summarily transgressed, broken, dissolved." On the ground that iconoclasm is "entangled in the very sorts of symbolic action that may issue in idolatry," he concludes that in *The Faerie Queene* "iconoclasm itself becomes just as much of a threat as idolatry."[54] Unlike Gross, who concludes that Spenser practices a subversive "poetics of idolatry" (Gross, p. 27), Ernest Gilman extrapolates a "poetics of Reformation iconoclasm" out of the theological controversy over image-breaking. By calling the utility of the imagination into question, the iconoclastic controversy created a poetic "dilemma [that] may seem to be a formula for poetic paralysis," according to Gilman, who concludes that the resolution of this problem lies in the general Protestant shift away from external images of late medieval popular devotion and toward the internalized imagery of metaphor and poetic language.[55] Gilman rejects as a too "tidy con-

[53] Collinson, *From Iconoclasm to Iconophobia: The Cultural Impact of the Second English Reformation*, The Stenton Lecture, 1985 (Reading: University of Reading, 1986), p. 8.

[54] Kenneth Gross, *Spenserian Poetics: Idolatry, Iconoclasm, and Magic* (Ithaca, N.Y.: Cornell University Press, 1985), pp. 16, 18–19; hereafter cited as Gross.

[55] Gilman, *Iconoclasm and Poetry*, pp. 1, 31, and ch. 2, passim; cited hereafter as Gilman. Although the present chapter was in draft before Gross and Gilman were published, it has been revised to address their arguments. See also my review of these books in *Spenser Newsletter* 17 (1986): 55–59.

clusion" (Gilman, p. 151) the ahistorical view that "idolatry is itself iconoclastic" (Gross, p. 160).

Gilman builds upon Carol Kaske's finding that the rhetorical figure of *epanorthosis* or *correctio* is a fundamental "structuring principle" of the epic, according to which successive cantos or books correct their predecessors. A misunderstanding of the relation of this practice to the Protestant habit of doubling "images *in bono* and *in malo*" has led readers, in Kaske's opinion, to misinterpret iconoclastic actions like the destruction of the Bower of Bliss as evidence of Spenser's "Puritanical" hostility to sensuality and art. "Self-correction of thought" instead characterizes the way in which the Garden of Adonis corrects the Bower of Bliss and the Temple of Venus then corrects both the "evil Bower" and the "good Garden."[56] David Norbrook defines this procedure in terms of "a series of what amount to alienation effects" whereby Spenser discourages his audience from accepting

> . . . the interpretations they are offered immediately on trust. It is the idolatrous magicians Archimago and Acrasia who encourage readers to take sign for reality, representation for thing represented; the alert reader is reminded . . . to keep experience under constant rational scrutiny.[57]

Norbrook's masterly analysis grounds both iconoclasm and the Reformation attack against the mass in the semiotics of " 'natural' and 'artificial' signs." According to the Roman rite, the host undergoes transubstantiation from an artificial to a natural sign that partakes "of that which it represented"; indeed, it *is* what it shows. While Catholic theologians did not confer equivalent status upon religious images, Norbrook argues that the "underlying concept of the natural sign undoubtedly reinforced the general reverence paid to all mediators and religious symbols, giving rise in the popular mind to all kinds of magical beliefs." Protestant theologians criticized what they regarded as an "idolatrous confusion between sign and thing signified" on the ground that "sacramental signs seemed 'natural' only because of the corruption of the imagination which was always ready to draw false analogies."[58]

[56] Kaske, "Surprised by Puritanism," an unpublished paper delivered at the session on English Reformation literature at the 1980 meeting of the Modern Language Association, pp. 1–4. The distinction between the right use and the abuse of images in Peter Martyr's *Common Places*, pt. 2, 2L5 (fol. 341), is central to the proper understanding of Spenserian iconoclasm; cited by Kaske, p. 5. On the principle of use and abuse, see Alastair Fowler, "Protestant Attitudes to Poetry, 1560–1590," dissertation, Oxford University 1957, pp. 34–36; and Whitaker, *Religious Basis*, pp. 24–25, 27–28.

[57] Norbrook, *Poetry and Politics*, p. 111.

[58] Ibid., pp. 35–36.

Protestant iconoclasm furnishes a theoretical framework for Spenser's witty transfer of a theological problem to an aesthetic context by playing upon the analogy between the poetic imagination and religious idolatry, and by inviting the fusion of sacred and secular categories.[59] Spenser's uneasiness concerning the negative potential of the imagination results from the dialectical nature of iconoclasm as a force that has both a positive and a negative potential. Many early Protestants shared the Erasmian view that images in themselves are spiritually neutral because their value depends upon how they are applied. Just as the best defense of poetry against the charge of idolatry is the emphatic affirmation of the right use of poetic imagery, Spenser's destructive attacks against false images are embodied in intrinsically imagistic form. The echoing and re-echoing throughout the iconoclastic episodes of *The Faerie Queene* of terms like "image," "idol," "maker," "imitation," "art," and "fantasy" rest upon the same analogy between divine creation and artistic creativity that underlies E.K.'s conviction that poetic fiction in its truest sense is a "divine gift" and product of "celestiall inspiration" (argument to "October").

Spenser shares the uneasiness that contemporary Protestants felt toward the "fantasy" or "fancy"—he never uses the word "imagination"—as a deceptive faculty capable of undermining human understanding by transmitting false and misleading ideas.[60] The imagination may deceive not only by reflecting an inaccurate image of the external world, but also by actively creating false concepts. Thus the "false shewes" of Archimago's erotic dream readily deceive Redcrosse and lead him to abandon Una (1.1.46). Nevertheless, *The Faerie Queene* incorporates an urgent defense of poetic fiction and the imagination producing it.[61] Such views are implicit in an iconoclastic tract against pilgrimages, "The Fantassie of Idolatrie," written by William Gray, a protégé of Thomas Cromwell, at the time of the Dissolution of the Abbeys. Although the title of this polemic implicates the imagination in the production of "false" images, Gray's casting in ballad form of this attack on devotion to saints' relics and monastic shrines

[59] Gross concludes that Spenser "displaces the problem of idolatry into secular—political, erotic, and aesthetic—realms with a freedom that no ascetically theological discourse could allow itself" (p. 31).

[60] Puttenham distinguishes between true and false applications of the imagination in *The Arte of English Poesie*, ed. Gladys Willcock and Alice Walker (Cambridge: Cambridge University Press, 1936), pp. 19, 307, a work that treats "phantasie and imagination" as synonyms. See also Greenblatt, *Renaissance Self-Fashioning*, pp. 112–13.

[61] See Isabel G. MacCaffrey, *Spenser's Allegory: The Anatomy of Imagination* (Princeton: Princeton University Press, 1976), pp. 73–75.

indicates that he and other early Protestants harbored no hostility toward the appropriate application of poetry.[62]

*The Faerie Queene* illustrates profound suspicion and distrust of the imagination's potential for error by associating it with the falsifications of Phantastes' chamber, where may be found such shapes "as in the world were never yit, / Ne can devized be of mortall wit" (2.9.50):

> idle thoughts and fantasies,
> Devices, dreames, opinions unsound,
> Shewes, visions, sooth-sayes, and prophesies;
> And all that fained is, as leasings, tales, and lies.
>
> (st. 51)

Nevertheless, Phantastes (or the imagination) coexists with Eumnestes ("good memory"), a "man of infinite remembrance," within the rationally ordered soul embodied by the House of Alma (2.9.50–58). The true and false operations of the imagination engage in a dialectical interplay contingent upon Spenser's "dual citizenship in the realms of texts and images." The imagination and memory are not mutually exclusive, because the poet is a "part-time resident" of Phantastes' chamber who also "inhabits the chamber of memory, where he sits, like the ancient but vigorous Eumnestes."[63] In reply to the criticism that *The Faerie Queene* is the product of the falsifying imagination—"th'aboundance of an idle braine . . . and painted forgery"—the narrator claims that his work is "matter of just memory" (2.proem.1). Indeed, his acknowledged source of poetic inspiration is Clio, the Muse of history whom he describes as the "sacred Muse" and "noursling of Dame *Memorie*."[64] The portrayal of Contemplation associates memory with "true" vision and poetry (1.10.54).

The ambiguous status of the imagination leads Spenser to address a major problem that faced sixteenth-century Protestant poets and theologians, that of discriminating between "true" and "false" images in religion, psychology, and fictional art. The profound duality of *The Faerie Queene*, with its population of true and false women, knights, prophets, and hermits, reflects an apocalyptic worldview in

---

[62] Ernest W. Dormer, *Gray of Reading: A Sixteenth-century Controversialist and Ballad-Writer* (Reading, Pa.: Bradley & Son, 1923), pp. 66–75. Foxe interpolates Gray's poem into the "Book of Martyrs" (*A&M* [1877], 5: 404–9).

[63] Gilman, p. 61. See John Guillory, *Poetic Authority: Spenser, Milton, and Literary History* (New York: Columbia University Press, 1983), pp. 35, 37.

[64] *FQ* 1.proem.1; 1.11.5; 4.11.10. For counterarguments that Spenser invokes Calliope, the Muse of epic poetry, instead of Clio, see *Var.* 1: 506–14; and Cain, *Praise in "The Faerie Queene,"* pp. 44–47.

which competing churches made apparently equal claims to spiritual authority, and in which even concerned lay people and theologians could easily fall into error. The Protestant eradication of justification by good works and demotion of nonscriptural tradition made the search for truth an arduous process filled with danger. C. S. Lewis observes that Spenser draws back from any sense of absolute dualism, however, by reminding us "by delicate allegories that though the conflict seems ultimate yet one of the opposites contains, and is not contained by, the other."[65]

The scriptural model for this conflict is Revelation, in which commentators discovered prophecies of religious discord throughout the Middle Ages and Renaissance. Whereas Catholics scrutinized Revelation for signs of Protestant error,[66] Protestants like John Bale commandeered a medieval tradition of antipapal commentary when they read the text as a prophetic attack against the corrupt Church of Rome. Joachim de Fiore originated the identification of worldly popes with Antichrist during the twelfth century, an assertion that underwent elaboration in pseudepigraphous prophecies attributed to him in later centuries.[67] Unlike the Lollards and their Protestant successors, however, Joachimist commentators accepted the institutional ideals of the papacy and acknowledged that good popes could occupy a rightful place as leaders of Christendom; they regarded false pontiffs as types of Antichrist.[68] The title of Bale's commentary on Revelation, *The Image of Both Churches*, calls attention to the problem of discriminating between images of truth and falsehood, which the elect Christian, guided by faith, should be able to resolve by perceiving in Revelation, which is said to contain the whole of the Bible in small, types for one's own individual history and the collective history of humanity.[69] Bale draws eclectically from sources ranging from

[65] Lewis, *The Allegory of Love: A Study in Medieval Tradition* (Oxford: Clarendon Press, 1936), pp. 314–15. See also *ERL*, pp. 155–60.

[66] Cornelius á Lapide interprets the plague of locusts (Rev. 9:1–11), for example, as a prophecy directed against Luther, Calvin, and other Protestant heretics in *Commentaria in Acta Apostolorum, Epistolas Canonicas, et Apocalypsin* (Antwerp, 1647).

[67] On the pope as Antichrist, see Christopher Hill, *Antichrist in Seventeenth-Century England* (London: Oxford University Press, 1971), pp. 1–40. The Joachimist tradition and its relation to Bale and English Protestant thought are treated in Marjorie Reeves, *The Influence of Prophecy in the Later Middle Ages: A Study in Joachimism* (Oxford: Clarendon Press, 1969), pp. 107–8, 453–54, 459, 502–4; Richard Bauckham, *Tudor Apocalypse* (Abingdon: Sutton-Courtenay Press, 1978), pp. 24–27, 211–14; Katharine Firth, *The Apocalyptic Tradition in Reformation Britain, 1530–1645* (Oxford: Oxford University Press, 1979), pp. 4–5, 39–49, 68; and *ERL*, pp. 197–203.

[68] See Bernard McGinn, "Revelation," in *The Literary Guide to the Bible*, ed. Robert Alter and Frank Kermode (Cambridge, Mass.: Harvard University Press, 1987), p. 533.

[69] *Select Works of John Bale*, ed. Henry Christmas, Parker Society, vol. 36 (Cambridge:

Augustine's *City of God* to Joachimist writings and Lutheran commentaries. The view that Revelation predicts the return to true faith during the Reformation was well known during the Elizabethan age through Bale's commentary, Heinrich Bullinger's *A Hundred Sermons upon the Apocalips of Iesu Christe* (trans. publ. in London in 1561), and the annotations excerpted from Bullinger in the Geneva Bible.[70] Spenser was presumably familiar with this polemical context, if only through the antipapal commentary for the *Theatre for Worldlings* into which Jan van der Noot incorporated views derived from Bale and Bullinger.

Readers have long recognized that Spenser ostentatiously employs Revelation in Book 1 of *The Faerie Queene* as a model for characterization, imagery, and a broadly dualistic concern with Reformation controversy.[71] John Dixon was the first to note this connection in the earliest extant annotations on *The Faerie Queene*, which he inscribed into a copy of the first volume in 1597. (He was clearly an isolated interpreter whose views would have been disputed by recusants and other readers, but his notes are quite valuable for the sense that they provide of how at least one Protestant contemporary understood Spenser's work.[72]) The poet concentrates on major incidents that were illustrated with woodcuts in the *Theatre for Worldlings* (Rev. 13,

---

Cambridge University Press, 1849), p. 340. See *ERL*, pp. 62–64; and Hume, *Protestant Poet*, pp. 78–80. On Bale's place in Tudor apocalyptic thought, see Bauckham, *Tudor Apocalypse*, pp. 21–33, 68–75, 80–88; Paul Christianson, *Reformers and Babylon: English Apocalyptic Visions from the Reformation to the Eve of the Civil War* (Toronto: University of Toronto Press, 1978), chs. 1–2; and Firth, *Apocalyptic Tradition*, ch. 2.

[70] Bauckham, *Tudor Apocalypse*, p. 49.

[71] Thomas Warton, *Observations on the Fairy Queen of Spenser*, 2 vols., 2nd ed. (1762), 2: 98; Josephine Bennett, *The Evolution of "The Faerie Queene"* (Chicago: University of Chicago Press, 1942), pp. 112–14, and ch. 9, passim; Hankins, *Source and Meaning in Spenser's Allegory*, pp. 99–119, a revision of "Spenser and the Revelation of St. John," *PMLA* 60 (1945): 364–81 (reprinted in *Essential Articles*, ed. A. C. Hamilton, pp. 40–57); Florence Sandler, "*The Faerie Queene*: An Elizabethan Apocalypse," in *The Apocalypse in English Renaissance Thought and Literature: Patterns, Antecedents, and Repercussions*, ed. C. A. Patrides and Joseph Wittreich (Ithaca, N.Y.: Cornell University Press, 1984), pp. 160–67. Wittreich advances the sweeping view that the impact of Revelation extends beyond "image and theme or allegory and plot" to structural, rhetorical, and narrative strategies that may be documented "in one way or another, on every book of *The Faerie Queene*," in *Visionary Poetics: Milton's Tradition and His Legacy* (San Marino, Calif.: Huntington Library, 1979), p. 63; see pp. 3–78, passim. Frank Kermode argues that Book 1 functions as a poetic application of John Foxe's theory of providential history in *Spenser, Shakespeare, and Donne: Renaissance Essays* (London: Routledge and Kegan Paul, 1971), pp. 19–21, 40–41. See also Nohrnberg, *Analogy*, pp. 217–18, 238.

[72] Dixon, *Commentary*. O'Connell demonstrates how Dixon applies Spenser's allusions to Revelation as a grid for historical allegory in *Mirror and Veil*, pp. 49–65, passim.

17, 19, 21; Figs. 8, 6, 21, 5).[73] Of particular importance for Spenser is Bale's insistence that Revelation has a poetic texture because its apocalyptic visions should be read as a picture book full of "pleasant figures and elegant tropes."[74]

Spenser elaborates upon Revelation by invoking the widespread Protestant interpretation of the antithesis between the Woman Clothed with the Sun and the Whore of Babylon (Rev. 12, 17) as a prophecy of the division between "true" religion and the "false" church of Rome. Redcrosse's difficulty in differentiating between the respective claims of Una, whose "blacke stole" conceals her "heavenly beautie" (1.1.4, 1.12.22), and the gorgeously costumed Duessa, who disguises herself as truth, epitomizes the Reformation dilemma of choosing between "images" of competing churches. John Dixon recognizes Una's relationship to the apocalyptic woman who flees into the wilderness under attack from "the great dragon, that olde serpent, called the devil and Satan" (Rev. 12:6, 9) when he identifies her as the "true Church" (Dixon, *Commentary* 1.2.9n, 1.12.20n).[75] Dixon repeatedly comments on Duessa and the Seven-headed steed upon which she rides with glosses like "Romish harlot" (1.7.1n), "a discription of the whor of babylon" (st. 17n), and "Antichrist Compared to a harlot whose beautie only standeth in outward pompe and impudencie" (1.2.34n; see also st. 40n).

Dixon's annotations on Archimago identify him as "a falste profite" (1.1.29n) and "Antichriste" (1.12.24n). Under its guise as the False Prophet (Rev. 19:20), the Beast from the Land, "which had two hornes like the Lambe, but he spake like the dragon" (Rev. 13:11; Fig. 8), provides the likely model for Archimago and his ability to change appearance at will. The Beast's ability to disguise itself as the Lamb of God fulfills the exhortation from the Sermon on the Mount that the faithful "beware of false prophetes, which come to you in shepes clothing" (Matt. 7:15). Dixon's interpretation of Orgoglio as another variation of "Antichriste" (1.8.2) accords with S. K. Heninger's identification of the giant as a type for papal pride.[76] Dixon reinforces Spenser's own association of the vision of the "goodly Citie" from Mount Contemplation (1.10.55–57) with the descent of the New Jerusalem (Rev. 21:2, 10) by commenting that "the hevenly Jerusalem"

---

[73] See Bennett, *Evolution*, p. 112.

[74] Bale, *Select Works*, p. 252.

[75] See Sandler, "*The Faerie Queene*: An Elizabethan Apocalypse," pp. 165–66.

[76] Heninger, "The Orgoglio Episode in *The Faerie Queene*," *ELH* 26 (1959): 171–87; reprinted in *Essential Articles*, ed. A. C. Hamilton, p. 132. See also Hume, *Protestant Poet*, p. 93.

is "purchased by the blood of our Saviour Christe for us sinners" (see Fig. 5).

Redcrosse is a variation of a warrior named Faithful and True, that is, Christ, who rides upon a white horse and defeats the forces of Antichrist (Rev. 19:11–16). Dixon concludes that Redcrosse's restoration by the "trickling streame of Balme" is "a fiction of the incarnation of Christe" (1.11.48n). The annotator celebrates the knight's defeat of the great Dragon by reference to the apocalyptic victory recounted in Revelation 18:20–21: "o heavens, holy appostles and profitts rejoyce, for god hath given Judgment and over throwen the great citie babylon" (1.11.55n). Just as the Dragon succeeds Archimago and Orgoglio as a type of Antichrist, who "rainged through the world befor the Cominge of Christe," the Dragonets it has spawned may be identified with "the popes Cardnalls, munkes and fryers" (1.12.9–10nn). Dixon views the joyful celebration of Redcrosse's "happie victorie" (1.12.4 and n) as a re-creation of "a great voyce of a great multitude" heard in heaven (Rev. 19:1). The knight's

**5.** *The Vision of the New Jerusalem.* Jan van der Noot, *A Theatre for Worldlings* (1569)

betrothal to Una re-creates the relationship of Christ the Bridegroom and the Spouse as a type for the "true" church (1.12.19n).

Archimago plays the role of false prophet by deceiving the Redcrosse Knight during his sleep, when "false shewes" have the greatest power to "abuse his fantasy" (1.1.46). As Spenser's prototype for demonic artistry, this master of false appearances heads a series of necromancers, conjurers, *and* poets, including Busirane and Bonfont/ Malfont, the false poet at Mercilla's court (5.9.25–26). Archimago's expertise as a teller of tales and crafter of blasphemous "verses" and "true-seeming lyes" contributes to his portrait as a guileful "maker" (1.1.35–38, 45), an epithet that parodies the roles of the creator God, the recusant priest, and the right poet who, according to Sidney, creates his "golden" world as a "maker" who is secondary to God.[77] Archimago's mastery of disguise and his shape-changing ability align him with Proteus (1.2.10), who, like Phantastes, is the "father of false prophecis" (3.4.37). The witch who creates the false Florimell is a variant of Archimago as a demonic imitator who conjures the counterfeit beauty of an "Idole faire" (3.8.4–11).

The repeated creation of false images involves a self-reflexive consideration of the nature of the poet and poetic fiction because Spenser, too, is maker of images. Like his own Merlin and Shakespeare's Prospero, Spenser himself plays the role of a magus devoted to crafting a portrait of our world by means of competing images of truth and falsehood. Merlin as a model prophet is identified with "true" imagination, in contrast to Archimago and Busirane.[78] In line with Spenser's dialectical conception of the poetic imagination, the hermit Contemplation represents an alternative type for the poet as a visionary seer. In its conformity to scriptural testimony, his insight characterizes the prophetic vision of the Protestant poet whose exalted standing accords with Peter Martyr's judgment that "somtimes the phantasie or imagination that is in men, was fashioned by the holie Ghost, and help of angels, at the commandement of God." According to Martyr's *Common Places*, "true" dreams and poetry correspond to divine revelation, whereas "evill prophets" and the dreams that they produce are misleading visions (pt. 1, E1, F1) comparable to those generated by Archimago.

With its "shadows" and "false appearances," allegorical fiction shares the dubious epistemological status of the imagination in general. Although Puttenham acknowledges the problematic nature of

[77] G. Smith, *Elizabethan Critical Essays*, 1: 156–57.

[78] On Archimago and Merlin as poets and magicians, see A. Bartlett Giamatti, *Play of Double Senses: Spenser's "Faerie Queene"* (Englewood Cliffs, N.J.: Prentice-Hall, 1975), pp. 118–20; Nohrnberg, *Analogy*, pp. 103–5, 119; and Gilman, p. 75.

interpretation when "the wordes beare contrary countenaunce to th'intent," he exempts poetic fiction from the charge that it departs from "plainnesse and simplicitie to a certaine doublenesse, whereby our talke is the more guilefull and abusing." Puttenham's definition of *allegoria* as "false semblant or dissimulation"[79] was doubtlessly in current use as a rhetorical term, but it may also have reminded some Tudor readers of the False Semblaunt who personifies religious abuses in *The Romaunt of the Rose*. Archimago's status as a disseminator of false "semblances" accordingly associates religious dissembling with an undisciplined multiplication of meanings in allegory.

The recurrence of the word "semblance" ("outward appearance," "superficial aspect," "copy," from Old French *sembler*, "to resemble, seem") and its derivatives "semblant," "dissemblance," and "resemblance" in passages contrasting the false fictions of Spenser's doubles with the true images of right poetry identifies a fundamental concern with the validity of metaphor and allegory as vehicles for knowledge and truth.[80] Archimago creates a "semblance" of Una "under feigned hew" to introduce into Redcrosse's dream (1.1.46). Just as Duessa-Fidessa, Una's second double, offers "simple shew and semblant plaine" (2.1.21) or "faire semblance" of a woman "under maske of beautie and good grace" (4.1.17), the dream image of the false Una that imitates "that Lady trew" (1.1.46) sounds suspiciously like a forbidden image of the Blessed Virgin. Similarly, Duessa's paramour, Paridell, employs "good semblance" as a means of "dissembling his disease and evill plight" (4.1.38). The world of deceptive appearances, in which Lucifera delights in "her selfe-lov'd semblance" (1.4.10) and the false Genius entices passersby with "semblaunce pleasing" (2.12.46), parodies the perfection of the unfallen world, where true beauty directly represented the "great Creatours owne resemblance bright" (4.8.32). At the court of Mercilla as a manifestly Protestant queen, however, "fayned semblance" is "warded" away by the porter, Awe (5.9.22).

It is erroneous to presume that "Protestant suspicion" of allegory makes this mode "a peculiar form" for Spenser to use as a "self-consciously Reformed poet."[81] His contemporaries and the English Protestant authors of the preceding generation found ample precedent in the writings of William Tyndale for their use of allegorical fiction as

[79] Puttenham, *Arte of English Poesie*, ed. Willcock and Walker, pp. 154, 186. See Nohrnberg, *Analogy*, p. 93.
[80] See Guillory, *Poetic Authority*, p. 183 n. 20.
[81] Waller, *English Poetry of the Sixteenth Century*, p. 186.

a pleasing vehicle for conveying religious and moral truth.[82] While Tyndale's *Obedience of a Christian Man* follows Lutheran precedent in opposing the kind of multilevel scriptural interpretation that flourished during the Middle Ages, it does so on the ground that scholastic commentators obscured the all-important literal meaning of the scriptures. According to Tyndale's view, the Bible contains allegories as part of the "literal sense, which . . . [the reader] must seek out diligently." He further endorses allegorical application of the scriptures with the caveat that such interpretations "are no sense of the scripture, but free things besides the scripture," which must be governed by the rule of faith.[83] Tyndale accepts the Augustinian view that the literal sense provides the basis for theological interpretation, a position that had been assimilated by those late medieval commentators who affirmed that the literal sense *contains* the various figurative senses. Erasmian humanists and those influenced by them, Luther included, shared their view that all scriptural interpretation must accord with the literal and grammatical sense of the text.[84]

Spenser's conception of the imagination internalizes Tudor strictures based upon "fear of anthropomorphism or 'humanizing' the holy," in contrast to the Thomistic approval of images because people require "sensible signs in order to arrive at true spirituality."[85] Protestant hostility toward Catholic images is rooted in the failure of late medieval popular devotion to distinguish between image and archetype. According to Roger Hutchinson's *Image of God, or Laie-Mans Booke* (1550), to conceive of any physical or visual likeness between human and divine is to commit the heresy of the "Anthropomorphites, or humaniformianes" (C4, S4ᵛ). His attack follows Zwingli's disapproval of the "Anthropomorphytes" who attribute "mans shape and forme" to God.[86] The Church of England observed Melanchthon's distinction that because religious images and ceremonies in themselves are spiritually neutral, their value depends upon how they are applied.[87] Although one must be alert to the abuse commit-

---

[82] For profuse examples of Protestant allegorical poetry, drama, and sermon exempla, see ch. 5, below; and *ERL*, pp. 142–43, 174, 252–70, 284–89, 310–18, 339–57.

[83] Tyndale, *Doctrinal Treatises*, ed. Henry Walker, Parker Society, vol. 42 (Cambridge: Cambridge University Press, 1848), pp. 304–5.

[84] G. R. Evans, *The Language and Logic of the Bible: The Road to the Reformation* (Cambridge: Cambridge University Press, 1985), pp. 42–43, 46. On Luther's acceptance of "allegory, tropology, and anagogy" when they are part of the "historical" or literal sense of the Bible, see *Works*, ed. Pelikan et al., 10: 3–5.

[85] Phillips, *Reformation of Images*, pp. 2, 41.

[86] Zwingli, *A short pathwaye to the ryghte and true understanding of the holye & sacred Scriptures*, trans. Jean Veron (Worcester, 1550), B1.

[87] See *Melanchthon on Christian Doctrine*, trans. and ed. Manschreck, pp. 306–16.

ted when the creator of an idol designs it "of his owne vaine fancies thought," according to Belge (*FQ* 5.11.19), who is a victim of Catholic persecution, images could be retained if they focused attention on holy events and doctrines. Thus the Royal Injunctions of Edward VI forbade images "devysed by mennes phantasies" because they deny the centrality of the scriptures in religious life, but they endorsed images that serve as objects of "remembraunce, whereby, men may be admonished, of the holy lifes and conversacion of theim, that the sayde Images do represent."[88]

The legitimate power of the imagination to feign is a result of its "invention" (i.e., discovery) of archetypal ideas in conjunction with the memory. Many early Protestants believed that subjection of the imagination to the control of reason is essential to the production of "true" images and "right" poetry.[89] According to Calvin, "phantasye" (i.e., imagination) is the lowest of the "thre powers of the sowle, that rest in knowledge" (*Institution* 1.15.7; fol. 55ᵛ). Although Cranmer's "Sermon of Good Workes Annexed Unto Faith" attacks the displacement of faith through the worshipping of "images" and "phantasies" (*Book of Homilies*, 1: 33), the memory in association with the higher faculties may reunite one with truth through spiritual understanding. Under the influence of Augustine's Neoplatonic doctrine of memory (*Retractiones* 1.8), Cranmer identifies true images with the recovery of what mankind has lost as a consequence of the Fall. Peter Martyr similarly argues that although images "ought not to be worshipped nor adored," they may properly be used "to renew the memorie of things which have beene doone." Martyr denies the Gregorian sanction that "images be the bookes of laie men," arguing instead for the primacy of "the holie scriptures" and "godlie sermons."[90]

The controversy over the nature of idolatry spilled over the boundary of theological discourse into the late Elizabethan argument over the validity of fiction and the stage. Critics echoed the division between moderates like Peter Martyr, who condoned images so long as they were rightly used, and Protestant radicals who agitated for an outright ban against religious images and other ceremonial obser-

---

[88] *Injunccions Geven by Edward the VI* (1547), a3ᵛ. See also *ERL*, p. 146; and Gilman, p. 35.

[89] William Rossky stresses the importance of rational control in overcoming deepseated suspicion of imagination in sixteenth-century defenses of poetic fiction in "Imagination in the English Renaissance: Psychology and Poetic," *Renaissance News* 5 (1958): 64–73.

[90] Martyr, *Common Places*, pt. 2, 2M1, 2M6; see also 2L1ʳ⁻ᵛ, 2L4ᵛ–5ᵛ, 2M1ᵛ–2ᵛ; and *ERL*, p. 146.

vances (see Gilman, pp. 33–40). At the iconophobic extreme, William Perkins sees the adoration and worship of external "idols" as an abuse of "internall images rightly conceived."[91] Fulke Greville offers an instructive example of the way in which a zealous Protestant poet could convert radical charges into a defense of the poetic imagination. Although the corruption of human faculties (sense, imagination, reason, and understanding) as a consequence of the Fall leads him to a skeptical denial of the sufficiency of human knowledge and art as "vaine Idols of humanity," his Neoplatonic scheme does hold out the possibility of true poetry that transcends idolatry in order to describe truth or pure "Ideas" of divine revelation.[92] Sidney's *Apology for Poetry* addresses the disordered state consequent upon the Fall, whereby "our erected wit maketh us know what perfection is, and yet our infected will keepeth us from reaching unto it." The moral superiority of the "right" poet inheres for Sidney not in the ability to improve upon fallen nature (whose "world is brasen"), but in the ability to undo the Fall by creating a second Nature, a "golden" world, thus moving the audience to right action.[93]

## True Idols and False

Spenser's fashioning of a dense pattern of iconoclastic episodes in which destruction alternates with construction, and demolition with creation, manifests a dialectical consideration of the use and abuse of art. Although Stephen Greenblatt suggests that the dismantling of the Bower of Bliss raises the possibility that "art itself . . . [is] idolatrous,"[94] Spenserian iconoclasm affirms the validity of "true" images and art at the same time that it dismisses their "demonic" falsifications. One may argue further for the *necessity* of "diabolical fictions" because their presence "helps to chasten and make innocent the great fiction that is *The Faerie Queene*."[95] The Augustinian principle that evil functions as a negative argument for good, of which it is the

[91] Perkins, *A Warning against the Idolatrie of the Last Times* (Cambridge, 1601), C7, D5. On Perkins's iconophobia, see Siemon, *Shakespearean Iconoclasm*, p. 45. After 1580 some Protestant groups shifted toward an intrinsic hostility toward literature and art, according to Collinson, *From Iconoclasm to Iconophobia*, p. 8 et seq.

[92] From Greville's *A Treati[s]e of Humane Learning*, in *Poems and Dramas*, ed. Geoffrey Bullough, 2 vols. (Edinburgh, 1939), pp. 163, 167, 173–74, 181–82.

[93] G. Smith, *Elizabethan Critical Essays*, 1: 156–57, 159.

[94] Greenblatt, *Renaissance Self-Fashioning*, p. 189.

[95] I. MacCaffrey, *Spenser's Allegory*, p. 115.

privation,[96] furnishes a context for episodes where evil vanishes away (1.8.24, 3.12.42) and for the narrator's apology for the risqué fabliau of Malbecco and Hellenore:

> But never let th'ensample of the bad
> Offend the good: for good by paragone
> Of evill, may more notably be r[e]ad,
> As white seemes fairer, matched with blacke attone.

(3.9.2)

An iconoclastic pattern informs many of the memorable setpiece scenes where imagery is intensified and concentrated "into great, simple iconographic symbols."[97] Characteristically, Spenser gathers into a composite whole a set of apocalyptic images that recur in Protestant attacks against the mass: the temple, altar, idol, and cup (see Rev. 6:9, 11:1, 17:4). Such imagery may be located at the dwellings of Orgoglio and Busirane, Geryoneo's Church, the sites of the Blatant Beast's depredations, and other locales, where it tends to constellate into examples of *ekphrasis*, that is, literary descriptions of "real or imagined works of visual art" like statues on altars.[98] These figures tend to be ambivalent, as is the case of the elaborate tapestries portraying "*Cupids* warres" (3.11.29) and the Masque of Cupid at the House of Busirane, where both works are "products of an enchanter's artfulness which intends to deceive, although both, in the context of the larger fiction, may be seen to figure a kind of truth."[99] When Spenser attempts to synthesize contradictory iconographical materials, he may seem to verge upon the iconophobic mode favored by some Puritans. The iconoclastic episodes incorporate a dialectical pattern whereby the narrator describes a beautiful object or individual in intricate and alluring detail before reporting its shattering, destruction, or death.[100]

The major iconoclastic episodes occur toward the ends of books

---

[96] St. Augustine, *City of God* 11.9. See Etienne Gilson, *The Christian Philosophy of St. Augustine*, trans. L.E.M. Lynch (New York: Random House, 1960), pp. 144–45.

[97] See Thomas P. Roche, Jr., *The Kindly Flame: A Study of the Third and Fourth Books of Spenser's "Faerie Queene"* (Princeton: Princeton University Press, 1964), p. 60. Like Gross, I consider the working out of an iconoclastic pattern in the battle between Arthur and Orgoglio, the House of Busirane, Isis Church, and the activity of the Blatant Beast.

[98] John B. Bender, *Spenser and Literary Pictorialism* (Princeton: Princeton University Press, 1972), pp. 35, 51n.

[99] I. MacCaffrey, *Spenser's Allegory*, p. 104.

[100] Germs for this pattern may be found in the destruction of a temple and a monument in Spenser's *Visons of Bellay* (ll. 27–28, 41–42) and in the vision of an idolatrous image "upon an Altare faire" in *The Ruines of Time* (ll. 491–504).

when Arthur or another of Spenser's heroes (Redcrosse, Guyon, Britomart, or Artegall) razes an allegorical structure like Acrasia's palace grounds and bower or defeats a monstrous enemy like Orgoglio or Geryoneo. These symbols of pagan idolatry parody counterbalancing places of idealized vision like the Garden of Adonis, Mercilla's Palace, and Mount Acidale. The positive movement toward restoration and reconstruction that marks the endings of Books 1–4 is identified closely with the existence of other buildings that exemplify variant forms of "idolatry" identified with true imagery and art.[101] Thus Arthur's conquest of Orgoglio, which is recalled by Redcrosse's defeat of the great Dragon, precedes the return to Eden and restoration of Adam and Eve. The dismantling of the Bower of Bliss follows upon Guyon's visit to the restorative House of Alma; similarly, Britomart's disruption of the House of Busirane initiates a movement toward restoring positive values previously associated with the Garden of Adonis. Despite the displacement of Arthur in Book 4 by the manifold disguisings of Proteus, the Temple of Venus and Marriage of the Thames and Medway offer concluding images of true beauty, concord, and love. Isis Church and Mercilla's Palace counterbalance the defeats of Radigund, the Souldan, and Geryoneo. The open-ended disruption at the close of Book 6 represents a special case, as the Blatant Beast "raungeth through the world againe, / And rageth sore in each degree and state" (6.12.40), yet the model of Revelation suggests that such a demonic escape must precede the final resolution at the end of time (Rev. 20:7–10).[102]

Spenser applies the term "idol" both to personifications at the core of iconoclastic episodes and to contrasting images of "true" faith and art. Thus Arthur's destruction of Geryon's "Idoll . . . / Whom he did all to peeces breake and foyle" (5.11.33) offers a sharp contrast to Guyon's praise of Gloriana as "th'Idole of her makers great magnificence" (2.2.41), that is, as a Neoplatonic emanation of the divine. Through repetition and variation, an increasingly dense composite image of an idol that has a monster at its feet and rests upon an altar in a shrine-like "temple" or "church" becomes a conventional element in episodes of vision or destruction at the House of Busirane,

---

[101] See Giamatti, *Play of Double Senses*, pp. 68–69, 75–77; and his "A Prince and Her Poet," *Yale Review* 73 (1984): 330–32. Giamatti argues that this pattern is aligned with the contrasting impulses toward dissolution and unity in each book of *The Faerie Queene*. Characteristically, a disruptive movement that dominates the first half of every book is established in the first and second cantos, but soon after the midpoint (by the seventh or eighth canto in each instance save the third) Arthur appears to initiate a restoration of what has been dissolved or disrupted.

[102] See Kaske, "Surprised by Puritanism," p. 4; and Gilman, pp. 74, 81.

Venus's Temple, and Isis Church.[103] Characteristically, it manifests an affirmation or negation of faith in religion or love by playing wittily upon the Petrarchan cliché of the religion of love and its reversal in the exploration of profane love as a metaphor for true religion.

Clustered images of this kind were widely known in contemporary Bible translations and commentaries.[104] In illustrations of the Measurement of the Temple (Rev. 11:1–3), for example, the Beast frequently appears opposite an altar bearing an open Bible and candles that symbolize the illumination of the divine Word in an otherwise bare church (*ERL*, fig. 10). Many Protestants interpreted the cleansing of the Temple as a figure for the Reformation through the purgation of church ornamentation and external aids to devotion (Geneva Bible, dedicatory epistle). The apocalyptic Beast is an iconographical cousin of the Seven-headed Beast ridden by the Whore of Babylon. Spenser presumably recalled the woodcut in the *Theatre for Worldlings* that depicts the Great Harlot as a "Woman sitting on a beast" (Fig. 6). The dialectical nature of the combination of dragon and female may be noted in images of the Woman Clothed with the Sun, who appears in front of or above the Seven-headed Beast that opposes her (Figs. 7–8).

Spenser fuses imagery from Revelation and classical mythology when he combines Duessa's steed (and, later, the Blatant Beast) with the classical prototype for multiheaded beasts, "the hell-borne *Hydra*" (1.7.17, 6.12.32). The Echidna (see Hesiod, *Theogony* 295–305) is the ancestress of the serpentine females, Errour and Geryon's monstrous beast. Spenser's combination of Christian and pagan images for spiritual monstrosity finds a parallel in works like *A View of the Romish hydra confuted in seven sermons* (1588) by Laurence Humphrey, who was an associate of John Foxe. In comparing the conflict with the papacy to the labors of Hercules, Humphrey conflates the Hydra

---

[103] See Gross, p. 37.

[104] Rev. 6:9–11; 9:20; 11:19; 17:4. A rich iconographical tradition lies behind the confrontation between the portrayal of Una in the guise of the Woman Clothed with the Sun confronted by an apocalyptic beast (Figs. 7–8) and Duessa as a type of the Whore of Babylon riding on her Seven-headed Beast (Figs. 6, 11). Albrecht Dürer includes these scriptural figures in the series of twenty magnificent woodcuts, *Apocalypsis cum Figuris* (Nuremberg, 1498), that he modeled upon the manuscript tradition of Apocalypse illustration. It provides the prototype for the polemical designs of Lucas Cranach the Elder, Hans Holbein the Younger, and their German, Dutch, and English imitators, whose woodcuts were known widely in England because they appeared in the Coverdale Bible (1535), the "Matthew" version (1537), and different editions of Bale's *Image of Both Churches*. See Kenneth A. Strand, *Woodcuts to the Apocalypse in Dürer's Time* (Ann Arbor: Ann Arbor Publishers, 1968); *ERL*, pp. 46–47, 156; and Gilman, pp. 32, 34–35, 64.

**6.** *The Whore of Babylon.* Van der Noot, *A Theatre for Worldlings* (1569)

with the Beast of Apocalypse and allocates one sermon to each of its seven heads. Spenser's choice of Egyptian Typhon as the model for Orgoglio as the paramour of Duessa suggests a complex allegorical lineage for idolatry, because Orthrus, the two-headed dog of Geryoneo's cowherd, and the Hydra are both the offspring of Typhon and Echidna.[105]

Polemicism infiltrates a truncated version of this apocalyptic motif when Redcrosse encounters monstrous Errour, who is

> Halfe like a serpent horribly displaide,
> But th'other halfe did womans shape retaine,
> Most lothsom, filthie, foule, and full of vile disdaine.
>
> (1.1.14)

[105] Heninger observes that "if we identify Orgoglio with Typhon, we then see him properly as the monstrous sire of Duessa's seven-headed Beast, and closely related to the Blatant Beast and to the cruel dog of Geryon" ("The Orgoglio Episode," in *Essential Articles*, pp. 136–37). Henry Parker, eighth Baron Morley, introduces a polemical interpretation when he praises Henry VIII for "the vanquishyng of this monstruous hydra" of Rome in *The Exposition and declaration of the Psalme, Deus ultionum Dominus* (1539), B8.

Die offinbarung

**7.** Lucas Cranach the Elder. *The Seventh Trumpet: The Woman Clothed with the Sun and the Seven-headed Beast*. Luther's September Testament (1522)

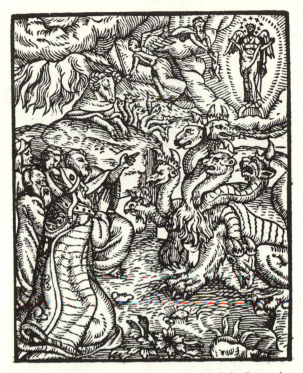

**8.** *The Woman Clothed with the Sun and the Beasts from the Sea and Land.* Van der Noot, *A Theatre for Worldlings* (1569)

The knight's victory over this repulsive female involves the iconoclastic destruction of erroneous learning symbolized by the intermingling in the creature's "vomit . . . of bookes and papers" with "loathly frogs and toades, which eyes did lacke" (st. 20). Although the association of these amphibians with heresy is traditional, the inclusion of publications in the demonic discharge is a witty invention, because Errour's apocalyptic prototype only spews forth "uncleane spirits like frogges" (Rev. 16:13; Fig. 9).[106] Errour's "bookes and papers" parody the Bible carried by Fidelia, a figure for true faith. The epithet "blacke as ink" (st. 22) further connects Errour's prolific offspring with religious propaganda spawned by the Reformation. The

[106] "Error in abhominable filthiness was the spirit which came from the beastly antichrist" according to *The Image of Both Churches*, which identifies the frogs with Roman Catholic practices (Bale, *Select Works*, p. 486). See Nohrnberg, *Analogy*, p. 101. Lapide's Catholic *Commentaria* identifies the frogs, by contrast, with Lutheranism and other Protestant heresies.

**9.** Lucas Cranach the Elder. *The Pouring of the Seven Vials*. Luther's September Testament (1522)

bookishness of contemporary religious turmoil may be noted as well in the "false" books that Archimago and Idleness prefer to the Bible.

As Spenser's prototype for infidelity, monstrous Errour provides an iconographical model for the tableaux where Lucifera is enthroned atop a "dreadfull Dragon with an hideous trayne" (1.4.10) and Duessa rides astride her "manyheaded beast" (1.8.6). The hyperbolic fecundity of Errour, in her double aspect as fearsome dragon and loathsome hag, prefigures the association of the biblical metaphor for idolatry—"whoring after false gods"—with Duessa.[107] Many of the "demonic" females of *The Faerie Queene* are emanations of "the great whore, which did corrupt the earth with her fornicacion" (Rev. 19:2). Errour's sinister maternality is ultimately sterile and self-defeating because she cannot nurture the spiritual needs of her famished brood of a "thousand yong ones" (1.1.15). They creep in and out of the mouth of the mother whom they eventually devour in a blasphemous parody of transubstantiation and the mass offered by yet another "mother," the Church of Rome:

> They flocked all about her bleeding wound,
> And sucked up their dying mothers blood,
> Making her death their life, and eke her hurt their good.
>
> (st. 25)

Milton pays homage to this lurid Reformation allegory when the many monstrous offspring of Sin, sired by Death and descended from Satan, creep in and out of the womb of the mother upon whom they feed (*PL* 2.795–800).

Lucifera and her prideful court offer the first extended instance of Spenser's idol imagery. The contradiction between her apparent beauty and the ill-concealed horror of the "dreadfull Dragon" beneath her feet anticipates the hypocrisy and prideful display of Duessa, Acrasia, and other false women of *The Faerie Queene*.[108] The falsity of Lucifera's appearance and her delight in using a "mirrhour bright" to view her "selfe-lov'd semblance" embody abuses attributed by the reformers to the uncontrolled imagination (1.4.10).

Lucifera's warm welcome of and conferral of a place of honor upon

[107] On the *topos* of "spiritual fornication," see Waters, *Duessa as Theological Satire*, pp. 62–93, passim. This argument reduces the complexity of Spenser's allegory by considering Duessa simply as a personification of the Roman mass. John Dixon glosses Sansloy's attempted rape of Una as "Idolatria, which is spirituall whordom" (Dixon, *Commentary* 1.6.3n).

[108] On Spenser's iconography of "biform Sirens and seemingly human Circe figures, who offer enticements to lust and other vices," see Joan L. Klein, "From Errour to Acrasia," *HLQ* 41 (1977–78): 173–99.

Duessa further identifies Lucifera's establishment with the Roman church, a connection supported not only by the presence of Idleness, the monastic member of the the Pageant of Pride, but also by Envie's hatred of "all good workes and vertuous deeds." Envie may sound like a Protestant when he attacks almsgiving because of "want of faith" (st. 32), but this charge is fraudulent because he must really believe in good works in order to envy them. Spenser's representation of this vice incorporates a witty slander at a time when Luther and Calvin declare that good works without faith do not count and that God rejects them. Envie's feigned hostility to charitable deeds contradicts Cranmer's insistence that good works are the necessary result of "true Faith" (*Book of Homilies* 1: 32).[109] (By way of contrast to Envie, Philotime is Lucifera's Catholic double as a personification of pride who offers advancement solely on the basis of "workes and merites just" [2.7.49].)

The "weake foundation" of Lucifera's palace upon a "sandie hill" (1.4.5) indicates that her dwelling furnishes the first instance of Spenser's extended application of Christ's Parable of the House on the Rock and the House on the Sand:

> Whosoever then heareth of me these wordes, and doeth the same, I wil liken him to a wise man, which hathe buylded his house on a rocke: And the raine fell, and the floods came, and the windes blewe, and beat upon that house, and it fell not: for it was grounded on a rocke. But whosoever heareth these my wordes, and doeth them not, shalbe likened unto a foolish man, which hathe buylded his house upon the sand: And the raine fell, and the floods came, and the windes blewe, and beat upon that house, and it fell, and the fall thereof was great.
>
> (Matt. 7:24–27)

In its shoddy construction and the ease of access that it offers to vain worldlings, the Palace of Pride is the antithesis of the House of Holiness, a fortress-like establishment built upon a firm foundation where the door is "fast lockt" and "warely watched night and day, / For feare of many foes" (1.10.5). Spenser's allegorization of this scriptural text is comparable to a more narrowly polemical application in Stephen Bateman's *Christall Glasse of Christian Reformation*, where a woodcut allegorizes folly as a monastic house filled with tonsured friars and flying a papal banner as it is swept away by a flood (S2;

---

[109] Calvin declares that "we do not justifie a man by workes before God: but we say that all they that are of God, are regenerate and made a newe creature, that they may passe out of the kingdome of sinne into the kingdome of righteousnesse, and that by this testimonie thei make their callyng certayne, and are judged as trees by the frutes" (*Institution* 3.16.8; fol. 196).

Fig. 10). The gloss comments upon the contrast between the fortress on the hill, which embodies wisdom, and the ruined dwelling down below:

> The house which standeth on the rocke, signifieth the stedfast beliefe of the faythfull: The other which standeth in the valy and on sandy ground, is the church of Antichrist and all popishe preaching, whiche house by violence of the water which falleth from the heigth [sic], overturneth it, and so lieth voyde and empty.[110]

Although Lucifera's palace is the sort of establishment that the reader learns to expect to see destroyed through an iconoclastic attack like the dismantling of the Bower of Bliss, Redcrosse's weak faith renders him incapable of purging idolatrous display. He may recognize and estrange himself from its "glorie vaine" and "joyaunce," and even flee from the "perill" against which the Dwarf warns (1.4.15, 37; 1.5.52), but his continuing failures prevent him from exemplifying "true" holiness. We may therefore regard Redcrosse's sojourn to the Palace of Pride as an aborted iconoclastic incident that will be completed in the assault on Orgoglio's Castle by Prince Arthur, who embodies holiness along with his other virtues.

Although Lucifera thrives on a deliberate cult of false adoration, idolatry may also result from a naive confusion of an image with its sacred archetype. The mistaken worship of Una by the "salvage nation" of fauns and satyrs (1.6.11) illustrates the fundamental epistemological danger of misperceiving truth, because her devotees first attempt to make "her th'Image of Idolatryes" and then, when she restrains their "bootlesse zeale," to worship the ass upon which she rides (st. 19) in a scene evocative of the Israelites' idolatrous worship of the Golden Calf (Exod. 32:4, 24). The worship directed by the fauns and satyrs toward Una "as Queene, with olive girlond cround" (st. 13) fuses iconography associated with the cult of the Virgin Mary with conventions of pastoral romance. Because catechetical instruction is the proper antidote to idolatry, Una eventually accomplishes her own act of "iconoclasm" by inculcating "trew sacred lore" and "faith and veritie" in both the satyrs and Satyrane (sts. 30–31).[111] When, in a later book, Serena's capture by a "salvage nation" of cannibals recalls the idolatry of the satyrs in a more demonic form, their priestly "Altar . . . [of] sacrifice divine" and "divelish ceremonies"

---

[110] For a Lutheran woodcut that portrays the Reformation conflict in terms of Christ's parable, see Chew, *Pilgrimage*, fig. 65.

[111] Satyrane responds to her "as the True Church and also as a type of queen," according to Cain, *Praise in "The Faerie Queene,"* p. 73.

## *Of wiſedome.*

## *Of wiſdome.*

### *The ſignification.*

*T*He houſe which ſtandeth on the rocke, ſignifieth the ſted-
faſt beliefe of the faythfull : The other which ſtandeth in
the valy and on ſandy ground, is the church of Antichriſt and
all popiſhe preaching, whiche houſe by violence of the water
which falleth fró the heigth, ouerturneth it, and ſo lieth voyde
and empty.

S.ij. Seperate

**10.** *The Parable of the Two Houses.* Bateman, *A Christall Glasse of Christian Reformation* (1569)

(6.8.42, 44) are reminiscent of Protestant attacks against transubstantiation and the Roman-rite mass:

> But of her dainty flesh they did devize
> To make a common feast, and feed with gurmandize.
>
> (st. 38)

Arthur's defeat of Orgoglio and the capture of Duessa by his squire (1.8.3–25) fulfills expectations established at the episodes at Archimago's hermitage and Lucifera's palace, where iconoclastic attacks are postponed. All of the elements of the idolatrous image cluster are present: idol, altar, monster, and an unholy shrine or "temple" (see st. 36). Duessa assumes the posture of the Whore of Babylon atop her monstrous apocalyptic steed, the bloodying of whose many mouths "with late cruell feast" (st. 6) is modeled on the shedding of the "blood of Saintes . . . [and] Martyrs" (Rev. 17:6). The altar on which the martyrs "were killed for the worde of God" (Rev. 6:9) supplies the prototype for the site within Orgoglio's Castle where "true Christians bloud was often spilt, / And holy Martyrs often doen to dye." (Surely, this episode also alludes to accounts of persecution contained in Foxe's "Book of Martyrs.")

Spenser's palpable allusion to the scriptural description of the harlot "araied in purple and skarlat, and guilded with golde, and precious stones, and pearles" (Rev. 17:4) confers a stridently polemic edge upon the scene. In a tradition going back to St. Augustine's *City of God*, Babylon as the embodiment of sophisticated corruption and depravity is a type for the untrue religion of the sinful City of Man, whereas unfallen Eden or Jerusalem typify the City of God. A broad Protestant consensus accepted the Joachimist elaboration of this view whereby the Scarlet Whore "is the Antichrist, that is, the Pope with the whole bodie of his filthie creatures . . . whose beautie onely standeth in outwarde pompe and impudencie and craft like a strumpet" (Geneva Bible gloss on Rev. 17:4).[112] No single site in *The Faerie Queene* exemplifies Babylon, because Duessa and the "demonic" characters for whom she is the prototype dwell in scattered habitations, but her overlapping origins in both Babylon and Rome are recreated in many of the allegorical houses of the fallen world, notably the Palace of Pride and Orgoglio's Castle.

The iconoclastic component of the episode at Orgoglio's Castle

---

[112] Bale's *Image* identifies the Fall of Babylon (Rev. 18:1–3) with the dissolution of the monasteries and the advent of "the faithful preachers of our age" (Bale, *Select Works*, pp. 516–17). By way of contrast, Cornelius à Lapide connects Babylon to the capital of the pagan world rather than to papal Rome in his *Commentaria*. See also Hankins, *Source and Meaning in Spenser's Allegory*, pp. 100–104.

may be noted in the "golden cup" that Duessa brandishes when she rides into battle against Prince Arthur. The "magick artes" that fill it (1.8.14, 25) link her both to the Protestant attack against transubstantiation and to Archimago as a priest-magician (1.1.36). Finding its origin in the Great Whore's "cup of golde . . . ful of abominations, and filthines of her fornication" (Rev. 17:4), this vessel is a prominent feature in contemporary woodcuts (Figs. 6, 11). Reformation iconography identified elaborate chalices of this kind with the Roman mass of one kind in which the sacrament of wine was denied to the laity. That Protestants like Spenser attacked not the cup but its misuse may be noted in a woodcut in Richard Day's *Booke of Christian Prayers* that portrays the personification of "Love of God" rising in iconoclastic triumph over "Idolatry" or "Spirituall adultery" and the cult objects of Roman ritual (Fig. 12). While the cup in the left border is appropriate to observance of the Roman rite because it is too small to offer to communicants, the broad-mouthed cup in the woodcut situated beneath the text is suitable for congregational use during a Protestant communion service.[113] The "cup of gold" that Fidelia carries at the House of Holiness is a vessel of the latter kind because it contains sacramental "wine and water" (1.10.13), in pointed contrast to the "secret poyson" filling Duessa's cup (1.8.14). Although the serpent in Fidelia's goblet recalls Duessa's "manyheaded beast" (1.8.6), the principle of use and abuse underlies the association of true faith with a serpent in Christian iconography. Spenser applies the medieval symbolism of the snake in the cup of St. John of Patmos, the power of whose faith enabled him to drink poison without harm. The contemporary currency of this symbol may be noted in a polemical woodcut in Bateman's *Christall Glasse of Christian Reformation*, which features a cup containing a serpent that is extended by a friar who signifies "treason" (Fig. 13). The recipient of this offering, the "man which standeth lyke a Prophet [who] signifieth godlines," would presumably undergo no harm from drinking the "poyson" within the cup (C4ᵛ).[114]

The tiara that Duessa has received from Orgoglio adds an antipapal nuance to this episode:

[113] On the symbolism of the two cups, see Davies, *From Cranmer to Hooker*, pp. 366–67. In contrast to the private cups featured in Fig. 2 above, an allegorical woodcut in Foxe's "Book of Martyrs" employs an oversize cup to symbolize Protestant communion. See King, *Tudor Royal Iconography*, fig. 28; and Kellogg and Steele, p. 35.

[114] Snakes may symbolize either wisdom or evil. On the Protestant application of serpent symbolism, see Gertrud Schiller, *Iconography of Christian Art*, trans. Janet Seligman, 2 vols. (Greenwich, Conn.: New York Graphic Society, 1971–72), 2: 125. Note the presence of the Serpent of Wisdom (Matt. 10:16) in the hand of Prudence in Fig. 17.

**11.** Hans Holbein the Younger. *The Whore of Babylon*. German New Testament (Basel: T. Wolff, 1523)

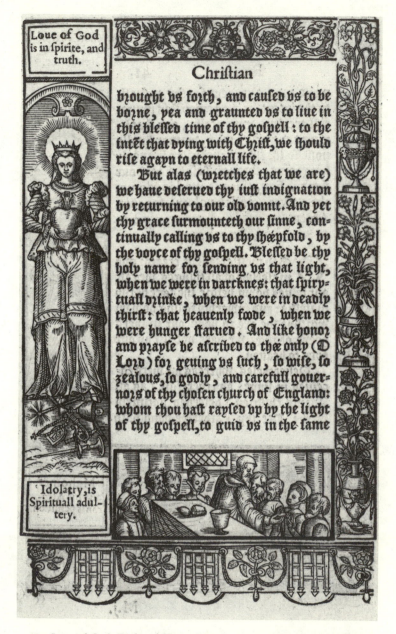

**12.** *Love of God.* Richard Day, *A Booke of Christian Prayers* (1578)

## *The deſcription*

Pythagoras.

{ *They which to ſlaunder or to kil,*
*The dead haue their delight:*

## ¶ *The ſignification.*

*T*He man which ſtandeth lyke a Prophet ſignifieth godlines : the Fryer treaſon : the cup with the Serpent poy-
ſon : the other which ſtriketh with the ſworde murder: and
he which is wounded is peace.

𝕹𝖔𝖙𝖍𝖎𝖓𝖌

**13.** *Of Wrath.* Bateman, *A Christall Glasse of Christian Reformation* (1569)

> He gave her gold and purple pall to weare,
> And triple crowne set on her head full hye,
> And her endowd with royall majestye.

(1.7.16)

Her pontifical display recalls Thomalin's harangue against the wearing of "purple and pall" and "belts of glitterand gold" by false shepherds ("July," ll. 173–77) and the grounding of that attack in Revelation and *The Plowman's Tale* (see above, pp. 21–22, 91). Although even a simple regal crown is absent from the scriptural description of the Whore of Babylon, that detail is a standard component of woodcut illustrations of the harlot (Fig. 6) and the Seven-headed Beast (Figs. 7–8).[115] Duessa's wearing of a "triple crowne" (1.7.16) represents a signal departure from the Great Harlot's traditional representation, however, because the papal headpiece is added to Protestant satirical woodcuts in the Cranach-Holbein tradition (Fig. 11). Lucas Cranach the Elder transformed the crown into a papal tiara in an illustration (Fig. 9) for Luther's translation of Revelation in the September Testament (Wittemberg, 1522); unlike other woodcuts in this edition, it is original to Cranach and not modeled upon Dürer.[116] Spenser presumably drew Duessa's tiara from Reformation visual propaganda, directly or indirectly, because it goes without mention in the text of Revelation, Bale's *Image of Both Churches*, and the glosses of the Geneva Bible. The precedents for Duessa's wearing of pontifical headgear are found in the violently antipapal woodcuts in the September Testament and other Lutheran texts. The eventual stripping away of her "royall robes, and purple pall" (1.8.46) further conforms to the prophecy of the time when people "shal hate the whore, and shal make her desolate and naked" (Rev. 17:16). It is important to note that Spenser postpones the "iconoclastic" destruction of Duessa until Book 5.

The defeat of Orgoglio and Duessa recalls another iconoclastic scene that was a familiar component of Tudor Protestant satire: the toppling of the pope by a monarch. (The giant's name associates him implicitly with papal dominion because it means "pride" in Italian.) Prince Arthur's victory reverses the earlier defeat of Redcrosse, whose fortunes had ebbed completely when he fell "full low" before

---

[115] On the manuscript tradition, see Rosemond Tuve, *Allegorical Imagery: Some Medieval Books and Their Posterity* (Princeton: Princeton University Press, 1966), figs. 21–22, 24 (pp. 103–5).

[116] Heimo Reinitzer, *Biblia deutsch: Luthers Bibelübersetzung und ihre Tradition* (Wolfenbüttel: Herzog August Bibliothek, 1983), p. 133. Cranach and members of his atelier executed the woodcuts in this series.

the giant and his paramour (1.7.12). Because of the knight's identity as England's patron, St. George, his conquest at the feet of Duessa evokes England's history of domination by the Church of Rome, "either during the Middle Ages" or during the recent reign of Mary Tudor.[117] Thus Spenser is polemically accurate in noting that the harlot's papal tiara "her endowd with royall majestye" (1.7.12, 16). When she and Orgoglio meet their downfall before Arthur as an embodiment of British royalty, the symbolic defeat of temporal government by the papacy is reversed when the "crowned mitre [she] rudely threw aside" (1.8.25). The triumph of the Crown over the Tiara is a conventional iconographical device for the establishment of complete royal authority over both church and state by the Protestant Tudor monarchs. This *topos* is incorporated into the woodcut in Foxe's "Book of Martyrs" that portrays the primal scene of Tudor iconoclasm at the time of Henry VIII's break with the Church of Rome by showing the monarch treading upon Clement VII as a "footstool" at the same time that the pope's tiara falls from his head; this scene reverses the movement of the text's earlier woodcut depictions of popes deposing emperors.[118] The initial capital C of the "Book of Martyrs" also depicts the toppling of the pope, who is entwined with demonic serpents in the lower bar, beneath the enthroned figure of Queen Elizabeth (Fig. 14).

Spenser's presentation of Orgoglio's porter, Ignaro, demonstrates how iconoclasm is wedded to a countermovement to adapt old images and generate new ones rather than simply to destroy traditional forms of religious iconography. The principle of use and abuse underlies the spiritual ignorance that the giant's "foster father" personifies (1.8.31), which inheres in his inability to manipulate a symbolic "bounch of keyes":

> The which unused rust did overgrowe:
> Those were the keyes of every inner dore,
> But he could not them use, but kept them still in store.
>
> (st. 30)

The allegory rejects not the keys, but their disuse. The spiritual blindness of Ignaro, who is described as an "old, old man," refers back to the superstition of Corceca and Abessa, and more generally to St.

---

[117] O'Connell, *Mirror and Veil*, pp. 54–55. He rightly cautions that it is unlikely that "Elizabethans would have countenanced any explicit connection of Mary with the whore of Babylon" (p. 199 n. 19). For a contemporary identification of Duessa and Queen Mary, see Dixon, *Commentary*, notes on 1.12.argument and st. 18.

[118] See King, *Tudor Royal Iconography*, pp. 157–64, figs. 22 and 51; and Heninger, "The Orgoglio Episode," in *Essential Articles*, pp. 132–33.

**14.** *Elizabeth I as Emperor Constantine.* John Foxe, Actes and Monuments of these Latter and Perillous Dayes (1563)

Paul's admonition to "put of[f] the olde man with his workes" and to "put on the newe, which is renewed in knowledge after the image of him that created him" (Col. 3:9–10). Zwingli identifies the Old Man with sin and corruption, explaining that "the ymage of god, doth every day shine furth more and more" in the New Man.[119] Protestants identified the Old Man of carnal corruption with Catholic tradition and the doctrine of good works. Thus the gatekeeper's inability to open the doors of Orgoglio's Castle demonstrates the alleged failure of the Church of Rome to provide effective spiritual instruc-

[119] Zwingli, *Short pathwaye*, C6.

tion, because Ignaro lacks knowledge sufficient to unlock the "doors" of understanding and salvation.[120]

Arthur's appropriation of the keys functions in the historical allegory as an allusion to the royal denial of the authority of the popes as the self-proclaimed heirs to the keys of St. Peter. His iconoclastic action is aligned with the portrayal in the "Book of Martyrs" of the downfall of the pope, who bears a pair of broken keys beneath the enthroned figure of Queen Elizabeth as head of state and governor of the Church of England (Fig. 14). The Reformation monarchy claimed to combat the ignorance of the laity by providing adequate religious instruction through public preaching and worship and by promoting individual reading of the vernacular Bible. Spenser reflects royalist iconography when Prince Arthur, as a type for Tudor monarchy, demonstrates the proper function of the previously unused and rusted keys of Ignaro by unlocking the doors of Orgoglio's Castle:

> Then to him stepping, from his arme did reach
> Those keyes, and made himselfe free enterance.
> Each dore he opened without any breach;
> There was no barre to stop, nor foe him to empeach.

> (st. 34)

Like Arthur, the reverend figure of Contemplation understands the correct use of the keys, which are conferred upon him by Fidelia. Fidelia and Contemplation represent the moral opposite of Ignaro as personifications of the introspective faith and knowledge fostered by scriptural understanding (1.10.50). In contrast to Contemplation's prophetic "foresight," which counterbalances his blindness to the material world, the "wrincled face" of unseeing Ignaro is turned "backward still" (1.8.31).

Ignaro is not a type of St. Peter, whom Protestants honored, but he does typify the papal claim to supremacy through apostolic succession from Christ through Peter. Spenser's reinterpretation of the keys of St. Peter is grounded in Protestant exegesis. The commentary in the Geneva Bible explains that the doctrine of papal supremacy— the "aut[h]oritie chiefly . . . committed to the Pope in signe whereof he beareth the keyes in his armes"—wrongly alludes to the "keye of the bottomles pit" (Rev. 9:1). Instead, the papal insignia parodies "the keyes of the kingdome of heaven" (Matt. 16:19), which were delegated to Peter (and by extension all true ministers) as a sign of apostleship. The Geneva Bible glosses the right use of the keys as a

---

[120] See Kellogg and Steele, p. 36.

reference to "preachers of the Gospel [who] open the gates of heaven with the worde of God, which is the right keye: so that where this worde is not purely taught, there is nether key, nor autoritie."[121] E.K. shares these views when he interprets Piers's attack of the "greedie governaunce" of false shepherds in *The Shephearde's Calender* as a reference to "the Pope, and his Antichristian prelates, which usurpe a tyrannical dominion in the Churche, and with Peters counterfet keyes, open a wide gate to al wickednesse and insolent government" ("May," l. 121 and gloss).

The thickest texture of iconoclastic images and actions is to be found in the most theologically and politically engaged parts of *The Faerie Queene*: Books 1 and 5. Because hypocrisy and idolatry are antithetical to true faith, Spenser places iconoclastic concerns in the foreground of the "Legend of Holiness." The recurrence of related iconoclastic episodes in the other books indicates that the first serves as a paradigm for later attacks on idolatry; abundant cross-references invite the reader to compare and contrast later incidents to the respective generation and destruction of idolatrous images by Archimago and Arthur. Surely this is the case in Book 2, where iconoclastic expectations lead the reader to anticipate Guyon's destruction of Acrasia's Bower from the moment that Amavia testifies about the nature of that "false enchaunteresse" (2.1.51). The intrusion into Guyon's quest of Archimago—"that cunning Architect of cancred guile" (st. 1)—forges a tight link between the first two books. Although the description of Phaedria's *"Idle lake"* (2.6.10–13) contains the undeveloped hint that she "floats in the lake of idolatry," it is the attack on the Bower itself that results in the ruin of what may be regarded as Archimago's "most lavish creation."[122] Stephen Greenblatt aptly notes that Acrasia's standing "as demonic artist and whore combines the attributes of those other masters of disguise, Archimago and Duessa."[123] Acrasia's possession of a "charmd" cup (2.1.55) and the "Cup of gold" (2.12.56) borne by her retainer, Excesse, are among the details that connect those seductresses to the great harlot, Duessa, and her poisonous cup.[124] The iconoclastic action of Book 2 repeats the shattering of cups and destruction of idols. Just as Arthur's attack forces Duessa to cast her "golden cup . . .

---

[121] On the Protestant redefinition of the iconography of the keys, see Jewel, *Apology*, p. 28; O'Connell, *Mirror and Veil*, p. 58; and King, *Tudor Royal Iconography*, pp. 61, 63–69.

[122] Gilman, p. 77.

[123] Greenblatt, *Renaissance Self-Fashioning*, pp. 189–90.

[124] Milton imitates the Spenserian use of the "enchanted cup" in *Comus*, according to Norbrook, *Poetry and Politics*, p. 252.

unto the ground" (1.8.25), Guyon harshly rejects Excesse's intemperate offer of wine: "The cup to ground did violently cast, / That all in peeces it was broken fond" (2.12.57).[125]

Among the many details that invite the reader to expect the destruction of the Bower are the presence of a goddesslike temptress in an artificial locale whose gilding (2.12.55) recalls the "golden foile" that conceals the surface of Lucifera's palace (1.4.4). (Guyon's experience at the House of Richesse, where Mammon's "roofe, and floore, and wals were all of gold" and where Philotime is enthroned in "glistring glory" [2.7.29, 46], refers likewise to the deflection of an iconoclastic attack upon the Palace of Pride, because the questing knight shares Redcrosse's lack of spiritual understanding sufficient to complete the assignment he had received at the court of Gloriana.) Acrasia may not possess a dragon, but she does transform her lovers into bestial "figures hideous, / According to their mindes like monstruous" (2.12.85), in a witty synthesis of the image of the Great Harlot of Revelation and the classical myth of Circe. Spenser also alludes to the gardens of love in Tasso and Ariosto.

Acrasia's destructive eroticism accords with her status as a variant of Duessa, just as the voluptuous imagery associated with her enchanted bower suggests religious apostasy as well as sexual pleasure. Acrasia's voyeuristic delights and her vicarious "feeding" upon Verdant constitute a seductive manifestation of visual idolatry (from *eidola*, "images, things seen") when she casts "hungry eies" upon her enervated lover (st. 78). Guyon's iconoclastic assault is motivated by the "close parallel between the evils of the Bower and the evils attributed to the misuse of religious images." The tableau in which the witch cradles Verdant in her arms may even suggest an "uncanny parody of the Pietà."[126] The scene recalls not only the classical myth of Mars and Venus, but also the sinister maternity of Errour and Duessa's seduction of disarmed Redcrosse in a parodic *locus amoenus* not unlike Acrasia's bower (1.7.1–3; see 2.12.80–81). Because the suspension of rational control during Verdant's sleep accords with the capacity of the imagination to create deceptive images, the Bower and its gaudy delights are implicated in the free play of the "fantasie" (2.12.42), whose power to falsify renders this place of "guilefull semblaunts" (st. 48) capable of transforming men into beasts. The false "art" and "spectacle" of this parody of Eden are to be noted in the

---

[125] A variation of this motif may be noted in Abessa's casting down of her "pot of water," according to Kathryn Walls, "Abessa and the Lion: *The Faerie Queene*, 1.3.1–12," *SSt* 5 (1984): 11–12.

[126] Greenblatt, *Renaissance Self-Fashioning*, p. 189; see also Nohrnberg, *Analogy*, p. 245.

"over-wrought" fountain at the center of the garden, whose "curious imageree" (st. 60) may remind the reader of idolatry (compare the "cunning imagery" of the altar of the "holy Martyrs" at Orgoglio's Castle [1.8.36] and the "antickes and wild Imagery" of Mammon's coat [2.7.4]).[127]

Although it is difficult to accept Harry Berger's view that the dismantling of the Bower of Bliss is a kind of "Puritan frenzy,"[128] the very beauty of its seductive *carpe florem* song ("Gather the Rose of love, whilest yet is time"; 2.12.74–75) exemplifies the complicated nature of Protestant iconoclasm. This virtuoso imitation of Tasso's *Gerusalemme liberata* (16.14–15) succeeds *as a work of art* at the same time that it provides a vehicle for attacking *the abuse of art*. C. S. Lewis has shown why it is a mistake to "think that Spenser is secretly on Acrasia's side" by demonstrating how the Bower's artifice subverts nature and parodies the natural artistry of the Garden of Adonis by means of a precise set of antitheses: "The one is artifice, sterility, death: the other, nature, fecundity, life."[129] Instead of functioning as a purely destructive act, the dismantling of the too neatly manicured gardens and ornamental groves surrounding Acrasia's palace offers a means of advancing toward the places of true vision and art that are to be discovered in the Garden of Adonis, where nature creates its own "artful" display, or Temple of Venus. Guyon's act of demolition may include an allusion to Josiah's destruction of paganism and the Canaanite cults in Jerusalem (2 Kings 23:4–20), an event that was often cited as an iconoclastic precedent under Edward VI and Elizabeth I:[130]

> But all those pleasant bowres and Pallace brave,
>   *Guyon* broke downe, with rigour pittilesse;
>   Ne ought their goodly workmanship might save
>   Them from the tempest of his wrathfulnesse,
>   But that their blisse he turn'd to balefulnesse:
>   Their groves he feld, their gardins did deface,
>   Their arbers spoyle, their Cabinets suppresse,
>   Their banket houses burne, their buildings race,
> And of the fairest late, now made the fowlest place.
>
> (2.12.83)

[127] See Helgerson, *Self-Crowned Laureates*, pp. 9, 86–87 n. 40.

[128] Berger, *The Allegorical Temper: Vision and Reality in Book II of Spenser's "Faerie Queene"* (New Haven: Yale University Press, 1957), p. 218. Alan Sinfield echoes Berger's charge in *Literature of Protestant England*, pp. 36–37.

[129] Lewis, *Allegory of Love*, pp. 325–26. See also Wells, *Spenser's "Faerie Queene" and the Cult of Elizabeth*, p. 66.

[130] See *FQ*, ed. Hamilton, 2.12.83n; and *ERL*, pp. 161, 177, 185–86.

Iconoclastic concerns permeate the House of Busirane, where the necromancer's "wicked bookes" and measuring of "many a sad verse" identify him, like his prototype Archimago, with false authorship and "art" (3.12.31–32, 36). The gilded façade and false display of the dwelling's second chamber, with its imagery of "wilde Antickes" and a "thousand monstrous formes" (3.11.51), align it with the idolatrous "dwellings" of Lucifera, Mammon, and Acrasia. As a construct of Busirane's mind, the pageant of Cupid, projected in the form of Amoret's fears, is perceived in terms of "phantasies / In wavering wemens wit" (3.12.26). Prior to Britomart's entry into this chamber, she encounters a projection of Busirane's falsifying imagination when she witnesses "fowle Idolatree" paid to Cupid's blindfolded "Image . . . / Of massy gold," which is poised atop a precious "Altar" with a "wounded Dragon" twined about his feet (3.11.47–49). Because Spenser "literalizes the metaphors of the religion of love," we find that instead of a metaphoric reference to "arrows that 'have pierst the trembling harts,' a palpitating pierced heart is presented to our very eyes." According to this view, Busirane's demonic art embodies the power of the imagination to reify "invisible or psychic sufferings . . . in dramatic images."[131] This inversion of Spenser's figures of the temptress and the dragon wittily confers a kind of metaphoric "hermaphroditism" upon Cupid. The association of these clichés with a winged god of love who peeks out from beneath his blindfold (3.12.22)—like Acrasia he is a kind of voyeur, albeit a sadistic one—suggests yet another correction of the Petrarchan religion of love. The entire presentation of the false Cupid offers a sharp contrast to the true Cupid of the Garden of Adonis, who lives in harmony with principles of cosmic order.

Fancy's leadership of Cupid's masque embodies iconoclastic suspicions of the power of the uncontrolled imagination and, by extension, of the ability of poetry itself to produce deceiving images. As one who follows in the train of Fancy, Hope is the antithesis of Speranza as a theological virtue. The personification of false Hope as a priestly maid with a "holy water Sprinckle" links Cupid's procession with the parodic monasticism of Archimago and Idleness. This "handsome Mayd, / Of chearefull looke and lovely to behold" (st. 13) contradicts Spenser's association of chastity with the three theological virtues, notably charity, at the House of Holiness.

The iconoclastic principle of use and abuse applies directly to Cupid and Busirane, both of whom Spenser conceives as morally neutral. It is therefore possible to resolve "some apparent inconsistencies

---

[131] I. MacCaffrey, *Spenser's Allegory*, pp. 111–12.

in Book III" by interpreting Cupid as "a *power* in the world, operating under an overarching Providence (as does the medieval Fortuna) and *appearing* true or false, good or bad, according to the narrative and poetic context."[132] In this sense Cupid is related to the power of poetry as Spenser and Sidney define it. If the reader is invited to recognize the masque of Cupid as a "demonic" imitation of Petrarch's *Triumph of Love*, Britomart's victory may evoke contemporary praise of the reign of Queen Elizabeth as a *Triumph of Chastity*. On analogy to the complete sequence of six Petrarchan triumphs, the power of love cannot be destroyed, but it is controlled by and contained within that of chastity.[133]

Britomart's conquest of Busirane corresponds to the earlier iconoclastic attacks by Prince Arthur and Guyon, except that she restrains her wrath at Amoret's behest:

> So mightily she smote him, that to ground
> > He fell halfe dead; next stroke him should have slaine,
> > Had not the Lady, which by him stood bound,
> > Dernely unto her called to abstaine.

> > (3.12.34)

The scene provides an inversion of Acrasia's defeat wherein "the feminine is freed rather than bound" (*FQ*, ed. Hamilton, st. 34n). Like the "wilde Bore" that remains forever bound, as a necessary part of nature, in the cave beneath the Mount of Venus within the Garden of Adonis (3.6.48), Busirane must survive in order to release Amoret from enchantment. He is akin both to Archimago and to the Blatant Beast as a disruptive force that may be contained for a moment only to erupt again in a continuation of the cyclical pattern of victory and defeat, destruction and renewal, birth and death that marks life in the fallen world. Despite Britomart's restraint, her actions result in what looks like yet another iconoclastic purgation of false art when the masque procession vanishes upon her penetration into Busirane's innermost chamber:

> Returning backe, those goodly roomes, which erst
> > She saw so rich and royally arayd,
> > Now vanisht utterly, and cleane subverst
> > She found, and all their glory quite decayd,
> > That sight of such a chaunge her much dismayd.
> > Thence forth descending to that perlous Porch,

---

[132] Elizabeth Story Donno, "The Triumph of Cupid: Spenser's Legend of Chastity," *YES* 4 (1974): 37–48.
[133] Yates, *Astraea*, pp. 112–13, 215.

> Those dreadfull flames she also found delayd,
> And quenched quite, like a consumed torch,
> That erst all entrers wont so cruelly to scorch.
>
> (3.12.42)

The vanishing of the enchanter's misleading display recalls the disappearance of Orgoglio, "like an emptie bladder," under attack from Arthur (1.8.24).

Spenser's iconoclastic stance necessitates no opposition to "idols" or "idolatry" rightly conceived.[134] With its enclosed garden and temple, the Island of Venus accords with the harmonious agreement between nature and art typical of visionary locales like the Garden of Adonis and Mount Acidale:

> For all that nature by her mother wit
> Could frame in earth, and forme of substance base,
> Was there, and all that nature did omit,
> Art playing second natures part, supplyed it.
>
> (4.10.21)

Carol Kaske observes that the Bower of Bliss and the Garden of Adonis "did not constitute Spenser's last word on the subject of art," because the Temple of Venus surpasses those locales as a dialectical synthesis of "art with Nature."[135] The description of this locale invokes the language of idolatry to define the appropriate relationship between nature and art. "An hundred Altars" fume with ritual sacrifices in the innermost recesses of the shrine, close to the altar bearing an enigmatically veiled statue of Venus, whose beauty excels all "other Idoles" (sts. 38–40). The serpent twining about the goddess's legs and feet mirrors her hermaphroditic union of male and female in yet another inversion of Spenser's motif of the temptress and her beast:

> But for, they say, she hath both kinds in one,
> Both male and female, both under one name:
> She syre and mother is her selfe alone,
> Begets and eke conceives, ne needeth other none.
>
> (st. 41)

Spenser attempts to resolve the antinomy inhering in this scene with one of his cosmic visions of the reconciliation of opposites. As a place where "Priests were damzels" and where a "bevie of fayre damzels"

---

[134] See Hans Guth, "Allegorical Implications of Artifice in Spenser's *Faerie Queene*," *PMLA* 76 (1961): 474–79.

[135] Kaske, "Surprised by Puritanism," p. 4.

waits upon the time when the "Antheme should be sung on hye" (sts. 38, 48), the Temple dramatizes the Petrarchan religion of love. According to Scudamour's account of his courtship of Amoret within the shrine of her foster mother, this sanctuary is vulnerable only to a kind of erotic "iconoclasm": "For sacrilege me seem'd the Church to rob" (st. 53). Within the Neoplatonic frame of this episode, the fulfillment of sexual desire in a metaphoric sense constitutes a destructive act. Even though Spenser may reject Catholic sacramentalism, he joins zealous coreligionists like Greville and Sidney in continuing to use metaphors from the old religion to explore the nature of erotic desire.

Spenser projects alternative sides of iconoclasm onto the paired sanctuaries of Isis Church (5.7.2–24) and the "Chapell" or "Church" of Geryoneo (5.10.13, 28–29; 5.11.19–33), which are among the set-piece scenes in his most explicitly topical book, the "Legend of Justice." In the historical allegory, these locales very wittily emblematize the Reformation conflict between "true" and "false" churches. Like its antitype, the Temple of Venus, the gilded Church or "Temple" of Isis (5.7.5) harbors a priestly cult devoted to the honor of an "Idoll," whose placement of a foot upon her crocodile provides a further inversion of the apocalyptic motif of the temptress and her beast. This tableau functions as a syncretic variation of the Woman Clothed with the Sun poised above the Seven-headed Beast (Fig. 8), the Virgin Mary stepping on a serpent, or St. Margaret of Antioch trampling upon a dragon.

The mitre-wearing priests of Isis who make "rites and daily sacrifize" at altars (st. 4) evoke not only the image of Duessa, with the "crowned mitre" upon her head (1.8.25), but the entire thrust of the Protestant attack upon the mass. The placement of Isis Church in the "antique world" (5.7.2) rescues it from any charge of idolatry, however, because Spenser's syncretic habit of mind leads him to reconcile the apparent falsity of its religious practices and those of the church of his own age. The cult of Isis contains parodies that are directed against Catholic sacramentalism, because the asceticism of Isis's priestly order better conforms to the ideals of monastic life than to those of Spenser's self-indulgent clerical types: Archimago, Idleness, and Abbessa. The continent priests of Isis observe vows of "chastity" rather than celibacy, and they mortify the "proud rebellious flesh" by sleeping "uppon the cold hard stone" (st. 9). Their meager vegetarian diet and abstinence from wine vividly reverses the doctrine of transubstantiation that defines the Roman mass in terms of eating Christ's flesh and drinking his blood: "for wine they say is blood" (st. 10).[136] All of these details coalesce in an image of sacramental purification centered upon priests celebrating a true "Mas" that is involved with "holy things" (st. 17). Britomart's "wondrous vision" during her visit to this shrine confirms the sanctity of this cult, because she initially envisages herself in the guise of one of the priests of Isis, prior to the transformation of her "Moone-like Mitre to a Crowne of gold." Not only does her dream align Britomart with British royalty, according to the chief priest's interpretation, but it epitomizes the operation of the well-ordered imagination by "feeding her fantasie" with a "thousand thoughts" (sts. 12–13, 17).

Antithetical to the practices of the Isis cult are the rites at the shrine dedicated by Geryoneo to "his monstrous parent *Geryone*," which symbolize the reputed horrors of the Spanish Inquisition in the historical allegory. As "an Idole of his owne," one framed "to Gods owne likenesse" by "his owne vaine fancies thought," this image of Geryon emblematizes the idolatrous attribution of anthropomorphic features to the divine. Honor that is properly "dew / To God" is here dedicated instead "unto his Idole most untrew." The "powring forth" of blood offerings from daily sacrifices of the "flesh of men" at the ivory altar of this Church (or "Temple") directs a satirical attack against the Roman mass and doctrine of transubstantiation.[137] The hidden presence beneath the altar of "an hideous monster" that is reputed to devour the god's human sacrifices, "both flesh and bone," contributes to Spenser's final reversal of his apocalyptic motif of the temptress and the beast (5.10.13, 27–29; 5.11.19). Even though the image of Geryoneo's "monstrous father" (5.10.11) is "of massy gold / Most richly made" (5.11.21), it lacks the perverse femininity and seductive appeal of earlier gilded idols and temples. It is altogether appropriate that Prince Arthur's attack on Geryoneo's "Temple" should recall earlier instances of Spenserian iconoclasm, notably his own assault on Orgoglio's Castle:[138]

> And eke that Idoll deem'd so costly dere;
> Whom he did all to peeces breake and foyle
> In filthy durt, and left so in the loathely soyle.
>
> (5.11.33)

Many recollections of Redcrosse's battles with both Errour and the Dragon associate Arthur's attack upon Geryon's beast with contemporary ecclesiastical conflict, most notably the prince's thrust with a

---

[136] See Clifford Davidson, "The Idol of Isis Church," *SP* 66 (1969): 72.

[137] *FQ, Book V*, ed. Alfred B. Gough (Oxford: Oxford University Press, 1921), 5.10.28n.

[138] Davidson, "Idol of Isis Church," p. 73.

"fatall sword" (5.11.31) reminiscent of Redcrosse's dispatch of the monster in Eden. Although Geryon's beast is descended from "the brooding of *Echidna*," its possession of the "body of a dog," a "Lions clawes," a "Dragons taile," and "Eagles wings" multiplies the attributes of that classical prototype for biform females (sts. 23–24). By mirroring Errour's nature as a serpentine woman, this "huge great Beast" personifies idolatry as a bestial perversion of all that is sacred:

> For of a Mayd she had the outward face,
> To hide the horrour, which did lurke behinde,
> The better to beguile, whom she so fond did finde.
>
> (st. 23)

Altogether lacking in the seductive allure of Duessa or Lucifera, this monster is an unambiguous embodiment of the lurid horrors of idolatry that the Protestant English, with their sense of persecution and encirclement by hostile powers and penetration by Jesuit spies and missionary priests, attributed to foreign Catholicism. Its leaping upon Arthur's shield recalls Errour's seizure of Redcrosse's Shield of Faith (st. 27). The bursting of the monster when Arthur rips open its "wombe" provides a further recollection of Errour's sinister maternity and its vomiting forth of a "floud of poyson horrible and blacke, / Full of great lumpes of flesh and gobbets raw" (1.1.20):

> And powred out of her infernall sinke
> Most ugly filth, and poyson therewith rusht,
> That him nigh choked with the deadly stinke.
>
> (5.11.31)

This episode fails to terminate the enduring pattern of construction and destruction that underlies Spenser's iconoclastic scenes. By concluding with an aborted iconoclastic incident, Book 6 leaves open the final resolution of this cycle in a manner that accords with the unfinished state of the 1596 *Faerie Queene*. Indeed, the ambiguity of the Blatant Beast's despoilment of a monastery recalls the two-sidedness of Spenserian satire in the antimonastic scenes in the "Legend of Holiness." In this instance, the monster's invasion of a holy place exemplifies the negative potential of iconoclasm:

> From thence into the sacred Church he broke,
> And robd the Chancell, and the deskes downe threw,
> And Altars fouled, and blasphemy spoke,
> And th'Images for all their goodly hew,
> Did cast to ground, whilest none was them to rew.
>
> (6.12.25)

Ben Jonson interprets the creature as a vehicle for satire against the Puritans (see p. 237). Although Calidore's conquest of the Blatant Beast initially contains its destructive energy, that embodiment of blasphemy wins its "liberty" in the closing stanzas of "The Legend of Courtesy" through the breaking of its "yron chaine" (st. 38). As yet another outbreak in an enduring cyclical conflict, this event is not unlike the escape of Antichrist, which will precede the end of time according to Revelation 20:7–8.

The appearance of the Blatant Beast as a parodic iconoclast recalls the complicted presentation of abuses of monasticism in the early cantos of the "Legend of Holiness." In contrast to the clear deficiencies of Archimago and Idleness, whose status as parodic monastics is indicated by their devotional books and the habits that they wear, Kirkrapine's robbery of churches lodges a double-edged satire against both the monastic misappropriation of alms and tithes and, presumably, the failure of the English monarchy to redistribute ecclesiastical wealth to the poor following the Dissolution of the Monasteries. Kirkrapine shares the beast's external aspect as an iconoclast. All of these elements indicate that the eradication of religious "error" did not ensure the introduction of "pure" religion. The iconoclastic motive of *The Faerie Queene* is grounded not only in negative satire of this kind but also in the didactic presentation of Protestant theological ideals in the House of Holiness, which counterbalances the failures of Spenser's parodic monastics.

Although *The Faerie Queene* incorporates an iconoclastic attack against the abuse or misapplication of art, Spenser never equates art with idolatry. Instead, he juxtaposes the eradication of "false" products of the imagination with the reciprocal construction of "true" literature and art. This position is akin to the views of early English Protestants, who clearly distinguished between the rejection of forbidden religious images and the kind of iconophobia that increasingly gained favor among some sectarians late in the reign of Elizabeth I and in the seventeenth century. The ambiguous status of the imagination, which may generate both truthful and deceptive images, underlies the alternation of the destruction and construction of art throughout *The Faerie Queene*. This iconoclastic pattern informs many of the work's memorable scenes.

# THREE

## SPENSER'S ROYAL ICONS

QUEENLY ICONOGRAPHY fills space that is left empty by iconoclastic outbursts at locations like the Bower of Bliss or the "blasphemous" shrine of Geryoneo, whose golden idol ("The image of his monstrous parent *Geryone*"; 5.10.13) and devouring beast invert imagery characteristic of a truly regal court like that of Mercilla. It is no accident, then, that Britomart—a type for Queen Elizabeth in her capacity as a "warlike Britonesse" (4.1.36)— rushes into the chamber left vacant when the fantastic projections of Busirane have "vanisht utterly" (3.12.42). Spenser's comment in the *Letter to Ralegh* that Gloriana is only one type for "our soveraine the Queene"—"in some places els, I doe otherwise shadow her"—provides a basis for relating many iconic representations of feminine majesty, notably Una, Belphoebe, Britomart, and Mercilla, as well as lesser figures like Fidelia, Caelia, and Alma, to Gloriana as the type both for "glory" in general and for Elizabeth as its particular embodiment. Because *The Faerie Queene* is centered upon the queen, to whom Spenser attributes all virtue, we may link her to the work's feminine personifications of faith, hope, charity, justice, mercy, fortitude, temperance, and prudence. Elizabeth's private virtues as a woman and her public virtues as a queen are embodied in Belphoebe and Gloriana respectively.[1]

Spenser's effort to harmonize an iconoclastic program with reverence toward iconic images of the queen shares the rhetorical difficulties facing contemporary apologists for royal sovereignty over the church.[2] In the broad context of Spenser's praise of Elizabeth as a militant Protestant heroine (an image from which the queen attempted to distance herself), Guyon's homage to Gloriana as the "Great and most glorious virgin Queene alive" indicates that she is a worthy alternative to false idols as an object of "sacred reverence." In line with *The Faerie Queene*'s iconoclastic strategy, this knight's envisagement of the Fairy Queen "As th'Idole of her makers great magnificence" (2.2.40-41) accords with the Neoplatonic sense of *eidolon* as

[1] Yates, "Queen Elizabeth as Astraea," in *Astraea*, pp. 53, 65, 69; Norbrook, *Poetry and Politics*, p. 109.

[2] Roy Strong, *Portraits of Queen Elizabeth I* (Oxford: Clarendon Press, 1963), pp. 37–39.

a true idea or "image" in the mind rather than the kind of "idol" that St. Paul attacked as a demonic object (1 Cor. 10:19-20). Gloriana supersedes the Virgin Mary as an object of veneration, in contrast to the False Una, who so resembles a forbidden statue of the Blessed Virgin (1.1.46). The proems of many books of the epic articulate a Neoplatonic scheme that identifies the ideal image of Elizabeth with true glory, divinity, and the defense of poetry (i.e., fiction). By openly celebrating artifice as a complement to nature, these prefaces avoid the furtive concealment of art and falsification of nature intrinsic to idolatrous locales like Acrasia's bower. The queen, as the "true glorious type" and "Mirrour of grace and Majestie divine" (1.proem.4), provides a worldly pattern and a means of aspiring toward supernatural truth. In presenting the image of true queenship as an accommodation of regal majesty to the imperfect vision of mortal sight, the second proem describes the "covert vele" of allegory as a means of wrapping "in shadowes light" a queenly image that would otherwise blind "feeble eyes . . . with exceeding light" (st. 5). The representation of Una also features this scriptural and Neoplatonic figure of the veil.

In line with the improvisational strategy of "displacement and absorption" of prohibited ritual and imagery that the Protestant Tudors employed to supplant the Church of Rome,[3] Spenser fills generic space emptied by iconoclastic destruction with figures that praise Queen Elizabeth as a religious leader. Spenser's handling of queenly figures accords with the introduction of regal heraldry into the vacuum created when repeated outbursts of iconoclasm swept away images of the Blessed Virgin, statues of saints, and pilgrimage shrines. Because monarchal images and badges inherited the veneration that cult objects had acquired by the late Middle Ages, the royal arms replaced crucifixes on the rood screens of English churches at the same time that biblical texts were inscribed over whitewashed religious murals.[4]

This displacement of traditional religious art may be noted in the illustrated title pages of many Tudor Bibles. Portrayals of Elizabeth as a "godly" queen in the Bishops' Bible (Figs. 16–17), for example, supplanted cult images of the Virgin Mary at the same time that they assimilated Mary's presentation as the Queen of Heaven. Frances Yates and Roy Strong have demonstrated how Elizabethan iconography transferred praise of the Blessed Virgin's exceptional state to a cult of "sacred" monarchy focused on England's Virgin Queen. Royal

---

[3] Greenblatt, *Renaissance Self-Fashioning*, p. 230.
[4] Phillips, *Reformation of Images*, pp. 88, 119, 128–29, 138, 204–5.

propaganda adapted formulaic praise once associated both with the medieval cult of sacred kingship and with queens as types of the Virgin Mary as a celestial queen.[5] According to Strong, this "position was thus a somewhat peculiar one, for on the one hand the use of religious images was denounced as popish superstition, while on the other, the sacred nature of the royal portrait image was to be maintained." The queen was praised variously as the Virgin giving birth to the gospel and as the Virgin Mother of the English people.[6]

In extending this iconographical argument to Spenser, Robin Wells qualifies the position of Yates and Strong by arguing that Mariological images survive in the *The Faerie Queene* in a more or less undiluted form. In the face of the Tudor eradication of such vestiges, however, this claim goes too far. The "Catholic" element in the poem is not a simple survival, but an iconoclastic redefinition of traditional images. The adaptation of the traditional royal symbolism of the Tree of Jesse is a case in point. Based upon the messianic prophecy that "there shal come a rod forthe of the stocke of Ishai [Jesse], and a grase [i.e., flower] shal growe out of his roote" (Isa. 11:1), visual portrayals of the genealogy of Jesus from the royal house of David were a familiar component of medieval religious art. Even though the gospels present Joseph rather than Mary as a descendent of David (Matt. 1:2–16), medieval commentators viewed the rod as a symbol for the Virgin Mother from whom Christ sprang as a flower. Wells discovers an analogy to Spenser's procedure in a contemporary revision of the Jesse Tree, the woodcut border of John Stow's *Chronicles of England* (1580) (Fig. 15), which portrays the genealogy of the House of Tudor rising as a winding rose arbor from its stock, the sleeping figure of Edward III, to Queen Elizabeth. The poet likewise praises the queen as "the royal flower 'enraced,' like the Blessed Virgin, in 'stocke of earthly flesh' " (3.5.52).[7] Nevertheless, this title page incorporates a distinctively English variation of medieval typology. The Jesse Tree discovered by Wells is actually mediated by the dynastic arbor on the title page of Edward Halle's *Unyon of the Twoo Noble and Illustre[ous] Famelies of Lancastre & Yorke* (1550; 4th ed.), which rises upward to Henry VIII, who unites the white rose of York and red rose of Lancaster, from the recumbent figures of John of Gaunt and his brother,

---

[5] Yates, "Queen Elizabeth as Astraea," in *Astraea*, pp. 78–79. See also Strong, *Cult of Elizabeth*, p. 125. The cult of Elizabeth assimilates Mariological imagery associated with Catholic queens like Mary I as well as the evangelical iconography of Henry VIII and Edward VI, as discussed in King, *Tudor Royal Iconography*, pp. 81–84, 203, 241, 266.

[6] Strong, *Portraits*, p. 39; see also Phillips, *Reformation of Images*, pp. 119–24.

[7] Wells, *Spenser's "Fairie Queene" and the Cult of Elizabeth*, pp. 14–21, 32, 86, 89.

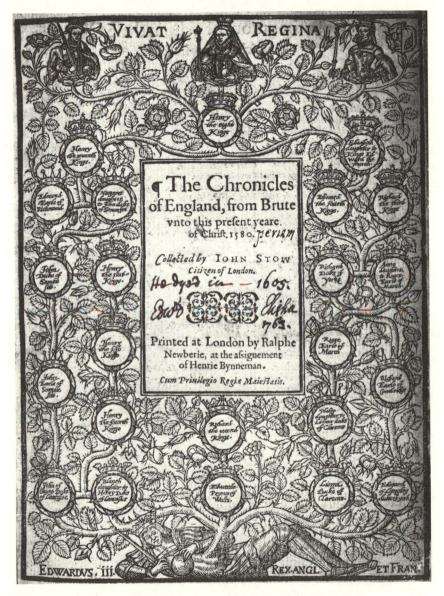

**15.** *The Tudor Rose Arbor.* John Stow, *Chronicles of England* (1580)

Edmund, Dukes of Lancaster and York. The Tree of Jesse survives in these symbolic images of dynastic succession not because they identify Tudor monarchs with the Virgin Mary, but because they preserve the medieval interpretation of the flower of Jesse as a symbol for Christ. If one interprets the border for Stow's *Chronicles* allegorically,

Elizabeth succeeds her predecessors, both male and female, in a place of honor as a Christlike sovereign.[8]

The iconoclastic habit of displacing Mariological imagery while absorbing it into queenly iconography may be noted in the symbolic portrayal of knightly armor during the encounter between Redcrosse and Guyon at the outset of Book 2. Guyon's spontaneous refusal to enter battle after recognizing the "sacred badge of my Redeemers death" on his opponent's shield of faith assimilates classical temperance into the framework of Christian holiness (2.1.27). (This act of deference to the cross is comparable to the position taken by Queen Elizabeth in favor of the valid use of religious ornaments.) The complementary decoration of Guyon's shield with a portrait of Gloriana—"that faire image of that heavenly Mayd"—suggests a witty variation of late medieval chivalric devotion to the Blessed Virgin (st. 28). The designs on their shields align these warriors with the badges of the members of the Order of the Garter, which included the red cross of St. George and the image of the Virgin Mary that decorated "their shields, Armour, and Ensigns."[9] The Palmer clearly subordinates Guyon and his shield-image of Gloriana to "that deare Crosse" on the shield of Redcrosse (st. 31). Displaced vestiges of Mariological devotion and the adoration of saints are to be seen when Guyon forces Pyrocles to do homage to his shield-image of "Saint" Gloriana (2.5.11). In an inversion of this scenario, Pyrocles later employs the stolen shield of Guyon to ward off Prince Arthur, whose adoration of "the Faery Queenes pourtract" prevents him from striking at his opponent (2.8.43).

## Demonic "Queens"

Because opposition is an essential component of a generic and iconographical system that internalizes iconoclastic forces, *The Faerie Queene* accommodates many "dark doubles" of Queen Elizabeth.[10] Accordingly, the figures who threaten Gloriana's knights are often

[8] On the connection between the Tree of Jesse and royal iconography, see Emile Mâle, *The Gothic Image: Religious Art in France of the Thirteenth Century*, trans. Dora Nussey (New York: Harper and Row, 1958), pp. 165–68.

[9] *The Register of the Most Noble Order of the Garter, From Its Cover in Black Velvet, usually Called the Black Book*, 2 vols. (1724): 1: 38. Michael Leslie comments that Redcrosse and Guyon bear Garter badges and that the Order had definite Protestant associations under Elizabeth in *Spenser's "Fierce Warres and Faithfull Loves": Martial and Chivalric Symbolism in "The Faerie Queene"* (Cambridge: D. S. Brewer, 1983), pp. 189, 191–92.

[10] I owe this epithet to Susan Snyder.

perversions of regal magnificence that parody ideals embodied positively in Elizabeth.[11] The most potent attack against a "demonic"
queen or princess is directed against Duessa as a personification of
the Roman church in general or its localized manifestation in the
Catholic queens, Mary I or Mary, Queen of Scots. Although Spenser's iconoclastic habit of doubling "true" and "false" images prevents us from discovering unambiguous blame of Elizabeth in
Duessa and her kind, his negative images of queenship sometimes
provide cautionary examples or critical glimpses of a queen who resisted the militantly Protestant foreign policy favored by her privy
council and whose power to govern as a female was the subject of
strenuous controversy.

Despite the overall design of *The Faerie Queene* as an epideictic
poem in praise of Queen Elizabeth, whom the dedication lauds as
the "MOST HIGH, MIGHTIE And MAGNIFICENT EMPRESSE RE-
NOWMED FOR PIETIE, VERTUE, AND ALL GRATIOUS GOVERN-
MENT," recent criticism has emphasized that the work also contains
cautious criticism of the queen or her policies. One must acknowledge that the poem is complicated in ways that have not previously
been explored; it is a heterogeneous and open-ended work. David
Norbrook observes that in spite of Spenser's "general celebration of
female rulers, his poem does hint at the problems some radical humanists and Protestants had believed to inhere in giving supreme
power to a woman." He concludes that "the cult of Elizabeth was
often, in effect, a cult of Elizabeth imagined as following the advice
of firm Protestants."[12] Judith Anderson offers a persuasive case that
Spenser's reverence for his queen is tempered "by a cautionary
awareness of the temptations and dangers of queenly power." With
reference to Sclaunder's vilification of Arthur and his companions,
Amoret and Aemylia (4.8.23–36), Anderson lodges the caveat that "it
should be obvious from the poet's virulent description" that the vituperative hag, Sclaunder, "is not an image of the Virgin Queen."
The way in which the "image of the bitter old woman glances at the
living Queen" exemplifies the delicacy of Spenser's handling of a parodic queen in an incident that recalls Corceca's accusation of inchas-
tity against Una. In noting the harsh presence of a pun that a Tudor
auditor might have heard in the attack against Sclaunder as a
"queane so base and vilde" (st. 28), Anderson acknowledges that
Sclaunder is akin to Lucifera not as "a missing side of Una or of the

[11] On the identification of queenly images with thematic opposites, see O'Connell,
*Mirror and Veil*, pp. 53–54; Norbrook, *Poetry and Politics*, pp. 151–54.
[12] Norbrook, *Poetry and Politics*, p. 113; see also p. 119.

Queen but [as] a denial of what they truly are."[13] Indeed, the previous rescue of Amoret and Aemylia from Lust praises Elizabeth through her identification with the rescuer, Belphoebe (4.7.31). Sclaunder joins the company of Spenser's parodic "queens," including Acrasia, of whom one critic observes that "she is truly Spenser's 'faery quean.' "[14] Their viciousness reflects a deficiency of regal magnificence.

The conventions of parody dictate that Elizabeth's dark doubles, who include Lucifera, Acrasia, Malecasta, and Radigund, satirize abuses opposed to "true" majesty. These evil females are associated with *vituperatio*, a species of rhetorical blame that negates epideictic praise (*laus*). Blame is a conventional component of the poetry of praise because it can be used to intensify the force of eulogy. Indeed, Thomas Cain argues that Gloriana "is made even more desirable when we see detailed images of what she is not in the fake queens Lucifera and Philotime." Lucifera's establishment is accordingly the "demonic opposite" of "the only other court in the poem," that of Mercilla. Cain concludes that the courts of Lucifera and Mercilla are both "types, negative and positive, of the unseen court of Gloriana." When Britomart defeats Radigund (5.7.25–45), the former is a type for Elizabeth as an "exception to the rule" of male supremacy, while the latter's status as a vituperative parody inverts the fundamental principles of masculine supremacy and patriarchal government.[15]

Any conclusion that *The Faerie Queene* contains one-sidedly negative portrayals of Queen Elizabeth ignores the late medieval and Renaissance satirical convention of portraying both the positive and the negative capabilities of the ruler. It was standard practice both to depict "allegorically certain sins of the court" and to recognize that

---

[13] Anderson, " 'In living colours and right hew': The Queen of Spenser's Central Books," in *Poetic Traditions of the English Renaissance*, ed. Maynard Mack and George deForest Lord (New Haven: Yale University Press, 1982), pp. 47, 62–64. The variable pronunciation of "quean" ("hag," "harlot") would have left the poet with the tactful disclaimer that he intended no pun. Anne Lake Prescott has informed me that Gervase Markham rhymes the word with "entertain" in *The Famous Whore, or Noble Curtizan* (1609): "And for this purpose I did entertaine, / A beldame old, a crafty cunning Queane" (C3ᵛ).

[14] David Lee Miller, "Spenser's Poetics: The Poem's Two Bodies," *PMLA* 101 (1986): 177. For the implausible view that Acrasia actually reflects Elizabeth, see Maureen Quilligan, *Milton's Spenser: The Politics of Reading* (Ithaca, N.Y.: Cornell University Press, 1983), p. 69.

[15] Cain, *Praise in "The Faerie Queene,"* pp. 112, 140–41, 150–53. See also Wells, *Spenser's "Faerie Queene" and the Cult of Elizabeth*, p. 125. Definition by negation is a characteristic Spenserian technique, according to both Wells (p. 32), and Jeffrey Knapp, "Error as a Means of Empire in *The Faerie Queene*," *ELH* 54 (1987): 820.

"these sins were themselves conventional."[16] Tudor literature is filled with cautious criticism of kings as well as queens. Inversion and indirection are essential ingredients in satires that acknowledge that the failures of monarchy need not reflect blame upon the institution as such. Thus More's *Utopia* moves from an opening analysis of monarchy's potential for misrule to the abstract praise of regal magnificence at the close of Book 2. In *Philargyrie of Greate Britayne* by Robert Crowley, the moral vacuum created by the misgovernment of Philargyrie and his ministers is filled by the ideal King who eventually collaborates with Truth, the Protestant counselor who urges an iconoclastic attack against idolatry, in restoring good government. Imperial Majesty similarly returns the realm to order at the close of Bale's *King Johan*, a work concerned with the progress of the Henrician Reformation. Sackville and Norton direct *Gorboduc*, an admonitory work that was restaged at the court of Elizabeth by royal command, not at monarchy as an institution, but against the queen's abuse of royal prerogative in failing to marry in order to perpetuate the Tudor dynasty. Political analysis of the ruler's potential for both good and evil may be found in two vastly influential *specula principis*, Machiavelli's *The Prince* and Erasmus's *The Education of the Christian Prince*.

As the court of a "mayden Queene," the Palace of Pride might seem to reflect England's Virgin Queen unfavorably were it not that this is the only negative application of this epithet throughout Spenser's poetry (1.4.8). The same phrase is applied positively to Eliza, Una, and Mercilla. Unlike the falsity of Lucifera's apparent brightness, Una's radiance as "a goodly maiden Queene" makes her "selfe-resemblance . . . seeme such, as she was" (1.12.8). Mercilla appears as "a mayden Queene of high renowne" (5.8.17) in a reversal of the vices of Lucifera and other demonic queens.

Nevertheless, the episode at the Palace of Pride does raise politically charged questions concerning the legitimacy of female government in particular, as well as the general tendency of royal courts to harbor hypocrisy and false display. Lucifera's panoply of "royall robes and gorgeous array" and her enthronement beneath a "cloth of State" distort queenly iconography because she lacks a legitimate claim to the "rightfull kingdome" that truly regal attributes represent. Her power derives from "wrong and tyrannie" rather than a "heritage of native soveraintie" (1.4.8, 12). Although the self-made nature of Lucifera's government contrasts sharply with Elizabeth's orthodox claim to govern by divine sanction, it cannot be denied that

---

[16] Heiserman, *Skelton and Satire*, p. 45.

any autocracy ultimately rests upon an assertion of self-will. Robin Wells observes that Lucifera's "pomp is not condemned in itself. Indeed it is precisely in this respect that she most resembles Elizabeth." The bright mirror in her hand symbolizes the pride for which she is blamed.[17] (In different contexts, the mirror may symbolize the opposed virtue of prudence.) She is a "great Princesse" only in an ironic sense, because she is "too exceeding prowd" (st. 15).[18] The generational allegory concerning Lucifera's "parentage" by Pluto and Proserpina (1.4.11) represents a favorite device by which Spenser indicates "relationships along the ontological scale,"[19] in this case suggesting that illegitimacy and false display are the inevitable results of the usurpation of temporal authority by regal pretenders.

Duessa's allegorical "kinship" to Lucifera may be noted in the entrée that the harlot has at the Palace of Pride, and in the place of honor that she assumes beside Lucifera's throne on the chariot of Satan. Duessa's portrayal as a false queen inverts epideictic categories that Spenser applies elsewhere in praise of Queen Elizabeth. John Dixon noticed this soon after the publication of *The Faerie Queene*, when he commented on Duessa's description as

> the sole daughter of an *Emperour*,
> He that the wide West under his rule has
> And high hath set his throne, where *Tiberis* doth pas.

(1.2.22)

Duessa's geographical origins identify her with false religion, according to Dixon, who observes that she is the antithesis of Queen Elizabeth as an evangelical prince: "Antichriste taketh one hir the nam of Truth, fained to be the daughter of a persian kynge: but truth is only ment, to our Soverainge Eliz. Christe and his gospell" (Dixon, *Commentary* 1.2.22–23n). One must grant that Dixon cannot reconstruct a

---

[17] Wells, *Spenser's "Faerie Queene" and the Cult of Elizabeth*, p. 33. The emphasis on Lucifera's virginity represents not an insult to Queen Elizabeth, but an allegorical sign that "Pride brooks no consort, no rival; she reigns alone," according to Chew, *Pilgrimage*, p. 95. See also O'Connell, *Mirror and Veil*, pp. 52–53.

[18] The term "princess" could carry a double meaning late in Elizabeth's reign, when the queen referred to herself as a "prince" and reserved the term "princess" for disgraced rulers like Mary, Queen of Scots. See Leah S. Marcus, "Shakespeare's Comic Heroines, Elizabeth I, and the Political Uses of Androgyny," in *Women in the Middle Ages and the Renaissance: Literary and Historical Perspectives*, ed. Mary Beth Rose (Syracuse, N.Y.: Syracuse University Press, 1986), p. 140. Elizabethan subjects might address the queen as "princess." Spenser refers to Elizabeth and Mercilla as princesses (e.g., 2.proem.4, 5.8.18).

[19] I. MacCaffrey, *Spenser's Allegory*, p. 144. See Cain, *Praise in "The Faerie Queene*," p. 75.

consistent allegory for Tudor political and ecclesiastical history; his commentary is haphazard, and he confuses episodes in the poem. Nevertheless, he consistently reads the opposition between Una and Duessa as a nationalistic allegory concerning the victory of Protestantism in England that is modeled upon the Revelation conflict between the Woman Clothed with the Sun and the Whore of Babylon.[20] His notation on Duessa as a "Romish harlot" (Dixon, *Commentary* 1.7.1n) aligns her correctly with anti-Catholic satire, because her search for the "blessed body" of Christ associates her with the ritual of the Roman mass that Protestants attacked as an idolatrous sacrifice (1.2.24). Dixon's interpretation of Duessa as a false queen is flexible in the extreme, because he indicates elsewhere that she is a type for Mary I. Thus he interprets Duessa's abortive effort to disrupt the betrothal of Una and Redcrosse as a "fiction" concerning the postponement of Elizabeth's betrothal "unto Christe" during the six-year period of her sister's reign. He likewise takes the six-year duration of Redcrosse's return to the court of Gloriana as a reference to "the time of the raingne of phil[ip]: and marye" (Dixon, *Commentary* 1.12.argument n and st. 18n).[21]

*The Faerie Queene* contains an array of parodic queens who recall their prototype, Duessa, whose scarlet attire identifies her as an imperial pretender.[22] The proximity of Philotime's court to Garden of Proserpina aligns her with the ancestress of Lucifera, just as her advancement of favorites "for works and merites just" (2.7.49) adds an anti-Catholic nuance to the House of Mammon.[23]

The false glory of Malecasta, who "glistred all with gold and glorious shew, / As the proud *Persian* Queenes accustomed" (3.1.41), recalls not only the prideful display of Lucifera and Philotime, but also Duessa's mitrelike "*Persian*" headpiece and her costume of "gold and pearle of rich assay" (1.2.13). The hidden side of Duessa as a loathsome hag affords a parallel both to Sclaunder's presentation as a "queane so base and vilde" (4.8.28) and to her own associate, Ate, as the embodiment of public discord:

> But Ladies none they were, albee in face
> And outward shew faire semblance they did beare;

[20] Sandler, "*The Faerie Queene*: An Elizabethan Apocalypse," pp. 165–66.

[21] One gloss refers ambiguously either to Mary I or to Mary, Queen of Scots: "Antichristian religion over throwne, and the maintainer their of Q ma: by death victored" (Dixon, *Commentary* 1.11.argument n).

[22] Eliza's attire "in Scarlot like a mayden Queene" ("April," l. 57) conforms to the legitimate use of this color in royal praise (see *FQ* 1.12.13).

[23] Wells, *Spenser's "Faerie Queene" and the Cult of Elizabeth*, p. 57, states that the throne room of this hellish chatelaine represents a "parody of Elizabeth's own court."

For under maske of beautie and good grace,
Vile treason and fowle falshood hidden were.

(4.1.17)

The respective encounters of Redcrosse and Guyon with Lucifera and Philotime indicate that pride and false magnificence are enemies of both holiness and temperance. The deficiencies of these queenly doubles make it clear that they parody regal ideals later attributed to Elizabeth in the guise of Mercilla. By way of contrast, the *Letter to Ralegh* explains that these knights of Gloriana personify virtues that are contained in regal magnificence as it is represented by Prince Arthur. Led by Duessa to the Palace of Pride, Redcrosse enters the court of Lucifera, whose pomp *exceeds* truly regal glory: "Ne *Persia* selfe, the nourse of pompous pride / Like ever saw" (1.4.7). Lucifera's gaudy display of "glistring gold" and jewels "too exceeding shone" (st. 8). The "glistring glory" (2.7.46) of the court of Philotime ("love of honor") recreates the Palace of Pride as a travesty of majesty. Although Philotime emanates "great brightnes" through the "dim shade" of her throne room (2.7.45), her fallen state and the artificiality of her radiance associate her with Lucifer and original sin. The diametrically opposed imagery of Una's theophanic veiling is akin to the shielding of divine radiance.

## "Mirrour of grace and Majestie divine"

Praise of Elizabeth tends to coalesce into static and compressed "icons" or moments of vision in which the narrative is suspended in order to provide a focused verbal portrait of a queenly figure by means of an elaborate allegorical device.[24] "Icon" is a poetic figure, according to Puttenham, that defines "resemblaunce by imagerie or pourtrait, alluding to the painters terme, who yeldeth to th'eye a visible representation of the thing he describes and painteth in his table [i.e., tableau or picture]." He cites the distinctively royal symbols of the serpent, lion, and angel, which may be applied in praise of Queen Elizabeth's "wisedome bewtie and magnanimitie" because of their proverbial association with those qualities.[25] Many queenly figures of *The Faerie Queene* resemble Elizabeth's visual portraits in the

[24] Cain, *Praise in "The Faerie Queene,"* p. 59. See also Bender, *Spenser and Literary Pictorialism,* p. 51n.
[25] Puttenham, *Arte of English Poesie,* ed. Willcock and Walker, p. 243.

hieratic rigidity that they share with religious icons.[26] The duality that permits Spenser to juxtapose iconic praise and iconoclastic attack within the same work, indeed within some of the same episodes, may find a precedent in the New Testament use of *eikon* ("image," "likeness," "portrait") to describe both Christ as "the image of God" (2 Cor. 4:4) and the Beast of the Apocalypse (Rev. 13:15; 15:2).[27]

Spenser embeds his praise of Elizabeth as a Protestant queen within a circular pattern of iconic types who resemble each other and refer back to archetypes of virtue assigned to the queen. Thus he repeatedly styles queenly figures like Una, Caelia, Fidelia, Alma, Cambina, and Gloriana herself, in terms of the Reformation image of the "godly" woman or queen, which was widely known from woodcuts, literature, and pageantry of the time. This figure was modeled on scriptural images of the Bride of the Song of Songs and the Woman Clothed with the Sun as well as "purified" images drawn from the medieval Mariology.[28] David Norbrook accordingly observes that "Spenser's Faerie Queen is presented as a mirror or image of Queen Elizabeth who is in turn imaged by other female figures—Belphoebe, Britomart, Mercilla, Medina—all of whom are emanations of the glory of the Virgin Queen."[29] Even Belphoebe has many Christian associations that may be concealed by her "classical name and foster-parentage."[30] As the summation of the virtues personified by the heroes of the separate books of the epic, Prince Arthur serves as a masculine counterpart to Gloriana.[31]

An analogy to Spenser's presentation of Elizabeth as the epitome of all virtue, notably the "three theological virtues and the four cardinal virtues" (especially the imperial attributes of justice and mercy),[32] may be located in the well-known title pages of the Bishops' Bible. Spenser repeatedly· identifies Elizabeth with scriptural truth along the lines of the frontispiece in the first edition of 1568, where female personifications of faith and charity flank a portrait of the

---

[26] See Camille A. Paglia, "The Apollonian Androgyne and *The Faerie Queene*," *ELR* 9 (1979): 45 n. 7.

[27] Florence Sandler, "Icon and Iconoclast," in *Achievements of the Left Hand: Essays on the Prose of John Milton*, ed. Michael J. Lieb and John T. Shawcross (Amherst: University of Massachusetts Press, 1974), p. 161.

[28] King, *Tudor Royal Iconography*, pp. 195–201.

[29] Norbrook, *Poetry and Politics*, p. 109. In *FQ* "all instances of a virtue necessarily resemble each other, and all partake" of a Christian archetype, according to I. MacCaffrey, *Spenser's Allegory*, p. 102.

[30] Wells, *Spenser's "Faerie Queene" and the Cult of Elizabeth*, p. 52, and n. 5.

[31] Tuve, *Allegorical Imagery*, p. 350. See also Giamatti, "A Prince and Her Poet," p. 329; and Miller, "Spenser's Poetics," p. 171.

[32] See Yates, "Queen Elizabeth as Astraea," in *Astraea*, p. 65.

queen (Fig. 16). The epigraph from Romans 1:16 ("For I am not ashamed of the Gospell of Christ, because it is the power of God unto salvation to all that beleve") identifies Elizabeth as the completion of St. Paul's triad of theological virtues. This envisionment of the queen as England's only "hope" for implementing and completing the Reformation was assimilated into propaganda that her government authorized, even though Elizabeth herself shrank from assuming a militantly Protestant posture. The congruence of Una with Fidelia and Speranza, whose "kind speeches" greet Una's entry into the House of Holiness, makes that queenly type look like a temporary member of the triad of theological virtues (1.10.15). Spenser's procedure also finds an analogy in the woodcut border of the 1569 Bishops' Bible, where female personifications, Justice and Mercy, crown the queen while Fortitude and Prudence gaze upon the scene (Fig. 17).

As the embodiment of Truth (arguments to 1.2 and 1.3), Una looms in the foreground as Spenser's prototype for a faithful queen. She is the scion of a royal house

> Of ancient Kings and Queenes, that had of yore
> Their scepters stretcht from East to Westerne shore,
> And all the world in their subjection held;
> Till that infernall feend with foule uprore
> Forwasted all their land, and them expeld.

(1.1.5)

John Dixon discovers in the "blazing brightnesse" of Una's unveiled face an image of a "Crowned quene" (Dixon, *Commentary* 1.12.23n). Idealized females had personified virtue in medieval romances and romantic love poetry—Beatrice and Laura leap to mind—but Una's portrayal combines such models with the scriptural figure of the Woman Clothed with the Sun, whose flight from the Seven-headed Beast into the wilderness was viewed as the antitype for the true church under attack from Antichrist (Fig. 7; see above, pp. 73, 82, 119). As a crowned matron bearing a "man childe, which shulde rule all nations with a rod of yron" from a heavenly throne (Rev. 12:5; Christ according to the Geneva Bible gloss), the Woman Clothed with the Sun offers a prototype for pious queens, including the Virgin Mary, who bears the heir to a heavenly throne, and royal consorts, who bear the heirs to worldly thrones.

John Dixon's identification of Una as "a fiction of o[u]r Queene Eliz[abeth]: the maintainer of the gospell of Christe" is aligned with well-known Christian iconography (Dixon, *Commentary*, note on

**16.** *Elizabeth as Hope.* Bishops' Bible (1568)

**17.** *Elizabeth I and the Four Virtues.* Bishops' Bible (1569)

1.12.argument).[33] Spenser's familiarity with the typology of the apocalyptic woman may be noted in the Revelation woodcut that accompanied his earliest published verse in the *A Theatre for Worldlings* (Fig. 8); her figure rises on a vertical axis that suggests that she will experience ultimate victory over the Seven-headed Beast beneath her.[34] Although the beleaguered woman who confronts the forces of evil by trampling upon a dragon or serpent was identified in medieval and Counter-Reformation art with the Blessed Virgin (or St. Margaret), Elizabethan apologists adapted this apocalyptic image in order to praise Elizabeth as the leader of the Church of England. The connection between Una's name and the Nicene Creed's definition of the church as " '*unam*, sanctam, catholicam' " corresponds to Spenser's envisionment of "the return of the truth of a single apostolic church through the person of a unique royal virgin."[35] One need only contemplate the initial capital C of Foxe's "Book of Martyrs," with its historiated image of Elizabeth crushing the pope and serpents that intertwine in the lower arm, to understand that the queen has displaced the Virgin Mary and inherited her iconography (Fig. 14). Richard Vennard forges a direct link between the queen and the maiden whom St. George rescued from a dragon in verses that face an illustration of that victory (Fig. 18):

> A Virgin Princesse and a gentle Lambe,
>> domb'e [i.e., doomed] both to death to gorge this ugly beast:
> This valiant victor like a Souldier came,
>> and of his owne accord, without request:
> With never daunted spirit the Fiend assaild,
>> perserv'd [sic] the Princesse, and the Monster quaild.

> (*The Right Way to Heaven* [1601], A2)[36]

Both these verses and the captions treat St. George as "the figure of our Saviours force" as it is enlisted on the side of England and her queen.

The opening tableau of the "Legend of Holiness" includes an ex-

---

[33] Dixon also annotates Una as Truth (Dixon, *Commentary* 1.1.4n) and as the "daughter and heir to a persian kinge . . . [who] is rightly to be understod the daughter of Israel or the true Church, which was led by the wylldernese 140 yeares" (1.2.9n). See also 1.3.2n, 1.12.40n.

[34] Truth tramples upon the serpent of Error in a woodcut that appears in *The Vocacyon of Johan Bale* (1553), ed. Peter Happé and John N. King, Renaissance English Text Society, 7th ser. vol. 14 (1989) (Binghamton, N.Y.: Medieval and Renaissance Texts and Studies, vol. 70, 1990), l. 284.

[35] O'Connell, *Mirror and Veil*, pp. 45–46.

[36] Quoted from the second edition of 1602; cited in *Var.* 1: 390.

**18.** *St. George.* Vennard, *The Right Way to Heaven* (1602)

tended iconic portrait of Una as the embodiment of faithful "queen-ship." Una's accompaniment by St. George associates her with a saint who had been brought in line with Reformation ideology through the association of his antagonist with the apocalyptic Beast. Despite the hostility that Edward VI showed toward the saint, Elizabeth retained his image on the device of the royalist cult of the Order of the Garter (see below, pp. 191–93). Spenser's first scene is akin to the St. George's Day tableaux that were pushed around English towns on pageant carts. Flanked by Redcrosse and the Dwarf, this "lovely Ladie" rides

> Upon a lowly Asse more white then snow,
> Yet she much whiter, but the same did hide   ·
> Under a vele, that wimpled was full low
> And over all a blacke stole she did throw,
>
> .   .   .   .   .   .   .   .   .   .   .   .   .   .
>
> And by her in a line a milke white lambe she lad.

(1.1.4)

As narrative this scene is unrealistic—after all, Una and her slow-moving entourage keep up with the galloping knight—but it makes allegorical sense because her humble steed associates her with the humility of Christ, who entered Jerusalem upon an ass.[37] Una's teth-ered lamb is a familiar part of the iconography of St. George (see Fig. 18), but it also signifies Christ as the *agnus dei* (see Fig. 2). Redcrosse's quest to defend Una's native land of Eden from attack by an "infer-nall feend" (st. 5) provides a sign that she is the antithesis of Duessa, the witch who rides her diabolical steed in the manner of a perverse mirror image (see Fig. 6).

Una exemplifies many virtues that were conventionally attributed to Queen Elizabeth, just as their shared traits are consistently re-versed in the parodic "queens" of *The Faerie Queene*. Spenser high-lights a heraldic link between the first woman in his epic and the leading woman in England by having Una appear in the personal colors of Queen Elizabeth—white and black—which respectively sig-nify virginity and constancy.[38] The fusion of scriptural and Neopla-tonic images of the clouded light of divine revelation (or the blinding light of truth) and the whiteness of innocence in Una's iconic image is a conventional element in portraits praising Queen Elizabeth. These iconographical details may be noted, for example, in the

---

[37] Cain, *Praise in "The Faerie Queene,"* p. 60. Una's steed is a variation of *asinus portans mysteria*, a figure for true gospel ministry, according to John Steadman, "Una and the Clergy: The Ass Symbol in *The Faerie Queene,"* *JWCI* 21 (1958): 134–37.

[38] Strong, *Cult of Elizabeth*, pp. 71, 74.

"Ditchley Portrait" (c. 1592), in which the white-garbed queen is poised between a clouded sun and black clouds.[39] The narrator associates the Neoplatonic figure of the veil, an attribute of Una, with the dazzling brightness of Queen Elizabeth (2.proem.5). Just as the somber blackness of Una's attire accords with the sobriety and sanctity of Truth, in contrast to her opposite's ostentatious attire and mitrelike headpiece, "the unveiling of Una has its demonic parody in the stripping of Duessa."[40] Duessa and her associates are promiscuous in the extreme, and their blatantly scarlet and gold costumes are antithetical to the cloaking of Una's preternatural whiteness.

Una's name calls attention to the affinity between Spenser's "royall virgin" (1.2.7) and Elizabeth I because it was one of the queen's epideictic epithets.[41] Una's constancy evokes the undividedness of both truth and queenly majesty, and her invulnerability to the vicissitudes of time corresponds to the royal motto, *Semper Eadem*.[42] The concealment of her brilliant whiteness under a veil is a variation of the standard Reformation use of the sun shielded by a circle of clouds as a symbol for divinity and, by extension, royalty. The iconoclastic sanction of the abstract symbolism of the sun in place of anthropomorphic images of the deity may be noted in the frequent placement of the Tetragrammaton within a sunburst on the title pages of Tudor Bibles and other Protestant books (see Fig. 20; *ERL*, fig. 2). Una's eventual unveiling at the royal court in Eden associates her with the apocalyptic image of the rising sun:

> As bright as doth the morning starre appeare
> Out of the East, with flaming lockes bedight,
> To tell that dawning day is drawing neare.

> (1.12.21)

The Geneva Bible gloss on Christ as "the bright morning starre" (Rev. 22:16) explains that he is "the light that giveth light to everie one that commeth into this worlde."

Una's initial encounter with the Lion exemplifies Spenser's handling of iconic tableaux, for he arrests the narrative to focus on the instinctive reverence of the beast for its acknowledged mistress.[43]

---

[39] National Portrait Gallery, London, no. 2561. See Strong, *Portraits*, pp. 75–76 and pl. 15; and Yates, *Astraea*, pp. 106, 218. O'Connell identifies "the sun bursting through a veil of clouds" as an Elizabethan symbol in *Mirror and Veil*, pp. 47–48 and n. 11.

[40] Cain, *Praise in "The Faerie Queene,"* p. 74.

[41] See Wells, *Spenser's "Faerie Queene" and the Cult of Elizabeth*, pp. 31–32.

[42] This formulaic phrase is a variation of the queen's Phoenix device (Yates, "Queen Elizabeth as Astraea," in *Astraea*, p. 65). See Apteker, *Icons of Justice*, p. 78.

[43] See Cain, *Praise in "The Faerie Queene,"* pp. 66–67.

Una's removal of her stole just before this encounter had already likened her to a divine sunburst:

> Her angels face
> As the great eye of heaven shyned bright,
> And made a sunshine in the shadie place;
> Did never mortall eye behold such heavenly grace.
>
> (1.3.4)

The narrator's apostrophe—"O how can beautie maister the most strong, / And simple truth subdue avenging wrong" (st. 6)—ponders the paradoxical power of abstract virtue over physical strength. At this point, John Dixon identifies Una with Queen Elizabeth as a godly monarch who ought "Love Christe the sone of david" (Dixon, *Commentary* 1.3.5n). The placement of this scene as an introduction to the episode at the house where Corceca "sate in eternall night" (st. 12) draws a sharp contrast between the alleged "blindness" of Catholic superstition and the Protestant claim to spiritual "vision" and "light" of revelation consonant with the truth of the early Christian church.

Spenser's association of solar and lunar imagery with Elizabeth Tudor may be noted as early as the "April" eclogue, where Hobbinol sings Colin Clout's praise of Eliza for outshining Phoebus, the god of the sun:

> But when he sawe, how broade her beames did spredde,
>    it did him amaze.
> He blusht to see another Sunne belowe,
> Ne durst againe his fyrye face out showe:
>    Let him, if he dare,
>    His brightnesse compare
> With hers, to have the overthrowe.
>
> (ll. 75–81)

This conceit is an example of "the outdoing *topos*" in evidence throughout the poem, whereby the poet elevates "the queen above all possibility of comparison."[44] The celestial figure highlights the political power of the queen's feminine beauty because the "angelick face" of Eliza ("April," l. 64) is comparable to the goddess of the Moon, Phoebe or Cynthia. Elizabeth resembles the sun in her public capacity as "king" of England, but her private nature as a woman

---

[44] Cain, *Praise in "The Faerie Queene,"* p. 16. See also O'Connell, *Mirror and Veil*, p. 47. Spenser's metaphor corresponds to the allegory of the "Ditchley Portrait," which bears the explanation that the queen outshines "The prince of light, The Sonn." Quoted in Strong, *Portraits*, p. 75.

also makes her a nighttime figure who is ever alluring, changeable, and chaste.[45] In this she is like the Virgin Mary, whose Litanies celebrated her as the antitype of the Spouse: "Pulchra ut luna, electa ut sol" ("faire as the moone, pure as the sunne"; Song of Sol. 6:9). Spenser's combination of sun and moon symbols is akin to the concealment of Una's brilliant whiteness beneath a "blacke stole" (1.1.4), which suggests the lunar aspect of the Woman Clothed with the Sun, who has "the moone . . . under her feete" (Rev. 12:1). (Medieval art often portrays the Virgin Mary above the crescent moon symbolic of chastity.) The subordination of the masculine sun to the feminine moon in Spenser's queenly iconography may be noted as well in Britomart's dream at Isis's Church, where the Crocodile (i.e., Osiris, who "signifies the Sunne") submits to Isis, "who doth the Moone portend" (5.7.4).

Cynthia played a prominent role in royal panegyric during the latter part of Elizabeth's reign, when Spenser was actively engaged in his political and poetic career. A nocturnal portrait of his patron, Sir Walter Ralegh, compliments the queen's ability to govern the male by depicting the crescent moon, Luna, as the goddess controlling the tides of this seafaring courtier; like Una, he wears Elizabeth's colors of black and white. This allegorical portrait defines Ralegh's relationship to the queen as Cynthia, who in turn gave him the punning nickname of "Water."[46] Spenser's *Letter to Ralegh* acknowledges that he models Belphoebe, his name for the queen in her private capacity as "a most vertuous and beautifull Lady," upon his patron's compliment to Elizabeth as goddess of the moon: "this latter part in some places I doe expresse in Belphoebe, fashioning her name according to your owne excellent conceipt of Cynthia (Phoebe and Cynthia being both names of Diana.)" Spenser presumably refers to a lost section of the fragmentary manuscript of *Ocean to Cynthia* that preceded Ralegh's disgrace in 1592. Ralegh does speak of Elizabeth as Belphoebe in "The 11th [i.e. 21st]: and last booke of the Ocean to Scinthia," which manifestly postdates his fall from favor.[47]

In opposition to the way in which Duessa and Lucifera parody Una as a type for both true queenship and religious truth, Dame Caelia

[45] See Donald V. Stump, "Isis Versus Mercilla: The Allegorical Shrines in Spenser's *Legend of Justice*," *SSt* 3 (1982): 89.

[46] National Portrait Gallery, London, no. 7; attributed to the monogrammist H. See Strong, *Cult of Elizabeth*, pp. 74, 217; illus. 50.

[47] Agnes Latham, ed., *The Poems of Sir Walter Ralegh* (Cambridge, Mass.: Harvard University Press, 1951): ll. 271, 327. See Stephen Greenblatt, *Sir Walter Ralegh: The Renaissance Man and His Roles* (New Haven: Yale University Press, 1973), pp. 60–62; and James Bednarz, "Ralegh in Spenser's Historical Allegory," *SSt* 4 (1983): 49–70.

and her household embody many of Una's positive values. Just as Una attempts to teach "trew sacred lore" to the Satyrs (1.6.30), Caelia's "auntient house" is "renowmd throughout the world for sacred lore" (1.10.3). Unlike the gaudy splendor of the Palace of Pride, the House of Holiness represents a "true" courtly establishment that is well governed by Caelia as a place associated with piety and chastity. Its firm grounding in spiritual "wisedome" contrasts with the "weake foundation" of Lucifera's palace upon a "sandie hill" (1.4.5; Fig. 10). The porter of the House of Holiness, Humiltá, shares Una's virtue of humility in contrast to Lucifera's gentleman usher, Vanitie.[48] Although Caelia's fortresslike gate is locked "for feare of many foes," Humiltá freely admits the few saved souls who knock (1.10.5; see Matt. 7:7), unlike Ignaro, who cannot open the doors of Orgoglio's Castle. Reverence's rejection of courtly "nicetie" in favor of a plain speaking style and "comely sad attire" confer upon him a ministerial "demeanure" appropriate to one who guides Una into the presence of Caelia, who instinctively greets her visitor as one "Whom well she knew to spring from heavenly race" (sts. 7–8).

Una may be only a visitor at the House of Holiness, but Fidelia's visual appearance establishes that she is Una's double as a queenly type. As a personification of Una's attribute of fidelity, Fidelia has a kindred standing as a figure for the "true" church (see st. 15 on the interrelationship of faith and truth). An elaborate iconic portrait anticipates the unveiling of Una at the royal court of Eden by presenting Fidelia's white-clad appearance ("She was araied all in lily white"; st. 13) as an emanation of celestial revelation:

> Like sunny beames threw from her Christall face,
> That could have dazd the rash beholders sight,
> And round about her head did shine like heavens light.
>
> (st. 12)

Spenser assimilates traditional Christian imagery into Fidelia's portrayal with an aureole akin to the elaborate nimbus of the Virgin Mary, whom medieval artists and theologians associated with Holy Church.[49]

Fidelia's carrying of a Bible or New Testament is closely tied to queenly iconography. Although symbolic books also appear in medieval and Renaissance images of saints and other pious women, they were linked closely to Elizabeth as a Protestant queen. The in-

---

[48] See Cain, *Praise in "The Faerie Queene,"* p. 75; and *FQ*, ed. Hamilton, 1.10.3n.

[49] Alma is another queenly type who wears a "robe of lilly white" and is "crowned with a garland of sweete Rosiere" (2.9.19). On her grounding in the Bible and Protestant scriptural commentary, see Hume, *Protestant Poet*, pp. 122–24.

clusion of Elizabeth's portrait on the title pages of the Bishops' Bible was modeled on the use of the Bible as a royalist emblem during the reigns of Henry VIII and Edward VI, when portraits of kings bearing the scriptures appeared in the Coverdale Bible, the Great Bible, and other translations. The depiction of Faith as the "bearer" of an open Bible in the 1568 Bishops' Bible parallels the portrayal of Fidelia (Fig. 16). As a Protestant variation of her traditional representation with a cross and chalice, the woodcut portrayal of Faith holding an open copy of the scriptures and a cross constitutes an endorsement of the reformist insistence on the free circulation of the vernacular Bible.[50] (Fidelia retains the chalice but not the cross.) Poised between flanking female personifications of faith and charity, the queen's image clearly completes St. Paul's triad of theological virtues (see above, pp. 121–23).

The unveiling of Una furnishes a prototype for the revelation of virtue in a cluster of related monarchal types including Prince Arthur, Artegall, and Britomart. Arthur appears as a solar figure at his first encounter with Una:

> His glitterand armour shined farre away,
> Like glauncing light of *Phoebus* brightest ray.

> (1.7.29)

The corona around his gilded helmet gives him the appearance of "a sun god, specifically a *Sol iustitiae*."[51] By outshining the sun, "As when a cloud his beames doth over-lay" (st. 34), Arthur's shield assimilates the imagery of the pagan shield of Aeneas with the "sunnebright shield" of Christian faith (1.11.40) at the same time that it identifies the prince as an agent of divine justice.[52] Spenser typically associates a sunburst with the unveiling of Prince Arthur's enchanted shield in battle against idolatry. Thus its blinding light defeats Orgoglio:

> that heavens light did pas,
> Such blazing brightnesse through the aier threw,
> That eye mote not the same endure to vew.

> (1.8.19)

---

[50] See above, pp. 63–64; and King, *Tudor Royal Iconography*, pp. 105–7. The "book is an attribute which Faith shares with Truth," according to Chew, *Pilgrimage*, p. 128.

[51] Douglas Brooks–Davies, *Spenser's "Faerie Queene": A Critical Commentary on Books I and II* (Manchester: Manchester University Press, 1977), p. 75. On the application of the biblical figure of the "sun of justice" as a Tudor symbol, see Sydney Anglo, *Spectacle, Pageantry, and Early Tudor Policy* (Oxford: Clarendon Press, 1969), pp. 79–83; and King, *Tudor Royal Iconography*, pp. 36–37.

[52] See Gilman, pp. 64–65.

The Souldan meets his defeat when Arthur withdraws the "vaile, which did his powrefull light empeach" (5.8.37). This syncretic figure mixes pagan and Christian imagery in a reversal of the solar symbolism of Philip II's impresa, which portrays Apollo driving the chariot of the sun over both sea and land as a symbol of his mission to spread faith across the pagan world. Spenser inverts Hapsburg iconography by identifying the fraudulent Souldan with Phaeton's destruction by the thunderbolt of Jove.[53] The sun similarly appears as a device on the shield of Artegall, who, in Britomart's initial vision of him in Merlin's mirror, is seen to look "foorth, as *Phoebus* face out of the east" (3.2.24).[54] The etymology of Artegall's name relates him to the prince whom he "equals."

Britomart is labeled as a type for Elizabeth by her name ("martial Britoness"), by her dream at Isis Church, and by the virginity and chastity that she shares with the queen.[55] The chief priest of the Isis cult rightly interprets her "vision" as a revelation that her warlike arms mask her "royall blood" because she travels in disguise that is designed, like that of Una, to protect rather than deceive. She is presented as the ancestress of Queen Elizabeth (3.4.3). Like Elizabeth, she is the heir to a "Crowne" and a worthy giver of "royall gifts of gold and silver wrought" (5.7.20–24). Britomart's encounters with parodic "queens" infuse considerations of chastity and religious faith into episodes concerning government. At the Castle Joyeous, she fends off the false chatelaine, Malecasta, whose ostentatious state recalls Duessa's infidelity and prideful wearing of a *"Persian mitre"* (1.2.13). John Dixon notes a connection to the religious allegory of Book 1 when he glosses Malecasta both as "Duessa; or falshood" and as "duessa im'odeste luste" (Dixon, *Commentary* 3.1.47n, 3.1.57n). Malecasta's posture recalls Lucifera's enthronement and the languorous ease of Acrasia's "bed of Roses" (2.12.77) as she sits

> on a sumptuous bed,
> That glistered all with gold and glorious shew,
> As the proud *Persian* Queenes accustomed.
>
> (3.1.41)

---

[53] See *FQ*, ed. Hamilton, 5.8.37–38nn; and Apteker, *Icons of Justice*, pp. 82–83. See also René Graziani, "Philip II's 'Impresa' and Spenser's Souldan," *JWCI* 27 (1964): 322–24.

[54] See Wells, *Spenser's "Faerie Queene" and the Cult of Elizabeth*, pp. 84–86.

[55] Chastity acquired a religio-political dimension during the reign of Elizabeth when apologists transferred the symbolism of Petrarch's *Triumph of Chastity* to the queen and her conflict with Rome (Yates, *Astraea*, pp. 113–15, 215–16). See Wells, *Spenser's "Faerie Queene" and the Cult of Elizabeth*, pp. 84–85.

Unlike the removal of armor by Redcrosse and Verdant, actions that signify their respective conquest by Duessa and Acrasia, Britomart's "disrobing" at Castle Joyeous is a chaste act that incites passion incapable of fulfillment in Malecasta. When Britomart removes her armor, by way of contrast, her kinship to Una (and Fidelia) is established by the imagery of the sun bursting through a cloud-like veil as a symbol of chastity or concord.[56] At the removal of her helmet, for example,

> Her golden locks, that were in tramels gay
> Upbounden, did them selves adowne display,
> And raught unto her heeles; like sunny beames,
> That in a cloud their light did long time stay,
> That vapour vaded, shew their golden gleames,
> And through the persant aire shoote forth their azure streames.

> (3.9.20)

When during battle Artegall shears away her armored neckpiece,

> her yellow heare
> Having through stirring loosd their wonted band,
> Like to a golden border did appeare.

> (4.6.20)

The martial maiden personifies militant chastity akin to that of Elizabeth, to whom men were obligated to submit. (Her unveiling reverses Acrasia's retention of a "vele of silke and silver thin" [2.12.77] in an act of false modesty that is actually intended to incite desire.)

Britomart exposes the perversity of yet another false queen when she defeats Radigund, the ruler of the Amazons who embodies abuses of female government of the kind that John Knox assailed, shortly before Elizabeth's accession, in the *The First Blast of the Trumpet against the Monstruous Regiment of Women* (Geneva, 1558). Radigund's injustice calls into question the right of women to govern and the very legitimacy of the Elizabethan regime, not least in her status as a dark double of Britomart.[57] The militancy of the Amazon queen resembles that of Britomart, just as her subjugation of men recalls Elizabeth's imposition of a Petrarchan code of romantic love as a means of political control. In explicit contrast to Britomart, however,

---

[56] Roche, *Kindly Flame*, pp. 56–57.

[57] See Louis A. Montrose, "*A Midsummer Night's Dream* and the Shaping Fantasies of Elizabethan Culture: Gender, Power, Form," in *Rewriting the Renaissance: The Discourses of Sexual Difference in Early Modern Europe*, ed. Margaret Ferguson et al. (Chicago: University of Chicago Press, 1986), p. 78.

"no hair falls" when Artegall removes Radigund's helmet after battle (5.5.11–12).[58] Radigund's disarming of Artegall, after his willing surrender, and her replacement of his apparel with "womans weedes" (st. 20), label her as a tyranness who shares Acrasia's habit of "emasculating" victims whom she has stripped of warlike attire. Although the Amazon episodes might seem to undermine the principle of rule by women, the narrator reverses himself to make an exception for queens like Elizabeth who succeed by just inheritance:

> But vertuous women wisely understand,
> That they were borne to base humilitie,
> Unlesse the heavens them lift to lawfull soveraintie.
>
> (st. 25)

This position is in accordance with that of Calvin and his followers, who disagreed with Knox by allowing that God may except certain outstanding women from the norm of masculine supremacy.[59] Spenser's comparison of Britomart and Radigund provides a cautionary portrait of the choice faced by Elizabeth (and other queens) between justice and injustice.

The argument that queens may govern as exceptions to the rule of masculine supremacy reaffirms the patriarchal assumptions of this age, paralleling the political conduct of Elizabeth and her predecessor, Mary Tudor, who governed England as "kings" and relegated all other women to submissive positions. Broad sexual comedy inheres in the resolution of Artegall's captivity, however, when Britomart repeals the Amazons' law of feminine supremacy and restores them to "mens subjection" (5.7.42). Susanne Woods observes that by conquering Radigund and liberating Artegall, Britomart becomes "the perfect ruler" who leads the Amazons "to deny women's rule. . . . [yet she] may be seen to continue female rule" over their land. Woods finds an example of Spenser's "poetics of choice" in his alternation of "the surface condemnation of woman's rule" with ironic views that may suggest "the potential for woman's authority." Here

---

[58] Simon Shepherd notes that "hair revelation" symbolizes the fusion of "feminity and knighthood," in *Amazons and Warrior Women: Varieties of Feminism in Seventeenth-Century Drama* (New York: St. Martin's Press, 1981), p. 10. According to his view, Radigund personifies a "version of the Catholic threat" associated with female rulers like Mary, Queen of Scots, and Catherine de Medici, by way of contrast to the English Protestant associations of Britomart (pp. 22–23). See also O'Connell, *Mirror and Veil*, pp. 140–41, 147, on parallels between Radigund and Queen Elizabeth's Scottish rival.

[59] See James E. Phillips, Jr., "The Woman Ruler in Spenser's *Faerie Queene*," HLQ 5 (1942): 211–34; and Cain, *Praise in "The Faerie Queene,"* p. 153. See also Pamela J. Benson, "Rule, Virginia: Protestant Theories of Female Regiment in *The Faerie Queene*," ELR 15 (1985): 292.

again, we see Spenser's habitual imposition of double meanings and apparent contradictions in an attempt to engage the reader in a dynamic consideration of alternative possibilities.[60] This pattern is connected to Spenser's dialectical opposition between iconoclastic destruction and artistic construction, a process in which succeeding perspectives correct what has gone before without providing complete closure. Although Radigund undergoes defeat and Talus slaughters her followers, Arthur and Artegall go on to pay homage to Mercilla as a "gratious Queene" (5.9.27). The implicit contrast between Mercilla and Radigund as true and false queens enables Spenser to develop his fullest analysis of the working of justice under the reigning monarch. The juxtaposition of the Radigund and Mercilla episodes incorporates issues involved in the contemporary debate over the ability of women to govern, which was a vital political question at a time when women were the crowned rulers of both England and Scotland.

The portrait of Mercilla as a "mayden Queene of high renowne" (5.8.17) represents the most complex royal icon in *The Faerie Queene* (5.9.27–50). The presence of a chained lion beneath her feet provides one sign that she is a positive antitype for a succession of false idols and parodic queens. In a reversal of the iconoclastic motif of the idol and the monster, the iconography of the monarch enthroned above a lion symbolizes the merciful restraint of absolute power.[61] The explicit contrast between Mercilla's sunlit court and the nighttime vision of Isis Church helps to define mercy as "a distincively Christian virtue . . . [that] is as far above equity as revealed religion is above pagan philosophy."[62] The opposition between Mercilla's piety and the portrayal of idolatrous observances in the succeeding episode further highlights her standing as a Protestant queen. In Canto 10 Arthur goes directly from her court to mount his iconoclastic attack against Geryoneo's Church, a shrine associated with hostility against the threat of Spanish Catholicism.[63]

By transferring the biblical and Neoplatonic image of sunlike Truth from Una to Mercilla, Spenser personifies mercy (a virtue decidedly absent from Radigund's regime) as a defining trait of Elizabethan

[60] Woods, "Spenser and the Problem of Women's Rule," *HLQ* 48 (1985): 146, 153, 155. Unlike Phillips and Cain, she concludes that Spenser "finds potential for rule inherent in women, not exceptional to them."

[61] Apteker, *Icons of Justice*, pp. 60–69. The scene may also recall the use of the lion as a heraldic supporter (Fig. 16).

[62] Stump, "Isis Versus Mercilla," pp. 87–88.

[63] See Cain, *Praise in "The Faerie Queene,"* p. 141.

government. Like Una, Mercilla partakes of the imagery of the clouded sun by virtue of the cloth of estate that shields her

> like a cloud, as likest may be told,
> That her [i.e., its] brode spreading wings did wyde unfold;
> Whose skirts were bordred with bright sunny beams,
> Glistring like gold, amongst the plights enrold,
> And here and there shooting forth silver streames,
> Mongst which crept litle Angels through the glittering gleames.

(5.9.28)

Mercilla's enthronement invokes the vision of divine majesty in Revelation 7:11: "And all the Angels stode rounde about the throne, and about the Elders, and the foure beastes, and they fell before the throne on their faces, and worshiped God." The scene recalls the rapt adoration of the angelic host surrounding the celestial throne, except that Mercilla sits "on high, that she might all men see, / And might of all men royally be seene" (st. 27). This paradoxical combination of the visibility and invisibility of royal splendor has theophanic associations,[64] because the transcendent brightness of divine radiance blinds even the seraphim closest to the throne of heaven, who veil their eyes with wings (Isa. 6:1–2; see also Rev. 4:5). Visual analogues to Mercilla's canopy appear in contemporary portraits of Queen Elizabeth (see Fig. 14).[65]

In contrast to the false grandeur of the Palace of Pride or Bower of Bliss, Mercilla's court complements certain values introduced in the House of Holiness. As "Patronesse" of the hospital of the seven Bead-men (1.10.44), Dame Mercie furnishes a prototype for Mercilla as a private embodiment of a virtue that Mercilla manifests in the political sphere. The residence of both Reverence and Zele at the courts of Caelia and Mercilla provides a tight allegorical link between the two establishments. Although Spenser varies the gender of the two personifications of Reverence, the "gentle Squire" who waits in Caelia's antechamber (1.10.7) and the virginal maiden attending Mercilla's throne, both figures manifest the devout respect for the sacred that is appropriate at a pious court (5.9.32).

The personification of Zele is twofold: he is both an easygoing freeman ("a franklin faire and free"; 1.10.6) at the House of Holiness and a dogged prosecutor at Mercilla's court. His characterization may allude in the first instance to the Lutheran conception of spiritual lib-

---

[64] Ibid., p. 139. Cain likens Mercilla's royal court to the Temple in Jerusalem and her throne to the seat of divine judgment (p. 138). See above, note 39 and related text.

[65] On the scriptural imagery of this scene, see Hume, *Protestant Poet*, pp. 136–37.

erty as "that freedome which Christ has purchased for us by his death" rather than the right to accept erroneous belief or to practice unlimited civil liberty.[66] The first Zele avoids the pitfall of religious "enthusiasm" when he guides Una and Redcrosse into the inner recesses of Dame Caelia's establishment.[67] Their movement demonstrates the close association between ardent devotion to true religion, which specifically opposes irreverence and blasphemy, and the Protestant doctrine of justification by faith alone as Fidelia personifies it. The first Zele's presentation in the moral allegory of Book 1 is consistent with the role of the second Zele as a prosecuting attorney full of "earnest fervour" at Duessa's trial (5.9.46); in each instance their discourse is notable for its persuasiveness. The narrator points out the way in which the first Zele matches words to deeds: "in his speeches and behaviour hee / Did labour lively to expresse the same" (1.10.6). This bluntness resembles that of Protestant pastors in the *Calender*, Piers and Diggon Davie. When the second Zele manifests political justice rather than its ostensible complement, holiness, he is closer to a sophisticated rhetorician than a plain-speaker as

> a person of deepe reach,
> And rare in-sight, hard matters to revele;
> That well could charme his tongue, and time his speach
> To all assayes.

> (5.9.39)

There may be a trace of ambiguity here, because Zele's ability to "charme" resembles the use of magic by Archimago and Busirane (1.1.45; 3.12.41); but his devotion to truth marks him as a rhetorician rather than a sophist. The capital charges of incontinence, adultery, and "lewd *Impietie*" that the second Zele lodges against Duessa set up a stark opposition between religious ardency and idolatry. Her other transgressions include murder and sedition (5.9.48). Zele's allegations recall the crimes of Sclaunder, because the charges include "vyld treasons, and outrageous shame, / Which she against the dred *Mercilla* oft did frame" (st. 40). The pun heard in the earlier description of Sclaunder as a railing "queane so base and vilde" (4.8.28) echoes when "false *Duessa*" is arraigned as a "now untitled Queene" (5.9.42; see above, pp. 115–16). The names of Zele's fellow advocates (Kingdomes Care, Authority, Religion, and Justice) allegorize sober political and religious values associated with true zeal. Religion

---

[66] Luther, *Commentarie upon Galathians*, 2E6ᵛ. See *FQ* ed. Hamilton, 1.10.6n.

[67] These personifications assimilate the approved view of "zeal" in the New Testament (2 Cor. 9:2). The ease with which apparent zeal may disguise irreligion is noted in *FQ* 1.6.19, and *Mother Hubberds Tale*, ll. 491–93.

claims that Duessa's execution accords with "High Gods beheast, and powre of holy lawes" (st. 44).

The enthroned figure of Mercilla reduplicates the nationalistic image of Elizabeth in her presence chamber, variations of which appeared incessantly in woodcuts, seals, and portraits, and on coins of the realm:

> Thus she did sit in soverayne Majestie,
>> Holding a Scepter in her royall hand,
>> The sacred pledge of peace and clemencie,
>> With which high God had blest her happie land,
>> Maugre so many foes, which did withstand.
>> But at her feet her sword was likewise layde,
>> Whose long rest rusted the bright steely brand;
>> Yet when as foes enforst, or friends sought ayde,
> She could it sternely draw, that all the world dismayde.

> (st. 30)

Among the heraldic symbols surrounding the queen are the "Lyons and Flourdelice" decorating her throne (st. 27), which signify Elizabeth's claim to sovereignty over France as well as England. Featuring the royal lion, the scepter, and the sword of state, this tableau bears a particularly close resemblance to the seal of the Court of Common Pleas, which portrays the queen on the obverse and the royal arms and its supporters, the dragon of Cadwallader and greyhound of Richmond, on the reverse. These symbols flank Mercilla in the form of the dragon crest worn by Arthur and the greyhound worn by Artegall. Michael Leslie concludes that although Mary, Queen of Scots, was not arraigned before this tribunal, the seal image is symbolically appropriate to a view of treason as "a crime against the whole commonwealth" rather than the "individual monarch." The court had jurisdiction over claims lodged by ordinary citizens.[68]

While mercy has clear antecedents in classical and Christian iconography, Mercilla's portrayal may be related to other definitive images of Elizabeth, like the illustrated capital C in Foxe's "Book of Martyrs," in which the queen wields the sword of justice (Fig. 14), or the title page of the 1569 Bishops' Bible, in which the regal sword is detached from the queen herself as an attribute of Justice in the upper left (Fig. 17). The placement of Mercilla's sword at her feet, where it has tarnished from disuse, figures power that is reserved rather than

[68] Leslie, *Spenser's "Fierce Warres and Faithfull Loves,"* pp. 65–68. Henry VII introduced the Tudor badges of the dragon and greyhound to English royal heraldry. The dragon joins the lion as a supporter of the text at the base of Fig. 16. See also O'Connell, *Mirror and Veil*, p. 151.

denied. The contemporary testimony of Sir John Harington, the queen's godson, records that Elizabeth kept such a sword in her privy chamber. Regardless of whether a corroded sword was actually kept in the royal household, however, it was a conventional iconographical figure for a queen who claimed to prefer peace to bloodshed or war.[69] Her weapon is antithetical to the rusty keys that Ignaro surrenders to Prince Arthur, however, because the queen's sword has rusted as a sign that she has chosen to reign in "peace and clemencie" (st. 30).

The presentation of Mercilla and her rusted sword introduces the thinly veiled topical allegory of the trial of Duessa, whose experience demonstrates that Mercilla retains the capacity of executing stern justice. The identification of these antagonists with Elizabeth, the Protestant queen of England, and Mary, the Catholic queen of Scotland, has gone unchallenged ever since James VI of Scotland (later James I of England) demanded that Spenser be "dewly tryed and punished" for defaming "himself and his mother deceassed."[70] John Dixon's topical identification of Duessa as a "fiction" for Mary, Queen of Scots (Dixon, *Commentary* 1.12.26n) recognizes a layer of historical allegory in the "Legend of Holiness" that is developed fully in the trial scene at the court of Mercilla (5.9.38–50).[71] The contradiction between the ending of the trial scene with Mercilla shedding tears (st. 50) and the ensuing execution of Duessa reflects the delicate political problem of attempting to bridge the gap between Elizabeth's public desire to avoid the beheading of a crowned queen and the insistence upon Mary's death by the Protestant progressives who dominated the privy council and controlled Parliament.[72] Mercilla weeps, yet Duessa stands condemned and dies. As a fiction of sovereign power, this image conceals whatever political machination lies behind the outward display of royal magnificence.

This episode's lack of resolution hinges upon the inherent reluc-

[69] William Nelson, "Queen Elizabeth, Spenser's Mercilla, and a Rusty Sword," *Renaissance News* 18 (1965): 113–17. For a portrait going back to the early part of her reign that depicts Elizabeth's attendant, Peace, trampling upon weapons of discord, including a sword, see King, *Tudor Royal Iconography*, p. 223, fig. 74.

[70] From a 12 November 1596 letter to William Cecil from Robert Bowes, as quoted in *Var.* 5: 244. See Richard McCabe, "The Masks of Duessa: Spenser, Mary Queen of Scots, and James VI," *ELR* 17 (1987): 224–25.

[71] Richard McCabe finds "narrative and thematic continuity" in the portrayals of Duessa in Books 1 and 5 in "Masks of Duessa," p. 227.

[72] David Norbrook analyzes the explosive political dynamics that Spenser attempts to reconcile in *Poetry and Politics*, pp. 136–39. See also Jonathan Goldberg, *James I and the Politics of Literature: Jonson, Shakespeare, Donne, and Their Contemporaries* (Baltimore: Johns Hopkins University Press, 1983), pp. 12–17.

tance of Elizabeth to undermine the regal claim to transcendent power by openly countenancing even the *possibility* of regicide. She faced special difficulty as a queen whose government as an unmarried female was virtually lacking in historical precedent (Mary I married soon after her accession), and whose virginity resulted in an unsettled line of succession. For Elizabeth openly to countenance the execution of the queen of Scotland would have undercut not only her own claim to rule as a divine instrument, but the legitimacy by which she governed as an exception to masculine supremacy. Instead of vacillating, Elizabeth decisively opposed the agitation in favor of Mary's death. David Norbrook attributes Spenser's sympathetic portrayal of Elizabeth's revulsion against "the ugly anti-Catholic campaign" and his minimizing of the execution to a deliberate effort to construct "an image of Elizabeth's mercy and compassion."[73] Even if her anger at Burghley and other officials was disingenuous, the queen's posture would have constituted a pragmatic displacement upon her counselors of blame for the execution of the Scottish queen. Surely Mercilla weeps, but her tears signify delicate awareness of political exigency on the part of both Elizabeth and the poet.

Spenser's equation of justice and mercy, which "meriteth to have as high a place" (5.10.1), complements the portrayal of these imperial virtues in the 1569 Bishops' Bible (Fig. 17). Female personifications of these virtues unite in the act of placing the crown on Queen Elizabeth's head in this well-known representation of Reformation queenship. The woodcut's identification of Elizabeth with divine revelation suggests an analogy to the Four Daughters of God (see Ps. 85:10): Truth, Mercy, Righteousness (or Justice), and Peace. (Prudence and Fortitude appear at the base of the woodcut instead of Truth and Peace.) Two of these personifications join the virgin maidens attending Mercilla's throne in a syncretic fusion of scriptural imagery with the pagan myth of the daughters of Jove, Dice and Eirene, who respectively signify Justice and Peace (5.9.32).[74] Guyon's recollection that mercy and peace may be seen in Gloriana's visage (2.2.40) underscores their connection to the cult of sacred majesty. Peace is the chief attribute of Cambina, yet another queenly type who possesses the ability to reconcile opposites (4.3.41–43). The interpretation of Psalm 85 in the Geneva Bible headnote as "a figure of Christs kingdome, under the which shulde be perfite felicitie" could have prompted Protestants to apply this messianic text to the new Israel

---

[73] Norbrook, "Panegyric of the Monarch," p. 81.

[74] Apteker, *Icons of Justice*, pp. 18–19; O'Connell, *Mirror and Veil*, p. 151. Iconographical evidence undercuts Hume's claim that it "would be a mistaken view" to conclude that Mercilla "especially represents mercy," in *Protestant Poet*, p. 133.

of Elizabethan England. The royalism of the image is traditional, however, because it had been used for many generations in the pageantry of queens like Margaret of Anjou.[75]

## Truth, the Daughter of Time

John Jewel begins his defense of the Elizabethan settlement of religion with the "old complaint . . . that the truth wandereth here and there as a stranger in the world and doth readily find enemies and slanderers amongst those that know her not."[76] Through the figure of Una, Spenser similarly associates Queen Elizabeth with the restoration of the true faith of the apostolic church after an extended period of spiritual exile. Unlike the timeless radiance of Fidelia, Una's brightness is cloaked, aligning her with the historical movement of truth in the temporal world. As a revelation of unadorned truth after a period of concealment and distress, her unveiling at the court of her father, Adam, exemplifies Spenser's alignment of the politically charged proverb *Veritas Filia Temporis* ("Truth is the Daughter of Time") with certain royal icons. This tag fuses a classical phrase with the text of Psalm 85:11, "Trueth shal bud out of the earth," which Christians generally interpreted as a reference to Christ. The related text of Isaiah 53:2, "he shal growe up before him as a branche, and as a roote out of a drye grounde," is glossed in the Geneva Bible as a messianic prophecy of how "Christs kingdome . . . shal growe wonderfully, and florish before God."

During the Reformation, warring creeds identified Truth with either traditional orthodoxy or the newly reconstituted Church of England. Father Time's welcome of his daughter, Truth, who emerges out of the cave of envy and calumny, was adapted as a slogan by Protestant partisans who supported Henry VIII's disestablishment of the Church of Rome. They claimed that contemporary changes in religion constituted an apocalyptic revelation of truth, which had endured despite the "distortions" of late medieval popular devotion. John Byddell includes a woodcut modeled on this tag as the frontispiece of a reformist primer that he printed on behalf of William Marshall at the time of the breach with Rome. It portrays Father Time revealing naked Truth, who has remained hidden in a cave, while a

---

[75] Gordon Kipling, "The London Pageants for Margaret of Anjou: A Medieval Script Restored," *Medieval English Theatre* 4 (1982): 20.

[76] Jewel, *Apology*, ed. Booty, p. 7; quoted in Kellogg and Steele, p. 23.

demonic figure hovers above (Fig. 19).[77] The polemical caption aligns this personification of Catholic orthodoxy with Archimago and the many parodic monastics who go by the name of Hypocrisy in Reformation interludes (see pp. 51–52). That Truth is generally conceived as a female personification made it an easy step to convert the iconography of *Veritas Filia Temporis* to the personal praise of Queen Mary and the abortive Counter Reformation that she fostered. Cardinal Pole greeted her accession as the revelation of Truth as "a virgin, helpless, naked and unarmed." The queen adopted the phrase as her personal motto, converting it into an argument for the validity of Catholic tradition that has been rescued by time from oppression.[78]

Although Elizabeth's choice of "Semper Eadem" ("Always the Same") as her own motto represented a perfect summary of her attitude toward religious and governmental policy, her apologists also appropriated the motto of her late sister, Mary Tudor, in a return to the standard Protestant use of that phrase.[79] The discovery of Elizabeth as the Daughter of Time provided a dramatic introduction to her reign when her precoronation procession passed before a pageant representation of the motto in the City of London. Spenser may have known the printed account of the pageantry, which had been prepared by his former schoolmaster, Richard Mulcaster of Merchant Tailors' School.[80] This tableau represented Father Time's emergence from a cave leading a girl costumed as Veritas, who wore the inscription *"Temporis filia*, the daughter of Tyme." The girl then presented Elizabeth with a copy of the Bible (*"Verbum veritatis*, the woorde of trueth"). The queen, who had already identified herself as Truth with the remark "Tyme hath brought me hether [sic]," actively joined in the spectacle. By embracing the scriptures, she also played the role of Faith, whose conventional attribute is an open Bible (see Fig. 16). The queen provided a living enactment of evangelical iconography

[77] Marshall, *A Goodly Prymer in Englyshe, newly corrected* (1535). See Charles C. Butterworth, *The English Primers (1529–1545): Their Publication and Connection with the English Bible and the Reformation in England* (Philadelphia: University of Pennsylvania Press, 1953), pp. 60–65.

[78] On the competing reinterpretations of this phrase during the reigns of Henry VIII and his daughters, see Fritz Saxl, "Veritas Filia Temporis," in *Philosophy and History: Essays Presented to Ernst Cassirer*, ed. Raymond Klibansky and H. J. Paton (Oxford: Clarendon Press, 1936), pp. 203–10; and Norbrook, *Poetry and Politics*, p. 38. Milton varied this symbolism yet again by arguing that Truth "was 'the daughter not of Time, but of Heaven' " (Norbrook, *Poetry and Politics*, p. 236).

[79] See King, *Tudor Royal Iconography*, pp. 191–95. For a woodcut portraying Elizabeth as "the naked Truth which Time has brought to light," see Yates, "Queen Elizabeth as Astraea," in *Astraea*, p. 80, pl. 11a.

[80] Norbrook, *Poetry and Politics*, p. 121.

**19.** *Truth, the Daughter of Time.* John Byddell for William Marshall, *A Goodly Prymer in Englyshe, newly corrected* (1535)

when she struck a dramatic pose as the restorer of religious truth: "But she as soone as she had received the booke, kyssed it, and with both her handes held up the same, and so laid it upon her brest, with great thankes to the citie therfore."[81] Fidelia's display of her "sacred Booke" at the House of Holiness (1.10.19) recalls Elizabeth's famous public gesture.[82]

An early Spenserian allusion to "Truth, the Daughter of Time" may exist in the woodcut for the "April" eclogue, where the solitary flower before Eliza may compliment Elizabeth as Truth budding "out of the earth." Although Colin's lay includes a catalogue of flowers and references to olive branches, these details are omitted in favor of the visual portrayal of a single flower in a tableau that incorporates mythological attendants (Muses and Graces).[83] The allusions in *The Faerie Queene* are more clearly demonstrable. Because Una is the embodiment of Truth as a faithful princess, Adam plays the role of Time at the royal court in Eden when he restores her to her rightful place:[84]

> The fairest *Un'* his onely daughter deare,
> His onely daughter, and his onely heyre;
> Who forth proceeding with sad sober cheare,
>
> . . . . . . . . . . . . . .
>
> So faire and fresh that Lady shewd her selfe in sight.

(1.12.21)

The punning repetition of "onely" underscores the uniqueness of Truth. In line with Elizabeth's precoronation pageantry, the conflict

---

[81] Mulcaster, *The Quenes Majesties Passage through the Citie of London to Westminster the Day before Her Coronacion*, facs. ed. James M. Osborn (New Haven: Yale University Press, 1960), C2ᵛ C4–D1 (pp. 44, 47–49). See note 50, above, and related text; and King, *Tudor Royal Iconogaphy*, pp. 228–31. Mark Breitenberg concludes that the pageantry for Elizabeth's entry into London "relies upon an essentially iconic mode of representation," in " '. . . The hole matter opened': Iconic Representation and Interpretation in 'The Quenes Majesties Passage,' " *Criticism* 28 (1986): 11.

[82] The queen struck a histrionic pose with the Bible on at least one other occasion, because Richard Vennard's *Right Way to Heaven* describes how she conferred "a Bible, Richly imbrothered [i.e., embroidered]" upon Charles Lord Mountjoy, Lord Deputy of Ireland, at the time that he set out to take command of her forces as the successor to the Earl of Essex. Verses interpret her action as a sign that the English policy of militant conversion of the Irish furthers God's providential design: "The Testament of Truth, this posie taught, / Given with hir counsell to that noble Lord, / Who hath in *Ireland* Gods glory sought, / By beating downe those *Rebbels* so abhord" (A2ᵛ).

[83] Anne Prescott has kindly offered this conjecture concerning the woodcut. Ruth Luborsky concludes that Spenser played a role in designing the woodcuts for the *Calender* in "The Allusive Presentation of *The Shepheardes Calender*," *SSt* 1 (1980): 53–57; and "The Illustrations to *The Shepheardes Calender*," *SSt* 2 (1981): 30–32, and fig. 2b.

[84] I. MacCaffrey, *Spenser's Allegory*, p. 226.

between Una and Duessa furnishes a historical allegory for the succession of a Catholic queen, Mary I, by her Protestant sister, Elizabeth.

In the first canto of *The Faerie Queene*, Spenser very wittily anticipates Una's ultimate revelation when Errour emerges from her den as a parodic *Veritas*.[85] Unlike Truth, who emerges from a cave, the monster is revealed when Redcrosse descends "unto the darksome hole" (1.1.14). Archimago may provide a perverse representation of Errour's father, because his appearance as an "aged Sire" in the *succeeding* episode inverts the iconography of Father Time (st. 29). The magician also plays the role of Hypocrisy (the enemy of Time's daughter in Fig. 19) when he subverts Truth during Una's visit to his false hermitage (headnote to 1.1.). Evidently, the moment for the apocalyptic revelation of truth is still far off. Although Spenser varies the gender of Time's offspring, royalist overtones remain when Arthur discovers from Merlin that he "was sonne and heire unto a king, / As time in her just terme the truth to light should bring" (1.9.5); Tudor historians like Arthur Kelton regarded this British monarch as the ancestor of Elizabeth. The position of Sclaunder, who sits "upon the ground" within her cottage (4.8.23), provides "a reminder of the chthonic aspect of slander" associated with the familiar portrayal of Time assisting his daughter out of the cave where she has remained hidden.[86] The narrator comments on the sojourn of Arthur, Amoret, and Aemylia at Sclaunder's hut that "antique age yet in the infancie / Of time, did live then like an innocent, / In simple truth" (st. 30).

Mutabilitie's rebellion against the realm where Cynthia "raignes in everlasting glory" (7.6.8) might seem to tarnish the glory of Elizabeth by subverting the figure of "Truth, the Daughter of Time." After all, Elizabeth was praised as the chaste moon-goddess, and the steeds who pull Cynthia's throne display Elizabeth's personal colors of black and white.[87] This invasion calls into question poetic assumptions concerning the timelessness of Cynthia. Spenser presumably worked on the fragmentary *Cantos of Mutabilitie* as Elizabeth was approaching the end of her long reign. Mutabilitie's standing as a dark double of the aging queen lends support to the view that the penultimate canto of *The Faerie Queene*, as it survives, contains "the eruption of all the suppressed discontent with the virgin queen that has

[85] See Brooks-Davies, *Critical Commentary*, p. 20.

[86] Anne Lake Prescott, "Sclaunder," forthcoming in *The Spenser Encyclopedia*.

[87] William Blissett, "Spenser's Mutabilitie," in *Essays in English Literature from the Renaissance to the Victorian Age, Presented to A.S.P. Woodhouse*, ed. Millar MacLure and D. W. Watt (Toronto: University of Toronto Press, 1964), pp. 31–34. See also Cain, *Praise in "The Faerie Queene*," pp. 181–82.

run through the poem." As the queen's life drew toward its close, the political anxieties that her mythology was designed to neutralize became increasingly difficult to stifle. Nevertheless, Spenser's acknowledgment of her mortality takes place on a cosmic scale that identifies her mutability with "the order of the entire universe."[88] This strategy may demonstrate the continuing impact of Petrarch's *Trionfi* upon Elizabethan iconography, because the victories of Death, Time, and Eternity inevitably follow upon the conquests of Love, Chastity, and Fame. It is important to remember that Mutabilitie's failed rebellion does not alter the constant attendance of Time, the "Old aged Sire," at the court of Cynthia as a virgin queen (st. 8).

Spenser's iconoclastic zeal helps to explain his reputation in the seventeenth century as a Protestant authority favored by Puritan groupings who increasingly opposed the monarchy.[89] Thomas Dekker's *Whore of Babylon* must have been met with patriotic roars of approval when, in the aftermath of the 1605 Gunpowder Plot, the playwright adapted well-known scenes from Elizabeth's coronation pageantry and *The Faerie Queene*, beginning with a show in pantomime portraying the queen's accession as a time of victory over the Church of Rome. "Uncrowned" Truth is revealed, "disheveld, and sleeping on a Rock," as her father, Time, enters carrying his hourglass and scythe. When Truth awakens after the passage of a pageant of friars, bishops, and cardinals preceding the hearse of a queen (evidently Mary I), Time joins Truth, who, as a variation of the Woman Clothed with the Sun, wears a "robe spotted with Starres." Newly awakened Truth then meets Titania, the Faery Queen, and presents her with a book symbolic of the Bible, which the queen kisses. Her counselors then reenact the primal scene of Tudor iconoclasm by drawing their swords and driving into exile the Roman clergy, with their images, croziers, statues, and other cult objects.[90] Dekker adopts Spenser's strategy of filling the space left by the exile of the Catholics with imagery associated with Elizabeth I, the Protestant queen of England.

[88] Norbrook, *Poetry and Politics*, pp. 152–54. See also Wells, *Spenser's "Faerie Queene" and the Cult of Elizabeth*, pp. 152, 155.

[89] Norbrook, "Panegyric of the Monarch," p. 71; and *Poetry and Politics*, pp. 60–61, 120, 198–99.

[90] Thomas Dekker, *Dramatic Works*, ed. Fredson Bowers, 4 vols. (Cambridge: Cambridge University Press, 1953–61), 2: 500.

# FOUR

## SPENSER'S ART OF MARRIED LOVE

### "So straunge ensample of conception"

BELPHOEBE'S STANDING as a personification of chastity is problematic because it tends to identify that condition with virginity, even though Spenser elsewhere associates chastity with marital eligibility or the consummation of love within marriage.[1] As an exception to the rule that the many chaste women of *The Faerie Queene* are either married or betrothed, she is an anomaly in a Protestant poem committed to celebrating married love. This divergence accommodates Belphoebe's status as a figure for Elizabeth I, the Virgin Queen of England, in her capacity as "a most vertuous and beautifull Lady" (*Letter to Ralegh*). Book 3, in particular, stands opposed to the medieval view that celibacy is superior to marriage because of the inherent sinfulness of carnal love. Because Spenser indicates the standing of sibling personifications by means of their relative age, Belphoebe as an elder sister appears to have higher status than her twin, Amoret, who arrived "in the second place" (*FQ* 3.6.4). Spenser may therefore seem to take a "Catholic" position by elevating the celibate life above wedded love in the mythic account of their birth. Nevertheless, the order of their birth may simply acknowledge that virginity always comes before marriage. Their twinship makes them more closely linked than are Dame Caelia's daughters, Fidelia, Speranza, and Charissa, who are widely separated in age. Although Belphoebe is eldest, Amoret participates equally in the innocence of their conception by Chrysogone:

> Pure and unspotted from all loathly crime,
> That is ingenerate in fleshly slime.
>
> (st. 3)

On one level, this allusion to the virgin birth represents yet another appropriation of Mariological imagery, but it also lodges the important point that Protestants accepted the humanistic view that *both* marital love and celibacy are valid states of life.[2]

---

[1] See Wells, *Spenser's "Faerie Queene" and the Cult of Elizabeth*, p. 74.

[2] On the association of Incarnational imagery with the twins' birth, see Roche, *Kindly*

Unlike her twin, Amoret is headed for wedlock, as are many other virgins: Una, Fidelia, Speranza, Britomart, Florimell, and Pastorella. Just as Amoret's career embodies Spenser's most extended consideration of married love, her twinship with Belphoebe explores the interrelationship of *eros* and *agape* as "twin" attributes of chastity that are to be united in Britomart. Amoret's name links her further to the consideration of chaste erotic love in *Amoretti*. The Incarnational imagery of the virgin birth that she shares with Belphoebe corresponds to the innocence of love in *Amoretti* 76–77, where the lady's bosom, the "neast" of love, is "exceeding sweet, yet voyd of sinfull vice." Amoret's commitment to erotic love participates in the displacement of the cult of the Virgin Mary, thus stressing positive aspects of sexuality. She is closer to St. Anne, who conceived sexually but without sin, than to Anne's daughter, Mary.

Although Belphoebe is a strong woman who vanquishes enemies and hunts with her bow and arrows and her spear, Spenser passes her over to choose the female knight, Britomart, as his chief personification of chastity. In pointed contrast to Belphoebe's withholding from love, Britomart is destined to marry from the advent of her search for Artegall, whose "image she had seene in *Venus* looking glas" (3.1.8). As the fictional ancestress of Elizabeth, this "Magnificke Virgin" embodies many of the queen's attributes as part of Spenser's epic purpose of dynastic praise (5.7.21). Her combination of the complementary sides of chastity found in Belphoebe and Amoret enables her to take over the role of Amoret's protector after the separation of the twins. As such, Britomart offers a means of analyzing the necessity that chastity include *both* virginity and married love. Whereas the female knight is "the champion of married love" in the 1590 *Faerie Queene*, she evolves into an embodiment of married love in the expanded 1596 edition.[3] We never do see her married, however, unlike Amoret, who is wed, albeit in a state of shock. In contrast to Belphoebe's impregnability, Britomart's dream at Isis Church centers on her impregnation by the crocodile-lover: "That of his game she soone enwombed grew, / And forth did bring a Lion of great might" (st. 16). The high priest of Isis interprets this vision as a prophecy of the union of Britomart and Artegall and her bearing of a "Lion-like" (i.e.,

---

*Flame*, pp. 105–6. He identifies Belphoebe and Amoret with "specifically Christian virginity and Christian marriage" (p. 103, et seq.). See also Mark Rose, *Heroic Love: Studies in Sidney and Spenser* (Cambridge, Mass.: Harvard University Press, 1968), p. 111; and Hume, *Protestant Poet*, pp. 126–27. Wells mistakenly compares Belphoebe's Christlike virgin birth to the Immaculate Conception of the Virgin Mary in Spenser's *"Faerie Queene" and the Cult of Elizabeth*, p. 52.

[3] Roche, *Kindly Flame*, p. 52.

royal) son. Her ability to control the crocodile and turn its "pride to humblesse meeke" illustrates the role of chastity in the control of desire (sts. 16, 23).

The anomalous aspect of Belphoebe's virginity invites the reader, almost automatically, to equate her unmarried state with that of Elizabeth I. The *Letter to Ralegh* defines the chaste huntress as the embodiment of the queen's private person as "a most vertuous and beautifull Lady." A gap exists, therefore, between Spenser's religious principles and his service to Elizabeth, whose "virginity conflicts with the broad sweep of the Protestant redefinition of the family. . . . He needs to celebrate his virgin patroness in a poem that elevates human sexuality to a sacred level and ennobles wedded love."[4] No dichotomy should exist, however, between Belphoebe and her counterpart, Gloriana, the titular heroine of the entire poem, because the narrator stipulates that Elizabeth may see herself "In mirrours more then one" (3.proem.5). The complementary aspect of the two figures invokes the constitutional *topos* of the "king's two bodies,"[5] wherein a monarch's political "body" is contained within a natural body:

> But either *Gloriana* let her chuse,
> Or in *Belphoebe* fashioned to bee:
> In th'one her rule, in th'other her rare chastitee.
>
> (3.proem.5)

Although the blankness and amorphousness of Gloriana are appropriate to the fluidity of Elizabeth's image, even the Fairy Queen's future presumably involves marriage, for there seems to be little doubt that she will eventually wed Prince Arthur.[6] (That Arthur will marry seems assured by the chronicle in which he learns about his descent from a line of British kings [2.10]; it was commonly assumed during Spenser's time that he was the ancestor of the Tudor dynasty.) The

---

[4] Quilligan, *Milton's Spenser*, p. 177. While it may be that Elizabeth's retention of virginity constituted a "political act" (p. 213), her celibate state was hardly "unique" (p. 177). See Keith Wrightson, *English Society: 1580–1680* (New Brunswick, N.J.: Rutgers University Press, 1982), p. 68.

[5] See Ernst H. Kantorowicz, *The King's Two Bodies: A Study in Mediaeval Political Theology* (Princeton: Princeton University Press, 1957); and Marie Axton, *The Queen's Two Bodies: Drama and the Elizabethan Succession* (London: Royal Historical Society, 1977), pp. 11–25, et seq.

[6] Norbrook argues that Spenser would have faced an awkward problem had he concluded *FQ*, because marriage would have challenged Elizabeth's "political supremacy" (*Poetry and Politics*, p. 116). Nevertheless, the treaty governing the marriage between Mary I and Philip of Spain provided a precedent for government by a wedded queen whose consort holds no political power. On this point, see *Statutes of the Realm*, 9 vols. in 10 pts. (1810–28): 4, i: 222–25.

ostentatious association of regal and nubile qualities in both Gloriana and Britomart makes it difficult to accept the militantly virginal Belphoebe as any *more* representative of Elizabeth than those other queenly types, or to invoke her as an unequivocal sanction of Elizabeth's virgin state. Although Belphoebe reflects Elizabeth's nature as a perpetual virgin, Britomart's commitment to wedlock may reflect a sense of nostalgic loss over the youthful queen's failure to marry and perpetuate her dynasty.[7]

Belphoebe's "vocational chastity"[8] offers a retrospective myth for the queen's failure to wed, one that postdates the collapse of her final effort at marriage. The emphasis on Belphoebe's remote untouchability during her involvement with Timias (3.5.18–55; 4.7.23–4.8.18) is particularly attuned to the circumstances of the last two decades of Elizabeth's reign, when she was praised increasingly as a type of the goddess Cynthia, who would never wed. Belphoebe's initial appearance stresses a different aspect of her character, however, when she participates in a broadly comic Ariostan episode involving the boastful coward Braggadocchio (2.3.20–46). The scene parodies the encounter between Venus, in the guise of a nymph, possibly a votaress of Diana, and her son, Aeneas, who greeted her with these words: "o—quam te memorem, virgo?" ("By what name should I call thee, O maiden?"). Trompart's words of homage, "O Goddesse" (st. 33), mimic the hero's response to his own question, "o dea certe" ("O Goddess surely").[9] Belphoebe possesses a "paradoxical doubleness" that combines attributes of Diana and Venus in a symbolic rather than a literal depiction of the queen.[10] The presence in her character of a Venerean aspect that reflects anything but perpetual virginity may identify this episode as either a survival of an early part of Spenser's composition, one written while marriage was still a realistic option for Elizabeth, or a representation of events that predated the publication of the 1590 *The Faerie Queene*. Indeed, the incident has been interpreted as an allegory of the queen's courtship by François d'Alençon, Duc d'Anjou, during her last serious marriage negotiations in 1579–83.[11]

[7] O'Connell sees Britomart as "a version of the Elizabeth who might have been, the Elizabeth upon whom the duty of marriage was so often urged in the first half of her reign" (*Mirror and Veil*, p. 88).

[8] Ibid., p. 100.

[9] *Aeneid* 1.327–28, in Virgil, *Eclogues, Georgics, Aeneid*, ed. and trans. H. Rushton Fairclough, 2 vols. (Cambridge, Mass.: Harvard University Press, 1924).

[10] O'Connell, *Mirror and Veil*, pp. 100–101.

[11] Ibid., pp. 101–3. See also Bennett, *Evolution*, pp. 49–51. On our inability to "prove" the presence of political allegory in the Braggadocchio episode and related sections involving Belphoebe, see Roche, *Kindly Flame*, pp. 97–98, 100. For a rejoinder

Composition of the Braggadocchio episode may have taken place close to the time when Hugh Singleton published *The Shepheardes Calender*, during the political storm triggered by the Anjou courtship. We know from Spenser's *Letters* that Gabriel Harvey had read a section of the epic by 1580, within one year of the *Calender*'s appearance (*Var.* 9: 17). The "April" eclogue disseminates an image of Eliza that is topically relevant to the contemporary debate over royal marriage. Her portrayal as an eligible queen is aligned in certain respects with that of Belphoebe in the Braggadocchio episode. E.K. identifies the "emblems" spoken respectively by Thenot and Hobbinol—"O quam te memorem virgo?" and "O dea certe"—as the same Virgilian allusion that Spenser applies to Belphoebe. The commentary explains that the utterance was made "in the person of Aeneas to his mother Venus, appearing to him in likenesse of one of Dianaes damosells: being there most divinely set forth." This allusion highlights the ambiguousness of Eliza's sexuality, because her likeness to Venus enhances her standing as an eligible woman, even as her affinity with Diana calls attention to the likelihood that she will retain her unwedded state. Piers's appeal in the "October" eclogue that Cuddie devote himself to romantic epic further celebrates Elizabeth's love for Robert Dudley, Earl of Leicester, and advances the possibility of his candidacy for her hand in marriage:

> Whither thou list in fayre *Elisa* rest,
> Or if thee please in bigger notes to sing,
> Advaunce the worthy whome shee loveth best,
> That first the white beare to the stake did bring.
>
> (ll. 45–48)

E.K.'s identification of this "worthy" as the Earl of Leicester reflects his knowledge of the Dudley device of the bear chained to the ragged staff. When members of Parliament and the privy council prodded the queen to marry during the 1560s, this royal favorite was her most eligible subject.

The *Calender* evokes the political milieu of the Anjou courtship, when Elizabeth was still remotely capable of bearing an heir to the throne. The text was entered into the Stationer's register on 5 December 1579, at roughly the time that the queen was facing the prospect of failure in her last effort to marry. (Desultory attempts at reviving the courtship marked the next three years.) Her taking of the initia-

---

to the widely held opinion that Elizabeth I took a vow of perpetual virginity at the outset of her reign, see John N. King, "Queen Elizabeth I: Representations of the Virgin Queen," *RQ* 43 (1990): 30–74.

tive with apparent eagerness after the arrival of Anjou's agent, Jean de Simier, in early 1579 suggests that she had every intention of wedding the duke, despite her recorded distaste for marriage and despite the opposition of powerful Protestant lords on the privy council who believed that the choice of a husband who was both an heir to a foreign throne and a Catholic would threaten England's religious settlement and its political autonomy. While Anjou was a pawn in the strategy of his mother, Catherine de Medici, to further an alliance with England, Elizabeth's main motivation was doubtless a desire to perpetuate the Tudor dynasty.[12] The prominence of Spenser's allusion to Dudley places the poet in the camp of the Protestant progressives who opposed the Anjou match, even though his patron's secret marriage during the previous year excluded him from any real hope as a potential mate for the queen.[13]

The appearance of the *Calender* during the immediate aftermath of the political explosion provoked by the publication of the most notorious appeal that Elizabeth spurn a foreign marriage, John Stubbs's *Discovery of a Gaping Gulf* (August 1579), may account for Spenser's last-minute alteration of his dedication from his patron to Dudley's nephew, Sir Philip Sidney.[14] Whereas the queen's anger over the appearance of this tract gave the earl every reason to disassociate himself publicly from the anti-Anjou faction, Sidney would soon go on record against the French marital alliance in a letter that he sent directly to the queen. According to Hubert Languet, Sidney withdrew from court because of his failure at swaying her. Even though this appeal recounts the manifold disadvantages of a match with a foreign Catholic whose family is tainted by its involvement in the St. Bartholomew's Day Massacre, he still adopts the stance that the queen should choose an appropriate husband and bear children who will be "the perfect mirror to your posterity."[15]

The contemporary assumption that the queen remained eligible *and interested* in marriage until well into her forties underlies Spen-

---

[12] Wallace T. MacCaffrey, *Queen Elizabeth and the Making of Policy, 1572–1588* (Princeton: Princeton University Press, 1981), pp. 254–66.

[13] See Norbrook, *Poetry and Politics*, pp. 83, 86–88. The present discussion of the "April" eclogue is generally indebted to Norbrook's argument.

[14] William A. Ringler, Jr., "Spenser, Shakespeare, Honor, and Worship," *Renaissance News* 14 (1961): 159–61.

[15] "A Letter Written by Sir Philip Sidney to Queen Elizabeth, Touching Her Marriage with Monsieur," in *Miscellaneous Prose*, ed. Katherine Duncan-Jones and Jan van Dorsten (Oxford: Clarendon Press, 1973), p. 57.7–8. Sidney's departure from court in 1580 was presumably the result of a personal decision rather than royal banishment (ibid., pp. 34–35). See *The Correspondence of Sir Philip Sidney and Hubert Languet*, trans. Steuart A. Pears (1845), p. 155.

ser's representation of Eliza in the "April" eclogue. It was not until
after the failure of Elizabeth's last effort at marriage, midway through
her reign, that the patriotic "cult" of an unmarried Virgin Queen
who would remain ever "wedded" to her nation took hold in offi-
cially sponsored propaganda, in poetry of praise generated outside
of the royal court, and in the popular imagination. How are we, then,
to interpret the praise of Eliza as "a mayden Queene" (l. 57)? Hobbinol's rendition of Colin Clout's blazon to Eliza obviously applies to
the queen iconography associated in the popular mind with the Virgin Mary:

> The flowre of Virgins, may shee florish long,
>  In princely plight.
> For shee is *Syrinx* daughter without spotte,
> Which *Pan* the shepheards God of her begot:
>  So sprong her grace
>  Of heavenly race,
> No mortall blemishe may her blotte.
>
> (ll. 48–54)

Although the ideological foundation of this lyric differs radically from
medieval hymns to the Blessed Virgin, the ostentatious allusions to
the Song of Solomon 4:7 ("there is no spot in thee") transfer the
iconography of the Spouse of Canticles from Mary, as Christ's
mother and his "bride" in heaven, to England's queen. Like Christ,
Eliza is the issue of a virgin birth. "April" exemplifies the way in
which Spenser fuses pastoral devices with patriotic themes, at a time
when the queen came increasingly to play Mary's role as the antitype
of Holy Church under persecution by agents of Antichrist.[16]

The argument for "April" declares that Colin's blazon "is pur-
posely intended to the honor and prayse of our most gracious sov-
ereigne, Queene Elizabeth." Although this eclogue was "a seminal
work in creating the image of the Virgin Queen,"[17] the French marriage remained a political "threat" (as it was perceived by the Leicester circle within which Spenser moved) until *after* publication of the
*Calender.* E.K.'s gloss cites the most readily accessible reason for the
synthesis of the classical myth of Pan and Syrinx with the virgin birth
of Christ. He notes that among other symbolic meanings, including
that of "Christ himselfe, who is the verye Pan and god of Shepheardes," the allusion to Pan refers to "the most famous and victori-

---

[16] L. S. Johnson, "Elizabeth, Bride and Queen," pp. 75, 82–83. See also Cain, *Praise
in "The Faerie Queene,"* p. 16.

[17] Norbrook, *Poetry and Politics,* p. 84.

ous King, her highnesse Father, late of worthy memorye K. Henry the eyght." What E.K. leaves *unstated* is more significant than his explanation of the Pan reference, because Syrinx must refer to Anne Boleyn, the mother of the queen who was executed on grounds of adultery during her daughter's infancy. Soon after her mother's death and Henry's remarriage to Jane Seymour in 1536, Princess Elizabeth was declared illegitimate in order to clear the way for the accession of the male heir expected of her father's third wife. When Elizabeth acceded to the throne as the "living symbol of her father's break with Rome," it was unthinkable that she would remain unmarried and fail to provide an heir to succeed her.[18] The "April" eclogue's emphasis on the queen's innocent virginity participates in the Elizabethan rehabilitation of Anne Boleyn from charges of unchastity at the same time that it defends Elizabeth herself against longstanding Catholic accusations of bastardy.

Spenser's praise of Eliza as a virgin queen is poised at a liminal moment in the development of Elizabethan iconography. On the one hand, it enhances the queen's standing as an eligible woman at virtually the last moment when she is still capable of marriage and childbearing; on the other hand, it may also be read as a covert appeal that she retain her unwedded state. Colin's blazon praises a marriageable queen who is on the verge of a decision to remain unmarried. E.K. acknowledges the eclogue's manifest concern with dynastic politics by interpretating Colin's iconic description of Eliza's cheeks, where the "Redde rose medled with the White yfere" (l. 68), as an allusion to "the uniting of the two principall houses of Lancaster and of Yorke" in the marriage of Henry VII and Elizabeth of York, who "begat the most royal Henry the eyght aforesayde, in whom was the firste union of the Whyte Rose and the Redde." The reunion of the two dynasties was an important feature of Tudor iconography until Elizabeth's childless death brought an end to her dynasty (see Fig. 15).

## Matrimonial Chastity

Spenser accepts the high valuation that Protestants placed upon marriage, as opposed to the idealization of virginity by the Church of Rome.[19] Nevertheless, it is important to recognize that the common

---

[18] Norman L. Jones, "Elizabeth's First Year: The Conception and Birth of the Elizabethan Political World," in *Reign of Elizabeth*, ed. Haigh, pp. 28–29.

[19] Davies, *From Cranmer to Hooker*, pp. 318–19.

view that Protestants (or Puritans) invented praise of wedded love ignores "the stress on mutuality within marriage" throughout Christian tradition.[20] Although Erasmus's *Matrimonii encomium* and other humanist texts anticipated the Protestant sanctification of wedlock,[21] such views were proscribed following the Council of Trent because they criticized the celibate ideal.[22] Because the international Protestant movement attacked the abuse of celibacy rather than its pure observation, however, Calvin observes that virginity may be as holy a state as marriage: "For they by the certaine Word of God are called to mariage, to whom the power of continence is denyed."[23] Belphoebe's character accordingly accommodates the *Book of Common Prayer's* sanction of the virgin state as a valid alternative to marriage, albeit one available only to some individuals,[24] and the absorption of Mariological imagery into her portrayal provides an enduring Christian figure for Elizabeth's decision to remain unwed.

Spenser's love poetry accords in almost every respect with the presentation of marital ideals in the *Book of Homilies* and the prayer book, much of whose language comes from the pre-Reformation use of Sarum and the scriptural texts that it employs. The liturgical revision that Thomas Cranmer originally supervised during the reign of Ed-

[20] Wrightson, *English Society*, p. 91. The earlier viewpoint is represented by William and Malleville Haller, "The Puritan Art of Love," *HLQ* 5 (1942): 235–72; and Roland Mushat Frye, "The Teachings of Classical Puritanism on Love in Marriage," *Studies in the Renaissance* 2 (1955): 148–59. Steven Ozment notes that it was a distinctively Protestant position "to set the family unequivocally above the celibate ideal and to praise the husband and the housewife over the monk and the nun," in *When Fathers Ruled: Family Life in Reformation Europe* (Cambridge, Mass.: Harvard University Press, 1983), p. 7.

[21] Richard Taverner translated a portion of the Erasmian text, *Ryght Frutefull Epystle, . . . in Laude and Prayse of Matrymony* (c. 1536) under the patronage of Thomas Cromwell. Its call for married chastity, endorsement of clerical marriage, and attack against the abuse of monastic celibacy (C1ᵛ–C2) offered support for the Cromwellian campaign to dissolve the monastic houses. Virginity is praiseworthy, in Erasmus's view, but not to the exclusion of marriage. The Protestant partisan Thomas Wilson incorporated a different translation of "An Epistle to perswade a young jentleman to Mariage, devised by Erasmus in the behalfe of his frende" into *The Arte of Rhetorique* (1553).

[22] See Bruce Mansfield, *Phoenix of His Age: Interpretations of Erasmus c. 1550–1750* (Toronto: University of Toronto Press, 1979), p. 41. The Sorbonne proscribed some Erasmian writings in 1526.

[23] Calvin, *Institution* 4.13.17 (fol. 89); see also 4.12.27 (fol. 82). Despite the divinely ordained state of matrimony, Heinrich Bullinger acknowledges "howe holy and excellente a thing virgenite is," in *The Christian State of Matrimony*, trans. Miles Coverdale, 5th ed. (c. 1546), E6ᵛ. See also Roche, *Kindly Flame*, p. 114.

[24] *BCP*, p. 290. On the introduction of praise of the "gift of continencie" into the second *BCP* of Edward VI, see F. E. Brightman, *The English Rite*, 2 vols. (London: Rivingtons, 1915): 2: 803.

ward VI also incorporates elements of the Lutheran order of worship and the Protestant church service prepared for Cologne by Bucer and Melanchthon (see *BCP*, pp. 352–54, 407–9). Although Spenser accepts the Protestant denial of sacramental status to marriage, in line with the view that "marriage itself is not an exclusively Christian act,"[25] the wedding ceremony at the center of *Epithalamion* reflects the favored place granted to wedlock by the prayer book's "Form of Solemnization of Matrimony." (Some radical Protestants countered that marriage should be little more than a civil ceremony.)

Because the Bride of the Song of Solomon was commonly interpreted as an allegorical figure for the Virgin Mary, the church, and the individual soul during the Middle Ages, the Church of England inherited a network of epithalamic imagery based upon the scriptures and mediated through the Roman-rite liturgy that was ready-made for transfer from the Blessed Virgin to individual brides. According to an addition to the Sarum rite in the *Book of Common Prayer*, the union between Christ and individual Christians is fulfilled in the married state because "holy matrimony" was "instituted of God in paradise in the time of man's innocency, signifying unto us the mystical union, that is betwixt Christ and his Church."[26] This viewpoint received broad support within the Protestant movement.[27] Spenser could have derived the formulaic praise of the virginity of Eliza, Belphoebe, *and Amoret* ("without spotte"; "No mortall blemishe may her blotte"; "Pure and unspotted from all loathly crime, / That is ingenerate in fleshly slime") either directly from the Song of Solomon or indirectly through the prayer book's encomium of the bride as a participant in "a glorious congregation, not having spot or wrinkle."[28]

A belief stubbornly persists that Spenser shared Queen Elizabeth's opposition to clerical marriage.[29] Little more is offered in evidence,

[25] Rose, *Heroic Love*, p. 80. The Church of England reduced the seven sacraments of the medieval church to the two ordained by Christ: baptism and Holy Communion or the Lord's Supper (Matt. 28:19; Luke 22:14–20). No longer included were confirmation, penance, ordination, marriage, and extreme unction.

[26] *BCP*, p. 290. See Brightman, *English Rite*, 2: 801.

[27] Coverdale's translation of Heinrich Bullinger's *The Christian State of Matrimony* accordingly declares that wedlock is "an holye mysterye or secreate of the Unyon and couplynge together of Chryste and of the Chrysten Congregacion"; republished in Thomas Becon's *Worckes*, 3 vols. (1560–64), 1: 3I1ᵛ. A cursory examination of Spenser's *Epithalamion* and Donne's "Canonization" disproves Alan Sinfield's contention in *Literature in Protestant England*, pp. 49–50, that Protestants "insisted upon disjunction" between love sacred and profane.

[28] *BCP*, p. 297. This part of the wedding ceremony follows the order of worship prepared for Cologne on behalf of its reformist archbishop, Hermann von Wied, according to Brightman, *English Rite*, 2: 814.

[29] See Whitaker, *Religious Basis*, p. 19; and Rose, *Heroic Love*, 111.

however, than Piers's echoing of Edmund Grindal's attack against those married clergy who attempt to emulate lay people by leaving large bequests to their descendents:

> But shepheard must walke another way,
> Sike worldly sovenance he must foresay.
> The sonne of his loines why should he regard
> To leave enriched with that he hath spard?

("May," ll. 81–84)

Although it is important to note that Piers does not attack clerical marriage per se, the abuse of clerical vows does consistently appear as an issue in Spenser's ecclesiastical satire. For example, *Mother Hubberds Tale* satirizes the worldly priest who boasts that "We be not tyde to wilfull chastitie," not because he wishes to marry, but because of his advocacy of clerical entitlement ("free libertie") promiscuously to share the beds of "our lovely Lasses, or bright shining Brides" (ll. 476–77).[30] His laxness is of the same order as the "whoredome" resulting from Abessa's failure to observe the vow of celibacy taken by nuns (*FQ* 1.3.18). Surely the quasimonastic practices at Isis Church cannot be taken as a call for a celibate clergy, because the faithful observance of religious vows that bind *female* priests to "stedfast chastity, / And continence of life" (5.7.9) wittily contradicts clerical incontinence, be it Catholic *or* Protestant.

Spenser's verse accommodates the position of Protestant clerics who countered Queen Elizabeth's desire for a celibate ministry with the argument that the unusual ability to remain abstinent was granted to preachers no more often than to laity. They interpreted St. Paul's strictures against marriage as a commendation of chastity, not as a rule of celibacy. John Jewel states the normative position of the Elizabethan Church of England: "We say that matrimony is holy and honorable in all sorts and states of persons, as . . . in the ministers of the church, and in bishops. . . . We say that a good and diligent bishop doth serve the ministry never the worse for that he is married, but rather the better, and with more ableness to do good."[31] Although some clergy followed the example of Archbishops Grindal and Whitgift in remaining unwed, the prominent marriages of Archbishops Cranmer and Parker (like those of Luther and his close associates) constituted a public declaration of the acceptability of wedlock and a rejection of the clerical vow of celibacy. It is worthy of note

---

[30] Anthea Hume overlooks this cleric's reference to concubinage by interpreting his bawdy boast as a reference to "his married state" in *Protestant Poet*, p. 18.

[31] Jewel, *Apology*, p. 29.

that Spenser's patron, Bishop Young of Rochester, decided to marry.[32] By way of contrast to the hostility toward marriage and idealization of virginity that Catholic thinkers derived from St. Paul and patristic authorities,[33] Peter Martyr argues that clerical marriage is permitted on the authority of "the primitive church," where ministers "had wives and used them" (*Common Places*, 2R1). As part of his argument that the "matrimoniall lyfe excelleth all orders of lyfe invented by man," Heinrich Bullinger criticizes the Roman church for slandering marriage and extolling the single life. His view of celibacy as an invitation to sexual license and depravity leads to an invective attack against hypocritical clergy who polymorphously practice "whordome, adulterye, incest, Sodomitrie, abusinge of theym selves with male kynde, embrasinge of brute beastes, etc."[34]

While emphasis upon "mutuality in marriage" is "part of the Christian mainstream,"[35] Protestants place special emphasis on matrimonial companionship. "Chastitie and cleannesse of life" are extolled in the authorized "Sermon Against Whoredome and Uncleannesse," which exhorts communicants, "whether they be married or unmarried, . . . to eschew fornication, adultery, and all uncleannes" (*Book of Homilies*, 1: 88). The wedding service in the *Book of Common Prayer* accordingly differentiates between chaste wedded love and the satisfaction of "men's carnal lusts and appetites." It declares that God instituted wedlock to provide for "the procreation of children"; to offer a "remedy against sin, and to avoid fornication, that such persons as have not the gift of continency might marry"; and to enable man and woman to live together in "mutual society, help, and comfort" (*BCP*, pp. 290–91). The homily "Of the State of Matrimony" similarly declares that the purpose of that institution is "as well to avoide sinne and offence, as to encrease the kingdome of GOD" (*Book of Homilies*, 2: 239), a goal that the reformers interpreted as a

---

[32] Judson, *Biographical Sketch of John Young*, p. 14.

[33] Juan Luis Vives exemplies this position in *A Very Fruteful and Pleasant Boke Called the Instruction of a Christen Woman*, trans. Richard Hyrde (5th ed., 1547), E1r–Fv, 2N2v.

[34] Bullinger, *The Christian State of Matrimony*, republished in Becon's *Worckes*, 1: 3H4v, 3I5v–6v, 3P4v; see 3N5r. John Bale contends that in the Roman church "were false wurshippinges commaunded for Gods holy service / and monstrouse buggery for a professed virginite / in our consecrate clergye admitted" (*Vocacyon*, ll. 544–46). Van der Noot's *Theatre for Worldings* declares that "wedlocke is called of them [the Roman clergy] uncleane, notwithstandyng it was instituted as a good and undefiled ordinaunce of God him selfe, no papistical vowes of Monkes and Friers may be broken, although it be sufficiently proved to be the most wicked and divelish and hath ingendred a thousande Sodomites" (H3v).

[35] Wrightson, *English Society*, p. 91. See Greenblatt, *Renaissance Self-Fashioning*, pp. 247–49.

means of reforming the church and reestablishing a well-ordered commonwealth. William Perkins acknowledges this social orientation when he states that marriage "was made and appointed by God himselfe, to be the fountaine and seminarie of al other sorts and kinds of life, in the Common-wealth and in the Church."[36]

## Amoretti and Epithalamion

By writing a sequence of love sonnets, Spenser joined in the Petrarchan vogue of the 1580s and 1590s that produced cycles by Sidney, Shakespeare, Drayton, and many others. Although Sidney follows tradition in filling *Astrophil and Stella* with the paradoxical complaints of the unrequited lover, he delicately parodies Astrophil's inability to impose rational restraints upon erotic desire. Spenser joins Shakespeare in violating convention, on the other hand, by considering marriage and reproduction in a literary genre traditionally dedicated to *unmarried* love. Whereas Shakespeare flouts romantic tradition by addressing sonnets to a male rather than a female auditor, Spenser strikingly addresses them to the woman whom he weds. The express concern of his sonnets with courtship and marriage—the yearning to "knit the knot" (*Am.* 6) pervades the entire cycle—and their conclusion in an epithalamium represent a radical innovation. In looking back to *Amoretti* from the perspective of *Epithalamion*, one may note a powerful emphasis upon married chastity.[37]

The title of the 1595 edition of *Amoretti and Epithalamion* indicates that these texts are to be read not as separate works, but as an integrated collection that is concerned throughout with the growth of love and marriage.[38] The circumstances of publication of this volume are related to Spenser's redefinition of imported genres in English and Protestant terms. William Ponsonby published the text soon after the arrival from Ireland of a manuscript "Written not long since by Edmunde Spenser." The wedding of the poet on 11 June 1594 represents a *terminus ad quem* for the completion of this work, and the

---

[36] Perkins, *Christian Oeconomie*, trans. Thomas Pickering, in Perkins's *Workes* (Cambridge, 1609), 3: 671.

[37] C. S. Lewis, *Allegory of Love*, p. 360, says that Spenser's emphasis on a "romantic conception of marriage" distinguishes his contribution to English love poetry.

[38] "Spenser became the first poet to climax a sonnet-sequence with an epithalamion," according to Carol V. Kaske, "Spenser's *Amoretti and Epithalamion* of 1595: Structure, Genre, and Numerology," *ELR* 8 (1978): 271. See also G. K. Hunter, "Spenser's *Amoretti* and the English Sonnet Tradition," in *A Theatre for Spenserians*, ed. Judith M. Kennedy and James A. Reither (Toronto: University of Toronto Press, 1973), p. 124.

manuscript had evidently arrived in London by the time that Ponsonby entered the text in the Stationers' Register on 19 November 1594. These poems were therefore ready for the press at the approximate time that Ponsonby was preparing to publish the 1596 *Faerie Queene*. (*Am.* 80 exhaustedly notes that all six books were finished.) The printing of each stanza on a separate page decorated with an ornamental bar at the top and bottom gives *Amoretti and Epithalamion* the appearance of a complete unit, an impression that accords with the tight thematic and quasinarrative links between the two works.

The volume is uniquely unconcerned with Spenser's incessant search for patronage. Although it stands alone among his works in its lack of an authorial dedication, that gap is appropriate to the personal character of a collection in which a fictional record of courtship and marriage has a close bearing on the poet's relationship to his second wife, Elizabeth Boyle. (Elizabeth is the name of the sonnet lady, according to *Am.* 74.) It seems unlikely that the absence of a dedication stems from the convention that the writings of a gentleman should not appear in print, however, because Spenser had long since subjected his name to the "stigma" of publication. Ponsonby's dedication to Sir Robert Needham, a military man who had served in Ireland, has no connection to either author or text, other than the fact that this cavalry officer crossed over to England on board the ship that brought the manuscript to London. Needham set off on 25 September 1594.[39]

Spenser's modification of foreign poetic models in *Amoretti and Epithalamion* displays the impact of Protestant ideology. The volume should bring Petrarch's *Canzoniere* to mind, despite any misgiving that the provision of a title leaf for *Epithalamion* separates that poem as an autonomous work. Given the absence of an imprint, this leaf simply indicates that Spenser's *canzone* on marriage differs in genre from the love sonnets. Petrarch augmented his own sonnet cycle with interpolated *canzoni*, in which long stanzas of equal length are followed by an envoi that completes the song. A. Kent Hieatt argues that Spenser may have decided, "not least as a non-Catholic poet and a 'Christian humanist,' to crown his sequence with a *canzone* for an earthly marriage and for the beloved with whom he saw love as a part of Christian charity, just at the point where the great Catholic

---

[39] See *Var.* 7, ii: 417; and Spenser, *Daphnaida and Other Poems*, ed. W. L. Renwick (London: Scholartis Press, 1929), p. 196. My argument is generally indebted to the commentaries on *Amoretti and Epithalamion* in Renwick's edition and in Kellogg and Steele.

had crowned his sequence with a *canzone* to the Virgin."[40] In line with the Protestant idealization of wedded love, this work displaces Petrarch's veneration of the Blessed Virgin onto a husband's love for his wife.

Spenser departs from sonnet tradition in his conformity, on the one hand, to Petrarch's long-forgotten ideal that love may ultimately transcend the shifting instability of erotic desire, and in his rewriting of Petrarch, on the other hand, to celebrate love that may achieve satisfaction though marriage in the temporal world. Spenser differs from the line of imitators who applied the Petrarchan devices of antithesis and oxymoron to explore the paradoxicality of romantic love without recognizing the delicate counterpoise that their master achieved in the balancing of discordancies.[41] Elizabethan sonneteers like Sidney and Shakespeare fail to reach the point where Petrarch turns away from the irresolvable contrarieties of desire toward contemplation of the unchanging world of heavenly love. In his later sonnets *in morte*, Petrarch, "though still a lover, conforms to the higher spiritual life—for medieval Christianity—of celibacy."[42] Although Spenser imitates Petrarch in striving to abandon the oxymoronic mode of the earlier sonnets *in vita*—that domain of cold fire and heavy lightness that defines "Petrarchism" according to later convention—his turn toward marriage challenges tradition. Although both poets aim at a transcendent ideal, "Spenser's concept of 'Eros sanctified' enabled him to use the *stil novo* motifs while avoiding the drastic either/or attitude that made the death of the lady the price of love's fulfillment."[43]

Spenser's modification of the dynamics of the lover's complaint to his cruel lady enables one to read *Amoretti* as a text that eventually transforms the Petrarchan mode. The stale conceits of Petrarchan paradoxy dominate *Am.* 10 ("See how the Tyrannesse doth joy to see / the huge massacres which her eyes do make") and *Am.* 30 ("My love is lyke to yse, and I to fyre"), for example, not because Spenser is unable to write good lyrics, but as part of an effort to parody the conventional stance of the unrequited lover. The adaptation of the clichés of the religion of love is countergeneric in the sense that Spenser *reapplies* them to a state of grace achievable only through married

[40] Hieatt, "A Numerical Key for Spenser's *Amoretti* and Guyon in the House of Mammon," *YES* 3 (1973): 15.

[41] See Leonard Forster, *The Icy Fire: Five Studies in European Petrarchism* (Cambridge: Cambridge University Press, 1969), pp. 4–8.

[42] Reed Way Dasenbrock, "The Petrarchan Context of Spenser's *Amoretti*," *PMLA* 100 (1985): 38–41, 46.

[43] O. B. Hardison, Jr., "*Amoretti* and the *Dolce Stil Novo*," *ELR* 2 (1972): 215.

love. *Am.* 22 provides a case in point in its dedication to the higher valuation of love directed toward marriage that characterizes the Reformation. The speaker affirms that the chaste purgation of his lust accords with Lenten devotion and self-denial. Because Elizabeth's saintly "ymage" is an idea within the "temple" of the speaker's mind, the worshipful service of the lover's thoughts, "lyke sacred priests," to his "sweet Saynt" dramatizes St. Paul's declaration that the Holy Spirit dwells within the human soul as a "Temple of God" (1 Cor. 3:16–17).

Spenser reassesses romantic love within the overarching pattern of the Christian year as one means of bridging the Petrarchan chasm between worldly and spiritual love. The imagistic and thematic correspondence of individual sonnets to the liturgical calendar for 1594, the year of Spenser's marriage to Elizabeth Boyle, provides an allegorical sign of the interpenetration of religion and love in *Amoretti*. Conclusive evidence exists for the presence of a central group of forty-seven "Lenten" sonnets whose limits are marked by the poems referring to Ash Wednesday (13 February; *Am.* 22) and Easter (31 March; *Am.* 68). The introductory and concluding sequences each contain exactly twenty-one poems. The central group corresponds precisely to the period of forty weekdays in Lent, when fasting is observed in commemoration of the duration of Christ's temptation in the desert, in addition to seven Sundays (including the post-Lenten celebration of Easter). As a New Year's poem, *Am.* 62 calls for the amendment of "our mynds and former lives" and avoidance of "the old yeares sinnes" in celebration of the Feast of the Annunciation or Lady Day (25 March), which still marked the beginning of the English legal year. More general calendric associations inform the sonnets that date the beginning of the courtship in January (*Am.* 4), and refer to springtime (*Am.* 19), to the conclusion of the first year of love (*Am.* 60), and to May (*Am.* 76).[44] Anne Lake Prescott demonstrates

---

[44] Alexander Dunlop argues that *Am.* 22–68 form a closely related Lenten group in "The Unity of Spenser's *Amoretti*," in *Silent Poetry: Essays in Numerological Analysis*, ed. Alastair Fowler (New York: Barnes and Noble, 1970): 153–69; and idem, "The Drama of *Amoretti*," *SSt* 1 (1980): 107–20. William C. Johnson points out that this group contains forty Lenten poems in addition to a set of festive "Sunday sonnets" (*Am.* 26, 33, 40, 47, 54, 61, 68) in "Spenser's *Amoretti* and the Art of the Liturgy," *Studies in English Literature* 14 (1974): 51–52. O. B. Hardison likens the three parts of *Amoretti* to "the panels of a triptych" in which the Lenten group resolves romantic conflicts introduced in the opening sequence and leads to a concluding sequence concerning fulfillment in love, in "*Amoretti* and the *Dolce Stil Novo*," p. 209. See also Hieatt, "A Numerical Key for Spenser's *Amoretti*," p. 23. For opposed views, see Josephine Bennett, "Spenser's *Amoretti* LXII and the Date of the New Year," *RQ* 26 (1973): 433–36; G. K. Hunter,

further that *Am.* 67–70 form a tightly interconnected cluster of sonnets that are informed by scriptural and liturgical texts appropriate to Holy Saturday, Easter, and the ensuing Easter season. She makes the convincing case that investigation of *Amoretti* "too exclusively in terms of the Elizabethan Book of Common Prayer" has led to the neglect of Spenser's allusion to the Sarum missal, related scriptural texts, and contemporary religious poetry.[45]

It is appropriate that a sonnet cycle so thoroughly dedicated to the idealization of married love should contain specific echoes of the language and rhetoric of the *Book of Common Prayer* and the Sarum rite upon which it is largely based. Explicit parallels to the collects, epistles, and gospels assigned by the prayer book are found in the poems for Ash Wednesday and Easter. The connection established in *Am.* 22 between a "holy season fit to fast and pray" and the lover's sacrificial "burning in flames of pure and chast desire" parallels the dedication of Lent to fasting and penitence in the readings for Ash Wednesday.[46] The heavily scriptural language of the Easter sonnet (*Am.* 68) takes on the structure of a formal prayer imbued with the rhetoric of the prayer book collects.[47] It also anticipates the liturgical readings for the period between Easter and Ascension Day in both the Sarum missal and the prayer book.[48] The union of sacred and profane love in the speaker's call to "let us love, deare love, lyke as we ought, / love is the lesson which the Lord us taught" alludes to Christ's definition of the New Law: "This is my commandement, that ye love one another, as I have loved you. Greater love then this hathe no man, when any man bestoweth his life for his friends" (John 15:12–13). An intriguing note of anticipation may be inferred from the designation of this text as the gospel reading for St. Barnabas Day (11 June), the very day of Spenser's wedding according to *Epithalamion*. *Am.* 68 celebrates the betrothal as the initiation of a movement that will lead to a union of worldly and divine love in the closing marriage poem.[49]

Arguments for the existence of the Lenten group have been confirmed and extended by Kenneth Larson's documentation of Spenser's consistent use of the scriptural readings for morning and eve-

---

[44] " 'Unity' and Numbers in Spenser's *Amoretti*," *YES* 5 (1975): 39–45; and Kaske, "Spenser's *Amoretti and Epithalamion*," pp. 293–95.

[45] Prescott, "The Thirsty Deer and the Lord of Life: Some Contexts for *Amoretti* 67–70," *SSt* 6 (1985): 53.

[46] W. C. Johnson, "Spenser's *Amoretti* and the Art of the Liturgy," pp. 50–55. See *BCP*, pp. 108–9.

[47] Hardison, "*Amoretti* and the *Dolce Stil Novo*," p. 214.

[48] Prescott, "The Thirsty Deer," pp. 43–44, 56–57.

[49] Carol V. Kaske, "Another Liturgical Dimension of '*Amoretti*' 68," *N&Q* 222 (1977): 518–19.

ning prayer in the proper lessons of the *Book of Common Prayer* as a grid for almost all of the sonnets.[50] Larson argues that in addition to the 21–47–21 pattern of *Amoretti* as a whole, the poems fall into two sections that reflect the worship service in the period leading up to Spenser's wedding day. By reflecting upon the lessons for morning and evening prayer on 23 January, *Am.* 1 functions as a frontispiece that initiates an unbroken sequence of liturgical references that continues until *Am.* 75, whose language reflects the readings for Low Sunday (7 April), the first Sunday after Easter. Although other critics have read the opening line of *Am.* 4 as a celebration of New Year's Day, Larson finds that it alludes to the second lesson for evening prayer on 26 January. The couplet's view of the lady as a "faire flowre" accordingly refers to St. Paul's permission for a man to marry an older woman who has passed "the flowre of her age" (1 Cor. 7:36). The contrast between Elizabeth Boyle and her middle-aged suitor injects a "private joke" into the poem, according to Larson, because it is she who is young while he is old. The sober warning against "th'assurance that weake flesh reposeth / In her owne powre" in *Am.* 58 parallels the concern with human frailty in Christ's refusal to judge the woman taken in adultery (John 8:1–11; second reading for morning prayer on 21 March). Allusion to Philippians 2:5–12 associates *Am.* 61 with the epistle for Palm Sunday (24 March), just as *Am.* 66 is identified as a Good Friday poem by reference to the second lesson for evening prayer on 29 March (Philemon 1). After an unexplained break of nearly one month, *Am.* 76 initiates a new round of prayer-book allusions by reference to the "early fruit in May" in a poem dedicated to the third day of that month. The mixture of joy and sadness prior to the wedding on 11 June is appropriate to the final cluster of sonnets, which are modeled, in Larson's view, upon the scriptures for Expectation Week (13–17 May; *Am.* 85–89). This interval between Ascension Day and Whitsunday is a period of liturgical anticipation that parallels the lover's plaintive "expectation" in *Am.* 87. This season of the church year commemorates the anticipation by the apostles of the descent of the Holy Spirit on Pentecost.

The opening sequence (*Am.* 1–21) initiates Spenser's modification of Petrarch's treatment of the lady as "a visionary instrument in the Platonic mode" by joining spiritual love to romantic union in the temporal world.[51] Conventional hyperbole colors the portrayal of

---

[50] I am indebted to Larson's forthcoming book, *"To Knit the Knot": An Account of Spenser's "Amoretti,"* from which he has given permission to cite several examples.

[51] John D. Bernard, "Spenserian Pastoral and the *Amoretti*," *ELH* 47 (1980): 422. O. B. Hardison observes, in "*Amoretti* and the *Dolce Stil Novo*," p. 215, that Spenser

Elizabeth both in this section and in the Lenten group as one who is unmoved by the lover's appeals, but it also suggests a corrective aspect whereby she is an uplifting spiritual agent capable of inspiring his "fraile spirit" away from the "basenesse" of lust (*Am.* 3). (Astrophil, of course, stands in a corrective relationship to Stella, but his corrections are ironic versions of typical Petrarchan conventions, and they are not given a theological cast.[52]) From the early stages of the courtship, the suitor exculpates the lady's "self-pleasing pride" (*Am.* 5) on the ground that this trait actually manifests constancy that spurs him to look beyond "lusts of baser kynd" to the "chast affects" of wedlock "that naught but death can sever" (*Am.* 6). The poet's stock exercise at discovering "to what I might compare / those powrefull eies, which lighten my dark spright" results in the lady's identification with heavenly grace as a counterforce to human self-sufficiency and as a means of spiritual illumination that "doth lighten all that here we see" (*Am.* 9). *Am.* 13 highlights a theological explanation for her haughtiness by aligning it with the paradoxicality of the Incarnation, which provides a model for her "myld humblesse mixt with awfull majesty" and "lowlinesse [that] shall make you lofty be." By lowering herself to love the speaker, she may alternately rise higher along the lines of "Christ's exaltation, love, humility, and resurrection" (Kellogg and Steele, p. 454).

The Lenten sequence (*Am.* 22–68) plays a central role in Spenser's articulation of a theology of love that accords with Protestant doctrine concerning grace and justification by faith. The lady's condemnation for "th'assurance that weake flesh reposeth / In her owne powre" (*Am.* 58) builds upon a thick texture of biblical admonitions concerning the frailty of the flesh.[53] Her spiritual autonomy carries the stamp of original sin, and this sonnet accordingly censures her pride as an impediment to true faith dedicated to the love of God—or man. Nevertheless, the contrary movement of *Am.* 59 reveals that her apparent pride actually represents proper "assurance" (contemporary Protestants used this term to define election).[54] This palinode emphasizes faith, predestination, and the individual's total dependence upon external grace rather than free will. *Am.* 61 argues that what may have appeared to be "pride" is actually the spiritual elevation of one who

---

joins together "the 'cruel fair' and *donna angelicata* motifs" that Petrarch associated with the living and the dead Laura respectively.

[52] Here and elsewhere in this discussion of *Amoretti*, I am indebted to conversations with Anne E. Imbrie.

[53] See 1 Cor. 10:12, 2 Cor. 1:9, 1 Peter 1:24 (*Var.* 7, ii: 439), and Isa. 40:6.

[54] Sinfield, *Literature in Protestant England*, p. 67. See also Bernard, "Spenserian Pastoral and the *Amoretti*," p. 424.

is "divinely wrought, / and of the brood of Angels hevenly borne."
"Fayth" in married love wherein "spotlesse pleasure builds her sacred bowre" (*Am.* 65) parallels the justifying faith of Protestant salvation theology. The lady imitates Christ's redemptive sacrifice in the Good Friday sonnet when she "stoup[s] unto so lowly state" to return her suitor's love; the mutuality of their feeling mirrors the reciprocal operation of grace and faith:

> for now your light doth more it selfe dilate,
> and in my darknesse greater doth appeare.
> Yet since your light hath once enlumind me,
> with my reflex yours shall encreased be.
>
> (*Am.* 66)

The explicit concern with "election" in *Am.* 84 aligns the speaker's ultimate assurance of fulfillment in wedlock, when contemplation of the lady in "pure affections" and "modest thoughts" displaces "filthy lustfull fyre," with the pleasures of those faithful souls who are the recipients of the providential gift of salvation (see Kellogg and Steele, note to *Am* 84).

Only recently has "Lyke as a huntsman after weary chace" (*Am.* 67) been related convincingly to the liturgy for Holy Saturday, despite its proximity to the climactic Easter sonnet. Its literary connections have instead been traced to antecedents in Renaissance love poetry. In a reversal of the standard expectation that sonnet ladies should remain aloof (Shakespeare's "dark lady" is a comically promiscuous exception), Elizabeth accepts her suitor in Spenser's adaptation of the conventional use of the deer hunt as a poetic conceit for romantic pursuit. Although Petrarch's "Una candida cerva sopra l'erba"[55] and its rewriting by Wyatt, "Whoso list to hunt, I know where is an hind," are immediately recognizable as the best-known models for *Am.* 67, Spenser's sonnet differs from these poems in almost every respect except the celebration of the loved one's virtuous chastity. Because Laura was married, the "white doe" envisioned by Petrarch has been set "free" ("libera") in the sense of being bound by the laws of Caesar (i.e., God) concerning chaste marriage.[56] The diamond collars in the poems by Petrarch and Wyatt indicate that the deer wearing them are obedient to Caesar, who protects them from hunters. Wyatt develops a hunting conceit that is no more than im-

---

[55] Robert M. Durling, ed. and trans., *Petrarch's Lyric Poems: The "Rime sparse" and Other Lyrics* (Cambridge, Mass.: Harvard University Press, 1976), "Canzoniere" 190.

[56] Prescott, "The Thirsty Deer," pp. 33–35.

plicit in the original in order "to amplify despair at failure,"[57] and he transforms Petrarch's explicitly Christian context by inviting the reader to liken the deer's wildness to her fidelity to a worldly Caesar (i.e., an emperor or king):

> And graven with diamonds in letters plain
> There is written, her fair neck round about,
> "*Noli me tangere*, for Caesar's I am,
> And wild for to hold, though I seem tame."

Her inability to be tamed connotes constancy because both the text and its generic context dictate that "wildness means chastity and tameness submission to a lover's will."[58] According to tradition, Wyatt's sonnet alludes to the love relationship between Henry VIII and his second wife, Anne Boleyn.

Spenser reorients the conventional relationship between the suitor and the sonnet lady by frankly dedicating *Am. 67* to the eventual fulfillment of erotic desire. The "gentle deare" surrenders out of "her owne goodwill," in implicit contrast to the prey whom hunters can neither catch nor tame. This acquiescence departs from the unapproachable remoteness of the deer of Petrarch and Wyatt. Unlike the "candida cerva," the Spenserian doe returns to the hunter's resting place in order "to quench her thirst at the next brooke":

> There she beholding me with mylder looke,
>     sought not to fly, but fearelesse still did bide:
> till I in hand her yet halfe trembling tooke,
>     and with her owne goodwill hir fyrmely tyde.
> Strange thing me seemd to see a beast so wyld,
>     so goodly wonne with her owne will beguyld.

Her paradoxical submissiveness must be attributed not to the successful suit of the amorous male, but to her own change of heart and willing participation in a delicate act of self-conquest.

Anne Lake Prescott has recently shown that the religious associations of *Am. 67* are at least as important, if not more profound, than its connection to secular verse. She demonstrates that the closest known parallel to Spenser's combination of a hunter who "chases the deer with dogs, gives up, sits down by water to rest, and then finds the deer comes to him to be bound" is found in Marguerite de Navarre's "Un jeune Veneur demandoit," the sixth poem in her *Chan-*

---

[57] Alastair Fowler, *Conceitful Thought: The Interpretation of English Renaissance Poems* (Edinburgh: Edinburgh University Press, 1975), p. 4.

[58] Ibid., p. 6.

*sons spirituelles* (1547). It seems either that Spenser was aware of these verses or that he "independently arrived at a similar conceit with similar religious implications embedded in a similar series of poems with seasonal and liturgical significance." In addition to this model for a Christlike "cerf" whose sacrifice figures in an allegory of religious faith, chanson 30 provides a prominent parallel to the thirstiness of Spenser's doe. The imagery of these poems alludes to biblical texts and to the Roman rite for Good Friday and the following days in a manner that provides a striking parallel to Spenser's linkage of the growth of love in *Am.* 67–70 to Eastertide. In particular, the deer shared by Spenser and Marguerite is akin to the thirsting hart of Psalm 42 (Vulg. Ps. 41), which is featured in the liturgy for Easter Eve according to the use of Sarum; St. Augustine records that penitent catechumens who were baptized at this time sang this Psalm on their way to the font. The allegorical interpretation of this deer as a type for Christ, as substantiated by Marguerite's chanson, is altogether appropriate to Spenser's timing of the betrothal to coincide with the anniversary of the Crucifixion. The liturgical context is suited to the fusion of human and divine love in *Am.* 68 because the "deer can be the accepted penitent or the yielding savior thirsty from slaying vices, or both."[59]

Spenser's emphasis upon the doe's surrender out of "goodwill" incorporates a refined theological nuance that enables one to read *Am.* 67 as the second half of a poetic diptych. The lady has undergone a change of heart since *Am.* 10, where she scorns her suitor "of her freewill." This accusation was highly charged at a time when Protestants attacked the church of Rome for subscribing to the Pelagian heresy, which denied original sin and affirmed the human ability to attain righteousness through the free operation of the will. The declaration "Of free will" in the *Thirty-nine Articles* fittingly declares that "we have no power to do good workes pleasaunt and acceptable to God, without the grace of God by Christe preventyng [i.e., coming before] us, that we may have a good wyll, and workyng with us, when we have that good wyll" (*Article* 10). The lady's acquiescence out of "her owne goodwill" accords with the right operation of that human faculty in accordance with divine grace, by contrast to the prideful state of *Am.* 10. Indeed, her surrender is Christlike as a completely free and gracious gift that bears no relationship to "the merit, improvement, or psychological development of the lover/speaker."[60] The lover may testify, however, to his faith in Christ—and the lady.

[59] Prescott, "The Thirsty Deer," pp. 37, 42, 46, 55.

[60] Ibid., p. 47; see also p. 44.

The prayerlike address to the "Most glorious Lord of lyfe" in the climactic Easter sonnet (*Am.* 68) aligns the betrothal with Christ's resurrection as an event that purges and renews human love, and makes possible its fusion with the divine:

> And that thy love we weighing worthily,
>   may likewise love thee for the same againe:
>   and for thy sake that all lyke deare didst buy,
>   with love may one another entertayne.

Addressing the speaker and lady as a couple for the first time, the couplet calls upon them to fulfill the "lesson which the Lord us taught" in the mutuality of their love relationship. This sonnet initiates a frank anticipation of the joys of wedlock in the postbetrothal sequence (*Am.* 69–89), which insists that sexuality may be innocent and chaste, as it was said by theologians to be for Adam and Eve before the Fall,[61] in conformity to the prayer-book vision of love that is pursued "reverently, discreetly, advisedly, soberly, and in the fear of God" rather than in satisfaction of "men's carnal lusts and appetites" (*BCP*, p. 290).

This sanctification of erotic love may be noted in two poems that revise a single sonnet by Tasso, "Non son sí belli." Spenser modifies Tasso's explicitly erotic blazon by chastely turning to the lady's "Fayre bosome" not through the speaker's eyes, but through "sweet thoughts" that wander to the "neast of love, the lodging of delight," where they find a "paradice of pleasure" that exemplifies the sinlessness of true sexual pleasure:

> And twixt her paps like early fruit in May,
>   whose harvest seemd to hasten now apace:
>   they loosely did theyr wanton winges display,
>   and there to rest themselves did boldly place.
>
> (*Am.* 76)

The "happy rest" achieved by these thoughts contradicts the restlessness of erotic desire according to Petrarchan tradition, as does the imagery of fruition and "harvest." *Am.* 77 extends this anticipation of the bliss and fulfillment to be enjoyed in marriage, for the lover's thoughts contemplate his lady's bosom as "twoo golden apples of unvalewd price"; her breasts are "exceeding sweet, yet voyd of sinfull vice."[62]

---

[61] See James G. Turner, *One Flesh: Paradisal Marriage and Sexual Relations in the Age of Milton* (Oxford: Clarendon Press, 1987), pp. 40–62, passim.

[62] See Dasenbrock, "Petrarchan Context," pp. 44–45.

In their interrogation of Petrarchan conventions concerning sexual discord and the paradoxicality of desire, Spenser's sonnets participate in a movement to unify all the genres in *Amoretti and Epithalamion*—sonnets, Anacreontics, and epithalamium—by passing from disunity and strife to harmonious resolution and cosmic harmony.[63] The transitory disturbance over the lady's absence during the three final sonnets may be designed to create some sense of suspense prior to the final union in *Epithalamion*. Although critics have generally expressed puzzlement or dissatisfaction at the presence of the Anacreontics between *Amoretti* and *Epithalamion*, those verses comment upon issues important in the collection as a whole; they may be designed to enhance Spenser's reputation as a modish poet by linking him to a vogue that members of the Pléiade had made fashionable. His variation of praise that Catholic poets had accorded to the celibate ideal may be noted in a parody of the "Hail Mary," where Venus receives her son's homage:

> I Saw in secret to my Dame,
> How little Cupid humbly came:
> and sayd to her All hayle my mother.
>
> (st. 3, ll. 1–3)

Alert readers would recognize the close translation of Marot's "De Cupido et sa Dame" (*Var.* 7, ii: 456).

*Epithalamion* represents the culmination of Spenser's movement away from conventional Petrarchan norms. The proliferation of epithalamia during antiquity and the Continental Renaissance attests that such "ballades at the bedding of the bride"[64] belong not to a new genre, but to a form that Spenser introduces into print in its English vernacular form, thus defining its structure and motifs prior to its rich and complicated flowering during the seventeenth century.[65] The conventions of the lyric epithalamium were well defined by the time that Catullus wrote "Collis o Heliconii," the chief ancient model for Renaissance poets. Classical epithalamia established precedents for the references to the donning of the bridal veil, the invocation of Hymen, the bride's emergence from her parents' house, the groom's anxiety about the passing of the day, praise of the wedding bed, fes-

---

[63] Kaske, "Spenser's *Amoretti and Epithalamion*," p. 272, et seq.

[64] Puttenham, *Arte of English Poesie*, ed. Willcock and Walker, p. 50.

[65] Sidney's composition of the epithalamium sung by Dicus for Lalus and Kala in the *Old Arcadia* (written c. 1577–80) and Bartholomew Young's translation (written in 1583; published in 1598) of an epithalamium in Montemayor's *Diana* predate *Epithalamion*. Spenser's *Letters* refer to *Epithalamion Thamesis*, an early experiment that is no longer extant (*Var.* 9: 17).

tive celebration, fescennine jesting, the bedding of the bride, and the hope for posterity.[66] Spenser also conforms to the practice of contemporary humanistic and Protestant authors of hexameral poetry who amalgamated ancient pagan formulas with scriptural imagery and Christian matrimonial ideals. Conventional elements include the bashfulness of the bride, the congratulation of vernal Nature, and consummation as a private and natural act.[67]

Spenser's innovative fusion of the roles of bridegroom and singer allows for a striking variation of the original locus for epithalamic song at the door to the bridal chamber (*epi thalamou*) because the singer moves not only inside the chamber, but *into the bed*. In joining the heretofore divided roles of the fescennine jester and the bridegroom,[68] the poet modifies the ancient purpose of the epithalamium, according to Puttenham, of allowing that "there might no noise be h[e]ard out of the bed chamber by the skreeking and outcry of the young damosell feeling the first forces of her stiffe and rigorous young man, she being as all virgins tender and weake, and unexpert in those maner of affaires."[69] Spenser's emphasis on the stillness of the night departs from the conventional noisiness of more explicitly erotic versions of this genre:

> Let no lamenting cryes, nor dolefull teares,
> Be heard all night within nor yet without.

> (*Epith.*, ll. 334–35)

The chaste consummation is likened to a mythographic event in which the bridegroom plays the role of Jupiter in the begetting of the great hero, Hercules, or (in a newly invented myth) Majesty:

> Lyke as when Jove with fayre Alcmena lay,
> When he begot the great Tirynthian groome:
> Or lyke as when he with thy selfe [i.e., Night] did lie,
> And begot Majesty.

> (ll. 328–31)

This syncretic fusion of classical myth with Christian matrimonial ideals emphasizes the correspondence between marital union and cosmic order.

[66] *Catullus, Tibullus, and Pervigilium Veneris*, ed. and trans. F. W. Cornish et al., 3rd ed., rev. (Cambridge, Mass.: Harvard University Press, 1962), no. 61, ll. 7, 39–40, 76, 105–7, 122, 177–86, 207–11. See Lewalski, *Rhetoric of Literary Forms*, pp. 190–91.

[67] Gary M. McCown, "Milton and the Epic Epithalamium," *Milton Studies* 5 (1973): 44–45, 47, 49, 50–55, passim.

[68] Thomas M. Greene, "Spenser and the Epithalamic Convention," *Comparative Literature* 9 (1957): 222.

[69] Puttenham, *Arte of English Poesie*, ed. Willcock and Walker, p. 51.

Although Spenser preserves the mythological framework of pagan epithalamia, his interpolation of a dense network of allusions to the Bible and the wedding ceremony is indebted to the modification of the genre by the hexameral poets. The scriptural models for epithalamia include Psalm 45, which was sung for a royal wedding, and the fertile gardens of Eden and the Song of Solomon, whose imagery of the fruitful vine, seedtime, and harvest infiltrates the matrimonial service. Some of the tropes drawn from biblical pastoral may be noted in the following verses: "gay girland / For my fayre love of lillyes and of roses"; "Wake, now my love, awake"; and "Hark how the cheerefull birds do chaunt theyr laies" (ll. 42–43, 74, 78; Song of Sol. 2:1–2, 10, 12). While models for the iconic portrait of the bride exist among foreign and native blazons, Spenser chastely domesticates the scriptural portrayal of the Spouse: "Thy belly is as an heape of wheat compassed about with lilies. Thy two breastes are as two yong roes that are twinnes. Thy necke is like a towre of yvorie: thine eyes are like the fishpooles in Heshbon by the gate of Bath-rabbim" (Song of Sol. 7:2–5). Spenser constructs a blazon that moves in a Christian rather than a Platonic direction by emphasizing the Incarnational and not denigrating the flesh:

> Her goodly eyes lyke Saphyres shining bright,
> Her forehead yvory white,
> Her cheekes lyke apples which the sun hath rudded,
> Her lips lyke cherryes charming men to byte,
> Her brest like to a bowle of creame uncrudded [i.e., uncurdled],
> Her paps lyke lyllies budded,
> Her snowie necke lyke to a marble towre,
> And all her body like a pallace fayre,
> Ascending uppe with many a stately stayre,
> To honors seat and chastities sweet bowre.
>
> (ll. 171–80)

The emphasis on chastity accords with the honor paid to that virtue in *Amoretti*.

Spenser's vantage point is akin to the allegorization of the Song of Solomon in many Protestant sermons as "the divine archetype which human marriage should imitate."[70] By using that book of the Old Testament as a poetic model, he aligns *Epithalamion* with a scriptural work that had long been regarded as an epithalamium *par excellence*. From the patristic age onward, scriptural commentaries assimilated the love of the Bridegroom and the Bride to the nuptial imagery of

---

[70] George L. Scheper, "Reformation Attitudes toward Allegory and the Song of Songs," *PMLA* 89 (1974): 556, 558.

Genesis 1–3 and Revelation, with the result that the Song of Solomon came to be read allegorically as a mysterious dialogue between Christ and the church or the individual Christian. Regarding the work as a poem in a dramatic mode, Origen's commentary develops a powerful sense of colloquy between the Bride (Church) and the Bridegroom (Christ) in the context of choruses of their followers, notably the Daughters of Jerusalem.[71] This reading was widespread during Spenser's time in both Catholic[72] and Protestant commentaries, and it was assimilated into the prayer book (see *BCP*, p. 290) and the glosses in the Geneva Bible. Gervase Markham's *The Poem of Poems. Or, Sions Muse, Contayning the Divine Song of King Salomon, Devided into eight Eclogues* (1596) exemplifies the replication of this view of marriage as a symbol of the mystical union, "by most sweete and comfortable allegories and parables," of the perfect love of Christ the Bridegroom and "the faithfull soule or his Church" (A7ʳ).[73]

*Epithalamion* parallels *Amoretti* in its placement of Spenser's love relationship with Elizabeth Boyle within the cosmic context of time and eternity. A. Kent Hieatt brilliantly documents the many overlapping layers of temporal and calendric structure in the wedding poem, the most significant of which are the presence of 365 long lines that duplicate the number of days in the year, twenty-four stanzas that imitate the hours of the day, and the alteration of the refrain to accommodate the shift to night in the seventeenth stanza. These numerological patterns support his thesis that *Epithalamion* constitutes an allegory of time in all of its aspects.[74] Because the seventeenth hour of the day was the exact time of sunset when his wedding took place, Spenser clearly localizes this poem in Ireland at his manor of Kilcolman. The reference to the "Nymphes of Mulla" who tend the "silver scaly trouts" and "greedy pikes" (*Epith.*, ll. 56–58) incorporates his poetic name for the Awbeg, one of two rivers that border his estate.[75]

---

[71] Origen, *The Song of Songs: Commentary and Homilies*, trans. R. P. Lawson, Ancient Christian Writers, no. 26 (London: Longmans, 1957), p. 21, et seq.

[72] See Cornelius à Lapide, *Commentarii in Ecclesiasten* (Antwerp, 1657): ⁑1–6.

[73] See the related interpretations in Thomas Wilcox, *An Exposition uppon the Booke of the Canticles* (1585); and Dudley Fenner, *The Song of Songs translated out of the Hebrue into Englishe meeter* (Middelburgh, 1587).

[74] A. Kent Hieatt, *Short Time's Endless Monument: The Symbolism of the Numbers in Edmund Spenser's "Epithalamion"* (Port Washington, N.Y.: Kennikat Press, 1960), pp. 8–15.

[75] "*Mulla* the daughter of old *Mole*" is the sister of "her owne brother river, *Bregog*," according to *Colin Clouts Come Home Againe* (ll. 108, 117). The streams of the Awbeg and the Bregoge descend from the Ballahoura Mountains to the north of Kilcolman (*Var.* 7, i: 456).

The enactment of the wedding ceremony at the structural and temporal center of *Epithalamion* provides a nexus of symbolic meaning: "The church of these two stanzas is the sacred space in which all time is seminally implicit. The center of the poem's territory is the *telos* of its movement." The shift from the "human anthem in stanza 12 to the heavenly alleluya in stanza 13" anticipates the closing movement of the poem, which places the couple's life within the context of eternity.[76] Described from the vantage point of the groom, the bridal procession preserves a measured and reverent solemnity:

> Open the temple gates unto my love,
> Open them wide that she may enter in,
>
> . . . . . . . . . . . . .
>
> With trembling steps and humble reverence,
> She commeth in, before th'almighties vew.

(ll. 204–5, 210–11)

The Psalmic reference to the opening of the gates (Ps. 24:7–9) incorporates the familiar interpretation of the Temple in Jerusalem as a type for the Christian church (see Geneva Bible, dedicatory epistle). The realistic references to decorated pew "postes," garlanded "pillours," and the altar where "endlesse matrimony" is celebrated evoke the ambience of an Irish church. The organ music and choral singing of "the joyous Antheme" that merges with the refrain, "That al the woods may answere and their eccho ring," indicate that Spenser sympathized with the ritualism retained by the Church of England (ll. 206–7, 217, 221–22). Many Puritans demanded a simple worship service centered upon preaching and the singing of Psalms without instrumental accompaniment.[77] The ceremonial and quasi-sacramental nature of the "sacred ceremonies" administered by a "holy priest" at "th'high altar" would have been incompatible with Puritan ideology during the mid-1590s (ll. 215–16, 223). The angels hovering around the "sacred Altare" share more in common with the ubiquitous *putti* of Continental baroque art and architecture than with the liturgical simplicity demanded by some iconophobic Protestants (ll. 229–30).

The groom's urgency about the slow passage of time is evident

---

[76] Max A. Wickert, "Structure and Ceremony in Spenser's *Epithalamion*," *ELH* 35 (1968): 155. William C. Johnson observes that "the poet dramatizes at one time a fiction and a fact, the single instance of a wedding and the ritualistic reenactment of all weddings," in " 'Sacred Rites' and Prayer-Book Echoes in Spenser's 'Epithalamion,' " *Renaissance and Reformation*, o.s. 12, no. 1 (1976): 50.

[77] Davies, *From Cranmer to Hooker*, pp. 62–63; M. M. Knappen, *Tudor Puritanism: A Chapter in the History of Idealism* (Chicago: University of Chicago Press, 1939), p. 433.

from the beginning of the poem, in contrast to the leisurely attitude of the late-sleeping bride. His anxiety takes on an increasingly ludicrous edge as the nuptial merrymaking endures into the evening:

> Ah when will this long weary day have end,
> And lende me leave to come unto my love?
> How slowly do the houres theyr numbers spend?
> How slowly does sad Time his feathers move?
>
> (ll. 278–80)

Nighttime coincides with the reversal of the convivial refrain for the daytime stanzas. In place of their call for more music and song, the groom lodges an appeal that "The woods no more shal answere, nor your echo ring" (l. 314). The scheduling of the wedding on the feast of St. Barnabas the Apostle (11 June), when "the sunne is in his chiefest hight" (l. 265), coincided with the summer solstice, according to the old-style calendar. The marriage therefore took place during the Midsummer season of night vigils and merrymaking. (The bonfires and dancing of ll. 275–76 are associated with Midsummer Eve, 23 June.) The intersection of liturgical occasion with rural celebration redoubles the comedy in a very delicate injection of fescennine jesting when the groom finally laments the choice of wedding day to the "yong men of the towne" (l. 261):[78]

> But for this time it ill ordained was,
> To chose the longest day in all the yeare,
> And shortest night, when longest fitter weare.
>
> (ll. 270–72)

Even at the point of consummation, in the still privacy and darkness of the nuptial chamber after the departure of the guests, the astronomical calendar offers further occasion for jest when Cynthia, the goddess of the moon, peeps through the window to illuminate the scene. She might appear to be the rival of the goddess of love, Venus, whose rising as "the bright evening star" (l. 286) had marked the turn toward night, but quasivoyeuristic overtones diminish the "envy" that Cynthia experiences at the defloration of her devotee (l. 376), the bride who had risen that morning "Lyke Phoebe from her chamber of the East" (l. 149). The singer reorients Cynthia's conventional protection of virginity by lodging the mythographic caveat that the "fayrest goddesse" (l. 376), in her guise as Lucina, may also serve as a patroness of conception and childbirth. In a syncretic fusion of pagan myth and Christian theology, Spenser combines Cynthia's

---

[78] Hieatt, *Short Time's Endless Monument*, pp. 20, 58, 91.

watchful stance with the wedding ceremony's Old Testamental sanction of the "procreation of children, . . . that they may see their children's children" (*BCP*, p. 296):

> And sith of wemens labours thou hast charge,
> And generation goodly dost enlarge,
> Encline thy will t'effect our wishfull vow,
> And the chast wombe informe with timely seed,
> That may our comfort breed.
>
> (ll. 383–87)

The presiding role played at the wedding bed by Genius, the Roman god of generation, links the consummation to the consideration of love in *The Faerie Queene*, where twin Geniuses—one sterile and malevolent, the other fruitful and benevolent—officiate respectively at the Bower of Bliss and the Garden of Adonis. Internal rhymes and puns on the first syllable of "generation" (from Lat. *generare*, "to beget") fill the invocation to "glad Genius, in whose gentle hand, / The bridale bowre and geniall bed remaine, / Without blemish or staine" (ll. 398–400).[79] Reference to the "geniall bed" is of particular interest because of the combination of the fertility that the Romans associated with the marriage bed (*lectus genialis*) with the festive sense of the English word "genial" (see *OED*, 1–2). The utmost geniality of comic celebration infuses the singer's prayer that Genius "Send us the timely fruit of this same night" (l. 404). The final stanza contains a prayer for divine illumination ("to us wretched earthly clods, / In dreadful darknesse lend desired light"; ll. 411–12) in the hope that the couple may "raise a large posterity" (l. 417) that will attain salvation and heavenly grace:

> And for the guerdon of theyr glorious merit
> May heavenly tabernacles there inherit,
> Of blessed Saints for to increase the count.
>
> (ll. 421–23)

## Epic Epithalamia

"The Legend of Holiness" contains two epithalamic "sketches,"[80] the first of which functions as an antiepithalamium because it celebrates the False Una's temptation of Redcrosse:

---

[79] On the varied meanings of Genius, see Lewis, *Allegory of Love*, pp. 361–63.

[80] Hallett Smith, "The Use of Conventions in Spenser's Minor Poems," in *Form and Convention in the Poetry of Edmund Spenser: Selected Papers from the English Institute*, ed. William Nelson (New York: Columbia University Press, 1961), p. 137.

And eke the *Graces* seemed all to sing,
*Hymen io Hymen*, dauncing all around,
Whilst freshest *Flora* her with Yvie girlond crownd.

(1.1.48)

Although the "Hymen io Hymen" refrain is an ancient generic indicator for a nuptial song, this scene parodies values that are taken seriously in *Epithalamion* (see ll. 25, 140, 146, 256, 405). Rather than reflecting against marriage or the coventions of epithalamic verse, however, it satirizes moral and ecclesiastical corruption by analogy to the concealment of lust under the guise of chastity. Angrily misidentifying this seeming virgin with Una, Redcrosse, prompted into an act of excessive self-reliance that marks his state of sin, abandons his lady in an action that leads directly to the liaison with Duessa. The association of Flora, the classical goddess of springtime blossoming, with the succubus who invades the knight's dream is appropriate to the warping of nuptial imagery in Archimago's falsification of the image of a bashful bride ("the chastest flowre, that ay did spring / On earthly braunch"; st. 48), because the goddess had a reputation for unchastity. Her annual festival was marked by ribaldry and license according to Ovid (*Fasti* 5.331–54). E.K. notes that she was "a famous harlot, which with the abuse of her body . . . [had] gotten great riches" (gloss on "March," l. 16). Flora's meaning is equivocal because the classical goddess may symbolize either natural beauty or its distorted mirror image of artfully falsified display.

At the eventual betrothal of Una and Redcrosse, another epithalamium represents a point of intersection between heavenly and profane song by associating marriage with cosmic harmony. Although Adam acknowledges Una and Redcrosse's contracting of wedlock, he postpones celebration of the nuptials until after the knight's fulfillment of his obligation of six years' service to Gloriana. When Una lays "her mournefull stole aside" to don garments that are "lilly white, withoutten spot, or pride" (1.12.22), she appears in the guise of the Spouse in whom "there is no spot" (Song of Sol. 4:7). The celebration of the couple's "sacred rites and vowes" with the preparation of the bridal chamber and the singing of "a song of love and jollity" anticipate key elements in *Epithalamion* to the extent that we may even note the raining down of celestial influence in the "heavenly noise" heard throughout the palace (sts. 36–39; see *Epith.*, ll. 409–23). In accordance with Spenser's strategy of assimilating vestiges of Roman Catholic practice, the fire, water, and torch that accompany the betrothal (st. 37) apparently refer to the Sarum rite for

Easter.[81] Because this recreation of the marriage of the Bridegroom and the Bride, which is adumbrated in the Song of Solomon and fulfilled in Revelation, participates in the apocalyptic expectations of the Marriage of the Lamb (Rev. 21:9), which cannot be accomplished in the natural world, the narrator withdraws from the scene behind the inability *topos*:[82]

> That their exceeding merth may not be told:
> Suffice it heare by signes to understand
> The usuall joyes at knitting of loves band.

(st. 40)

The Bower of Bliss episode functions as an extended mock epithalamium that inverts the state of wedded bliss celebrated at the royal court in Eden and in *Epithalamion*. Like the antiepithalamic stanza associated with Redcrosse's temptation at Archimago's hermitage, the Bower sequence is a parody not in the modern sense of a literary imitation designed to make an original appear comical or ridiculous, but in the medieval and Renaissance sense of a composition that seriously transfers conventions from one genre to another.[83] This mock epithalamium denigrates the failures of Acrasia rather than ideals of wedded love. Among the more obvious epithalamic parodies in the Bower episode are the "Hymen io Hymen" refrain and the likening of Acrasia's garden of delights to a superfluously decorated bride:

> With all the ornaments of *Floraes* pride,
> Wherewith her mother Art, as halfe in scorne
> Of niggard Nature, like a pompous bride
> Did decke her, and too lavishly adorne,
> When forth from virgin bowre she comes in th'early morne.

(2.12.50)

The Flora allusion links this episode to Redcrosse's dream at Archimago's hermitage (1.1.48). Spenser reverses or negates other conventions of Renaissance epithalamia. Because Acrasia is a sterile variant of *Venus pandemos*, the generative goddess whose power may be a force for good or evil, we may recognize the Bower of Bliss as a perversion of the Bower of Venus that was associated with medieval gar-

---

[81] Harold L. Weatherby, "Una's Betrothal and the Easter Vigil: The Probable Influence of the Sarum Manual," in *Spenser at Kalamazoo, 1984*, ed. Francis G. Greco (Clarion, Pa.: Clarion University of Pennsylvania, 1984), pp. 6–16.

[82] See I. MacCaffrey, *Spenser's Allegory*, pp. 225–26.

[83] See Tuve, "Sacred 'Parody,' " 250–51, 254–55.

dens of love.[84] Spenser's parodies and his continuous contrast of Art and Nature find a precedent in his immediate model, Armida's garden of love in Tasso's *Gerusalemme liberata* 16.1–27. The easy access to this locale reverses the medieval allegory of the *hortus conclusus* as a figure for the enclosure, self-containment, and chastity of the Blessed Virgin.[85]

Having as little to do with virginity as Acrasia's innermost trysting place, her garden's lavishly parti-colored floral display contradicts the image of the bride whom Spenser describes in *Epithalamion* as being "Clad all in white, that seemes a virgin best" and walking "With trembling steps and humble reverence" (ll. 151, 210). The Bower's function as a place of single-minded sexual gratification inverts the traditional purposes of Christian marriage: procreation, avoidance of fornication, and mutual companionship. With the bareness of Acrasia's breasts emphasized by her transparent veil (2.12.77), the seductress denies the procreative impulse as she feeds upon Verdant "With her false eyes fast fixed in his sight" (st. 73) in a perverse parody of motherly nurturance (st. 78).[86] The voyeurism and musical accompaniment of this scene deny the chaste privacy and silence of the nuptial chamber in *Epithalamion* (ll. 296–314). In a sinister re-creation of the classical myth of Circe, Acrasia's transformation of her victims into "seeming beasts" and "figures hideous, / According to their mindes like monstruous" (st. 85) violates the prayer book's prohibition against simple satisfaction of "men's carnal lusts and appetites, like brute beasts that have no understanding" (*BCP*, p. 290).

Despite the negative associations of the Bower of Bliss as a place of erotic abandon, Spenser often describes places of honest sexual pleasure as alliterative variations of that locale, as for example in the descriptions of Venus's "blisful bowre of joy above" (3.6.11) or the lady's bosom in *Am.* 76 ("the bowre of blisse, the paradice of pleasure"). Venus's Bower offered a figure for sanctified bliss in Christian epithalamia.[87] *Prothalamion* anticipates the nuptial pleasures

[84] A. Bartlett Giamatti, *The Earthly Paradise and the Renaissance Epic* (Princeton: Princeton University Press, 1966), pp. 50–52. On the symbolism of the twin Venuses, see Erwin Panofsky, *Studies in Iconology: Humanistic Themes in the Art of the Renaissance*, pbk. ed. (New York: Harper and Row, 1962), pp. 152 and 160; Lewis, *Allegory of Love*, pp. 331–32; and Roche, *Kindly Flame*, pp. 101–3.

[85] Wells, *Spenser's "Fairie Queene" and the Cult of Elizabeth*, p. 68.

[86] Greenblatt, *Renaissance Self-Fashioning*, p. 189. See also Louis A. Montrose, "The Elizabethan Subject and the Spenserian Text," in *Literary Theory/Renaissance Texts*, ed. Patricia Parker and David Quint (Baltimore: Johns Hopkins University Press, 1986), p. 329.

[87] See Giamatti, *Earthly Paradise and the Renaissance Epic*, p. 50 n. 52. For further dis-

of the "lovers blisfull bower" (l. 93). Timias's perception of Belphoebe as an angel sent from heaven links even her "bowre of blis" to love devoid of sexual satisfaction (3.5.35). The wanton shamelessness and overly lush garden setting of Acrasia's bower negate such associations against the audible background of a seductive *carpe florem* song. This imitation of *Gerusalemme liberata* 16.14–15 issues a frankly hedonistic appeal to pluck "the Virgin Rose" (2.12.74) before it fades:

> Gather therefore the Rose, whilest yet is prime,
> For soone comes age, that will her pride deflowre:
> Gather the Rose of love, whilest yet is time,
> Whilest loving thou mayst loved be with equall crime.

> (st. 75)

The Bower of Bliss episode parodies values that are taken seriously elsewhere in *The Faerie Queene*, notably at the betrothal of Redcrosse and Una and throughout Book 3, by pointing out the deficiency of unbridled sensuality rather than the failure of ideals of virginity or wedded love. The lavishly ornamental display of Acrasia's gardens further contradicts the simple modesty of the bride and the stillness of the nuptial scene in *Epithalamion*. In certain respects, the witch resembles a dark double of Belphoebe, who is aligned with the private state of Elizabeth I as woman rather than queen. Accordingly, the full-blown display of the "Rose of love" (st. 75) in the seduction song heard in Acrasia's bower contradicts the modestly budded state of Belphoebe's "dainty Rose," which provides a diametrically opposed figure for "chastity and vertue virginall" (3.5.51, 53).

Spenser's attitude toward love reflects the honor paid both to virginity and to married love by the Church of England, in contrast to the idealization of celibacy by many medieval Christians as a state superior to marriage. As the adopted daughters of Diana and Venus, Belphoebe and Amoret personify the two sides of chastity that the poet associates respectively with the retention of the virgin state and the consummation of love within wedlock. The fusion of both of these aspects may be noted in Britomart, whose commitment to marriage may reflect a sense of nostalgic loss over Queen Elizabeth's failure to wed. (The combination of nubile and regal associations in Britomart recalls the marriageability of Eliza as maiden queen in the "April" eclogue.) The virtue of all of these characters provides a

---

cussion of Spenser's "bower" symbolism, see John N. King, "Milton's Bower of Bliss: A Rewriting of Spenser's Art of Married Love," *Renaissance and Reformation*, n.s. 10 (1986): 289–99. See also *Am.* 78.

counterbalance to the unchastity of Duessa, Acrasia, Malecasta, and other "false" women in *The Faerie Queene*.

Amoret's name links her further to the consideration of chaste erotic love in *Amoretti and Epithalamion*, a collection that features a distillation of Spenser's position concerning love and marriage and a modification of imported literary models in line with Protestant ideology. The climactic position of the betrothal poem (*Am.* 68) in the sonnet sequence represents an innovation during an age when other poets dedicated sonnet cycles to the consideration of unmarried love. In accordance with the liturgical pattern around which Spenser structures his sonnets, the occurence of the betrothal in an Easter poem signifies the interpenetration of religion and love throughout *Amoretti and Epithalamion*. Conclusion of the text with an epithalamium represents an equally radical innovation, one that places particular emphasis upon married chastity. Spenser's modification of literary genres and modes in line with Protestant attitudes occupies an equally prominent place in the poet's construction of Book 1 of *The Faerie Queene* as a Reformation saint's life.

# FIVE

## "TELL ON . . . THE WOFULL TRAGEDIE":
## SPENSER'S REFORMATION OF LITERARY
## GENRES AND MODES

IN ACCORDANCE WITH the Renaissance definition of epic as a
compendium of literary kinds, *The Faerie Queene* contains an encyclopedic array of genres, modes, and subjects. Whereas the definition of literary kinds in terms of their external form and structure
may lead to Sidney's censure of the "old rustick language" of *The
Shepheardes Calender* as a regrettable lapse in taste, a more flexible approach that takes into account internal elements like subject matter,
tone, and rhetorical stance is more compatible with the generic het-
erogeneity of Spenser's verse. Sidney himself relaxes prescriptive
standards in his detailed examination of the repertoire of literary
kinds, where he allows that genres like "Heroicall and Pastorall" contain "mingled matters . . . for, if severed they be good, the conjunction cannot be hurtfull."[1] In Book 1 of *The Faerie Queene*, in particular,
Spenser offers a critique of the Renaissance hierarchy of genres.
Within the comprehensive frame of allegorical romantic epic, Spenser incorporates a complexly layered pattern of allusion to the characteristic conventions, *topoi*, devices, and themes of a succession of
genres to evoke a broad movement from deficient and worldly forms
of romance, pastoral, and tragedy to a set of purged and elevated
Christian counterparts. This reformation of literary genres and
modes eventually results in an encompassing form of divine comedy
that anticipates the transcendence of worldly misery at the time of
the Last Judgment, when the tragic sufferings of the faithful are to
cease.[2]

---

[1] G. Smith, *Elizabethan Critical Essays*, 1: 175, 196. See Ann E. Imbrie, "Defining Non-
fiction Genres," in *Renaissance Genres: Essays on Theory, History, and Interpretation*, ed.
Barbara K. Lewalski, Harvard English Studies, vol. 14 (Cambridge, Mass.: Harvard
University Press, 1986), pp. 56–57; and Fowler, *Kinds of Literature*, p. 55.

[2] In *Paradise Lost* and earlier works, Milton displays a cognate "movement from less
to more noble genres (or varieties within a particular genre) as an emblem of a parallel
movement in moral understanding," according to Lewalski, *Rhetoric of Literary Forms*,
pp. 18–19.

The "Legend of Holiness" functions in the manner of a fictional-
ized defense of poetry through which Spenser exposes "false" genres
and defines "true" ones in order to resuscitate literary forms like
comedy and chivalric romance that were then under attack by humanist critics. According to the *Letter to Ralegh*, he proceeds by offering "doctrine by ensample, then [rather than] by rule." The overall
movement of Book 1 ascends the generic hierarchy that the Renaissance derived from classical authorities like Cicero and Horace by including most of the generic classes that Sidney terms "speciall de-
nominations" of true poetry (i.e., fiction) in *An Apology for Poetry*:
"Heroick, Lirick, Tragick, Comick, Satirick, Iambick, Elegiack, Pastorall."[3] It focuses on the major kinds defined by Renaissance genre
theory: pastoral, comedy, tragedy, and epic. The succession of examples enables the reader to discover a dialectical progression in
which genres assimilate their predecessors while correcting them. As
Rosalie Colie suggests, Spenser joins other authors of his time in employing literary composition for a kind of literary criticism whereby
poems symbolize other poems and efforts are made to surpass them.[4]
Spenser actively criticizes the models that he redefines as elements
in the generic mixture that the reader encounters by the conclusion
of Book 1.

This critique is fully compatible with Spenser's claim in the *Letter
to Ralegh* to be England's epic poet as the successor to Homer, Virgil,
Ariosto, and Tasso. While *The Faerie Queene* supplies little evidence of
the direct impact of the *Iliad* or *Odyssey*, the ambitious plan of writing
at least twelve books imitates the encyclopedic Homeric paradigm.
Like Virgil, the "Romish *Tityrus*" of the *Calender*, the poet abandons
the "Oaten reede" of pastoral song ("October," ll. 55–56) to sing
praise of Elizabeth I as England's new Augustus. The opening lines
of *The Faerie Queene* proclaim that Virgil's archetypal shift from pastoral to epic provides the model for the poet's graduation from
"lowly Shepheards weeds" to the "trumpets sterne" of heroic poetry,[5] but here again Spenser invokes the epic model through allusion rather than consistent structural imitation. Although Duessa undertakes a voyage to Hell, for example, her descent is not profoundly
Virgilian. The description of the lower world owes at least as much

---

[3] G. Smith, *Elizabethan Critical Essays*, 1: 159. On the hierarchy of genres, see Fowler,
*Kinds of Literature*, pp. 216–17.

[4] Colie, *Shakespeare's Living Art* (Princeton: Princeton University Press, 1974), pp. 11,
136–46.

[5] Knowledgable Renaissance readers would not have questioned the authorship of
the pseudo-Virgilian verses that Spenser imitates in the first proem. See Nelson, *Poetry
of Edmund Spenser*, p. 117.

to Ovid's *Metamorphoses* as it does to the *Aeneid*, but Natalis Comes's *Mythologiae* is probably Spenser's direct source (*Var.* 1: 231). Although the pronounced element of parody in this journey to the underworld might seem to "compromise" the classical frame of reference, Spenser's syncretic strategy incorporates pagan elements into a Christian frame of reference.[6]

The first proem announces a commitment to the mixing of literary genres in order to formulate a new type of heroic literature. Because *The Faerie Queene* is a "summational classic of mixed genre" like the *Commedia* or *Paradise Lost*, its allusions to preexisting genres "tend to constellate closely in the exordium."[7] By the middle of the first stanza Spenser turns from the example of Virgil to the romantic matter "of Knights and Ladies gentle deeds" on the precedent of Italian romantic epic. *Orlando furioso* and *Gerusalemme liberata* loom as the chief models for Spenser's fusion of "Fierce warres and faithfull loves" with epic convention and for his interlacement of episodes.[8] His strategy of embedding inset forms like "triumphal pageants, tapestry poems, [and] metamorphoses" reflects the practice of romantic epic.[9] Although the allegorical mode of *The Faerie Queene* distinguishes Spenser's work from that of Ariosto and Tasso, it was conventional to read romantic epic as an allegorical form.[10] Commentaries associated *Orlando furioso* with ideals of Christian heroism, and Tasso provided his own interpretation of *Gerusalemme liberata* as Christian allegory.[11] Although the invocation of the muse marks the conventional beginning of an epic, Spenser's designation of her as "the sacred Muse" aligns his work with the sacred poetry movement of the sixteenth century through an allusion to Urania, the Christian muse, at

[6] For an alternative view, see Anderson, *Growth of a Personal Voice*, p. 37. According to Wall, "The English Reformation," p. 160, *FQ* "claims precedence over classical epic because it derives its authority from constant allusion to its biblical sources."

[7] Fowler, *Kinds of Literature*, p. 89. Lewalski argues in the introduction to Rosalie Colie, *Resources of Kind*, p. viii, that the uncanonical combination of literary genres provided Renaissance authors with a means of creating "encyclopedic works of 'mixed genre' which incorporate and juxtapose virtually the entire range of generic conventions."

[8] See Lewis, *Allegory of Love*, pp. 304–5; Graham Hough, *A Preface to "The Faerie Queene"* (New York: Norton, 1963), pp. 9–81, passim.

[9] Fowler, *Kinds of Literature*, p. 179.

[10] Gordon Kipling states that Spenser's subordination of narrative to allegory results from a fusion of the conventions of Italianate romantic epic and Burgundian allegorical romance and pageantry; *The Triumph of Honour: Burgundian Origins of the Elizabethan Renaissance* (Leiden: Leiden University Press, 1977), pp. 152–57.

[11] See Michael West, "Spenser and the Renaissance Ideal of Christian Heroism," *PMLA* 88 (1973): 1013, 1026. The commentary that Sir John Harington added to his verse translation of *Orlando furioso* adduces moral, historical, and allegorical meanings.

the same time that he refers ambiguously to either Clio or Calliope, the respective muses of history and epic poetry. The poetry of Du Bartas supplies ample precedent for associating Urania with the reformation of existing forms in line with religious subject matter and purposes.[12]

Spenser's guidance of "the reader to asking questions about the Protestant meaning of the narrative"[13] leads to a thorough interrogation of literary genres and modes in the "Legend of Holiness." His effort to fuse the conventional interpretation of the *Odyssey* as an allegory of the progress of the human soul with the personification of Protestant religious and moral ideals was a familiar concern in early Elizabethan literature. The highly didactic quest narrative of *The Shippe of Safegarde* (1569) by Barnabe Googe provides an analogous example of how a contemporary English poet goes about incorporating Protestant ideology into "an encyclopedic moral-allegorical poem."[14] Like Book 1 of *The Faerie Queene*, it employs an exemplary structure of virtue and vice to portray the Christian journey to salvation. Stephen Bateman's *Travayled Pylgrime* provides an even more instructive precedent for the Spenserian combination of romance, quest narrative, allegory, and religious polemics. Like *The Faerie Queene*, this work is a Protestant allegory that describes "the journey of a knight from error to salvation while praising the Tudors and denouncing Rome." As a revision of a late fifteenth-century Burgundian allegory, Olivier de la Marche's *Le Chevalier délibéré* (1486), Bateman's heavily illustrated text combines the marvelous aspect of late medieval romance with iconoclastic anxiety, didactic earnestness, and Protestant moralism. As "England's only significant nondramatic Protestant quest allegory before Spenser," this work provides a case study of the impact of romance tradition upon a text completed not long before work began on *The Faerie Queene*. While *The Travayled Pylgrime* shares the antipapalism that permeates the "Legend of Holiness," its nationalistic celebration of Henry VIII and Edward VI, rather than Elizabeth, as the saviors of Protestant England falls short of Spenser's elaborate fictionality.[15]

[12] On the impact of Du Bartas and the "sacred poetry" movement, see Lily B. Campbell, *Divine Poetry and Drama in Sixteenth-Century England* (Berkeley: University of California Press, 1959), pp. 74–92; Prescott, *French Poets and the English Renaissance*, pp. 167–234.

[13] Norbrook, *Poetry and Politics*, p. 112.

[14] William E. Sheidley, *Barnabe Googe* (Boston: G. K. Hall, 1981), p. 92–93. On the early Protestant acceptance of allegory, see above, pp. 76–77.

[15] Prescott, "Spenser's Chivalric Restoration," pp. 169, 194, and passim. On analogies between *Le Chevalier délibéré* and *FQ*, see Kipling, *Triumph of Honour*, p. 154.

Book 1 of *The Faerie Queene* assimilates the formulaic concerns of romantic epic within the larger system of Christian epic, which supplies a higher view of the heroism, power, and glory that inhere in the magnificence of Arthur and Gloriana. Spenser's fusion of a romance knight and a Protestant hero in the character of Redcrosse puts into sharp contrast the traditional association of heroism with military victory versus the sacrifice entailed by Christian heroism.[16] It does not follow, however, that the contradiction between the Protestant emphasis on "human incapacity" and traditional definitions of the epic hero "by his marvellous accomplishments" causes Spenser to experience "conflict" between "puritan" ideology and a humanistic eagerness "to adapt the heroic poem."[17] Redcrosse's standing as both a sinner and a saint results from the Protestant view of human life as a continually sinful condition and from the redefinition of sainthood to include all of the elect rather than the superhuman miracle-workers who received honor in popular Catholic devotion. Although, according to the *Letter to Ralegh*, the knight is initially incapable of wielding the "armour of a Christian Man specified by Saint Paul" (Eph. 6:11–17), he completes his spiritual education when he commits himself to providential guidance and dedicates himself to a higher calling. Redcrosse learns from Contemplation that he must move beyond traditional chivalry, with its "deeds of armes" and code of courtly love, in order to attain sainthood (1.10.62).

Heroic ideals of martial prowess and battle glory are called into question as early as Una's counsel to Redcrosse, "Add faith unto your force," during his battle with Errour. The knight remains deficient in faith, however, by relying upon "all his force" to defeat the monster (1.1.19).[18] Just as Una attacks reliance upon external works, Redcrosse's strangling of Errour may provide a wry example of the doctrine of justification by good works because he has "excessive confidence in his own virtue" (Kellogg and Steele, p. 17). Michael West aptly notes that it is *because* a discrepancy exists between Christian truth and classical heroism that true courage "is essentially a form of religious faith." The worthiness of the hero remains ambiguous, however, because his eventual beheading of Errour (st. 24) owes as much to fury as to faith.[19]

Although the knight experiences momentary success, his early abandonment of Una attests to the insufficiency of his faith, both in religion and love. Although unwise wrath is a mark of fallen reliance

---

[16] Weiner, "Pattern as Structure," pp. 35–36.
[17] Sinfield, *Literature in Protestant England*, p. 37.
[18] See Mallette, "The Protestant Art of Preaching," p. 9.
[19] West, "Spenser and the Renaissance Ideal of Christian Heroism," pp. 1017, 1023.

upon his own strength, he is not totally flawed. In the course of a tragic descent that leads to eventual defeat and imprisonment by Orgoglio, Redcrosse backslides repeatedly when he allows himself to be governed by wrath (1.1.24, 50; 1.2.8). Archimago's deceptions similarly achieve success only when the knight is moved to "furious ire" and his "eye of reason was with rage yblent [i.e., blinded]" (1.2.5). Although Achillean wrath is not the defining trait of Redcrosse, both his temper and his reliance on human strength rather than divine grace are signs of degeneration and failure to live according to the all-important lesson of justification by faith.

Despite the deficiency of wrath when it is allowed to govern the higher human faculties, in conjunction with other virtues it can strengthen an individual. Because Sansfoy represents an unambiguous personification of faithlessness, Redcrosse can manifest true courage when, during battle with the Saracen, he becomes "wondrous wroth [and], the sleeping spark / Of native vertue gan eftsoones revive" (1.2.19). Still, the consequences of the knight's failure adequately to control his anger endure until his arrival at the House of Holiness, where he finally learns from Charissa the Christian truth that love is incompatible with rage, for she:

> Gan him instruct in every good behest,
> Of love, and righteousnesse, and well to donne,
> And wrath, and hatred warely to shonne,
> That drew on men Gods hatred, and his wrath,
> And many soules in dolours had fordonne.
>
> (1.10.33)

During the climactic battle in Eden, Redcrosse keeps his fury under control, in contrast to the Dragon's rage. Whatever supernatural force the knight possesses owes "less to his wrath than to the tree and fountain of life." Spenser's failure to achieve a complete resolution of war and peace may result from a metaphorical Protestant view of the human condition that sees "war as an inevitable and continuous part of strife with sin."[20]

## A Reformation Hagiography

The Palmer's contention that Redcrosse is an elect saint (2.1.32) accords with the ambivalent fusion of a saintly martyr and a chivalric

[20] Ibid., pp. 1016, 1023. According to West, a tendency toward pacifism makes it possible for Spenser to "admire the warlike qualities of his combatants while expressing their weariness of war" (pp. 1016–17).

knight in the first hero of *The Faerie Queene*.[21] The surprised welcome that he receives from Dame Caelia at the House of Holiness—"Strange thing it is an errant knight to see / Here in this place" (1.10.10)—calls attention to his abandonment of the mise-en-scène of quest romance in a manner that subsumes conventional romantic values within a new kind of saint's life. Spenser's redefinition of this literary form stands complete by the end of Book 1, when Redcrosse is revealed as an exemplar of Protestant sainthood and holiness. As one who is selected by divine grace for salvation, he corresponds to every believer whose suffering in the world constitutes a mark of election. Like any Protestant saint, he must learn the all-important lesson of justification by faith.[22]

Spenser's designation of each book of *The Faerie Queene* as the "legend" of a particular knight calls attention to his countergeneric strategy of providing an alternative to the legends of the saints that held an honored place in aristocratic and popular culture of the Middle Ages. The ironic account of Archimago's "pleasing" delivery of tales "of Saintes and Popes" (1.1.35) highlights a self-conscious authorial concern with purging a literary genre of Catholic associations in order to render it suitable for a Protestant readership. One critic wittily proposes that the false hermit reads to Una and her champion out of a copy of *The Golden Legend*.[23] The priority of the "Legend of Holiness" establishes the purified form of the saint's life as a generic context for the later books, despite their secular concerns. The alert reader is encouraged to remember the theological inception of *The Faerie Queene* by Spenser's comment on the Pauline armor in the *Letter to Ralegh* and the many returns of Redcrosse or references to him in later books (e.g., 2.1.23, 3.1.42, 5.11.53). Michael Drayton credits Spenser with transforming the "legend" from a prose form with an exclusively "Ecclesiasticall sense . . . touching the Lives of Saints" into "a Species of an Epick or Heroick Poeme." This title provides "a kind of Consecration," according to his view, for "a kind of sacred Nature" that is to be found in both the "Legend of Holiness" and other books of *The Faerie Queene*.[24]

Although the suffering of saints and concern with human salvation

---

[21] John Steadman, *Milton and the Renaissance Hero* (Oxford: Clarendon Press, 1967), p. xvii. See also West, "Spenser and the Renaissance Ideal of Christian Heroism," p. 1028.

[22] The present discussion of *FQ* 1 is indebted throughout to Kellogg and Steele, pp. 9–48. See also George and George, *The Protestant Mind*, pp. 101, 111.

[23] Nohrnberg, *Analogy*, p. 158.

[24] Drayton, *Works*, ed. J. William Hebel, 5 vols. (Oxford: Shakespeare Head Press, 1931–41), 2: 382.

are common elements in Protestant and Catholic legends, Spenser returns to the gospel conception of the saint as a "martyr" (from Greek *martus*, "witness") in styling George as one who learns to testify to his faith, to the point of death if necessary, rather than as the fabulous dragon-slayer who was venerated during the Middle Ages.[25] Erasmus led the way in lodging the humanistic attack against superstitious aspects of popular religion. In place of the acts of intercession, miracles, cures, and magical feats associated with the Catholic cult of saints,[26] faith is the essential precondition of Protestant sainthood, one that is imputed by God to every member of the elect.

We have been reminded that "no Renaissance humanist could have thought the legendary life of St. George a respectable literary model."[27] In place of the radical tendency to destroy saints' legends that may be noted in the prayer book's strictures against "uncertain stories . . . [and] legends" (*BCP*, p. 14), however, Spenser redrafts the life of St. George as the ground plan for his "Legend of Holiness." Archimago's ability to pose convincingly as the hero's double—"*Saint George* himself ye would have deemed him to be" (1.2.11)—identifies the magician with the "base Elfin brood" that a fairy substituted for the true Saint George soon after his birth (1.10.65). This changeling presumably became the mythic subject of the discredited saint's legend attacked by humanists and Protestants.[28] Spenser's countergeneric strategy assimilates an iconoclastic attack against *The Golden Legend* and other collections of saints' lives at the same time that it appropriates some of their conventions (see above, p. 48). While Caxton's translation of *The Golden Legend* contains the most readily available prototype for this tale, Lydgate and others provide versions as well.[29] Their lack of precedent for the assignment of the Armor of God to Redcrosse and his ultimate portrayal as a type of the Heavenly Bridegroom suggest that Spenser may have abandoned them in favor of extraliterary models.[30]

Native English models for the Protestant saint's life may be located in John Bale's hagiographies, sensational accounts of persecution in Foxe's "Book of Martyrs," and adaptations of Eusebian narratives that Barnabe Googe incorporated into his *Shippe of Safegarde*. Al-

[25] See Grace W. Landrum, "St. George *Redivivus*," *Philological Quarterly* 29 (1950): 381–88.

[26] See Thomas, *Religion and the Decline of Magic*, pp. 28–29.

[27] Nelson, *Poetry of Edmund Spenser*, p. 150.

[28] *FQ*, ed. Hamilton, 1.10.65n.

[29] See F. M. Padelford and Matthew O'Connor, "Spenser's Use of the St. George Legend," *SP* 23 (1926): 142–56; and *Var.* 1: 379–90.

[30] Harold L. Weatherby documents a set of tight parallels between Redcrosse and the liturgy of the Eastern Orthodox Church in "The True St. George," *ELR* 17 (1987): 122–33.

though Bale attacks saints' legends as nothing more than "fables / lyes / and fantasyes," he reorients the genre by grounding proper sainthood in a willingness to witness to one's faith in his life of Sir John Oldcastle and his edition of Anne Askew's *Examinations* (1546–47).[31] Foxe's apocalyptic rendering of human history not only assimilates the dualistic pattern of Bale's *Image of Both Churches*, but also transcribes Bale's accounts of Askew and Oldcastle. Foxe contends that the "Book of Martyrs" contains histories that differ in kind from old-fashioned saints' lives, which are unable "to abyde the touche of history" because they are mingled with "untrue additions and fabulous inventions of men" (*A&M* [1570], p. 132). The preface "Ad Lectorem" in the "Book of Martyrs" accordingly attacks *The Golden Legend* for containing lying "fabellis" (*A&M* [1563], B3ᵛ). Although the calendar for the "Book of Martyrs" omits the feast days of most nonscriptural saints whose reputations rest on early Christian and medieval legends of the saints, it retains an entry for the martyrdom of St. George in its redefinition of the sacred year by reference to the martyrdoms of biblical saints, apostles, and those who were persecuted during the period leading up to and including the reign of Mary Tudor. One of Foxe's major goals is to demonstrate that the sainthood of the elect is similar to the patristic conception of Ambrose and Jerome: "how cherefull and glad the remembrance of the holy Martirs of God was of olde time accustomed to be in the church" (B6). He explains that his accounts of the persecutions of the faithful should be useful to the reader, who should "imitate their death (as muche as we maye) with like constancy" (B6ᵛ).[32]

Nationalistic ideals play an important role in the definition of Redcrosse's character as a Protestant saint. Although generic allusion and his heraldic crest identify him to the reader as the patron saint of England at the outset of Book 1, the crucial element of his popular image—the dragon combat—is postponed until Canto 11. Despite the opposition of Edward VI, the mounted figure of St. George slaying the dragon was well known from woodcuts (Fig. 18) and from patriotic images like the pendant jewels of the Order of the Garter (the "Great George" and "Lesser George"), the highest honor that

[31] Bale, *A Mysterye of Inyquyte* (Antwerp, 1545), sig. I4ᵛ. See *A Brefe Chronycle concernynge the Examinacyon and Death of the Martyr Syr Johan Oldecastell* (Antwerp, 1544); *The First Examinacyon of Anne Askewe* (Marburg [i.e., Wesel], 1546); and *The Lattre Examinacyon of Anne Askewe* (Marburg [i.e., Wesel], 1547). In "The Vocacyon of Johan Bale and Early English Autobiography," *RQ* 24 (1971): 327–28, 332–33, Leslie P. Fairfield argues that Bale's *Vocacyon* (1553), an account of the author's one-year tenure as Bishop of Ossory in Ireland, is "an autobiographical saint's life."

[32] On the "Book of Martyrs" as a context for Spenser's historical allegory, see Kermode, *Shakespeare, Spenser, and Donne*, pp. 40–45.

the English sovereign may bestow. The patriotic associations of this figure are enhanced by the presence of a red cross on the Tudor battle flag. St. George's Day (April 23), the day upon which the Knights of the Garter meet in St. George's Chapel, Windsor, was celebrated with processions, plays, and pageants. All of these associations are brought to bear in the opening scene of *The Faerie Queene*, which evokes St. George's Day pageants and the tableaux staged during coronation celebrations.[33]

Spenser modifies the image of a saintly warrior whose armor was not only an unusual feature in Christian iconography, but also one of the few aspects of the medieval saint's cult to survive the English Reformation.[34] The legendary victory of St. George as a mounted knight who tramples upon a monster and slays it by driving his spear through its mouth or neck came under attack during the radical phase of the English Reformation. An anecdote in Foxe's "Book of Martyrs" illustrates the intensity of hostility to the saint's life as an inconsistent account filled with superstition. When Edward VI expressed skepticism about honoring the saint, his lord treasurer (presumedly Sir William Cavendish) allegedly replied that " 'I did never read in any history of St. George, but only in "Legenda Aurea," where it is thus set down: That St. George out with his sword, and ran the dragon through with his spear.' " Expressing great merriment at the inconsistency concerning weaponry, according to Foxe, the king made the witty rejoinder: " 'I pray you, my lord, and what did he with his sword the while?' " (*A&M* [1877], 6: 351–52). *The Golden Legend* describes how St. George "was upon his hors, and drewe out his swerde: and garnisshed him wyth the signe of the crosse, and rode hardely ayenste the dragon, whiche came toward hym and smote hym wyth his spere and hurte him sore, and threwe hym to the grounde." According to this version, the maiden led the dragon on a tether to the city of Sylene before her champion "slew the dragon and smote of[f] his hede." Caxton's woodcut in *The Golden Legend* portrays the saint slaying the dragon with spear rather than sword,[35] but other medieval pictures show his broken spear lying uselessly on the ground.

[33] On *FQ* and the Order of the Garter, see Leslie, *Spenser's "Fierce Warres and Faithfull Loves,"* pp. 139–46, 148–49, 151–52, 186–95. John Leland describes a pageant designed for Edward VI's coronation with "Seint George on Horsebacke in Compleat Harnes, with his Page in Harnes also, holding his Speare and Shield, and a faire Maiden holding a Lamb in a string" (*Var.* 1: 390).

[34] On the refounding of the Order after the Edwardian disestablishment, see Strong, *Cult of Elizabeth*, pp. 166, 182.

[35] Voragine, *Golden Legend,* 3rd ed. (1493), fol. 120$^{r-v}$; Edward Hodnett, *English Woodcuts: 1480–1535*, rev. ed. (Oxford: Oxford University Press, 1973), no. 272.

Spenser's redefinition of St. George resurrects evangelical iconography that failed to survive the accession of Elizabeth. A controversial Edwardian effort to eradicate the cult of the royal saint, whose apocryphal legend and observances were attributed by religious radicals to Antichrist, supplies an iconoclastic context for Redcrosse's wearing of the Armor of God. One mid-century proposal would have substituted for St. George the Pauline image of the Christian warrior, wielding a sword symbolic of the scriptures in one hand and the shield of faith in the other. Although the red cross emblazoned on the saint's silver shield was sufficiently noncontroversial to be retained in the proposed coat of arms, the revised statutes excluded the essential iconographical detail that had defined the St. George motif: the slaughter of the dragon as the embodiment of pagan evil. Although the knightly figure proposed for the new Garter jewels was identical in every other respect to the conventional visualization of the saint, the deletion of the dragon would have eradicated all reference to traditional iconography.[36] The Edwardian proposals would have supplanted the medieval dragon-slayer with a figure wielding allegorical armor appropriate not only to St. George, but to any member of the sainthood of the elect. By way of contrast, Spenser fuses the dragon-slayer of popular reputation with the Pauline warrior who wields the Armor of God.

Even though Redcrosse may not realize who he is initially, and formal announcement of his identity as St. George is postponed until the second canto (1.2.12),[37] his symbolic armament should enable the reader to recognize him from the outset as a Protestant Everyman. The *Letter to Ralegh* announces that Spenser alludes to the "armour of a Christian man specified by Saint Paul":

> Put on the whole armour of God, that ye may be able to stand against the assau[l]ts of the devil . . . and your loines girde about with veritie, and having on the brest plate of righteousnes, And your fete shod with the preparation of the Gospel of peace. Above all, take the shield of faith, wherewith ye may quench all the fyrie dartes of the wicked, And take the helmet of salvation, and the sworde of the Spirit, which is the worde of God.
>
> (Eph. 6:11–17)[38]

The Letter to the Ephesians and events like Christ's temptation in the wilderness (Matt. 4:1–11) provide antitypes for the "warfare" waged

---

[36] See King, *Tudor Royal Iconography*, pp. 100–101.

[37] See Fowler, *Kinds of Literature*, p. 82.

[38] For an argument that Spenser may refer to Eph. 5:15–16 as well as Eph. 6:10–17, see William Sessions, "Spenser's Georgics," *ELR* 10 (1980): 234–35.

by the individual Christian in everyday life.[39] The Protestant reorientation of spiritual life toward inward faith rather than good works in the external world indicates that the allegorical Armor of God should not be confused with conventional chivalric weaponry. The knight's initial inability to wield his symbolic weapons effectively renders the incapacity of human merit and total reliance of the elect upon divine grace. While the "silver shielde" symbolic of faith plays an important role in Spenser's allegory of holiness (1.1.1–2), the prominence of his offensive weapon, the Pauline sword symbolic of the scriptures, calls attention to the evangelical power of the Bible to regenerate the soul and implement salvation (see *Book of Homilies*, 1: 1). The complementary operation of scriptural revelation and a justifying faith is a standard Protestant theme.[40]

Martial imagery was a well-known feature of Christian iconography during the Middle Ages and Renaissance. From the end of the classical age, authors of "epic or romance-like" forms had fused the Pauline armor with the martial imagery of Revelation as an allegorical figure for "the Christian life as a warfare." Thus the Armor of God plays a crucial role in the incorporation of Virgilian and Prudentian conventions for epic battle between warriors or personified virtues and vices into a Christian framework.[41] Accordingly, the Christian "soldier" to whom Erasmus addressed the *Enchiridion Militis Christiani* (1503) was to engage in spiritual warfare rather than worldly battle. While Erasmus was by no means a Protestant, his work was readily adapted in defense of the Reformation.[42] The Dutch humanist's advocacy of the vernacular Bible and patristic theology complemented the reformers' attack against the ceremonialism and dogma of the Church of Rome. Albrecht Dürer transformed Erasmus's "soldier" into a Christian knight in his 1513 engraving of *The Knight*,

---

[39] The Geneva gloss on Eph. 6:12 states: "The faithful have not only to strive against men and them selves, but against Satan the spiritual enemie, who is moste dangerous: for he is over our heades so that we can not reache him, but he must be resisted by Gods grace." According to Calvin "faith doth armie [sic] and fortifie her self with the worde of God" and "serveth us for a sh[i]eld" (*Institution* 3.2.21; fol. 117r-v). Theological imagery of this kind underlies Lancelot Andrewes's *The Wonderfull Combate (for Gods glorie and Mans salvation) betweene Christ and Satan* (1592), a series of sermons "upon the Temptations of Christ, in the wildernes, etc." Andrewes regards the life of spiritual warfare as an imitation of Christ (B2v, C7v).

[40] See Knott, *Sword of the Spirit*, p. 147.

[41] Lewalski, *Protestant Poetics*, p. 92. See also Leslie, *Spenser's "Fierce Warres and Faithfull Loves,"* pp. 101–2.

[42] See Wells, *Spenser's "Faerie Queene" and the Cult of Elizabeth*, pp. 43–44, on Spenser's affinity with the Erasmian application of "the metaphor of Christian warfare." Miles Coverdale protestantizes Erasmus's text in *A Shorte Recapitulacion or Abridgement of Erasmus Enchiridion* (Antwerp[?], 1545). See also *ERL*, p. 44.

*Death, and the Devil,* in which a mounted warrior rides calmly through an apocalyptic landscape in the face of Death and the Devil. In later years, the German artist reinterpreted this pre-Reformation image in Lutheran terms.[43] This interpretation of the Armor of God informs an Elizabethan woodcut in *The Christall Glasse of Christian Reformation,* a compilation by Stephen Bateman, in which a caption emphasizes the priority of faith in the work of salvation (Fig. 20): "The man in armour signifieth all stedfast belevers of the veritie, being armed with constant zeale of Christianitie, and weaponed with the shielde of lively faith, the spere of continuaunce, and the sworde of the word of God: The Divil under him is temptation, being overcome by faith in Christ Jesus" (M4).

At the outset of his quest, Redcrosse has yet to learn that he can succeed only if he surrenders confidence in human power and relies, as an instrument of divine grace, upon faith and scriptural understanding. Although Redcrosse looks very much like a chivalrous saint of medieval legend in the opening tableau, upon arrival at Errour's cave he surrenders his "needlesse spere" to the Dwarf (1.1.11). Presumably he retains all of the Pauline weaponry for his descent underground, but only his shield and sword are mentioned specifically (sts. 14, 17–18). Nevertheless, is St. George quite wise to meet Errour? Una warns him to "beware,"[44] and the Dwarf urges him to flee the deathly locale (st. 13). A wiser Christian soldier might have stayed on his horse and kept on the right way.

A mock-heroic diminishment of the conventional battle between saint and beast signals Redcrosse's deficiency when Errour engages "his trenchand blade" in a duel with the "angry sting" upon her tail (st. 17). Ignorance of the scriptures renders Redcrosse incapable of winning victory through wielding "the sworde of the Spirit, which is the worde of God" (Eph. 6:17). Even though Errour's entwining tail pinions his arms, the shield retains its defensive capacity in line with Calvin's assurance that even weak faith is real: "So sone [soon] as any droppe of fayth, be it never so small, is poured into our heartes, we by and by beginne to beholde the face of God milde and pleasant, and lovyng toward us."[45] In a mock-heroic inversion of St. George's

[43] Erwin Panofsky, *Albrecht Dürer,* 2 vols. (Princeton: Princeton University Press, 1948), 1: 151; 2: fig. 207. Panofsky notes that Dürer's diary addresses Erasmus as a Christian warrior who may " 'ride forth at the side of Christ our Lord, protect the truth, [and] obtain the crown of the Martyrs!' " See also Weiner, "Pattern as Structure," p. 36.

[44] The cave of Errour affords a pun on Lat. *cave* ("beware"), according to Richard Mallette, "The Protestant Art of Preaching," p. 8.

[45] Calvin, *Institution* 3.2.19; fol. 116ᵛ.

# *Of Faith.*

*⁊Of fayth and the wonderfull working of the same: and stedfast beliefe of the fathers in olde tyme.*

## *The signification.*

⁊'He man in armour signifieth all stedfast beleuers of the veritie, being armed with constant zeale of Christianitie, and weaponed with the shielde of liuely faith, the spere of continuaunce, and the sword of the word of God: The Diuil vnder him is temptation, being ouercome by faith in Christ Iesus.

𝕸.iiij. 𝕱𝖆𝖎𝖙𝖍

20. *Of Faith.* Bateman, *A Christall Glasse of Christian Reformation* (1569)

conventional rescue of a maiden from the dragon, the distressed princess must intervene to rescue her own champion. Even when Una exhorts him to "Add faith unto your force, and be not faint" (st. 19), Redcrosse relies upon brute force rather than theological weaponry to strangle the beast. His use of his bare hands to defeat Errour represents a striking departure from the traditional iconography of St. George. Only after strangling the beast does the knight employ his sword to deliver the coup de grâce. Redcrosse does conquer Errour, but he has first erred.

Quite obviously, Redcrosse is not a type for Christ when he cannot wield the sword symbolic of the holy scriptures in open battle against religious falsehood. The formal course of scriptural instruction at the House of Holiness, where Fidelia teaches the knight to read her "sacred Booke," must necessarily precede his final victory over the great Dragon (1.10.18–19). Not until then does the characteristically inarticulate and illiterate knight learn to read the scriptures, to interpret them, and to apply them (see above, pp. 60, 63–64). His prior expertise at swordplay presumably extends to the conventional weaponry of chivalric combat rather than the Pauline blade. Although Redcrosse defeats Sansjoy through armed combat, for example, he misinterprets the perfectly ambiguous call that Duessa actually directs to his opponent: "Thine the shield, and I, and all" (1.5.11). This victory parodies spiritual battle because the shield hanging over the tournament ground is not the Pauline symbol for faith, but rather its moral opposite as the property of the slain Sansfoy ("without faith").[46] Redcrosse reaches his nadir when he willingly disarms himself, in a dalliance with Duessa that fuses romantic seduction with the spiritual "fornication" of religious apostasy (Rev. 17:2). His removal "of yroncoated Plate" and inability to take in hand "his unready weapons" or "get his shield" leave him defenseless before Orgoglio, the harlot's gigantic paramour, who personifies spiritual pride in general as well as the knight's own sexual arousal (1.7.2, 7–8).[47]

As the sole offensive component in the Armor of God, the "sword of the spirit" plays a paramount role in the climactic three-day battle

[46] Kellogg and Steele, p. 27, states that "his faith is real, but its object is not." See Mallette, "The Protestant Art of Preaching," p. 13.

[47] See John W. Shroeder, "Spenser's Erotic Drama: The Orgoglio Episode," *ELH* 29 (1962): 140–59. A comment in Calvin's *Sermons upon the Epistle of S. Paule too the Ephesians*, trans. Arthur Golding (1577), 2U1ᵛ–2, is appropriate to Redcrosse's apostasy: "Therefore if there bee such cowardlynesse in us as too bee so afrayd of the divell, that he makes us too tumble downe, and to start asyde, and too stray quyte out of the good way: we must impute all to our own rechlesnesse, bycause wee have not put on the armour that God giveth us, but have hanged them up upon a pin."

against the Dragon in Eden, a conflict that recalls Christ's three days in the grave prior to victory over death through the resurrection. The weapon remains unsheathed during the opening horseback charge, however, when Redcrosse relies unsuccessfully upon his spear (1.11.16, 20), a weapon conspicuously absent from Ephesians 6:10–17. Carol Kaske argues that the knight's weaponry lacks a fixed symbolic value, because the armor that enables a flame to sear his entire body on the first day of battle "can hardly represent 'the armour of a Christian man.'" Yet her finding that he is a figure for "unregenerate man" under the Old Law when he falls into the baptismal Well of Life at the end of the day violates his elect status as a newly converted knight who has finally learned the lesson of faith at the House of Holiness. On the second day the knight's shield fails to protect him fully from injury by the beast: "The mortall sting his angry needle shot / Quite through his shield, and in his shoulder seasd" (st. 38). According to Kaske's view, the knight's failures on the first and second day ready him to fulfill his calling as a Christian warrior in the final combat.[48] The armament is compatible with the Pauline allegory, however, if one acknowledges that religious belief is not always comfortable. The same faith that sustains the elect may also be a torment in this threefold allegory concerning the salvation of the soul. At the end of the first day, Redcrosse, as a figure for a sinful human being, falls into the baptismal Well of Life. Rising on the second day with the "baptized hands" of the believing Christian, he falters before the Dragon's onslaught and falls into the eucharistic "streame of Balme" trickling from the the Tree of Life (sts. 36, 48). The Geneva Bible identifies this tree with the "life everlasting" derived from Christ's sacrifice (gloss on Rev. 2:7). On the third day, as

---

[48] Kaske, "The Dragon's Spark and Sting and the Structure of Red Cross's Dragon-Fight: *The Faerie Queene*, I.xi–xii," *SP* 66 (1969): 609–38; reprinted in *Essential Articles*, ed. A. C. Hamilton, pp. 433–34, 446. For a critique of Kaske's argument, see Leslie, *Spenser's "Fierce Warres and Faithfull Loves*," pp. 105–14. In opposition to Kaske's view that Redcrosse becomes Christ by the third day ("Dragon's Spark," in *Essential Articles*, p. 439), Leslie responds that the knight is a "perfected" Christian who figures Christ but "is never equated with Christ, even on the final day" (*Spenser's "Fierce Warres and Faithfull Loves*," p. 114). See also Weiner, "Pattern as Structure," p. 56 n. 37; and Hume, *Protestant Poet*, p. 105. Calvin warns against the danger of seeking too much consistency in interpreting the Armor of God: "Now wee must not be curious in seeking heere why Saint Paule giveth the tytle of Helmet too one, the tytle of Brestplate too another, and the tytle of Sheeld too another. . . . Saint Paules intent heere, was not too decyfer particularly all the peeces of a Christen mans armour, but too shewe briefely that if wee receyve the meanes that God offereth us, and be diligent too serve him, we shall be furnished of all peeces, and wee neede not feare but wee shall have wherwith too withstand all our enemies, yea and too vanquish them" (*Sermons upon the Epistle of S. Paule too the Ephesians*, 2U1).

the faithful Christian bearing Christ within, Redcrosse slays the Dragon.

It is important to note that Redcrosse's role in the dragon combat is no more than instrumental, however, because it is the blade personifying the power of the Word that slays the beast:[49]

> The weapon bright
> Taking advantage of his open jaw,
> Ran through his mouth with so importune might,
> That deepe emperst his darksome hollow maw,
> And back retyrd, his life bloud forth with all did draw.
>
> (st. 53)

This scene reverses the episode at Errour's den, where the knight's unregenerate condition rendered him incapable of defeating his monstrous opponent through the simple agency of the sword. It is appropriate that the great Slanderer (*diabolos*) is slain through the mouth that undid humankind, and with the sword of the Word that undid his words. The metaphorical blade refers not only to the sword of Ephesians 6:17, but also to the double-edged weapon that Christ wields as a military commander named "Faithful and true," mounted upon a white steed, from whose "mouth went out a sharpe sworde, that with it he shulde smite the heathen" (Rev. 19:11–15). This "trope is self-referential" because it both embodies and refers to the powerful "force of the Christian message."[50] Illustrations for Bibles and commentaries often portray Christ with the spiritual sword emerging from his mouth (Fig. 21). The sword's autonomy from any element of knightly control accords with the narrator's invocation of the "sacred Muse" to enable him to praise the Armor of God rather than its wearer: "That I this man of God his godly armes may blaze" (sts. 5–7).[51] Like any member of the Protestant elect, Redcrosse remains powerless to perform good works capable of earning him salvation, which is wholly a gift of divine grace.

---

[49] Leslie, *Spenser's "Fierce Warres and Faithfull Loves,"* p. 105 n. 7. The stereotyped woodcut of St. George as a mounted knight slaying the Dragon by driving his spear through its neck in the 1590 *FQ* clashes with Spenser's narrative.

[50] Norbrook, *Poetry and Politics*, p. 278. See also *ERL*, fig. 9. John Dixon glosses the knight's "trenchand blade" (1.1.17) as "Christes Gospel" (Dixon, *Commentary*).

[51] According to William Perkins, *The Combat between Christ and the Devell Displayed* (1609), the "written word of God, rightly wielded by the hand of faith, is the most sufficient weapon for the repelling of Satan and vanquishing him in all temptations"; as quoted in Ann E. Imbrie, " 'Playing Legerdemaine with the Scripture': Parodic Sermons in *The Faerie Queene*," *ELR* 17 (1987): 149.

**21.** *The Man on the White Horse.* Van der Noot, *A Theatre for Worldlings* (1569)

## Romantic Error

Spenser initiates a critique of quest romance in the *Letter to Ralegh*. Because a "Poet historical" violates chronology by following the classical precedent of beginning *in medias res*—"a Poet thrusteth into the middest, even where it most concerneth him"—the *Letter* relates the starting point of the action at the annual feast of Gloriana. The first quest begins in a state of generic confusion because the rustic background of the candidate who brings himself forward for a chivalric "adventure" identifies him as a pastoral intruder in the romance world of chance encounters, desultory progress, and "interlaced multiplicity of action,"[52] in which deeds of combat, encounters with monsters and giants, marvelous rescues, and amatory exploits are governed by an elaborate code of courtly etiquette.[53]

[52] Fowler, *Kinds of Literature*, p. 28.
[53] As Weiner notes, in "Pattern as Structure," p. 37, it is unclear at the outset whether Redcrosse is a romance knight or a Christian hero.

The peasant's lack of armor highlights his predicament. Although the humility of this unnamed countryman offers a contrast to the elevated style and subject expected of romantic epic, the transforming effect of "the armour of a Christian man" provided by Una reveals his status as an elect saint chosen by God. In line with Una's view that Redcrosse "could not succeed in that enterprise" unless her armor "would serve him," no sooner does he don it than "he seemed the goodliest man in al that company." According to Una's own testimony during the poem proper, the repeated failures of "knights adventurous and stout" to rescue Eden, the kingdom of her parents, Adam and Eve, from the depredations of "an huge great Dragon" motivated her visit to the court of Gloriana. The shortcomings of knights clad conventionally in chivalric armor provide a key to understanding the moral deficiency of existing models for romantic epic, because their "want of faith, or guilt of sin" rendered them incapable of victory (1.7.44–45). In a paradoxical example of humility, it is Redcrosse's untested condition as a "clownishe person," according to the *Letter*, and his possession of a record unblemished by ill-gotten victories, that render him capable of heroic action defined in terms of Christian spirituality instead of simple deeds of combat.

Although Spenser clearly has the Italian models of Ariosto and Tasso in mind, Sir Thomas Malory compiled the best-known native exemplar for quest romance, *Morte Darthur*. By the late sixteenth century, Protestant humanists like Roger Ascham censured this work because they associated romance immorality with religious error:

> In our forefathers' time, when papistry as a standing pool covered and overflowed all England, few books were read in our tongue, saving certain books of chivalry, as they said, for pastime and pleasure, which, as some say, were made in monasteries by idle monks or wanton canons; as one for example, *Morte Darthur*, the whole pleasure of which book standeth in two special points—in open manslaughter and bold bawdry.[54]

Ascham makes no effort to conceal his disdain for medieval cultural practices, which he associates with Catholic "falsity." E.K. joins the humanistic attack by denouncing "the Authors of King Arthure the great and such like" as "fine fablers and lowd lyers" (gloss on "April," l. 120). It may be no accident, then, that no more than one edition of the *Morte Darthur* was published during the reign of Queen Elizabeth.

Rather than abandoning romance outright, however, Spenser

---

[54] Ascham, *The Schoolmaster*, ed. Lawrence V. Ryan (Ithaca, N.Y.: Cornell University Press, for the Folger Shakespeare Library, 1967), pp. 68–69.

cleanses it of "false" associations by adding layers of moral, religious, and political allegory.[55] In what looks like an implicit response to disapproving humanists, he attempts to reform literary conventions that others would destroy. His construction of Protestant allegorical romance accords with the contemporary English practice of Bateman's *Travayled Pylgrime* and Googe's *Shippe of Safegarde*.

Redcrosse's initial encounters with variant forms of Catholic "deceit," Errour and Archimago, reveal both his inability to cope with the mysterious world of chivalric romance and the distance that he must traverse before attaining true knighthood. As a sacred variation of the mistress of courtly romance, Una, in her involvement with Redcrosse, furnishes a poetic conceit for Christian faith as the love of every Christian for unitary truth. The entry of Una and Redcrosse into the "wandring wood" brings them into "the archetypal locus of romance, the *selva oscura*" in which the reader is expected to recognize heavily layered allusions to the *Aeneid*, the *Commedia*, and other seminal texts. Essential to their loss of way "is the romance experience of not knowing where lines are until they have been violated or crossed."[56] Redcrosse's reliance on physical prowess in battle with Errour contributes to an initial impression that he is yet another knight who may fail Una for "want of faith, or guilt of sin" (1.7.45).

The ensuing encounter with a more dangerous and covert form of falsehood, Archimago, indicates that Redcrosse has won a false victory over Errour. Although Archimago's secluded hermitage and disguise as a hermit reflect the conventional forest setting and character of the aged sire found in medieval romances like *Sir Orfeo*, Spenser's chief model is Ariosto's hypocritical hermit (*Orl. fur.* 2.12–13). Because of Redcrosse's inability, through a lapse in faith, to distinguish between Una and the false double conjured by Archimago, the magician succeeds in separating the lovers; the reader should recognize the irony inherent in this event. The knight's "inconstancie in love" (1.4.1) converts a romantic metaphor into an allegorical conceit for religious apostasy. The appearance of Duessa in the guise of Fidessa furnishes an easily recognizable form of error, not least because the headnote of the second canto identifies her as "falshood." Redcrosse's failure to recognize this seductress, whose character represents a fusion of an Arthurian witch similar to Morgan le Fay with the great harlot of Revelation, intensifies a sense of the moral failure of romance.

[55] On Spenser's adaptation of Arthurian tradition, see Hankins, *Source and Meaning in Spenser's Allegory*, p. 34.

[56] Patricia Parker, *Inescapable Romance: Studies in the Poetics of a Mode* (Princeton: Princeton University Press, 1979), pp. 64–65.

## Pastoral Ignorance

The *Letter to Ralegh* supplies an implicit authorial comment on the problem of infusing romantic epic with a pastoral mode, a mode that eventually undergoes a georgic shift. At Gloriana's court, Redcrosse represents a literary throwback because his description as "a tall clownishe younge man" aligns his character with the lowly style and subject matter of the *Calender*. ("Clownish" defines rusticity lacking in courtly refinement; *OED*, 1.) The intruder's ignorance and inexperience liken him to an uncultivated countryman comparable to a "gentle Shepheard" with "clownish hands" (1.1.23) or to a plowman urgently in need of the spiritual instruction that Redcrosse receives at the House of Holiness. Until his tutelage by Fidelia, Redcrosse remains almost completely inarticulate, lacking even the humble eloquence of Cuddie, whom Piers admonishes to transcend the "clownishness" of the pastoral eclogue in order to celebrate heroic achievement:

Abandon then the base and viler clowne,
Lyft up thy selfe out of the lowly dust:
And sing of bloody Mars, of wars, of giusts,
Turne thee to those, that weld the awful crowne.
To doubted [i.e., redoubted] Knights, whose woundlesse armour rusts,
And helmes unbruzed wexen dayly browne.

("October," ll. 37–42)

Redcrosse's transitional character reflects the poet's own commitment to discarding the "lowly Shepheards weeds" and "Oaten reeds" of pastoral eclogue to sing, instead, "of Knights and Ladies gentle deeds" (*FQ* 1.proem.1). The outlandish manner of this newcomer at Gloriana's court exemplifies what Alastair Fowler terms the "tertiary" stage of generic development, which "seems often to interiorize" a preexisting literary kind in line with a symbolic "interpretation of generic features."[57] When the unknown youth sits on the floor in mute recognition that his lack of armor and his "rusticity" render him "unfitte . . . for a better place," according to the *Letter to Ralegh*, his dilemma reflects the disparity between pastoral and epic as genres occupying the apex and base of the generic hierarchy. The youth's inarticulate resignation dramatizes the deficiency of pastoral in a scene that anticipates Spenser's effort to fashion a purified form of pastoral (or georgic) by the time the knight arrives at the Mount of Contemplation.

[57] Fowler, *Kinds of Literature*, p. 163.

Even though the pastoral scene may serve eventually as a *locus* for the revelation of truth, at the outset of the "Legend of Holiness" it is aligned with spiritual illusion or avoidance of truly heroic action. Before arriving at visionary places like Mount Contemplation or Eden, therefore, Redcrosse first enters into a series of anti-Edenic locales. Errour dwells within a green world that seems to offer shelter from "an hideous storme," but her immediate environs are deathly and "darksome" (1.1.6, 14). Although Redcrosse and Una make their way out of this dangerously shady grove, Archimago immediately leads them back into the land of pastoral error,[58] where his hermitage is situated:

> Downe in a dale, hard by a forests side,
> Far from resort of people, that did pas
> In travell to and froe.

(st. 34)

Fradubio and Fraelissa never hear the "mery oaten pipe" of pastoral song because shepherds shun "th'unlucky ground" in which they are rooted (1.2.28). Una's abandonment by Redcrosse consigns her, alternatively, to an extended episode of wandering in the wilderness, which is divided into two narrative sequences by his experience at the Palace of Pride. Although Una's encounters with the Lion and the fauns and satyrs may mimic idyllic scenes,[59] her experience emphasizes the reality of ignorance, death, and despair instead of pastoral escapism (1.3.1–44, 1.6.1–48). The scene represents a return to the harsh metaphorical landscape of "May" and "July," just as Una's role in teaching the satyrs recalls Piers's homiletic voice.

Like the Wood of Errour, the site of Una's sojourn reverses the languid associations of the *locus amoenus*, whose conventional description as an idealized landscape finds its antecedents in Roman pastoral poetry. This locale represents a departure from prelapsarian Eden, from which Una has been driven into exile by the depredations of the great Dragon, to the dreary landscape of the fallen world described in Revelation. As the biblical model for Una's experience as a damsel in distress, the Woman Clothed with the Sun and her retreat into the wilderness (Rev. 12:6) imply a topical context, because Protestants reinterpreted her suffering by reference to the conflict between the "true" church and the "false" church of Rome (see above, pp. 73, 82). Henry More recognizes this ecclesiastical allegory when

---

[58] On the Wood of Error and Archimago's glade as antipastoral places, see Knapp, "Error as a Means of Empire," pp. 803–11.

[59] See Bernard, "Spenserian Pastoral and the *Amoretti*," p. 420.

he declares that Una's "Entertainment by Satyrs in the Desart, does lively set out the condition of Christianity since the time that the Church of a Garden became a *Wilderness*."[60] Despite moments of relative tranquillity in this rural scene, where Una pauses to "gather breath in many miseries" (1.6.19), Spenser invites the reader to rethink the uses of pastoral by emphasizing the real danger, suffering, and woe that Una and her champions experience. As a place of ignorance and depravity, this landscape illustrates the sturdiness of Renaissance antipastoral sentiment. Sidney's *Arcadia* analogously reflects the hostility of a contemporary Protestant humanist to the mythic ideal of a life of idleness during a golden age devoid of "the real difficulties and hardships that life close to nature involves." Although Sidney's Arcadian landscape possesses the natural beauty of the *locus amoenus*, it is a place where rape is attempted, brigands lurk, and a wild lion suddenly attacks.[61]

Withdrawal into a self-contained world of contemplative enjoyment is incompatible with Una's commitment to Redcrosse and to the rescue of her parents and their kingdom. While her sudden encounter with the Lion that bursts "out of the thickest wood" might seem to be part of an antipastoral movement (1.3.5), Spenser parts from convention when the awestruck beast instinctively fills Redcrosse's place as the lady's protector. Corceca's household similarly inverts the conventional pastoral expectations of idleness and idyllic life. Her "cotage small" is hardly an Arcadian rural seat, and both she and her daughter, Abessa, personify ignorance and "blind" faith (sts. 14, 18). The depredations of Kirkrapine provide an antithesis to the rustic pleasures of shepherds and shepherdesses, just as his habit of robbing "Churches of their ornaments" and "holy Saints of their rich vestiments" evokes ecclesiastical issues familiar from the pastoral satires in Spenser's *Calender*. Although the Lion suppresses Kirkrapine's robbery of "holy things" (st. 17), Una's short-lived respite from suffering soon ends when Sansloy slays her protecting beast.

Una's providential rescue from Sansloy and her befriending by "a troupe of *Faunes* and *Satyres*" may seem compatible with pastoral escapism, but these spirits live in a world devoid of revelation (1.6.7) Their woodland habitat is reminiscent in some respects of the domain of Errour. The partly human and partly bestial nature of these spirits sets up a contrast between the limitations of pastoral ignorance and Christian revelation. The association of the woodland figures with

---

[60] More, *An Explanation of the Grand Mystery of Godliness* (1660), p. 169.

[61] Peter Lindenbaum, *Changing Landscapes: Anti-Pastoral Sentiment in the English Renaissance* (Athens, Ga.: University of Georgia Press, 1986), p. 12; see also pp. 42, 44, 75.

the desolation of Israel, when "the Satyrs shal dance there" (Isa. 13:21), emphasizes their spiritual deficiency and lack of scriptural understanding (see *FQ*, ed. Hamilton, 1.6.7n). Una's simple presence, however, is able to tame creatures whose proverbial lust drives them to rape unprotected nymphs (e.g., st. 22). The disruptive aspect of the satyrs' sudden appearance may be noted in Ben Jonson's *Entertainment at Althorpe* (perf. 1603) and *Oberon, the Faery Prince* (perf. 1611), where they appear as an unruly force alien to true courtliness. Modeled on *The Faerie Queene*, the latter masque dramatizes the taming of the satyrs, after they have danced a wild nighttime antimasque "full of gesture, and swift motion," when they witness the orderly rationality of the princely dance that greets the rising of the sun at Oberon's court.[62]

Una's sojourn in the wilderness passes into religious satire when the satyrs begin to worship "her heavenly grace" (st. 18), a misinterpretation that results from a collision between pagan ignorance and the veiled light of revelation associated with the lady. Their ignorance differs from that of Corceca's household, however, because it is based not on willful disobedience, but on the limitations of the natural world lacking in grace. Una's ability to supplant "old *Sylvanus*" (st. 7), the Roman god of uncultivated land, alludes to the eclipse of pagan lore by Christian wisdom. The Spenserian association of the pastoral mode with religious satire survives into Book 6, where Calepine rescues Serena from near-rape and sacrifice by "a salvage nation" whose "divelish ceremonies" evoke lurid Protestant attacks on the Roman-rite mass as a continuing sacrifice (6.8.35, 45).

The advent of Satyrane, a knight whose remoteness from civilization mirrors the rusticity of Redcrosse, might seem to underscore a shift to Christian pastoral. His ability to discipline his passions and his innate eagerness to accept Una's instruction in "Trew sacred lore" (1.6.30) set him apart from the satyrs, with whom he shares a woodland origin and a common descent through his satyr-father. As Una's champion, his epithets ("Plaine, faithfull, true, and enimy of shame"; st. 20) identify him as an incomplete double of Redcrosse (see *FQ*, ed. Hamilton, st. 20n), a knight who is "Right faithfull [and] true" (1.1.2). Donald Cheney notes that "it is appropriate that Una teaches him 'her discipline of faith and veritie' (I.vi.31), for it is in terms of discipline that his 'pagan' knowledge of truth must be formulated." Nevertheless, Satyrane plays no more than a minor role in the "Legend of Holiness" because "he stands outside the Christian

---

[62] Jonson, *Works*, ed. C. H. Herford, Percy Simpson, and Evelyn Simpson, 11 vols. (Oxford: Clarendon Press, 1925–52), 7: 351.

dispensation which alone makes Redcross' quest possible."[63] The lack of resolution in Satyrane's combat with Sansloy, fomented by Archimago disguised as a "false *Pilgrim*" (1.6.48), points to the inadequacy of unaided human nature. Despite his natural virtue, Satyrane falls short of Redcrosse, who, regardless of his manifold failures and deficiencies, has been singled out as an elect saint by divine providence.

## Tragedy of Salvation and Damnation

Una comments explicitly on literary genre when, upon her encounter with the Dwarf, she requests that he "Tell on . . . the wofull Tragedie, / The which these reliques sad present unto mine eie" (1.7.24). Their meeting marks the reunion of her subplot with the main line of action. She mistakenly assumes that the discarded armor carried off by her attendant when he took flight from Orgoglio's Castle indicates that her champion has suffered a tragic death. The Spenserian narrator compresses into one stanza the indirect discourse of Redcrosse's experience, which the narrator has already rendered in copious detail, from the time that Archimago succeeded in dividing him from Una:

> Then gan the Dwarfe the whole discourse declare,
>> The subtill traines of *Archimago* old;
>> The wanton loves of false *Fidessa* faire,
>> Bought with the bloud of vanquisht Paynim bold:
>> The wretched payre transform'd to treen mould;
>> The house of Pride, and perils round about;
>> The combat, which he with *Sansjoy* did hould;
>> The lucklesse conflict with the Gyant stout,
> Wherein captiv'd, of life or death he stood in doubt.
>
> (st. 26)

The Dwarf's narrative clearly lacks the formal dramatic attributes of Attic tragedy, but it does approximate some of its inner features; Spenser characteristically offers loose definitions of his embedded genres in terms of subjective qualities like mood and style. Redcrosse and his actions demonstrate the nobility of character, necessity of choice, discoveries, and reversals typical of the genre. Moreover, his thoughtless anger and abandonment of Una approximate the *hubris*

---

[63] Cheney, *Spenser's Image of Nature: Wild Man and Shepherd in "The Faerie Queene"* (New Haven: Yale University Press, 1966), pp. 63, 65.

of the tragic hero during the classical age. Both the taleteller and his solitary audience share the appropriately "wofull" emotions of pity, fear, sadness, and sorrow (1.7.19–20). This "Tragedie" is a fitting complement to the melancholy sadness that has dominated Una's mood from the beginning of the first canto, where she is described "As one that inly mournd: so was she sad, / And heavie sat upon her palfrey slow" (1.1.4). Redcrosse's mood corresponded to her own because his "cheere did seeme too solemne sad" (st. 2). When Prince Arthur learns about his experience, he adopts the somber view that "blisse may not abide in state of mortall men" (1.8.44).

When Una tells her own "storie sad" to Prince Arthur prior to his attack upon Orgoglio's Castle, repeated references to her "sorrow," "misfortunes," "grief," and "woes" (1.7.39–42) represent a fitting response to the experience of life in the fallen world. Her mournful mood derives from the repeated cycle of tragic misery, first of her parents, Adam and Eve, then of the series of champions who failed in her defense, and finally of Redcrosse. Her compressed retelling of his career constitutes an interpretation of prior events, one that accords with the version that she had heard from the Dwarf (sts. 49–51). Her view grounds the tragedy in original sin because Redcrosse has joined her prior champions who had failed "for want of faith, or guilt of sin" (st. 45).[64] As an instrument of divine grace, Arthur pulls Una back from despair, to which Redcrosse later succumbs, with the reminder that "Despaire breedes not . . . where faith is staid" (st. 41). This response indicates that faith makes it possible to transcend the tragic cycle of sin and damnation, if only after death. The narrator's summary at the beginning of the next canto sets Redcrosse's suffering within the context of Protestant theology of justification, whereby the elect are "imputed righteousness" even though they remain "radically sinful" in their mortal life.[65] The narrator avers that "heavenly grace" makes possible the undoing of the "daily fall" and "foolish pride" of the "righteous man" (1.8.1).

In grounding Redcrosse's fall in the sin of pride derived from Lucifer, Spenser adopts the well-known pyramidal pattern of *de casibus* tragedy, a narrative mode in which a descent from "height," like that of Algrind in the "July" eclogue, reverses a rise in fortune. It is exactly this kind of tragedy that the Dwarf witnesses in "his maisters fall" (1.7.19). On the model of Boccaccio's *Falls of Illustrious Men*,

---

[64] A. C. Hamilton remarks that the initial "tragedy" in *FQ* 1 culminates in Redcrosse's "fall into Orgoglio's dungeon" in *The Structure of Allegory in "The Faerie Queene"* (Oxford: Clarendon Press, 1961), p. 59. He argues further that the first part of Book 1 is structured as "the five acts in a tragedy" (p. 60).

[65] Lewalski, *Protestant Poetics*, p. 17.

works like *The Mirror for Magistrates* and a host of dramatic imitations made tragedy of this kind a familiar feature of Elizabethan literature. Such works relate spiritual failure to reliance upon fortune rather than to divine providence. Chaucer is of particular importance in establishing a tragic context for the "Legend of Holiness" because of his Tudor reputation as a religious reformer and because of the special deference that Spenser pays to him as a literary mentor. *The Monk's Tale* illustrates the potential of *de casibus* tragedy to differentiate between the falls of the reprobate and the saved, because the foregrounding of Adam's fall among many pagan examples holds out the implicit promise that God may choose to exempt certain individuals from damnation.

Redcrosse's inability to recognize the foreshadowing of his own fall in the exemplum of Fradubio and Fraelissa intensifies the irony growing out of the continuing failure of chivalric norms. It is the reader who must make the connection with a hero who remains tragically ignorant of his own fate. The knight's sojourn at Lucifera's court, his seduction by Duessa, and his defeat by Orgoglio offer a consistent portrait of different manifestations of spiritual pride. Marked by his armor as a disdainful stranger at Lucifera's Palace of Pride, Redcrosse can remain aloof from the vanity of the gathered throng, but his finding that their glory is "vaine in knightly vew" is grounded not in faith, but in the defining trait of "that great Princesse too exceeding prowd" (1.4.15). Although the knight lacks moral grounds for his judgment, the Dwarf discovers the carnage concealed behind the glittering façade of Lucifera's palace, a figure for hell where "huge numbers" of the damned are imprisoned. The Dwarf succeeds in averting Redcrosse's fall, at least temporarily, by making "ensample of their mournefull sight" by means of abbreviated *de casibus* tragedies that function as rhetorical warnings to flee from the "dreadfull spectacle of that sad house of *Pride*" (1.5.45, 52–53).

The succession of two separate portraits of pride provides a major crux: Why is Redcrosse able to escape from the Palace of Pride only to experience defeat at Orgoglio's Castle? The seduction of the backsliding knight by Duessa, his doffing of his armor and abandonment of his shield, leave him vulnerable to conquest. The Woodhouse hypothesis that Lucifera and Orgoglio represent "worldly pride" and "spiritual pride"[66] in Redcrosse's encounters with them fails to acknowledge the many references to religious error at Lucifera's domicile. By way of contrast, Patrick Cullen interprets the early phase of Redcrosse's quest as an integrated sequence in which the hero's "degeneration at the hands of Catholic tempters" constitutes a rejection

---

[66] Woodhouse, "Nature and Grace," in *Essential Articles*, p. 65.

of "the redemptive efficacy of works rather than faith." According to this view, Redcrosse exemplifies the special danger facing Protestants of relying on "a false faith in one's being numbered among the elect, which is in reality not true faith at all but a prideful perversion of faith into a presumptuous confidence in one's spiritual superiority."[67] The Dwarf's flight following Orgoglio's victory indicates that in spiritual affairs the individual Christian must fight a solitary battle aided by nothing more than inner faith and divine grace.

The rural setting where Redcrosse and Duessa fornicate beside a shaded fountain is an antipastoral locale reminiscent of the Wood of Errour. Religious and erotic allegory intermingle when Redcrosse willingly removes his armor in dalliance with his faithless paramour. His unwitting participation in his own defeat—"ere he could his armour on him dight, / Or get his shield" (1.7.8)—indicates that Orgoglio functions as a projection of the knight's own sinfulness, of his inward self. The giant's surprise attack externalizes the knight's own spiritual and physical state. The liaison of Orgoglio and Duessa, as a metamorphosis of the Whore of Babylon, associates the giant with human depravity, the "pride" of carnal desire, and theological error.[68] The giant is aligned with the "Kings of the earth" who "committed fornication" with the great harlot (Rev. 17:2; Fig. 11). Redcrosse's culpability for the very same transgression indicates an uneasy symmetry between the knight and Duessa's monstrous lover.[69]

The Orgoglio episode incorporates complementary tragedies of the reprobate and the elect. As a version of the fall of tyrants, the "Gyaunts fall" (1.8.23) represents an alternate side of Redcrosse's own defeat. The giant has every attribute of the "proud and presumptuous 'Other' " that Protestant sermons and manuals of meditation urged the elect to identify and purge as a means of distinguishing themselves by antithesis from the reprobate.[70] Arthur's beheading of Orgoglio exposes the giant's real impotence by means of a parodic "deflation" comparable to the self-consuming explosion of Errour's brood:

> But soone as breath out of his breast did pas,
> That huge great body, which the Gyaunt bore,

---

[67] Cullen, *Infernal Triad*, pp. 35–36.

[68] See Kellogg and Steele, pp. 30, 36; and Hamilton, *Structure of Allegory*, p. 76. Shroeder discusses the giant's phallic nature in "Spenser's Erotic Drama," pp. 140–59.

[69] On the topos of "spiritual fornication," see Waters, *Duessa as Theological Satire*, pp. 62–93, passim.

[70] Martha T. Rozett, *The Doctrine of Election and the Emergence of Elizabethan Tragedy* (Princeton: Princeton University Press, 1984), pp. 53, 58.

> Was vanisht quite, and of that monstrous mas
> Was nothing left, but like an emptie bladder was.
>
> (st. 24)

The giant's downfall, like that of the great Dragon in Eden, falls outside the limits of genuine tragedy, but within the overarching pattern of divine comedy.[71] The narrator's shift into a comic mode neutralizes any possibility for achieving pathetic effects similar to those experienced by Una, upon hearing the Dwarf's account of Redcrosse's "wofull Tragedie" (1.7.24), or by Arthur, who experiences "pitty deare" upon hearing the knight's lament within his prison cell (1.8.39). Duessa's unseating from the Seven-headed Beast immediately after Orgoglio's defeat constitutes a further variation of the motif of the toppling of the pope that pervades the iconography of the Protestant Tudor monarchs (see above, pp. 96–99).

The knight's tragedy departs from classical precedent in its lack of simultaneous *peripeteia* and *anagnorisis*. The reversal of fortune is a consequence of his seduction by Duessa, whereas recognition awaits his conviction of sin and his spiritual regeneration following his rescue by Arthur. In contrast to the spiritual emptiness of Orgoglio's demise, the proximity of the knight's place of imprisonment to a sacrificial altar aligns his experience with the slaughter of the martyrs who "were killed for the worde of God" (Rev. 6:9):

> And there beside of marble stone was built
> An Altare, carv'd with cunning imagery,
> On which true Christians bloud was often spilt,
> And holy Martyrs often doen to dye,
> With cruell malice and strong tyranny.
>
> (st. 36)

Because the dungeons at the Palace of Pride and Orgoglio's Castle represent alternate states of spiritual captivity, the unregenerate suffering of Lucifera's reprobate prisoners contradicts the experience of Orgoglio's victims. As martyrs, the latter are capable of regeneration and salvation. When Redcrosse overcomes his inarticulateness, he makes possible his rescue by directing Arthur to his cell (see *FQ*, ed. Hamilton, 1.8.38n). The knight is poised, at the lowest point in his tragic descent, to begin the strenuous ascent to spiritual understanding. Arthur's battering down of the "yron doore" (st. 37) of Red-

---

[71] On Milton's Satan as a "parodic tragic hero" who similarly moves "outside and below both the classical and the Elizabethan paradigms for tragedy," see Lewalski, *Rhetoric of Literary Forms*, pp. 64–65.

crosse's cell recalls the Harrowing of Hell, through which Christ rescued the souls of Adam, Eve, and the patriarchs:

> Where entred in, his foot could find no flore,
> But all a deepe descent, as darke as hell,
> That breathed ever forth a filthie banefull smell.

(st. 39)

Spenser's revision of the life of St. George presents Redcrosse as the successor of "holy Martyrs" (st. 36) whose tragic suffering is counterbalanced by the "happy fault" that holds out the promise of an eventual rise in fortune due to Christ's victory. As an agent of divine grace, Arthur rescues Redcrosse and makes it possible for the knight to "witness" to his own faith as a Protestant saint. G. K. Hunter notes that religious martyrdom is an important component of early Elizabethan tyrant plays in which the "flamboyant but brief trajectory of the tyrant figure" is set against the "inextinguishable ethos of his martyr-victim."[72] Accordingly, the complementary relationship of Redcrosse and Orgoglio parallels the "dual-protagonist scheme" of Reformation moral interludes, which enabled the playwright to resolve "the Calvinist's dilemma by permitting him directly to contrast the saved and the damned."[73] John Bale's *King Johan* provides an outstanding example of the tragedy of a "martyr" king who refused to submit to papal dominion. Like the "Legend of Holiness," this Protestant tragedy culminates in the reformation, formal forgiveness, and restoration of order characteristic of divine comedy. Redcrosse's survival to fight the Dragon differs, however, from the experience of King John and other martyred saints who win their victories only in death.

## Biblical Parody

The Augustinian theory of the setting forth in the Bible of a radically symbolic universe supplies a context for the epistemological dilemma that faces Redcrosse during much of Book 1, a dilemma that results from his initial inability to grasp the fundamental relationship between *res* and *signa* (*De doctrina Christiana* 2.1–2). By taking words and things as univocal phenomena, he ignores the symbolic or theological dimension by which they may point to concealed spiritual mean-

---

[72] G. K. Hunter, "Tyrant and Martyr: Religious Heroisms in Elizabethan Tragedy," in *Poetic Traditions of the English Renaissance,* ed. Mack and Lord, pp. 89–90.
[73] Rozett, *Doctrine of Election,* p. 89.

ings; more importantly, he cannot judge the corresponding power of words and deeds to deceive and confuse. From the beginning of the "Legend of Holiness," the narrator warns that despite Archimago's apparent humility ("Sober he seemde, and very sagely sad"; 1.1.29), both his words and deeds embody charms and magic that are also associated with Duessa and Despair (1.1.36, 1.8.14, 1.9.48). By way of contrast to these highly articulate speakers, among whom even the most "demonic" can quote scripture, Redcrosse remains strikingly inarticulate and silent. Because the knight relies on deeds of prowess rather than thought until his spiritual education at the House of Holiness, he is vulnerable to sophistical persuasions. The knight's inability to perceive hidden implications places him at grave disadvantage in his encounters with irreligious figures. Not until he learns that spiritual experience transcends the deceptive world of outward appearances does he finally learn to speak and read.

Despair dwells in yet another antipastoral locale, where vegetation withers and "carcases were scattered on the greene, / And throwne about the cliffs." Redcrosse discovers Despair in a cave set beneath a cliff in a barren landscape filled with "old stockes and stubs of trees, / Whereon nor fruit, nor leafe was ever seene" (1.9.34). This encounter follows immediately upon the knight's rescue by Arthur because conviction of sin represents only the first step toward true repentance. Indeed, predestinarian theologians warned against despair as a special danger to the elect. (The prince had already counseled Una that "Despaire breedes not . . . where faith is staid" [1.7.41].) The knight's experience accords with Calvin's warning that the elect soul is particularly vulnerable to despair when, upon first becoming aware of the enormity of its sinfulness, it feels unworthy of divine love and powerless to avoid divine punishment.[74] Because Redcrosse remains ignorant of the Bible and the true meaning of repentance until his course of instruction at the House of Holiness, Despair readily assumes the role of a parodic preacher who knows the scriptures intimately. More importantly, the process by which he distorts the Bible exemplifies by contrary example Protestant attitudes toward the correct application and interpretation of the Bible.

The temptation of Christ in the wilderness (Matt. 4:1–11) supplies the *locus classicus* for the wresting of the scriptures, because Satan misleadingly quotes an assurance of divine protection to the faithful (Ps. 91:11–12) in his attempt to convince Christ to test divine will by leaping from a high place. The Protestant polemical identification of

---

[74] Kellogg and Steele, pp. 38–39. See Daniel Doerksen, " 'All the Good Is God's': Predestination in Spenser's *Faerie Queene*, Book I," *Christianity and Literature* 32 (1983): 11, 13.

the mishandling of the Bible as a manifestation of Catholic error may be noted in John Bale's variation of a medieval mystery play, *A Brief Comedy Concerning the Temptation of Our Lord* (Wesel, c. 1547), in which Satan, costumed as a monk, declares to Jesus, during his forty-day sojourn in the wilderness, that God has charged his angels:

> that if ye leape at large
> They shall receyve ye    in their handes tenderly,
> Least ye dashe your fote    agaynst a stone therby.

Christ's rejoinder that his tempter has suppressed a key phrase demonstrates the proper application of the Bible as a guide to life:

> Yea, but ye omytted    foure wordes whych foloweth next,
> As 'in all thy wayes,'    whych if ye put out of syght,
> Ye shall never take    that place of scripture a ryght.[75]

The Geneva Bible similarly calls attention to Satan's practice of omitting key phrases "to deceive thereby the rather, and cloke his craftie purpose" (gloss on Matt. 4:6). Among the abuses of textual interpretation that Protestant commentators like Bale and William Perkins find in the temptation sequence are "quoting out of context, deleting verses, and reading too literally or too allegorically."[76]

In his encounter with Despair, Redcrosse's lack of both rhetorical expertise and scriptural knowledge leaves him vulnerable to devices of argumentation that he cannot even recognize. Identified as a skilled sophist by his "subtill tongue, like dropping honny" (1.9.31), Despair conceals his intentions behind a barrage of rhetorical questions in a riddling application of *pysma*, a scheme of amplification that is present, according to Henry Peacham the Elder, "when we ask often times together, and use many questions in one place, wherby we do make the oration sharp and vehement."[77] Despair accordingly

---

[75] *Complete Plays of John Bale*, ed. Happé, 2: 58, ll. 210–12, 226–28. Patrick Cullen identifies a Protestant temptation tradition between the time of Bale and Milton in *Infernal Triad*, pp. 62–63.

[76] Imbrie, " 'Playing Legerdemaine with the Scripture,' " p. 143. The ensuing discussion of scriptural parody is indebted throughout to Imbrie's discussion, in which she extrapolates Protestant hermeneutical practice from Bale's *Temptation of Our Lord* (Wesel, c. 1547), Bullinger's *Decades*, and Perkins's *Combat between Christ and the Devell Displayed: or a Commentary upon the Temptations of Christ*. Richard Mallette concurs that Despair is a parodic preacher in "The Protestant Art of Preaching," pp. 14–17. On the association of biblical parody with Phaedria and Mammon, see Whitaker, *Religious Basis*, pp. 25–26; Cullen, *Infernal Triad*, pp. 69–70; and William M. McKim, Jr., "The Divine and Infernal Comedy of Spenser's Mammon," *Essays in Literature* 1 (1974): 3–16.

[77] Peacham, *The Garden of Eloquence* (1577), L4. On the distortion of the tropes and schemes of Renaissance rhetoric in the discourse of Duessa, Archimago, and Despair,

collapses premise and conclusion in the balanced antitheses that climax his call to suicide:

> Sleepe after toyle, port after stormie seas,
> Ease after warre, death after life does greatly please.

(st. 40)

Despair exemplifies the fault of quotation out of context by piling up incomplete references to the scriptures in order to confound Redcrosse, who can neither reply effectively to the heaped-up proofs of his state of sin nor recognize that those arguments constitute a mismatched pastiche of texts drawn from the Epistle to the Romans and other scriptures in the Old and New Testaments. Although the naive knight is impressed by his opponent's "suddeine wit" (st. 41), a reader knowledgeable in the Bible should note the irony that the "Devill knowes the whole Scripture, and he will spare no text therein if he can corrupt it."[78]

Recognition of the Pauline foundation of the Despair episode compounds the irony, because the Epistle to the Romans is the primary source for the doctrine of justification by faith alone, the fundamental Protestant tenet that Redcrosse has thus far resolutely refused to learn. Luther and his followers gained confidence from St. Paul's assurance that justification follows as an immediate consequence of predestination: "Moreover whome he predestinate, them also he called, and whome he called, them also he justified, and whome he justified, them he also glorified" (Rom. 8:30).[79] By way of contrast, straightforward allusions to the Pauline epistles comprise the doctrinal core of the House of Holiness episode. Despair comes to the verge of victory by preaching a doctrine of damnation rather than salvation in "an infernal sermon" based upon Romans 3:23: ". . . for all have sinned, and are deprived of the glorie of God. . . ."[80] His discourse wrests the scriptures, however, by ignoring the conclusion of the scriptural sentence: "and are justified frely by his grace, through the redemption that is in Christ Jesus" (Rom. 3:24). The speaker's partial application similarly distorts the Pauline admoni-

---

see Herbert D. Rix, *Rhetoric in Spenser's Poetry*, Pennsylvania State College Studies, no. 7 (State College, Pa.: Pennsylvania State College, 1940), p. 68.

[78] Perkins, *Combat between Christ and the Devell*, in *Works*, 3 vols. (Cambridge, 1609), 3: 392. Because understanding of the scriptures is the sole antidote to Satanic sophistry, "true" preachers must not "wrest the same from the proper meaning of the holy Ghost to serve their own conceit" (p. 393).

[79] Doerksen, " 'All the Good Is God's,' " p. 12.

[80] Cullen, *Infernal Triad*, pp. 60–61. Cullen documents Spenser's extensive allusion to the Pauline epistles, notably Romans 6–7, as does Nohrnberg, *Analogy*, pp. 153–55.

tions that believers should accept that "the wages of sinne is death" (Rom. 6:23) and kill "our olde man . . . that the bodie of sinne might be destroyed" (Rom. 6:6). Redcrosse's impassioned response to this speech, as if "a swords point through his hart did perse" (st. 48), uneasily reflects Despair's ability to falsify the Bible because it distorts the familiar understanding of "the sworde of the Spirit" as a metaphor for "the worde of God" (Eph. 6:17; see Heb. 4:12). The knife offered by the tempter parodies the function of the Pauline sword that Redcrosse has such great difficulty in wielding,[81] just as Despair's words invert the truly penitential function of Remorse, who pricks the knight's heart at the House of Holiness so that "drops of bloud thence like a well did play" (1.10.27).

Una intervenes in this one-sided debate by completing the Pauline argument that Despair has left half-stated. For example, she points out that he has suppressed the merciful ending of a passage that declares that "the wages of sinne is death." This text concludes: "but the gifte of God is eternal life through Jesus Christ our Lord" (Rom. 6:23; see 1.9.46–47). Although Despair has brought Redcrosse to the brink of suicide by emphasizing his state of sin, Una proclaims the scriptural basis for salvation that the speaker has suppressed:

> In heavenly mercies hast thou not a part?
> Why shouldst thou then despeire, that chosen art?
>
> (st. 53)

The doctrine of election provides a response to despair bred of belief in predestination.[82] When Mercy guides the knight to Mount Contemplation in the next canto, she personifies the vital importance of this missing term of argument.[83]

## True Georgic

Despite Redcrosse's recovery of his voice at Orgoglio's Castle (1.8.38), he remains unfit for spiritual combat until after he undergoes instruction at the House of Holiness and visits Mount Contemplation. That his elect status as a "chosen" knight is no more than the starting point for the journey of salvation is acknowledged by the

[81] Nohrnberg, *Analogy*, p. 153.

[82] *Article* 17 (of *The Thirty-nine Articles of Religion*) warns that the fate of the reprobate "to have continually before their eyes the sentence of Gods predestination, is a most daungerous downefall, whereby the devyll doth thrust them either into desperation, or into rechelesnesse of most uncleane living, no less perilous then desperation."

[83] Ernest Sirluck, "A Note on the Rhetoric of Spenser's Despair," *Modern Philology* 47 (1950): 8–11; Doerksen, " 'All the Good Is God's,' " pp. 13–14.

narrator's moralization, which echoes Una's original admonition that Redcrosse rely on faith rather than physical prowess. The narrator's rhetorical question and comment apply the knight's own history as an exemplum for human powerlessness and the providential operation of divine grace:

> What man is he, that boasts of fleshly might,
>> And vaine assurance of mortality,
>> Which all so soone, as it doth come to fight,
>> Against spirituall foes, yeelds by and by,
>> Or from the field most cowardly doth fly?
>> Ne let the man ascribe it to his skill,
>> That thorough grace hath gained victory.
>> If any strength we have, it is to ill,
> But all the good is Gods, both power and eke will.
>
> (1.10.1)

With its foundation in scriptural understanding, the education of Redcrosse at the House of Holinesse (see above, pp. 60–65) marks a turn from a predominantly tragic to a predominantly comic mode of representation when, in the major breakthrough of the knight's progress, the hero rises to his highest point of spiritual ascent.

As a projection of the knight's inward mind, Contemplation is aligned with the mystical ideal of divine illumination, which plays a prominent role in medieval thought. St. Bonaventure's *Itinerarium mentis in Deum* furnishes a prototype for the rediscovery of the divine image within the mind and the soul's return to God. A fourfold ascent passes from sensual apprehension through intellectual judgment and introspection to mystical contemplation. The seraphic vision of St. Francis of Assisi on Mount La Verna provided Bonaventure with the structure for the *Itinerarium*'s ascent to a high place of vision.[84] Spenser's ideal hermit completes Redcrosse's spiritual education by leading him to reject a chivalric code grounded in simple battle deeds and honor and to rededicate himself to the higher values of Christian heroism. Despite the hero's new yearning to turn away from the world, however, he must learn that the way to sainthood lies through fulfillment of his spiritual quest not by withdrawal, but by action in the real world. Contemplation's insistence that he fulfill his worldly duty accords with "an emphasis shared by Protestantism and reforming elements of the medieval church on action as opposed to contemplation" (Kellogg and Steele, p. 43). *The Faerie*

---

[84] St. Bonaventure, *The Mind's Journey to God*, trans. Lawrence S. Cunningham (Chicago: Franciscan Herald Press, 1979), p. 9. See also Steven Ozment, *The Age of Reform 1250–1550: An Intellectual and Religious History of Late Medieval and Reformation Europe* (New Haven: Yale University Press, 1980), pp. 121–27.

*Queene* places action and contemplation on an equal footing.[85] This realignment of the active and contemplative lives gives priority to action in the world over the life of withdrawal emphasized in extreme forms of Roman Catholic piety. Nevertheless, contemplation retains its honored place in Christian spirituality.

As the endpoint of Redcrosse's spiritual education, "the highest Mount" (st. 53), from which he experiences a momentary glimpse of the New Jerusalem, constitutes a variation of the Christian "tradition of the mountain-top or hermitage experience." The narrator's deferential *occupatio*—"Too high a ditty for my simple song" (st. 55)—provides a "signal of literal reference to a Christian mystery."[86] Contemplation, whose inward vision enables him to read the book of God's foreknowledge, is a type of the seer of Revelation, who saw the heavenly city from a mountain peak on Patmos (Rev. 21:10; see Fig. 5).[87] That this peak is a sublime site of sacred vision is apparent from the triple simile that compares the Johannine mountain with Hebrew, Christian, and pagan places of prophetic inspiration: Mount Sinai, the Mount of Olives, and Parnassus. When the narrator turns to Moses and Christ as the chief scriptural prototypes for visionary ascent and prophecy, he also validates secular verse by subsuming the lesser inspiration of classical poetry within the context of biblical revelation:[88]

> That done, he leads him to the highest Mount;
>   Such one, as that same mighty man of God,
>   That bloud-red billowes like a walled front
>   On either side disparted with his rod,
>   Till that his army dry-foot through them yod,
>   Dwelt fortie dayes upon; where writ in stone
>   With bloudy letters by the hand of God,
>   The bitter doome of death and balefull mone
> He did receive, whiles flashing fire about him shone.

> Or like that sacred hill, whose head full hie,
>   Adornd with fruitfull Olives all arownd,

[85] West, "Spenser and the Renaissance Ideal of Christian Heroism," p. 1021.

[86] Carol V. Kaske, "Spenser's Pluralistic Universe: The View from the Mount of Contemplation (*F.Q.* I.x)," in *Contemporary Thought on Edmund Spenser*, ed. Richard C. Frushell and Bernard J. Vondersmith, (Carbondale and Edwardsville, Ill.: Southern Illinois University Press, 1975), pp. 132–33.

[87] Nohrnberg, *Analogy*, pp. 156–58. John Wall comments on Spenser's modification of classical precedent in this episode in "The English Reformation," pp. 143, 146.

[88] Alan Sinfield ignores syncretism when he misinterprets "the second, implicitly climactic half" of stanza 54 as an implication of "a radical validity in pagan imagery," in *Literature in Protestant England*, p. 30.

Is, as it were for endlesse memory
Of that deare Lord, who oft thereon was fownd,
For ever with a flowring girlond crownd:
Or like that pleasaunt Mount, that is for ay
Through famous Poets verse each where renownd,
On which the thrise three learned Ladies play
Their heavenly notes, and make full many a lovely lay.

(sts. 53–54)

The rudimentary personification of the Mount of Olives that is suggested by the "fruitfull Olives" crowning its "head" implies that a parallel exists between Christ's ministry and laureate poetry dedicated to the Muses. The ambiguous reference of the phrase "For ever with a flowring girlond crownd" suggests that both Jesus, as the greatest of the prophets, and the famous hill associated with his ministry wear not the laurel crown of the classical poets, but an olive wreath. (Wearing the olive victory wreath or *stephanos* was esteemed among the pagans, too.) This image of an olive crown associates Christ with poetic inspiration by linking this site to Parnassus, the home of the pagan Muses. A complicated series of correspondences relates "endlesse memory / Of that deare Lord" to the perpetual flowering of the olive trees, meditation, and the verse for which the pagan poets are "renownd." Sacred harmony and songs of worldly love ("full many a lovely lay") are assimilated into a complex identification of poetry and prophecy.

In contrast to the deficient satyr-world of Una's antipastoral wanderings, Mount Contemplation is a pastoral *locus amoenus* that has undergone a georgic modulation.[89] Spenser characteristically defines elevated locales of this kind as places of visionary insight. In style and subject matter, this episode has little in common with the Renaissance conception of pastoral as a lowly genre; instead, its literary affinities lie with the alternative tradition that associates pastoral of the classical Golden Age with the epoch of the biblical patriarchs.[90] Contemplation plays the role of the wise tutor in a Christianized version of the pastoral motif of the withdrawal of the hero in order to educate and return him to active life in the real world. The combination of pastoral and georgic conventions of character and thought may be noted in the hermit's unraveling of the mystery of Redcrosse's background by revealing his real name: Georgos (Greek for

---

[89] Anderson attributes a "witty pastoralizing of Revelation" to Contemplation's speech in "a curiously pastoral idiom" (*Growth of a Personal Voice*, p. 44).

[90] See Lewalski, *Rhetoric of Literary Forms*, p. 173.

"farmer"; st. 66). Contemplation's designation of Redcrosse as "thou man of earth" (st. 52) acknowledges the innate depravity that human beings share with their progenitor, Adam, whom God formed out of "the dust of the grounde" (Gen. 2:7).[91] At the hermit's mountaintop retreat, the knight learns to combine the gospel concerns of Christian husbandry with the labor that informs Virgil's *Georgics*.[92]

By infusing epic romance with conventions from the native English tradition of plowman satire, Spenser fashions Redcrosse as an idiosyncratically georgic knight. The fulfillment of his quest holds out not the pastoral expectation of a life of peacefulness, leisure, and abundance, but the georgic obligation of hard work. After long postponement of his heroic task, Redcrosse learns from Contemplation that he must postpone "that last long voyage" to the New Jerusalem in order to complete his quest in the land of Eden (st. 63). The knight learns further that he is a descendent of Saxon kings who, having been kidnapped in infancy by a fairy, was soon abandoned in "an heaped furrow" of a well-tilled field. The unexpected discovery of this foundling by a plowman and his upbringing "in ploughmans state" (sts. 65–66) align the knight's character with the native georgic tradition of *Piers Plowman*,[93] *Pierce the Plowmans Crede*, and the pseudo-Chaucerian *Plowman's Tale*. Surely the strident Protestantism of the sixteenth-century editions of these texts conditioned Spenser's incorporation of a humble English plowman into romantic epic. The knight's destiny to "walke this way in Pilgrims poore estate" (st. 64) suggests that his route combines the quest for spiritual understanding of Piers Plowman and the pseudo-Chaucerian Plowman with the Protestant way to salvation. Chaucer's idealization of the humble Plowman, whose failure to tell a story made it possible for Tudor editors to insert the apocryphal *Plowman's Tale* into the *Canterbury Tales*, and his brother, the Parson, who represents the exemplary cleric among the Canterbury pilgrims, were among the "proofs" that led Protestant ideologues to adopt the medieval poet as a crypto-reformer.[94]

---

[91] "The first man is of the earth, earthlie: the seconde man is the Lorde from heaven" (1 Cor. 15:47). See Cullen, *Infernal Triad*, p. 36.

[92] See Sessions, "Spenser's Georgics," pp. 235–36.

[93] For views that *Piers Plowman* provides a structural scheme for either the "Legend of Holiness" or the whole of *FQ*, see the respective arguments of A. C. Hamilton, "The Visions of *Piers Plowman* and *The Faerie Queene*," pp. 2–20; and Anderson, *Growth of a Personal Voice*, pp. 1–5, et seq.

[94] See above, pp. 20–27. Anthony Low notes that while the idealization of labor in *Piers Plowman* contains the "seeds of the Protestant Reformation," the work articulates an orthodox call for reform with a long medieval lineage, in *The Georgic Revolution* (Princeton: Princeton University Press, 1985), p. 186.

## Divine Comedy

The second invocation of the "sacred Muse" signals the final turning away from the limitations of traditional chivalry to the generic mixture of Christian epic, which places the purged forms of romance, pastoral, tragedy, and georgic within the larger frame of divine comedy. The poet modulates the Virgilian formula, *arma virumque cano*, into a prayer for inspiration to assume the "second tenor" or lower style appropriate to sacred song: "That I this man of God his godly armes may blaze" (1.11.5–7; compare 1.proem.1). The concluding episode of Book 1 incorporates a progressive movement toward the New Eden of Revelation rather than a return to the site of the Fall in Genesis. As types for baptism and holy communion, the Well of Life and the Tree of Life provide sacred landmarks for the climactic battle in which Redcrosse defeats the great Dragon. Although the monster that threatens humankind, figured by Una's parents, represents a fusion of a romance motif with the Beast of Revelation, argument for "complete identification" of Redcrosse "with the risen Christ" breaks down the crucial distinction between type and antitype.[95] His red cross marks the knight indelibly as a Christian soldier.

The pronounced turn toward "joy" following the defeat of the great Dragon (1.12.3–4, 7, 40–41) lodges the question of whether the knight's regeneration and victory make up a divinely inspired comic reversal of a tragic action. Like Milton, his self-proclaimed disciple, Spenser diverges from standards for tragicomedy that were formulated during the Renaissance debate over Guarini's *Il Pastor Fido*. As Barbara Lewalski notes, Milton centers *Paradise Lost* on "the Fall and the 'world of woe' it produces for Adam and Eve and all mankind."[96] In sharp contrast to works by Guarini and his English followers, Beaumont and Fletcher for example, the restoration of Eden in Canto 12 of the "Legend of Holiness" takes place in a world in which mortal danger and suffering abide. In place of the miraculous deliveries and absence of death in Renaissance tragicomedy, this conclusion portrays a world of human misery in which Una is "left to mourne" by the departure of her hero (st. 41). Closure remains impossible, however, until he has discharged his vow of six-year service "in warlike

[95] Kaske, "Dragon's Spark," in *Essential Articles*, pp. 445–46. For further discussion and alternative views, see Cullen, *Infernal Triad*, pp. 90–96; Kellogg and Steele, pp. 45, 47; and note 48, above.

[96] Lewalski, *Rhetoric of Literary Forms*, p. 222. See Hamilton, *Structure of Allegory*, p. 59, for an argument that a comic rise to the point of the betrothal in Eden compensates for Redcrosse's tragic fall; see also p. 79 there.

wize" to "that great Faerie Queene" (st. 18). Among the parallels that
*Paradise Lost* shares with the "Legend of Holiness" is its closing
movement, which looks forward to the millennial reversal of the tragedy of the Fall experienced by Adam and Eve and their descendents.[97]

Reformation drama furnishes abundant precedents for Spenser's
employment of Revelation as a model for interpreting human history
as a broad context for many particular "tragedies" of elect saints,
whose experience would undergo reversal at the millennium. These
plays dramatize the ability of the papal Antichrist to deceive the
faithful in a manner that parallels Redcrosse's experience with Archimago and Duessa. Protestant playwrights often used the term "tragedy" very loosely, but they sometimes applied it precisely to define
plays in which stage action concludes with a prophecy of a "comic"
reversal at the end of time that will restore faithful believers to hap-
piness.[98] Thomas Kirchmeyer's *Pammachius* (Wittenberg, 1538), a
"tragoedia nova" translated by John Bale, established a model for
apocalyptic tragedy.[99] Although humankind appears to suffer an ir-
reversible tragic fall as Pammachius, a papal Antichrist, rises in fortune, the abrupt breaking off of the play after the fourth act wittily
dramatizes millenarian expectations. In lieu of the fifth act dictated
by classical precedent, the epilogue announces that the Second Coming is at hand and that Christ will provide his own catastrophe,
which, if it could be represented on stage, would contain a double
reversal involving the tragic fall of the damned and the comic victory
of the chosen. In *King Johan*, Bale transfers Kirchmeyer's archetypal
pattern to the martyrdom of the medieval monarch whom he viewed
as a reformer who staunchly resisted papal tyranny. Bale's version of
events accords with his full-scale reading of human history in terms
of a conflict between the invisible church of the elect and the visible
church of the reprobate in *The Image of Both Churches*. "Comoedia
Apocalyptica" is the term that John Foxe applies to *Christus Triumphans* (Basel, 1556), another work modeled on *Pammachius*. The author evidently conceives of this form as a sublime genre containing
the manifold tragedies of the suffering faithful; the martyrological

[97] Lewalski, *Rhetoric of Literary Forms*, pp. 221–22. She notes that Milton's epic "has
a tragedy at its center and undertakes a complex fusion of the heroic and tragic modes"
(p. 29).

[98] On the Renaissance use of Revelation as a tragic paradigm, see Barbara K. Lewalski, "*Samson Agonistes* and the 'Tragedy' of the Apocalypse," *PMLA* 85 (1970): 1050–55;
and *Rhetoric of Literary Forms*, pp. 223–24 and nn. 17–20.

[99] Barnabe Googe's translation of Kirchmeyer's satire, *The Popish Kingdome, or Reigne
of Antichrist* (1570), was published during Spenser's lifetime.

structure of this work anticipates the embedding of individual tragedies within the comprehensive pattern of divine comedy in "The
Book of Martyrs."[100] The suffering of Protestant "saints," who are
destined for a heavenly reward according to the "Book of Martyrs,"
suggests furthermore that Foxe accepts tragedies of double issue of
the kind that Aristotle disapproved; this encyclopedic work defines
the contrasting downfalls of "reprobate" persecutors as "tragic"
events. Italian critical theory accepts that epic rather than drama is
the appropriate context for joining together the perpetual tragedy of
the damned and the averted tragedy of the elect.[101]

An even closer analogy to Spenser's assimilation of the tragic suffering of the faithful into epic may be found in Théodore Agrippa
d'Aubigné's *Les Tragiques* (1616), a work whose composition dates
back to the religious turmoil of the late 1570s. Although the narrator
invokes Melpomene, the tragic Muse, the title cannot be taken as an
adequate generic description of a work defined as epic poem. D'Aubigné's prefatory address "Aux Lecteurs" refers explicitly to his mixture of epic, tragedy, and satire. The explanation that the work
moves from a low tragic to a high tragic "style" refers not so much
to stylistic decorum as to the hybridizing of a variety of subgenres in
a work that ranges from polemical satire to consolatory divine comedy. The self-consciousness displayed by the Huguenot poet about
adopting this literary strategy suggests the likelihood that Protestant
authors like Spenser took a similar stance. Spenser similarly regards
religious warfare and the persecution of Protestants for their faith as
ongoing outbreaks of an apocalyptic conflict between Christ and Antichrist. D'Aubigné takes Revelation as the model for the seven-book
format of his work, which ranges from "Miseres," an opening account of contemporary religious conflict in France, to "Jugement," a
visionary prophecy concerning the coming end of corruption and the
reign of justice at the end of the world. The fifth and sixth books
constitute the generic hinge of the collection, because the former
("Les Fers") looks backward toward a depressingly tragic account of
the martyrdoms of the faithful from the limited point of view of
worldly experience. The shift to a heavenly vantage point in the fifth
book permits the narrator to reinterpret the suffering of the elect as
an example of divine testing that represents no more than a transi-

---

[100] Foxe, *Two Latin Comedies*, ed. and trans. John Hazel Smith (Ithaca, N.Y.: Cornell
University Press, 1973), pp. 212–13. See Norbrook, *Poetry and Politics*, pp. 38–39, 120.

[101] According to Lodovico Castelvetro's *Poetica d'Aristotele Vulgarizzata, et Sposta* (Basel, 1576), p. 696, the distinctive pleasure of epic is derived "d'all avenimento delle
due diverse persone buone, & ree, felice per le buone, e infelice per le ree." I am
indebted to William Lewis for this reference.

tory setback in the universal context of apocalyptic history. From the sixth book ("Vengeances") onward, "tragic" suffering loses its immediacy because it is placed within the "comic" context of God's providential design. By means of a series of *apophécies* (hindsight prophecies of events that have already taken place), the narrator "foretells" a future leading to the joyous victory of the "true" church. The conclusion anticipates a final and as-yet-unwritten book concerning the resolution of religious conflict, one that should recount the meting out of punishments to the reprobate and rewards to the faithful in heaven.[102]

As an outstanding example of the double *peripeteia* familiar from Protestant apocalyptic drama, the climax of the "Legend of Holiness" enfolds the multitude of tragic miseries throughout the book into the sweeping comic pattern of providential history. The rising action of Redcrosse's regeneration and victory as Una's champion counterbalances the downfall of the Dragon that had besieged the castle of her parents.[103] That the victory belongs to God alone is made clear, however, by the knight's new reliance on his Pauline armor and by the manner in which his sword, a figure for revelation through the scriptural Word, serves as an autonomous agent of retribution in slaying the monster. A recognition of the Reformation vogue for divine comedy helps to explain the high-spirited gathering of residents of Eden about the Dragon's carcass in what might seem to be a disconcerting shift from the more elevated apocalyptic handling of the battle itself. The superstitious fears of the "raskall many" (i.e., lowly mob) effect the by-now-conventional "deflation" of monstrosity that may be noted in the defeats of Errour and Orgoglio. Despite the Dragon's masculinity, rumors that the beast's "wombe" (i.e., belly) teems with "Dragonets" link it to Errour in a composite image of the proliferating fecundity of evil (1.12.9–10).

That comedy is the endpoint of Spenser's syncretic strategy in Book 1 is apparent from the songs and tales that celebrate Red-

---

[102] D'Aubigné, *Les Tragiques*, ed. I. D. McFarlane (London: Athlone Press, 1970). See Rosalie Colie, *Resources of Kind*, p. 100; J. A. Walker, "D'Aubigné's *Les Tragiques*: A Genre Study," *University of Toronto Quarterly* 33 (1964): 109–24; and Richard L. Regosin, *The Poetry of Inspiration: Agrippa D'Aubigné's "Les Tragiques,"* University of North Carolina Studies in the Romance Languages and Literatures, no. 88 (Chapel Hill: University of North Carolina Press, 1970), pp. 28–32, 66–78, passim. See also Richard M. Tresley, "Renaissance Commentaries on the Book of Revelation and Their Influence on Spenser's *Faerie Queene* and D'Aubigné's *Les Tragiques*," dissertation, University of Chicago, 1980.

[103] The device of *anaphora*, with its insistent repetitions, aligns the beast's defeat with the fall of Babylon (Rev. 14:8), "of which this dragon is a type," according to Upton, ed., *FQ* (1758): 1.11.54n. Cited in *FQ*, ed. Hamilton, 1.11.54n.

crosse's victory. The "joyous lay" of the maidens (st. 7), for example, fuses the laurel boughs of the classical poets with the timbrels that accompany Hebrew songs of divine praise (see Pss. 68:25, 149:3, 150:4; Isa. 24:8). Similarly, the "triumphant Trompets" send to heaven

> the ecchoed report
> Of their new joy, and happie victorie.
>
> (st. 4)

The stress on the *newness* of "joy" calls attention to the redefinition of pleasure and delight in accordance with Spenser's shift to Christian epic; "joy" is an appropriate response both to the tragedies of the faithful and to the outer frame of providential comedy that encloses them. (The Edenic celebration contradicts the joylessness personified by Sansjoy.) The recurrence of the term "joy" throughout Book 1 enables the reader to track a movement from its original identification with the worldliness of "vaine delight" (1.2.3) to the higher spiritual pleasures offered through the theological virtues of faith, hope, and charity. Comic references to "joy" culminating in the "exceeding merth" of the festival "proclaimd throughout the land" (1.12.40) cluster thickly throughout the final canto (sts. 3–4, 7, 41). After the conventional sharing of a meal that precedes the telling of tales in classical epic, Redcrosse adopts an elegaic manner akin to that of Una when he narrates his "perils sad" and "straunge adventures." In the fourth and final recounting of his downfall, the knight himself succeeds the Spenserian narrator, the Dwarf, and Una as the teller of his own "pittiful adventures." The tale's effect on the audience at the court of Adam is appropriate to providential comedy because the listeners respond with "Great pleasure mixt with pittifull regard." The only question on Adam's mind concerns the achievement of the proper balance between celebration and pathos: "whether prayse, or pitty more" (sts. 15, 17).

An epithalamium in celebration of the betrothal of Redcrosse and Una concludes Book 1 with a moment of still unification (see above, pp. 178–79). The knight's previously concealed descent from the ancient Saxon kings makes him a suitable candidate to wed Una, a biblical royal heiress. The Song of Solomon provides the scriptural model, because a tradition of allegorical interpretation going back to Origen assimilates the love of the Bridegroom and the Bride (a type for the true church) into the Marriage of the Lamb (Rev. 19:7). Origen interprets the Song of Solomon, moreover, as a model for drama, in the mode of pastoral idyll, which embodies dialogue between characters and twin choruses.[104] Reformation drama provides contemporary analogues to Spenser's practice. According to Kirchmeyer's *Pammachius*, the future union of Veritas and Christ as the Bridegroom and the Spouse holds out the possibility for a comic outcome of the tragic suffering of the faithful. In Foxe's *Christus Triumphans*, the concluding epithalamium and chorus of the virgins prophesy the resolution of apocalyptic conflict at the time of Christ's victory and the descent of the New Jerusalem. Ecclesia's designation as the Spouse carries with it intense apocalyptic expectations as the play concludes immediately prior to the promised double catastrophe that will follow upon the union of Christ the Bridegroom and his Spouse. In a dramatization of the song sung at the Marriage of the Lamb, the epithalamic chorus celebrates the anticipated return of Christ in the high comic mode of divine praise.

Generic boundaries disappear at the conclusion of Book 1 of *The Faerie Queene* within the all-embracing category of divine comedy. This ultimate simplification fittingly brings to a close a book that moves from generic multiplicity to the primal unity of truth embodied in Una. Although the celebration of the betrothal mirrors the union of Christ with the true church, Spenser's handling of this event is not chiliastic. The reappearance of Duessa and Archimago indicates that the trajectory of human history remains incomplete; the transcendence of time and space is located in a promised future. Because Spenser relates fairyland to the real world, the reader finds that Redcrosse must, at the end of his quest, return to where he began in order to complete his service to Gloriana. In the interim, Una is "left to mourne" (1.12.41) as her champion sets off to conclude his assigned task. His departure from Eden marks the shift in Spenser's emphasis from spiritual to secular affairs in the later books of *The Faerie Queene*.

## Continuities

Debate continues over whether the "Legend of Holiness" establishes an allegorical or theological paradigm for later books of *The Faerie Queene*. In response to the view that succeeding knights inherit the moral territory won by their predecessors, A.S.P. Woodhouse arrives at the influential hypothesis that Book 1 operates "upon the level of grace and deals with a specifically Christian experience and virtue," in opposition to later books that "move upon the level of nature and

---

[104] See above, pp. 173–74; and Kellogg and Steele, p. 47.

concern themselves with the natural virtues."[105] Other scholars have qualified or rejected this view by noting ways in which the careers of Guyon and other knights parallel that of Redcrosse, thus giving evidence of a fundamental harmony between the natural world and revealed theology. Alastair Fowler insists, therefore, that "each book after the first is built upon the preceding book, and takes for granted the spiritual territory already conquered."[106] While this argument has been formulated in largely theological terms, one may perceive ways in which Spenser extends his reformation of literary genres into the later books.

Evidence of continuity in no way implies that *The Faerie Queene* is a homogeneous or complete work. Although Books 5 and 6 parallel Books 1 and 2 in structural terms, they represent the culmination of a "general movement . . . from private to public virtues." One may accommodate the harsh political tenor of the final books by recognizing that the religious allegory of Book 1 provides an "extended prologue to the whole poem, setting secular values in a wider context." Arguing that Spenser locates fairyland "in the time between the decline of Roman rule and the triumph of the Saxons," David Norbrook points out that in Books 5 and 6, in particular, the "poem's present" depicts a time of such cultural backwardness "that it must be forcibly propelled into the sixteenth century." Merlin's prophecy that "order and civility . . . will one day be established by Elizabeth" therefore establishes a sharp contrast between a barbaric age and a narrative future that will witness the Reformation of Spenser's own historical present.[107] Book 5's explicit concern with setbacks suffered by the international Protestant cause supports the view that the "optimistic faith that had animated the early books, the faith that history was going the right way, seems to have left Spenser in the 1590s."[108]

While Spenser consistently styles no book except the "Legend of Holiness" as a Protestant hagiography, Book 5 in particular builds upon Book 1 as a model for religious iconography and a sequence of embedded "tragedies" that share much in common with the experiences of both Redcrosse and Una.[109] This is fitting because the social and cultural upheaval of the Reformation provides the topical occa-

---

[105] Woodhouse, "Nature and Grace," in *Essential Articles*, p. 81.

[106] Fowler, *Spenser and the Numbers of Time* (New York: Barnes and Noble, 1964), p. 85. See also Hamilton, *Structure of Allegory*, pp. 90–106; Cullen, *Infernal Triad*, pp. 68–96; and Hume, *Protestant Poet*, pp. 67–68.

[107] Norbrook, *Poetry and Politics*, pp. 119, 126, 148.

[108] Helgerson, *Self-Crowned Laureates*, p. 91.

[109] See Stump, "Isis Versus Mercilla," p. 88.

sion for both books.[110] The "Tragicke stowre" of widow Belge and her retreat into the fens for safety (5.10.13, 18) recalls Una's experience as a variation of the Woman Clothed with the Sun. Both figures seek haven in the wilderness because they are defenseless against irreligious enemies. In the manner of the land of Eden to which Una is heiress, Belge's territory has fallen under the dominion of a monstrous invader, Geryoneo, who governs tyranically like both his father Geryon, and Orgoglio (st. 12). Geryon, who "whylome in Spaine so sore was dred," and his son, who imposes a "yoke of inquisition" upon "a Citie farre up land" (i.e., Antwerp), are clearly identified with the extension of Hapsburg authority into the Low Countries (sts. 9, 25, 27). The sacrifice of Belge's sons (i.e., provinces) upon an altar bearing Geryon's idolatrous image evokes both the apocalyptic context of the slaughter of the "holy Martyrs" at Orgoglio's Castle (1.8.36) and the prophetic promise that the present suffering of the faithful will ultimately lead to a joyous outcome. Spenser models Arthur's slaughter of Geryoneo and destruction of the dragon-tailed monster within his idolatrous shrine (5.11.33–35) upon Redcrosse's battles against Errour and the great Dragon to the extent that he incorporates a comic celebration akin to the one that greeted the Edenic victory in the closing canto of Book 1.

Like Belge, Duessa suffers a "tragicke stowre" (5.9.45), but her misery manifests the truncated tragedy of the reprobate, whose damnation accords with the conventions of Protestant religious allegory. By using Una's familiar antagonist as a thinly veiled figure for Mary, Queen of Scots, Spenser invites the reader to connect the trial and execution of Elizabeth's rival to the religious allegory of Book 1. In the eyes of Elizabethan Protestant readers, these associations could only condemn the northern queen as a latter-day Whore of Babylon and agent of foreign Catholic aggression.[111] Mercilla differs sharply from both Una and Belge in her invulnerability and exercise of autonomous power, but she too is a variant of the Woman Clothed with the Sun. The stark contrast between her sun-bright majesty and the marred countenance of Duessa, whose "rare beautie" is "blotted with condition vile and base" (st. 38), recalls the apocalyptic opposition between "true" and "false" women that John Bale and others interpreted as a prophecy of the contemporary history of the church. Duessa's execution provides at least a partial resolution to the reli-

[110] Frank Kermode, *Shakespeare, Spenser, and Donne*, pp. 39–49; and O'Connell, *Mirror and Veil*, pp. 149–50.

[111] Dixon associates Duessa variously with Mary Tudor and Mary Stuart (Dixon, *Commentary* 1.12.argument n., and 1.12.26n).

gious crisis that remained open when she sent her lying letter to Adam at the end of the "Legend of Holiness" (1.12.25–29).

The fusion of the Armor of God with classical imagery furnishes an iconographical link between Books 1 and 5. By employing Chrysaor, the sword from "*Joves* eternall house" that ended the rebellion of the Titans (5.1.9), Artegall assumes an instrumental position analogous to Redcrosse's when he wielded the Pauline sword in the battle in Eden. Although Artegall repeatedly serves as an agent of divine vengeance (see 5.2.18), his defenselessness when "his sharpe sword he threw from him apart" (5.5.13) recalls Redcrosse's willful disarming in the company of Duessa prior to his capture by Orgoglio. Artegall's collaboration with Arthur similarly evokes the prince's earlier cooperation with Redcrosse. Arthur's enduring fidelity renders him capable of functioning as an instrument of providential victory when he unveils his adamantine shield, whose blinding light furnishes a figure for the brightness of divine revelation. According to Burbon's testimony, his own discarding of the Shield of Faith alludes to the Armor of God because Redcrosse "Gave me a shield, in which he did endosse / His deare Redeemers badge upon the bosse" (5.11.53). In the narrator's view, Burbon abandons Protestant faith on grounds that correspond to those which lead Geryoneo and Grantorto respectively to oppress Belge and Irena (i.e., Ireland). Burbon's abandonment of this shield refers explicitly to the recent conversion to Catholicism of Henri du Bourbon (later Henri IV^me) in order to cement his authority as king of France.

The "Legend of Justice" incorporates successive resolutions of the "tragic" suffering of the faithful through the defeats meted out by Arthur and/or Artegall to the Souldan, Geryoneo, and Grantorto, who collectively personify the menace posed to the international Protestant movement by foreign Catholicism. Nevertheless, enduring victory cannot be achieved, despite the celebrations that greet the rescues of Belge and Irena. The reconciliation of Burbon and Flourdelis (a transparent figure for France) is marred, for example, by the faithlessness that both have displayed. Although the local populace joyfully greets Artegall's decapitation of Grantorto and prevention of Irena's execution, no final resolution is achieved. On the level of historical allegory, Artegall's recall to the court of Gloriana and his encounter with Envy, Detraction, and the Blatant Beast signify the scandal that destroyed Lord Grey's career following the Smerwick massacre (1580), when he was recalled from Ireland following his failure to honor a pledge to spare the lives of captured Spanish and Italian mercenaries.[112]

---

[112] See O'Connell, *Mirror and Veil*, pp. 155–56.

Nevertheless, it is a convention of Reformation tragedy that the ultimate resolution of worldly misery cannot be attained prior to the Second Coming and the end of the world. Artegall's quest to rescue Irena accordingly fails to achieve a complete resolution of discord. Like the abrupt breaking off of Artegall's effort to implement "true Justice" and to reform Irena's land (5.12.26), Calidore's capture of the Blatant Beast evokes the "tragic" context of the Reformation experience. Although the knight of Courtesy succeeds in restraining the monster, its escape constitutes yet another outbreak in an enduring cyclical conflict. According to Revelation, such an escape must precede the Second Coming (Rev. 20:7–10). The coda for the entire poem provided by the *Cantos of Mutabilitie* is not unlike the ending of Book 1, because it circles around to apocalyptic expectation of the end of time:

> But thence-forth all shall rest eternally
> With Him that is the God of Sabbaoth hight:
> O that great Sabbaoth God, grant me that Sabaoths sight.
>
> (7.8.2)

Much recent Spenser criticism argues that Book 6 provides a sense of closure for *The Faerie Queene* as a literary whole.[113] Nevertheless, the incompleteness of the epilogue added in the posthumous folio edition (1609) and the conventional open-endedness of apocalyptic works as various as *Piers Plowman* and the dramas of Bale and Foxe suggest that the poet never abandons a compositional strategy based upon both aggregation and disjunction. At least one critic accordingly calls attention to evidence of disunity and lack of closure in *The Faerie Queene*.[114] The lack of resolution of the endings of Books 1, 5, and 6, and the apparently fragmentary nature of the *Cantos of Mutabilitie*, accord with the recognition that only at the end of time will the tragic misery of the faithful be placed within the surrounding frame of providential comedy.[115]

Spenser's reformation of literary genres is an example of his pervasive syncretism. The present book contends that a key to understanding Spenser lies in recognizing the diversity of his art rather than its unity. The poet's imagination attempts a synthesis of artistic elements from biblical and pagan, sacred and secular, classical and me-

[113] E.g., Richard Neuse, "Book VI as Conclusion to *The Faerie Queene*," *ELH* 35 (1968): 329–53; James Nohrnberg, *Analogy*, ch. 5; Susanne Woods, "Closure in *The Faerie Queene*," *JEGP* 76 (1977): 195–216.

[114] See Stanley Stewart, "Sir Calidore and 'Closure,' " *Studies in English Literature* 24 (1984): 69–86.

[115] See Lewalski, *Rhetoric of Literary Forms*, pp. 222–23.

dieval, Continental and British tradition in an effort to reconcile differing beliefs without denying either their divergencies or the primacy of Protestant theology. Because the native Protestant element in Spenser's verse has received relatively little attention, Renaissance scholarship has never adequately acknowledged the impact of Reformation imaginative literature on his poetic works. This gap probably results from the clearly evident richness of imported literary forms in vogue during Spenser's poetic career. Nevertheless, the native vernacular provided another fertile source of inspiration. Spenser's oeuvre gives evidence of his response to strictly religious texts, like the *Book of Common Prayer* and the English Bible, and his familiarity with themes and conventions of Protestant satire and allegory. Although this study is concerned with the native Protestant element in Spenser's art, it does not deny the importance of other layers in his syncretistic fusion.

We first note the importance of generic diversity in *The Shepheardes Calender*, where Spenser juxtaposes metrical and stanzaic features based upon foreign poetic models with the blunt language, humble characterization, and other conventions typical of native vernacular satire. In Tityrus, the apprentice poet emulates both Roman Virgil and English Chaucer as models for composing distinctively Protestant satirical eclogues. Spenser assimilates the widespread contemporary image of Chaucer as a religious reformer, whose works were aligned with the tradition of georgic satire spawned by *Piers Plowman*.

A satirical dimension also informs Spenser's pervasive concern with iconoclasm in many of the famous setpiece scenes of *The Faerie Queene*. Book 1 in particular shares the disapproval of the alleged abuses of the Roman church establishment that the reader encounters in "May," "July," and "September" from *The Shepheardes Calender*. Although *The Faerie Queene* incorporates an iconoclastic attack against the abuse of art, Spenser avoids the iconophobic extreme of equating art with idolatry. Like many earlier English Protestants, he attempts to supplant "false" images with purified alternatives. This iconoclastic strategy of juxtaposing the destruction and construction of art is related to the uneasy symmetry between iconic praise of Queen Elizabeth, through her affinity with such figures as Una, Belphoebe, Britomart, and Mercilla, and blame lodged against negative embodiments of "queenship" like Duessa, Lucifera, and Radigund.

The high valuation that Protestants placed upon marriage, as opposed to the idealization of celibacy in medieval Christianity, leaves its mark on Spenser's treatment of romantic love poetry. In *The Faerie Queene*, Belphoebe and Amoret personify chastity as it is manifested differently in lives dedicated to virginity and to married love. The high praise accorded to wedlock in *Amoretti and Epithalamion* represents a distinctive modification of Petrarchan convention. In place of the traditional dedication of romantic verse to unmarried love, Spenser takes the radically innovative step of grafting an epithalamium onto a sonnet sequence that culminates in betrothal.

"The Legend of Holiness" is the Spenserian text most firmly imprinted with Protestant ideology. The priority of Book 1 establishes the purified form of the saint's life as a context for the later books in *The Faerie Queene*, despite their secular concerns. The poet's countergeneric strategy assimilates an iconoclastic attack against saints' lives of the kind collected in *The Golden Legend* at the same time that it appropriates some of the conventions of medieval legends of the saints. Spenser's reworking of the legend of St. George, despite the hostility of Protestant humanists who also opposed romance as a form associated with immorality and religious error, incorporates evangelical iconography that predates the reign of Elizabeth I. Redcrosse's symbolic armament should enable the reader to recognize him from the outset as a Protestant saint. Acknowledging the deficiency of existing models for romantic epic, Spenser defines Redcrosse's heroic action in terms of Christian spirituality rather than simple deeds of combat. True romance therefore takes its place within the all-encompassing borders of divine comedy, which contains purged varieties of pastoral, georgic, tragedy, and epithalamium. Spenser's realignment of literary genres and modes in line with Protestant ideology is an important element within the encyclopedic diversity of his verse.

# APPENDIX

## WAS SPENSER A PURITAN?

A N ATTEMPT has been made to revive the notion that the writing of *The Shepheardes Calender* was motivated by Puritan zeal. The major external evidence cited in favor of this interpretation rests upon assumptions that Spenser shared the religious views of (1) Robert Dudley, Earl of Leicester; (2) Jan van der Noot, in whose *Theatre for Worldlings* (1569) Spenser's first verse appeared; and (3) Hugh Singleton, the printer of the first edition of the *Calender*.[1]

The Leicester connection is the easiest to address because it is overly reductive to define the progressive Protestant faction that he led as a Puritan clique. He was a great patron whom authors certainly aimed to please, but he neither determined the positions taken by his protégés or supplicants, nor did he necessarily share their views. He definitely patronized extreme Puritans and presbyterians, but "one could support Puritans fervently in the 1570s without accepting their definition of discipline."[2]

The case of van der Noot is more complex, but surely it is inappropriate to call him a Puritan. He was a Brabantine, native to Antwerp, who wrote in Flemish and French and emigrated to London after the invasion of the Netherlands by the Duke of Alva. Despite the possibly eirenic views of the *Theatre*, van der Noot attacks the "abhominations of the [pope as the] Romyshe Antechriste" (A3, G7ᵛ) and the papal endorsement of pardons, indulgences, relics, purgatory, pilgrimages, religious images, and clerical celibacy (G1ᵛ, G8–H1). Nevertheless, his views share little in common with *doctrinal* Protestantism; indeed, he favored the Pléiade poets and converted to Catholicism some years after publication of the *Theatre*. His commentary is charged not with a Puritan critique of English religion, but with the generalized (and presumably temporary) hostility toward Roman hegemony over the Christian church that all Protestants and some Catholics shared in common. Moreover, Spenser's translations of the "Sonets" that van der Noot drew out of Revelation are non-polemical. The four visions, including the description of the Whore of Babylon, for example, offer straightforward biblical paraphrases (see *Var*. 7, ii: 279):

---

[1] Hume, *Protestant Poet*, pp. 6–8. See above, pp. 18–20.
[2] Weiner, *Sidney and the Poetics of Protestantism*, p. 6.

She seemde with glorie of the scarlet faire,
And with fine perle and golde puft up in heart.
The wine of hooredome in a cup she bare.
The name of Mysterie writ in hir face.
The bloud of Martyrs dere were hir delite.

(*Var.* 7, ii: 23; see Rev. 17:4–6)

Despite his antipapal stance, van der Noot's own quietism and pacifism run against the grain of English Puritanism. The millennial prophecies that he gathers out of Bale's *Image of Both Churches* and Bullinger's *In Apocalypsim Iesu Christi* (Basel, 1557) are characterized instead by an amalgamation of medieval, Lutheran, and Swiss reformed scriptural commentary.[3]

According to long-standing tradition, the man who printed *The Shepheardes Calender*, Hugh Singleton, made his career by printing and publishing work by Puritans,[4] notably John Stubbs's *Discovery of a Gaping Gulf*.[5] Examination of all extant books imprinted by Singleton during his career of forty-five years fails, however, to substantiate this claim. Although he was an appropriate printer for both the *Gaping Gulf* and the *Calender*, his career was not marked by the Puritan partisanship of Robert Waldegrave or Richard Schilders.[6] The available evidence suggests further that although Singleton printed the *Gaping Gulf* and the *Calender*, he exercised no influence over the ideology, subject matter, or organization of the editions. There is,

[3] See Jan van Dorsten, *The Radical Arts: First Decade of an Elizabethan Renaissance* (Leiden: Leiden University Press, 1973), pp. 77–78; Prescott, *French Poets and the English Renaissance*, pp. 44–47.

[4] *The Shepherd's Calender*, ed. Renwick, p. 168; H. J. Byrom, "Edmund Spenser's First Printer, Hugh Singleton," *Library*, 4th ser., 14 (1933): 121–56. See also A. F. Scott Pearson, *Thomas Cartwright and Elizabethan Puritanism, 1535–1603* (Cambridge: Cambridge University Press, 1925), pp. 188–89.

[5] Soon after its publication in August 1579, *The Discovery of a Gaping Gulf* was suppressed by proclamation. See *Tudor Royal Proclamations*, ed. Paul L. Hughes and James F. Larkin, 3 vols. (New Haven: Yale University Press, 1964–69), no. 642. Stubbs was convicted at Westminster on 30 October 1579 of writing a seditious work and suffered the loss of his right hand on 3 November; he was imprisoned for more than one year. Although Singleton was prosecuted at the same time and sentenced to lose his hand, this penalty was never executed. See *John Stubbs's "Gaping Gulf" with Letters and Other Relevant Documents*, ed. Lloyd E. Berry (Charlottesville: University Press of Virginia, for the Folger Shakespeare Library, 1968), pp. xxvi–xxix; E. Gordon Duff, *A Century of the English Book Trade* (London: Bibliographical Society, 1905), p. 148; and Byrom, "First Printer," pp. 140–41.

[6] J. Dover Wilson comments in "Richard Schilders and the English Puritans," *Library*, 3rd ser., 11 (1909–11): 69, that "when the Puritans wished to publish anything dangerous they turned, and turned with confidence, to one or other of these two men." See also Collinson, *Elizabethan Puritan Movement*, pp. 273–75.

however, every reason to believe that he was probably the "instrument of the Leicester-Walsingham faction."[7]

The activities of Singleton are too diverse to be labeled simply as those of a "Puritan" member of the book trade. In 1548 Singleton began his career as a printer and publisher with translations of Lutheran writings and works written in support of the magisterial reforms implemented under Edward VI. His Edwardian output included John Foxe's first publication, *De Non Plectendis morte adulteris Consultatio*, a treatise opposing capital punishment for adultery that was written under the zealous patronage of Mary Fitzroy Duchess of Richmond, as well as translations by Foxe of works by Luther and two Rhineland reformers, Joannes Oecolampadius and Urbanus Regius (*STC* 16983, 18787, and 20847). Going underground during Mary Tudor's effort to advance the Counter Reformation, Singleton continued to publish Protestant tracts and translations, including writings by Bale, Calvin, Knox, and both English and German Lutheran reformers. Some of these fugitive publications may have been printed for him on the Continent, and their imprints bear some satirical colophons including "Rome, before the castel of s. Aungel at the signe of sainct Peter" (*STC* 1307, 4392, 13208, 13457, and 15059.5). Under Queen Elizabeth he continued to publish translations by Continental reformers and noncontroversial works of Protestant devotion, including Theodorus Beza's *Little Catechism* and some of the frequently published writings of Otto Werdmueller, the German Lutheran, in translations by Miles Coverdale (*STC* 2022–2023.5, 25250–25250.5, 25253, 25258–25258.5). The Werdmueller translations were first published during the reign of Queen Mary, except for the text of *A Spyrytuall and Moost Precyouse Pearle* that Edward Seymour edited soon after his deposition as Edward VI's Lord Protector. Singleton's output also included a funeral elegy, a tract against enclosures, a translation of a medieval contemplative manual, a handbook of accounting, and regulations that he printed for the City of London.[8]

Circular reasoning lies behind extrapolation from Singleton's "Puritanism" to that attributed to Spenser, because the originator of that view of the publisher's career cites Spenser's alleged Puritanism as one proof of Singleton's views.[9] Singleton, like many other "printers," often functions as a publisher for books printed by one or many undesignated hands. The word "printer" is used loosely at this time to describe the person undertaking to have books printed, and

---

[7] Byrom, "First Printer," p. 142.

[8] I am indebted to Katharine F. Pantzer's card index of English printers, 1475–1640.

[9] Byrom, "First Printer," p. 147. Byrom subscribes to the definition of Spenser's "Puritan" stance in Greenlaw, " 'The Shepheards Calender,' " pp. 436–38.

colophons often credit booksellers with books that they merely publish. Complicated business arrangements frequently lie behind apparently simple imprints, and it is these circumstances rather than ideological intention that often explain the publication process of works like Spenser's *Calender* and Stubbs's *Gaping Gulf.*[10] Singleton specialized in publication of texts compatible with the broad consensus of the Elizabethan church. Thus it should come as no surprise to find that hostility to the Roman Church permeates most of his publications, but taken as a group they fail to outline a "Puritan" program of reform.

Although some great printer-publishers like John Day and Richard Tottel commissioned works and collaborated with their authors, many other members of the book trade made their living by accepting whatever work came their way. Singleton was notoriously unsuccessful in his career, and his poverty would have made it extremely difficult for him to influence the content of books that he published. The Stubbs affair ruined Singleton, who, after giving up his press in 1581–82, continued to publish after his appointment as Printer to the City of London in 1584.[11] The most recent and thorough bibliographical studies of the *Calender* conclude that Singleton failed even to control decisions concerning layout and typography, and that Spenser determined the organization of the volume and program for the illustrations, which are integral to the text. Because Singleton had never before produced an illustrated book, he lacked both experience with woodcuts and regular access to the woodcutters who prepared the blocks.[12] It is virtually impossible that so impoverished a publisher would volunteer suddenly to undertake the major investment of capital required to produce an extraordinarily well-illustrated text. The woodcuts seem not to have been part of his printing stock, and they went as a unit to John Harrison the Younger, the publisher who commissioned the printing of the four editions of the *Calender* that were the work of four different printers between 1581 and 1597.

Not until the eve of the English Civil War were the ecclesiastical satires in the *Calender* reinterpreted as Puritan antiprelatical propaganda, when Milton concluded that it is the prelates of the Church of England whom "our admired *Spencer* inveighs against, not with-

[10] See W. W. Greg, *Some Aspects and Problems of London Publishing between 1550 and 1650* (Oxford: Clarendon Press, 1956), p. 83.

[11] Byrom, "First Printer," pp. 131–32; see also Stubbs, "*Gaping Gulf*," ed. Berry, pp. xxvi–xxxvi. Singleton was "one of the poorest of London stationers" (Byrom, "First Printer," p. 121).

[12] Luborsky, "The Allusive Presentation of *The Shepheardes Calender*," p. 41; and "The Illustrations to *The Shepheardes Calender*," p. 18 and n. 21.

out some presage of these reforming times."[13] Milton may have employed the *Calender* as a model for ecclesiastical satire in his own pastoral elegy, *Lycidas* (1638).[14] St. Peter's diatribe against "the grim Wolf with privy paw" (l. 128) resuscitates the Protestant satirical attack against "Romish" Wolves and Foxes that Spenser shares with William Turner.[15] Milton's approval of Spenser's satires suggests that Piers's defense of poetry in "October," ll. 19–20 ("*Cuddie, the prayse is better, then the price, / The glory eke much greater then the gayne*"), may provide one precedent for the first consolation in *Lycidas*:

> But not the praise,
> Phoebus replied, and touched my trembling ears;
> Fame is no plant that grows on mortal soil,
> Nor in the glistering foil
> Set off to the world, nor in broad rumor lies.
>
> (ll. 76–80)

During the Restoration Henry More interpreted "February" not as a Puritan attack, but as a prophecy of how presbyterians would suffer as a result of their attack on the episcopacy.[16] The variety of such readings offers a tribute to the open-endedness of Spenser's allegories.

Few have argued that Spenser's mature work in *The Faerie Queene* is marked by Puritan sentiment; indeed, opinion dating back to his own age identifies him with the conservative attack on late Elizabethan radicals. Ben Jonson supported this interpretation in conversation with Drummond, when he stated "that in that paper S. W. Raughly had of the Allegories of his Fayrie Queen by the Blating beast the Puritans were understood."[17] A version of the episode of the Giant with the Scales (5.2.29–54) that was issued separately during the Civil War sees Spenser as a supporter of monarchy and opponent of Puritanism.[18] This view was firmly in place a century later when Thomas Warton discovered in *Cantos of Mutabilitie* "a satirical

---

[13] Milton, *Animadversions against Smectymnuus* (1641), in *Complete Prose Works*, ed. Don M. Wolfe et al., 8 vols. in 10 (New Haven: Yale University Press, 1953–82 ), 1: 722–23.

[14] See Wittreich, *Visionary Poetics*, pp. 105–16, for the view that the *Calender* functions as "a general context for *Lycidas*."

[15] See pp. 36–38, above.

[16] More, *A Modest Enquiry into the Mystery of Iniquity* (1664), pp. 514–15.

[17] Jonson, *Works*, ed. Herford, Simpson, and Simpson, 1: 137.

[18] Anon., *The Faerie Leveller: Or, King Charles his Leveller descried and deciphered in Queene Elizabeths dayes* (1648). See John N. King, "*The Faerie Leveller*: A 1648 Royalist Reading of *The Faerie Queene*, V.ii.29–54," *HLQ* 48 (1985): 297–308.

stroke against the Puritans, who were a prevailing party in the age of Queen Elizabeth; and, indeed, our author, from his profession, had some reason to declare himself their enemy, as poetry was what they particularly stigmatiz'd, and bitterly inveigh'd against."[19]

Efforts to distinguish between the alleged Puritanism of *The Shepheardes Calender* and the Protestantism of *The Faerie Queene* fail to acknowledge that the latter work was under way in 1580 when Spenser collaborated with Harvey in publishing their correspondence. Harvey's comment on the poetic excellence of Revelation, the model for Spenser's most distinctively Protestant composition, "The Legend of Holiness," suggests that he may have seen a version of Book 1 of *The Faerie Queene* within one year of the publication of the *Calender* (*Var.* 9: 471–72). Piers's appeal to Cuddie to "abandon then the base and viler clowne" of pastoral eclogue and devote himself to romantic epic ("October," ll. 37–42) seems to indicate that Spenser thought about *The Faerie Queene* as he wrote his pastoral eclogues. The break between *The Shepheardes Calender* and the 1590 *Faerie Queene* is not as great as it has been made to seem.

[19] Warton's commentary on *FQ* 7.7.35, in *Observations on the Faerie Queene of Spenser*, 1st ed. (1754), p. 291.

# SELECT BIBLIOGRAPHY

## PRIMARY SOURCES

Ariosto, Ludovico. *Orlando furioso*. Translated by Sir John Harington (1591). Edited by Robert McNulty. Oxford: Clarendon Press, 1972.

*Articles of Religion*. See *The Thirty-nine Articles of Religion*.

Ascham, Roger. *The Schoolmaster*. Edited by Lawrence V. Ryan. Ithaca, N.Y.: Cornell University Press, for the Folger Shakespeare Library, 1967.

Bale, John. *The Complete Plays of John Bale*. Edited by Peter Happé. 2 vols. Cambridge: D. S. Brewer, 1985–86.

———. *Scriptorum illustrium maioris Brytanniae . . . catalogus*. 2 vols. Basel, 1557–59.

———. *Select Works of John Bale*. Edited by Henry Christmas. Parker Society, vol. 36. Cambridge: Cambridge University Press, 1849.

———. *The Vocacyon of Johan Bale* (1553). Edited by Peter Happé and John N. King. Renaissance English Text Society, 7th ser. vol. 14 (1989). Binghamton, N.Y.: Medieval and Renaissance Texts and Studies, vol. 70, 1990.

Bateman, Stephen. *A Christall Glasse of Christian Reformation*. 1569.

———. *The Travayled Pylgrime*. 1569.

Bible. See *The Geneva Bible*.

*The Book of Common Prayer 1559: The Elizabethan Prayer Book*. Edited by John E. Booty. Charlottesville: University Press of Virginia, for the Folger Shakespeare Library, 1976.

*Book of Homilies*. See *Certaine Sermons or Homilies Appoynted to be Read in Churches*.

Brightman, F. E. *The English Rite*. 2 vols. London: Rivingtons, 1915.

Bullinger, Heinrich. *The Christian State of Matrimony*. Translated by Miles Coverdale. 5th ed. C. 1546.

Calvin, Jean. *The Institution of Christian Religion*. Translated by Thomas Norton. 1561.

———. *Sermons upon the Epistle of S. Paule too the Ephesians*. Translated by Arthur Golding. 1577.

Catullus. *Catullus, Tibullus, and Pervigilium Veneris*. Edited and translated by F. W. Cornish et al. 3rd ed., rev. Cambridge, Mass.: Harvard University Press, 1962.

*Certaine Sermons or Homilies Appoynted to be Read in Churches*. 1633. Contains the two "tomes" in use after 1563. Personal copy.

Chaucer, Geoffrey. *Works* (1532). Facsimile edited by D. S. Brewer. London: Scolar Press, 1974

———. *The Works of Geoffrey Chaucer*. Edited by F. N. Robinson. 2nd ed. Boston: Houghton Mifflin, 1957.

Crowley, Robert. *Philargyrie of Greate Britayne* (1551). Edited by John N. King, in "*Philargyrie of Great Britayne* by Robert Crowley." *ERL* 10 (1980): 46–75.

Day, Richard. *A Booke of Christian Prayers*. 1578.

Dekker, Thomas. *Dramatic Works*. Edited by Fredson Bowers. 4 vols. Cambridge: Cambridge University Press, 1953–61.

Dixon, John. *The First Commentary on "The Faerie Queene."* Edited by Graham Hough. Stansted: privately published, 1964.

Drayton, Michael. *Works*. Edited by J. William Hebel. 5 vols. Oxford: Shakespeare Head Press, 1931–41.

Erasmus, Desiderius. *Colloquies*. Translated by Craig R. Thompson. Chicago: University of Chicago Press, 1965.

Foxe, John. *Actes and Monuments of these Latter and Perillous Dayes*. 1563.

———. *Actes and Monumentes of Thynges Passed in Every Kynges Tyme in this Realme*. 2nd ed., revised and enlarged. 2 vols. 1570.

———. *Acts and Monuments*. Edited by S. R. Cattley, revised and corrected by J. Pratt. 8 vols. 1877.

———. *Two Latin Comedies*. Edited and translated by John Hazel Smith. Ithaca, N.Y.: Cornell University Press, 1973.

*The Geneva Bible* (1560). Facsimile edition with introduction by Lloyd E. Berry. Madison: University of Wisconsin Press, 1969.

Gifford, George. *A Briefe Discourse of Certaine Points of the Religion, which is among the common sort of Christians, which may be termed the Countrie Divinitie*. 1581.

Googe, Barnabe. *Eglogs, Epytaphes, and Sonettes*. 1563.

———. *The Shippe of Safegarde*. 1569.

Greville, Fulke. *Poems and Dramas*. Edited by Geoffrey Bullough. 2 vols. Edinburgh, 1939.

Hooker, Richard. *Of the Laws of Ecclesiastical Polity*. 1593, 1597.

Hughes, Paul L., and James F. Larkin, eds. *Tudor Royal Proclamations*. 3 vols. New Haven: Yale University Press, 1964–69.

Jewel, John. *An Apology of the Church of England*. Edited by John E. Booty. Charlottesville: University Press of Virginia, 1963.

Jonson, Ben. *Works*. Edited by C. H. Herford, Percy Simpson, and Evelyn Simpson. 11 vols. Oxford: Clarendon Press, 1925–52.

Lapide, Cornelius á. *Commentaria in Acta Apostolorum, Epistolas Canonicas, et Apocalypsin*. Antwerp, 1647.

———. *Commentarii in Ecclesiasten*. Antwerp, 1657.

Latham, Agnes, ed. *The Poems of Sir Walter Ralegh*. Cambridge, Mass.: Harvard University Press, 1951.

Latimer, Hugh. *Selected Sermons*. Edited by A. G. Chester. Charlottesville: University Press of Virginia, for the Folger Shakespeare Library, 1968.

Leland, John. *Commentarii de Scriptoribus Britannicis*. Edited by Anthony Hall. Oxford, 1709.

Luther, Martin. *A Commentarie upon the Epistle of S. Paul to the Galathians*. Anonymous translation 1575.

———. *Luther's Works*. Edited by Jaroslav Pelikan, et al. 55 vols. St. Louis: Concordia Publishing House, 1958–76.

Martyr, Peter. See Vermigli, Pietro Martire.

Melanchthon, Philip. *Melanchthon on Christian Doctrine: "Loci Communes 1555."* Edited and translated by Clyde L. Manschrek. New York: Oxford University Press, 1965.

Milton, John. *The Poems of John Milton.* Edited by John Carey and Alastair Fowler. London: Longmans, 1968.

———. *Complete Prose Works.* Edited by Don M. Wolfe, et al. 8 vols. in 10. New Haven: Yale University Press, 1953–82.

More, Henry. *An Explanation of the Grand Mystery of Godliness.* 1660.

Mulcaster, Richard. *The Quenes Majesties Passage through the Citie of London to Westminster the Day before Her Coronacion.* Facsimile edited by James M. Osborn. New Haven: Yale University Press, 1960.

Noot, Jan van der. *A Theatre [for] Voluptuous Worldlings.* Translated by Theodore Roest and Edmund Spenser. 1569.

Order of the Garter. *The Register of the Most Noble Order of the Garter, From Its Cover in Black Velvet, usually Called the Black Book.* 2 vols. 1724.

Origen. *The Song of Songs: Commentary and Homilies.* Translated by R. P. Lawson. Ancient Christian Writers, no. 26. London: Longmans, 1957.

Petrarca, Francesco. *Petrarch's Lyric Poems: The "Rime Sparse" and Other Lyrics.* Edited and translated by Robert M. Durling. Cambridge, Mass.: Harvard University Press, 1976.

Piers Plowman. *The Vision of William Concerning Piers the Plowman.* Edited by W. W. Skeat. 2 vols. Oxford, 1886.

Puttenham, George. *The Arte of English Poesie.* Edited by Gladys Willcock and Alice Walker. Cambridge: Cambridge University Press, 1936.

Ripa, Cesare. *Iconologia.* Rome, 1603.

Sidney, Sir Philip. *Miscellaneous Prose.* Edited by Katherine Duncan-Jones and Jan van Dorsten. Oxford: Clarendon Press, 1973.

Skeat, Walter W., ed. *Chaucerian and Other Pieces.* Oxford: Clarendon Press, 1897.

Smith, G. Gregory, ed. *Elizabethan Critical Essays.* 2 vols. Oxford: Oxford University Press, 1904

Spagnuoli, Baptista. *A Lamentable complaynte of Baptista Mantuanus . . . wherin he famylyarly commoneth* [communes] *wyth his owne mynde, that Deathe is not to be feared.* Translated by John Bale. C. 1551

Spenser, Edmund. *Books I and II of "The Faerie Queene," the Mutability Cantos, and Selections from the Minor Poetry.* Edited by Robert Kellogg and Oliver Steele. New York: Odyssey Press, 1965.

———. *Daphnaida and Other Poems.* Edited by W. L. Renwick. London: Scholartis Press, 1929.

———. *The Faerie Queene.* 2 vols. 1590, 1596.

———. *The Faerie Queene.* Edited by A. C. Hamilton. London: Longman, 1977.

———. *The Faerie Queene.* Edited by Thomas P. Roche, Jr. Harmondsworth: Penguin Books, 1978.

———. *The Shepherd's Calender.* Edited by W. A. Renwick. London: Scholartis Press, 1930.

Spenser, Edmund. *The Poetical Works of Edmund Spenser*. Edited by J. C. Smith and Ernest de Sélincourt. 3 vols. Oxford: Clarendon Press, 1909–10.

———. *The Works of Edmund Spenser: A Variorum Edition*. Edited by Edwin A. Greenlaw, C. G. Osgood, F. M. Padelford et al. 10 vols. in 11 pts. Baltimore: Johns Hopkins University Press, 1932–57.

Spurgeon, Caroline, ed. *Five Hundred Years of Chaucer Criticism and Allusion: 1357–1900*. Rev. ed. 3 vols. Cambridge: Cambridge University Press, 1925.

Stubbs, John. *John Stubbs's "Gaping Gulf" with Letters and Other Relevant Documents*. Edited by Lloyd E. Berry. Charlottesville: University Press of Virginia, for the Folger Shakespeare Library, 1968.

Sylvester, Richard S., ed. *The Anchor Anthology of Sixteenth-Century Verse*. New York: Anchor, 1974.

*The Thirty-nine Articles of Religion* (1563 [Lat.], 1571 [Eng.]). Edited by Charles Hardwick. In *A History of the Articles of Religion*, pp. 289–353. London: George Bell and Sons, 1888.

Tyndale, William. *Doctrinal Treatises*. Edited by Henry Walker. Parker Society, vol. 42. Cambridge: Cambridge University Press, 1848.

Vennard, Richard. *The Right Way to Heaven*. 2nd ed. 1602.

Vermigli, Pietro Martire. *Common Places*. Translated by Anthony Marten. 1583.

Virgil. *Eclogues, Georgics, Aeneid*. Edited and translated by H. Rushton Fairclough. 2 vols. Cambridge, Mass.: Harvard University Press, 1924.

Voragine, Jacobus de. *The Golden Legend*. Translated by William Caxton. 1483.

———. *The Golden Legend*. Translated by William Caxton. 3rd ed. 1493.

Wever, R. *Lusty Juventus*. In *Four Tudor Interludes*, edited by J.A.B. Somerset, pp. 97–127. London: Athlone Press, 1974.

Wilson, Thomas. *The Arte of Rhetorique*. 1553.

Zwingli, Ulrich. *A short pathwaye to the ryghte and true understanding of the holye & sacred Scriptures*. Translated by Jean Veron. Worcester, 1550.

## SECONDARY SOURCES

Anderson, Judith H. *The Growth of a Personal Voice: "Piers Plowman" and "The Faerie Queene."* New Haven: Yale University Press, 1976

———. " 'In living colours and right hew': The Queen of Spenser's Central Books." In *Poetic Traditions of the English Renaissance*, ed. Maynard Mack and George deForest Lord, pp. 47–66.

Apteker, Jane. *Icons of Justice: Iconography and Thematic Imagery in Book V of "The Faerie Queene."* New York: Columbia University Press, 1969.

Axton, Marie. *The Queen's Two Bodies: Drama and the Elizabethan Succession*. London: Royal Historical Society, 1977.

Bauckham, Richard. *Tudor Apocalypse*. Abingdon: Sutton-Courtenay Press, 1978.

Bednarz, James. "Ralegh in Spenser's Historical Allegory." *SSt* 4 (1983): 49–70.

Bender, John B. *Spenser and Literary Pictorialism*. Princeton: Princeton University Press, 1972.

Bennett, Josephine. *The Evolution of "The Faerie Queene."* Chicago: University of Chicago Press, 1942.

Berger, Harry. *The Allegorical Temper: Vision and Reality in Book II of Spenser's "Faerie Queene."* New Haven: Yale University Press, 1957.

Bernard, John D. "Spenserian Pastoral and the *Amoretti.*" *ELH* 47 (1980): 419–32.

Bevington, David. *From "Mankind" to Marlowe: Growth of Structure in the Popular Drama of Tudor England.* Cambridge, Mass.: Harvard University Press, 1962.

Blissett, William. "Spenser's Mutabilitie." In *Essays in English Literature from the Renaissance to the Victorian Age, Presented to A.S.P. Woodhouse.* Edited by Millar MacLure and D. W. Watt, pp. 26–42. Toronto: University of Toronto Press, 1964.

Booty, John E., ed. *The Godly Kingdom of Tudor England: Great Books of the English Reformation.* Wilton, Conn.: Morehouse-Barlow Co., 1981.

Breitenberg, Mark. " '. . . The hole matter opened': Iconic Representation and Interpretation in 'The Quenes Majesties Passage.' " *Criticism* 28 (1986): 1–25.

Brooks-Davies, Douglas. *Spenser's "Faerie Queene": A Critical Commentary on Books I and II.* Manchester: Manchester University Press, 1977.

Byrom, H. J. "Edmund Spenser's First Printer, Hugh Singleton." *Library*, 4th ser., 14 (1933): 121–56.

Cain, Thomas H. *Praise in "The Faerie Queene."* Lincoln: University of Nebraska Press, 1978.

Campbell, Lily B. *Divine Poetry and Drama in Sixteenth-Century England.* Berkeley: University of California Press, 1959.

Cheney, Donald. *Spenser's Image of Nature: Wild Man and Shepherd in "The Faerie Queene."* New Haven: Yale University Press, 1966.

Chew, Samuel. *The Pilgrimage of Life.* New Haven: Yale University Press, 1962.

Colie, Rosalie. *The Resources of Kind: Genre-Theory in the Renaissance.* Edited by Barbara K. Lewalski. Berkeley and Los Angeles: University of California Press, 1973.

———. *Shakespeare's Living Art.* Princeton: Princeton University Press, 1974.

Collinson, Patrick. "A Comment Concerning the Name Puritan." *Journal of Ecclesiastical History* 31 (1980): 483–88.

———. *Archbishop Grindal, 1519–1583: The Struggle for a Reformed Church.* London: Jonathan Cape, 1979.

———. *The Elizabethan Puritan Movement.* Berkeley and Los Angeles: University of California Press, 1967.

———. "England and International Calvinism, 1558–1640." In *International Calvinism, 1541–1715*, edited by Menna Prestwich, pp. 197–223. Oxford: Clarendon Press, 1985.

———. *From Iconoclasm to Iconophobia: The Cultural Impact of the Second English Reformation.* The Stenton Lecture, 1985. Reading: University of Reading, 1986.

Collinson, Patrick. *Godly People: Essays on English Protestantism and Puritanism.* London: Hambledon Press, 1983.

Cullen, Patrick. *Infernal Triad: The Flesh, the World, and the Devil in Spenser and Milton.* Princeton: Princeton University Press, 1974.

———. *Spenser, Marvell, and Renaissance Pastoral.* Cambridge, Mass.: Harvard University Press, 1970.

Curtius, Ernst R. *European Literature and the Latin Middle Ages.* Translated by Willard Trask. 2nd ed. New York: Harper and Row, 1963.

Dasenbrock, Reed Way. "The Petrarchan Context of Spenser's *Amoretti.*" *PMLA* 100 (1985): 38–50.

Davidson, Clifford. "The Idol of Isis Church." *SP* 66 (1969): 70–86.

Davies, Horton. *From Cranmer to Hooker, 1534–1603.* Vol. 1 (1970) of *Worship and Theology in England.* 5 vols. Princeton: Princeton University Press, 1961–75.

Doerksen, Daniel W. " 'All the Good Is God's': Predestination in Spenser's *Faerie Queene,* Book I." *Christianity and Literature* 32 (1983): 11–18.

———. "Recharting the *Via Media* of Spenser and Herbert." *Renaissance and Reformation,* n.s. 8, no. 3 (August 1984): 215–25.

Donno, Elizabeth Story. "The Triumph of Cupid: Spenser's Legend of Chastity." *YES* 4 (1974): 37–48.

Dorsten, Jan van. *The Radical Arts: First Decade of an Elizabethan Renaissance.* Leiden: Leiden University Press, 1973.

Dunlop, Alexander. "The Drama of *Amoretti.*" *SSt* 1 (1980): 107–20.

———. "The Unity of Spenser's *Amoretti.*" In *Silent Poetry,* ed. Alastair Fowler, pp. 153–69.

Eire, Carlos M. N. *War against the Idols: The Reformation of Worship fom Erasmus to Calvin.* Cambridge: Cambridge University Press, 1986

Falls, Mother Mary Robert. "Spenser's Kirkrapine and the Elizabethans." *SP* 50 (1953): 457–75.

Firth, Katharine. *The Apocalyptic Tradition in Reformation Britain, 1530–1645.* Oxford: Oxford University Press, 1979.

Fletcher, Angus. *The Prophetic Moment: An Essay on Spenser.* Chicago: University of Chicago Press, 1971.

Forster, Leonard. *The Icy Fire: Five Studies in European Petrarchism.* Cambridge: Cambridge University Press, 1969.

Fowler, Alastair. *Conceitful Thought: The Interpretation of English Renaissance Poems.* Edinburgh: Edinburgh University Press, 1975.

———. *Kinds of Literature: An Introduction to the Theory of Genres and Modes.* Cambridge, Mass.: Harvard University Press, 1982.

———. "Protestant Attitudes to Poetry, 1560–1590." Dissertation, Oxford University, 1957.

———, ed. *Silent Poetry: Essays in Numerological Analysis.* New York: Barnes and Noble, 1970.

———. *Spenser and the Numbers of Time.* New York: Barnes and Noble, 1964.

George, Charles H., and Katherine George. *The Protestant Mind of the English Reformation: 1570–1640.* Princeton: Princeton University Press, 1961.

Giamatti, A. Bartlett. *The Earthly Paradise and the Renaissance Epic*. Princeton: Princeton University Press, 1966.

———. *Play of Double Senses: Spenser's "Faerie Queene."* Englewood Cliffs, N.J.: Prentice-Hall, 1975.

———. "A Prince and Her Poet." *Yale Review* 73 (1984): 321–37.

Gilman, Ernest. *Iconoclasm and Poetry in the English Reformation: "Down Went Dagon."* Chicago: University of Chicago Press, 1986.

Gless, Darryl. *"Measure for Measure," the Law, and the Convent*. Princeton: Princeton University Press, 1979.

Graziani, René. "Philip II's 'Impresa' and Spenser's Souldan." *JWCI* 27 (1964): 322–24.

Greenblatt, Stephen J. *Renaissance Self-Fashioning: From More to Shakespeare*. Chicago: University of Chicago Press, 1980.

———. *Sir Walter Ralegh: The Renaissance Man and His Roles*. New Haven: Yale University Press, 1973.

Greene, Thomas M. "Spenser and the Epithalamic Convention." *Comparative Literature* 9 (1957): 215–28.

Greenlaw, Edwin A. " 'The Shepheards Calender.' " *PMLA* 26 (1911): 419–51.

Gross, Kenneth. *Spenserian Poetics: Idolatry, Iconoclasm, and Magic*. Ithaca, N.Y.: Cornell University Press, 1985.

Guillén, Claudio. *Literature as System: Essays Toward the Theory of Literary History*. Princeton: Princeton University Press, 1971.

Guillory, John. *Poetic Authority: Spenser, Milton, and Literary History*. New York: Columbia University Press, 1983.

Guth, Hans. "Allegorical Implications of Artifice in Spenser's *Faerie Queene*." *PMLA* 76 (1961): 474–79.

Haigh, Christopher, ed. *The Reign of Elizabeth I*. London: Macmillan, 1984.

Hamilton, A. C. *The Structure of Allegory in "The Faerie Queene."* Oxford: Clarendon Press, 1961.

———. "The Visions of *Piers Plowman* and *The Faerie Queene*." In *Form and Convention in the Poetry of Edmund Spenser*, edited by William Nelson, pp. 1–34. New York: Columbia University Press, 1961.

———, ed. *Essential Articles for the Study of Edmund Spenser*. Hamden, Conn.: Archon Books, 1972.

Hankins, John. *Source and Meaning in Spenser's Allegory: A Study of "The Faerie Queene."* Oxford: Clarendon Press, 1971.

Hardison, O. B., Jr. "*Amoretti* and the *Dolce Stil Novo*." *ELR* 2 (1972): 208–16.

Heiserman, Arthur. *Skelton and Satire*. Chicago: University of Chicago Press, 1961.

Helgerson, Richard. *Self-Crowned Laureates: Spenser, Jonson, Milton, and the Literary System*. Berkeley and Los Angeles: University of California Press, 1983.

Heninger, S. K. "The Orgoglio Episode in *The Faerie Queene*." *ELH* 26 (1959): 171–87. Reprinted in *Essential Articles*, ed. A. C. Hamilton, pp. 125–38.

Herrin, Judith. *The Formation of Christendom*. Princeton: Princeton University Press, 1987.

Hieatt, A. Kent. "A Numerical Key for Spenser's *Amoretti* and Guyon in the House of Mammon." *YES* 3 (1973): 14–27.

——. *Short Time's Endless Monument: The Symbolism of the Numbers in Edmund Spenser's "Epithalamion."* Port Washington, N.Y.: Kennikat Press, 1960.

Hill, Christopher. *Antichrist in Seventeenth-Century England*. London: Oxford University Press, 1971.

Hough, Graham. *A Preface to "The Faerie Queene."* New York: Norton, 1963.

Hulbert, Viola. "Diggon Davie." *JEGP* 41 (1942): 349–67.

Hume, Anthea. *Edmund Spenser: Protestant Poet*. Cambridge: Cambridge University Press, 1984.

Hunter, G. K. "Spenser's *Amoretti* and the English Sonnet Tradition." In *A Theatre for Spenserians*, edited by Judith M. Kennedy and James A. Reither, pp. 124–44. Toronto: University of Toronto Press, 1973.

——. "Tyrant and Martyr: Religious Heroisms in Elizabethan Tragedy." In *Poetic Traditions of the English Renaissance*, ed. Mack and Lord, pp. 85–102.

——. " 'Unity' and Numbers in Spenser's *Amoretti*." *YES* 5 (1975): 39–45.

Imbrie, Ann E. "Defining Nonfiction Genres." In *Renaissance Genres: Essays on Theory, History, and Interpretation*, edited by Barbara K. Lewalski, Harvard English Studies, vol. 14, pp. 45–69. Cambridge, Mass.: Harvard University Press, 1986.

——. " 'Playing Legerdemaine with the Scripture': Parodic Sermons in *The Faerie Queene*." *ELR* 17 (1987): 142–55.

Johnson, Lynn Staley. "Elizabeth, Bride and Queen: A Study of Spenser's April Eclogue and the Metaphors of English Protestantism." *SSt* 2 (1981): 75–91.

Johnson, William C. " 'Sacred Rites' and Prayer-Book Echoes in Spenser's 'Epithalamion.' " *Renaissance and Reformation*, o.s. 12; no. 1 (1976): 49–54.

——. "Spenser's *Amoretti* and the Art of the Liturgy." *Studies in English Literature* 14 (1974): 49–61.

Jones, Norman L. "Elizabeth's First Year: The Conception and Birth of the Elizabethan Political World." In *Reign of Elizabeth*, ed. Christopher Haigh, pp. 27–53.

Judson, Alexander C. *A Biographical Sketch of John Young, Bishop of Rochester, with Emphasis on His Relations with Edmund Spenser*. Indiana University Studies, vol. 21, Study no. 103. Bloomington: Indiana University Press, 1934.

Kaske, Carol V. "Another Liturgical Dimension of 'Amoretti' 68." *N&Q* 222 (1977): 518–19.

——. "The Dragon's Spark and Sting and the Structure of Red Cross's Dragon-Fight: *The Faerie Queene*, I.xi–xii." *SP* 66 (1969): 609–38. Reprinted in *Essential Articles*, ed. A. C. Hamilton, pp. 425–46.

——. "Spenser's *Amoretti and Epithalamion* of 1595: Structure, Genre, and Numerology." *ELR* 8 (1978): 271–95.

——. "Spenser's Pluralistic Universe: The View from the Mount of Contemplation" (*F.Q.* I.x)." In *Contemporary Thought on Edmund Spenser*, edited by Richard C. Frushell and Bernard J. Vondersmith, pp. 121–49. Carbondale and Edwardsville, Ill.: Southern Illinois University Press, 1975.

———. "Surprised by Puritanism." Paper delivered at the annual meeting of the Modern Language Association, 1980.

Kendall, Ritchie D. *The Drama of Dissent: The Radical Poetics of Nonconformity, 1380–1590.* Chapel Hill: University of North Carolina Press, 1986.

Kermode, Frank. *Spenser, Shakespeare, and Donne: Renaissance Essays.* London: Routledge and Kegan Paul, 1971.

Kernan, Alvin. *The Cankered Muse: Satire of the English Renaissance.* New Haven: Yale University Press, 1959.

King, John N. *English Reformation Literature: The Tudor Origins of the Protestant Tradition.* Princeton: Princeton University Press, 1982.

———. "*The Faerie Leveller*: A 1648 Royalist Reading of *The Faerie Queene*, V.ii.29–54." *HLQ* 48 (1985): 297–308.

———. "Milton's Bower of Bliss: A Rewriting of Spenser's Art of Married Love." *Renaissance and Reformation*, n.s. 10 (1986): 289–99.

———. *Tudor Royal Iconography: Literature and Art in an Age of Religious Crisis.* Princeton: Princeton University Press, 1989.

Kipling, Gordon. "The London Pageants for Margaret of Anjou: A Medieval Script Restored." *Medieval English Theatre* 4 (1982): 5–27.

———. *The Triumph of Honour: Burgundian Origins of the Elizabethan Renaissance.* Leiden: Leiden University Press, 1977.

Klein, Joan L. "From Errour to Acrasia." *HLQ* 41 (1977–78): 173–99.

Knapp, Jeffrey. "Error as a Means of Empire in *The Faerie Queene*." *ELH* 54 (1987): 801–34.

Knott, John R., Jr. *The Sword of the Spirit: Puritan Responses to the Bible.* Chicago: University of Chicago Press, 1980.

Lake, Peter. *Moderate Puritans and the Elizabethan Church.* Cambridge: Cambridge University Press, 1982.

Leslie, Michael. *Spenser's "Fierce Warres and Faithfull Loves": Martial and Chivalric Symbolism in "The Faerie Queene."* Cambridge: D. S. Brewer, 1983.

Lewalski, Barbara K. *"Paradise Lost" and the Rhetoric of Literary Forms.* Princeton: Princeton University Press, 1985.

———. *Protestant Poetics and the Seventeenth-Century Religious Lyric.* Princeton: Princeton University Press, 1979.

———. "*Samson Agonistes* and the 'Tragedy' of the Apocalypse." *PMLA* 85 (1970): 1050–62.

Lewis, C. S. *The Allegory of Love: A Study in Medieval Tradition.* Oxford: Clarendon Press, 1936.

Lindenbaum, Peter. *Changing Landscapes: Anti-Pastoral Sentiment in the English Renaissance.* Athens, Ga.: University of Georgia Press, 1986.

Low, Anthony. *The Georgic Revolution.* Princeton: Princeton University Press, 1985.

Luborsky, Ruth. "The Allusive Presentation of *The Shepheardes Calender*." *SSt* 1 (1980): 29–67.

Luborsky, Ruth. "The Illustrations to *The Shepheardes Calender*." *SSt* 2 (1981): 3–53.

McCabe, Richard. "The Masks of Duessa: Spenser, Mary Queen of Scots, and James VI." *ELR* 17 (1987): 224–42.

MacCaffrey, Isabel G. *Spenser's Allegory: The Anatomy of Imagination*. Princeton: Princeton University Press, 1976.

MacCaffrey, Wallace T. *Queen Elizabeth and the Making of Policy, 1572–1588*. Princeton: Princeton University Press, 1981.

McCown, Gary M. "Milton and the Epic Epithalamium." *Milton Studies* 5 (1973): 39–66.

McGinn, Bernard. "Revelation." In *The Literary Guide to the Bible*, edited by Robert Alter and Frank Kermode, pp. 523–41. Cambridge, Mass.: Harvard University Press, 1987.

Mack, Maynard, and George deForest Lord, eds. *Poetic Traditions of the English Renaissance*. New Haven: Yale University Press, 1982.

MacLachlan, Hugh. "The Death of Guyon and the *Elizabethan Book of Homilies*." *SSt* 4 (1983): 93–114.

McLane, Paul. "Spenser and the Primitive Church." *English Language Notes*, 1 (1963): 6–11.

———. "Spenser's Political and Religious Position in the *Shepheardes Calender*." *JEGP* 49 (1950): 324–32.

———. *Spenser's "Shepheardes Calender": A Study in Elizabethan Allegory*. Notre Dame, Ind.: University of Notre Dame Press, 1961.

Mâle, Emile. *The Gothic Image: Religious Art in France of the Thirteenth Century*. Translated by Dora Nussey. New York: Harper and Row, 1958.

Mallette, Richard. "The Protestant Art of Preaching in Book One of *The Faerie Queene*." *SSt* 7 (1986): 3–25.

Marcus, Leah S. "Shakespeare's Comic Heroines, Elizabeth I, and the Political Uses of Androgyny." In *Women in the Middle Ages and the Renaissance: Literary and Historical Perspectives*, edited by Mary Beth Rose, pp. 135–53. Syracuse, N.Y.: Syracuse University Press, 1986.

Miller, David Lee. "Spenser's Poetics: The Poem's Two Bodies." *PMLA* 101 (1986): 170–85.

Milward, Peter. *Religious Controversies of the Jacobean Age: A Survey of Printed Sources*. London: Scolar Press, 1978.

Miskimin, Alice. *The Renaissance Chaucer*. New Haven: Yale University Press, 1975

Montrose, Louis A. "*A Midsummer Night's Dream* and the Shaping Fantasies of Elizabethan Culture: Gender, Power, Form." In *Rewriting the Renaissance: The Discourses of Sexual Difference in Early Modern Europe*, edited by Margaret Ferguson, Maureen Quilligan, and Nancy Vickers, pp. 65–87. Chicago: University of Chicago Press, 1986.

Mueller, Janel M. *The Native Tongue and the Word: Developments in English Prose Style, 1380–1580*. Chicago: University of Chicago Press, 1984.

Murray, J.A.H., Henry Bradley, W. A. Craigie, and C. T. Onions, eds. *A New English Dictionary on Historical Principles*. 11 vols. Oxford: Oxford University Press, 1884–1933.

Nelson, William, ed. *Form and Convention in the Poetry of Edmund Spenser: Selected Papers from the English Institute*. New York: Columbia University Press, 1961.

———. *The Poetry of Edmund Spenser: A Study*. New York: Columbia University Press, 1963.

———. "Queen Elizabeth, Spenser's Mercilla, and a Rusty Sword." *Renaissance News*, 18 (1965): 113–17.

Nohrnberg, James. *The Analogy of "The Faerie Queene."* Princeton: Princeton University Press, 1976.

Norbrook, David. "Panegyric of the Monarch and Its Social Context under Elizabeth I and James I." Dissertation, Oxford University, 1978.

———. *Poetry and Politics in the English Renaissance*. London: Routledge and Kegan Paul, 1984.

O'Connell, Michael. "The Idolatrous Eye: Iconoclasm, Anti-Theatricalism, and the Image of the Elizabethan Theater." *ELH* 52 (1985): 279–310.

———. *Mirror and Veil: The Historical Dimension of Spenser's "Faerie Queene."* Chapel Hill: University of North Carolina Press, 1977

Oetgen, Jerome. "Spenser's Treatment of Monasticism in Book I of *The Faerie Queene*." *American Benedictine Review* 22 (1971): 109–20.

Ozment, Steven. *The Age of Reform 1250–1550: An Intellectual and Religious History of Late Medieval and Reformation Europe*. New Haven: Yale University Press, 1980.

———. *When Fathers Ruled: Family Life in Reformation Europe*. Cambridge, Mass.: Harvard University Press, 1983.

Padelford, F. M., and Matthew O'Connor. "Spenser's Use of the St. George Legend." *SP* 23 (1926): 142–56.

Panofsky, Erwin. *Albrecht Dürer*. 2 vols. Princeton: Princeton University Press, 1948.

———. *Studies in Iconology: Humanistic Themes in the Art of the Renaissance*. Paperback ed. New York: Harper and Row, 1962.

Parker, Patricia. *Inescapable Romance: Studies in the Poetics of a Mode*. Princeton: Princeton University Press, 1979.

Patrides, C. A., and Joseph Wittreich, eds. *The Apocalypse in English Renaissance Thought and Literature: Patterns, Antecedents, and Repercussions*. Ithaca, N.Y.: Cornell University Press, 1984.

Patterson, Annabel. "Re-opening the Green Cabinet: Clément Marot and Edmund Spenser." *ELR* 16 (1986): 44–70.

Peter, John. *Complaint and Satire in Early English Literature*. Oxford: Clarendon Press, 1956.

Phillips, James E., Jr. "The Woman Ruler in Spenser's *Faerie Queene*." *HLQ* 5 (1942): 211–34.

Phillips, John. *The Reformation of Images: Destruction of Art in England, 1535–1660*. Berkeley and Los Angeles: University of California Press, 1973.

Porter, H. C. *Puritanism in Tudor England*. Columbia, S.C.: University of South Carolina Press, 1971.

Prescott, Anne Lake. *French Poets and the English Renaissance: Studies in Fame and Transformation*. New Haven: Yale University Press, 1978

———. "Spenser's Chivalric Restoration: From Bateman's *Travayled Pylgryme* to the Redcrosse Knight." *SP* 86 (1989): 166–97.

———. "The Thirsty Deer and the Lord of Life: Some Contexts for *Amoretti* 67–70." *SSt* 6 (1985): 33–76.

Quilligan, Maureen. *Milton's Spenser: The Politics of Reading*. Ithaca, N.Y.: Cornell University Press, 1983.

Reeves, Marjorie. *The Influence of Prophecy in the Later Middle Ages: A Study in Joachimism*. Oxford: Clarendon Press, 1969.

Regosin, Richard L. *The Poetry of Inspiration: Agrippa D'Aubigné's "Les Tragiques."* University of North Carolina Studies in the Romance Languages and Literatures, no. 88. Chapel Hill: University of North Carolina Press, 1970.

Ringler, William A., Jr. "Spenser, Shakespeare, Honor, and Worship." *Renaissance News* 14 (1961): 159–61.

Rix, Herbert D. *Rhetoric in Spenser's Poetry*. Pennsylvania State College Studies, no. 7. State College, Pa.: Pennsylvania State College, 1940.

Roche, Thomas P., Jr. *The Kindly Flame: A Study of the Third and Fourth Books of Spenser's "Faerie Queene."* Princeton: Princeton University Press, 1964.

Rose, Mark. *Heroic Love: Studies in Sidney and Spenser*. Cambridge, Mass.: Harvard University Press, 1968.

Rossky, William. "Imagination in the English Renaissance: Psychology and Poetic." *Renaissance News* 5 (1958): 49–73.

Rozett, Martha T. *The Doctrine of Election and the Emergence of Elizabethan Tragedy*. Princeton: Princeton University Press, 1984.

Sandler, Florence. "*The Faerie Queene*: An Elizabethan Apocalypse." In *Apocalypse in English Renaissance Thought and Literature*, ed. C. A. Patrides and Joseph Wittreich, pp. 148–74.

———. "Icon and Iconoclast." In *Achievements of the Left Hand: Essays on the Prose of John Milton*, edited by Michael J. Lieb and John T. Shawcross, pp. 160–84. Amherst: University of Massachusetts Press, 1974.

Saxl, Fritz. "Veritas Filia Temporis." In *Philosophy and History: Essays Presented to Ernst Cassirer*, edited by Raymond Klibansky and H. J. Paton, pp. 197–222. Oxford: Clarendon Press, 1936.

Scheper, George L. "Reformation Attitudes toward Allegory and the Song of Songs." *PMLA* 89 (1974): 551–62.

Schiller, Gertrud. *Iconography of Christian Art*. Translated by Janet Seligman. 2 vols. Greenwich, Conn.: New York Graphic Society, 1971–72.

Sessions, William A. "Spenser's Georgics." *ELR* 10 (1980): 202–38.

Sheidley, William E. *Barnabe Googe*. Boston: G. K. Hall, 1981.

Shepherd, Simon. *Amazons and Warrior Women: Varieties of Feminism in Seventeenth-Century Drama*. New York: St. Martin's Press, 1981.

*A Short-Title Catalogue of Books Printed in England, Scotland, and Ireland, and of English Books Printed Abroad, 1475–1640*. First compiled by A. W. Pollard and G. R. Redgrave. 2nd ed., rev. and enlarged, begun by W. A. Jackson and F. S. Ferguson, completed by Katharine F. Pantzer. 2 vols. London: The Bibliographical Society, 1976–86.

Shroeder, John W. "Spenser's Erotic Drama: The Orgoglio Episode." *ELH* 29 (1962): 140–59.

Siemon, James R. *Shakespearean Iconoclasm*. Berkeley and Los Angeles: University of California Press, 1985.

Sinfield, Alan. *Literature in Protestant England, 1560–1660*. London: Croom Helm, 1983.

Sirluck, Ernest. "A Note on the Rhetoric of Spenser's Despair." *Modern Philology* 47 (1950): 8–11.

Smith, Hallett. *Elizabethan Poetry: A Study in Conventions, Meaning, and Expression*. Cambridge, Mass.: Harvard University Press, 1952.

———. "The Use of Conventions in Spenser's Minor Poems." In *Form and Convention*, ed. William Nelson, pp. 122–45.

Steadman, John. "Una and the Clergy: The Ass Symbol in *The Faerie Queene*." *JWCI* 21 (1958): 134–37.

Stein, Harold. "Spenser and William Turner." *MLN* 51 (1936): 344–51.

Stewart, Stanley. "Sir Calidore and 'Closure.' " *Studies in Engish Literature* 24 (1984): 69–86.

Strand, Kenneth A. *Woodcuts to the Apocalypse in Dürer's Time*. Ann Arbor, Mich.: Ann Arbor Publishers, 1968.

Strong, Roy. *The Cult of Elizabeth: Elizabethan Portraiture and Pageantry*. London: Thames and Hudson, 1977.

———. *Portraits of Queen Elizabeth I*. Oxford: Clarendon Press, 1963.

Stump, Donald V. "Isis Versus Mercilla: The Allegorical Shrines in Spenser's Legend of Justice." *SSt* 3 (1982): 87–98.

Thomas, Keith. *Religion and the Decline of Magic: Studies in Popular Beliefs in Sixteenth- and Seventeenth-Century England*. Harmondsworth: Penguin Books, 1973.

Turner, James G. *One Flesh: Paradisal Marriage and Sexual Relations in the Age of Milton*. Oxford: Clarendon Press, 1987.

Tuve, Rosemond. *Allegorical Imagery: Some Medieval Books and Their Posterity*. Princeton: Princeton University Press, 1966.

———. "Sacred 'Parody' of Love Poetry, and Herbert." *Studies in the Renaissance* 8 (1961): 249–90

Wall, John N., Jr. "The English Reformation and the Recovery of Christian Community in Spenser's *The Faerie Queene*." *SP* 80 (1983): 142–62.

———. "Godly and Fruitful Lessons." In *The Godly Kingdom of Tudor England*, ed. John E. Booty, pp. 47–135.

Wallace, Dewey D., Jr. "George Gifford, Puritan Propaganda and Popular Religion in Elizabethan England." *Sixteenth Century Journal* 9, no. 1 (1978): 28–38.

———. *Puritans and Predestination: Grace in English Protestant Theology, 1525–1695*. Chapel Hill: University of North Carolina Press, 1982

Waller, Gary. *English Poetry of the Sixteenth Century*. London: Longman, 1986.

Walls, Kathryn. "Abessa and the Lion: *The Faerie Queene*, 1.3.1–12." *SSt* 5 (1984): 1–30.

Warton, Thomas. *Observations on the Fairie Queene of Spenser*. 2 vols. London, 1754.

———. *Observations on the Fairie Queene of Spenser*. 2 vols. 2nd ed. London, 1762.

Waters, D. Douglas. *Duessa as Theological Satire*. Columbia, Mo.: University of Missouri Press, 1970.

Weatherby, Harold L. "The True St. George." *ELR* 17 (1987): 119–41.

———. "Una's Betrothal and the Easter Vigil: The Probable Influence of the Sarum Manual." In *Spenser at Kalamazoo, 1984*, edited by Francis G. Greco, pp. 6–16. Clarion, Pa.: Clarion University of Pennsylvania, 1984.

Weiner, Andrew. " 'Fierce Warres and Faithfull Loves': Pattern as Structure in Book I of *The Faerie Queene*." *HLQ* 37 (1973): 33–57.

———. *Sir Philip Sidney and the Poetics of Protestantism: A Study of Contexts*. Minneapolis: University of Minnesota Press, 1978.

Wells, Robin H. *Spenser's "Faerie Queene" and the Cult of Elizabeth*. London: Croom Helm, 1983.

West, Michael. "Spenser and the Renaissance Ideal of Christian Heroism." *PMLA* 88 (1973): 1013–32.

Whitaker, Virgil. *The Religious Basis of Spenser's Thought*. Stanford University Publications, University Series, Language and Literature, vol. 7, no. 3. Stanford: Stanford University Press, 1950.

Wickert, Max A. "Structure and Ceremony in Spenser's *Epithalamion*." *ELH* 35 (1968): 135–57.

Wickham, Glynne. *Early English Stages 1300 to 1660*. 4 vols. London: Routledge and Kegan Paul, 1959–.

Wittreich, Joseph. *Visionary Poetics: Milton's Tradition and His Legacy*. San Marino, Calif.: Huntington Library, 1979.

Woodhouse, A.S.P. "Nature and Grace in *The Faerie Queene*." *ELH* 16 (1949): 194–228. Reprinted in *Essential Articles*, ed. A. C. Hamilton, pp. 58–83.

Woods, Susanne. "Spenser and the Problem of Women's Rule." *HLQ* 48 (1985): 140–58.

Wrightson, Keith. *English Society: 1580–1680*. New Brunswick, N.J.: Rutgers University Press, 1982.

Yates, Frances. *Astraea: The Imperial Theme in the Sixteenth Century*. London: Routledge and Kegan Paul, 1975.

———. "Queen Elizabeth as Astraea." *JWCI* 10 (1947): 27–82. Reprinted in idem, *Astraea*, pp. 29–87.

# SPENSERIAN PASSAGES CITED

# INDEX OF CHARACTERS AND PLACES

# INDEX OF BIBLICAL TEXTS CITED

# GENERAL INDEX